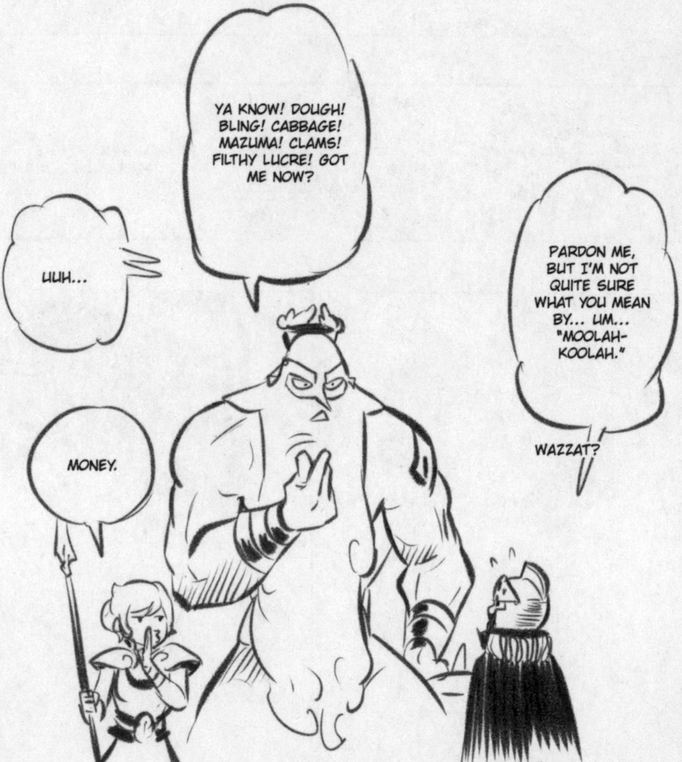
PARDON ME, BUT I'M NOT QUITE SURE WHAT YOU MEAN BY... UM... "MOOLAH-KOOLAH."
WAZZAT?
YA KNOW! DOUGH! BLING! CABBAGE! MAZUMA! CLAMS! FILTHY LUCRE! GOT ME NOW?
UUH...
MONEY.

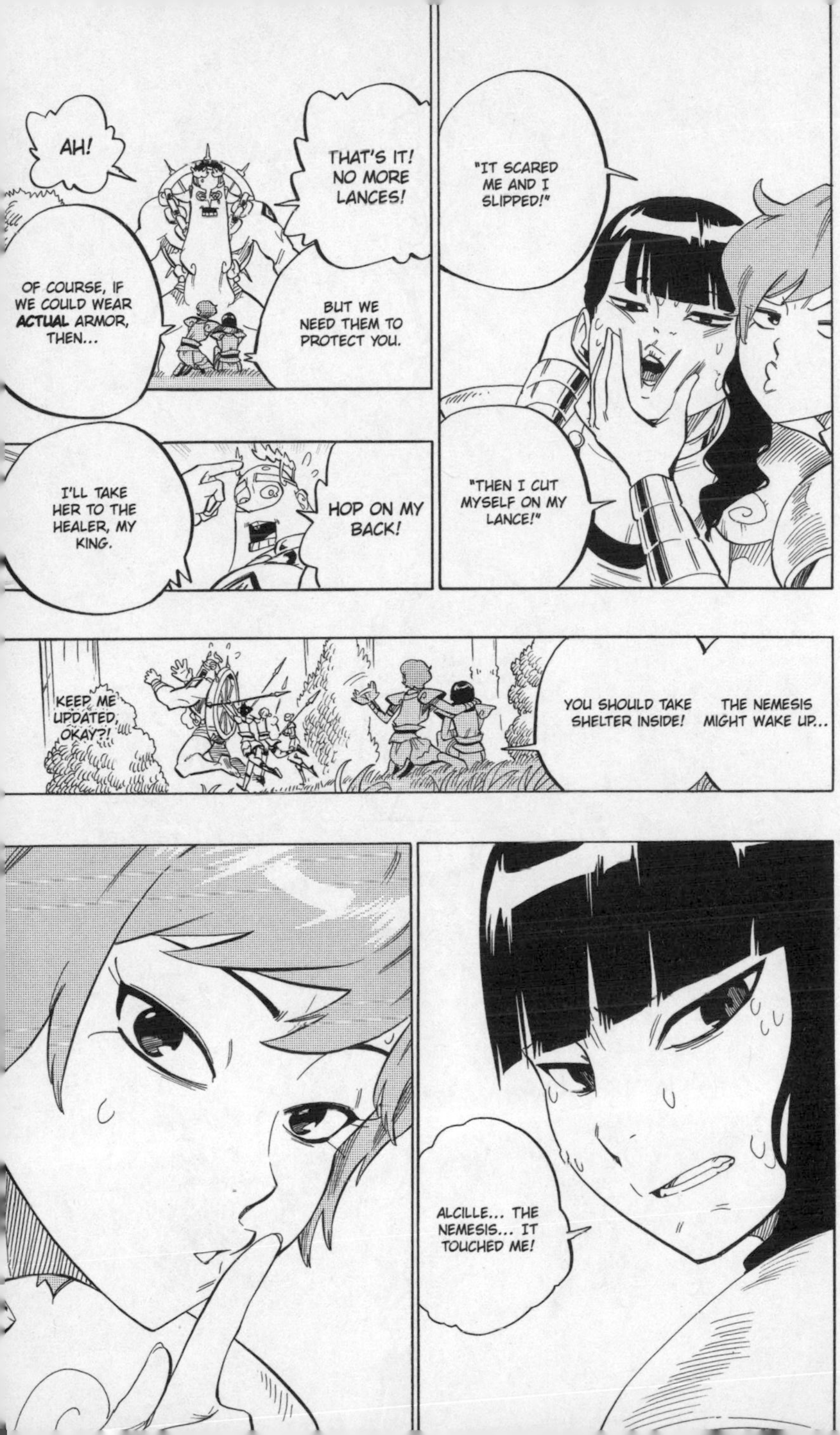
"IT SCARED ME AND I SLIPPED!"
"THEN I CUT MYSELF ON MY LANCE!"
THAT'S IT! NO MORE LANCES!
AH!
BUT WE NEED THEM TO PROTECT YOU.
OF COURSE, IF WE COULD WEAR **ACTUAL** ARMOR, THEN...
HOP ON MY BACK!
I'LL TAKE HER TO THE HEALER, MY KING.
YOU SHOULD TAKE SHELTER INSIDE! THE NEMESIS MIGHT WAKE UP...
KEEP ME UPDATED, OKAY?!
ALCILLE... THE NEMESIS... IT TOUCHED ME!

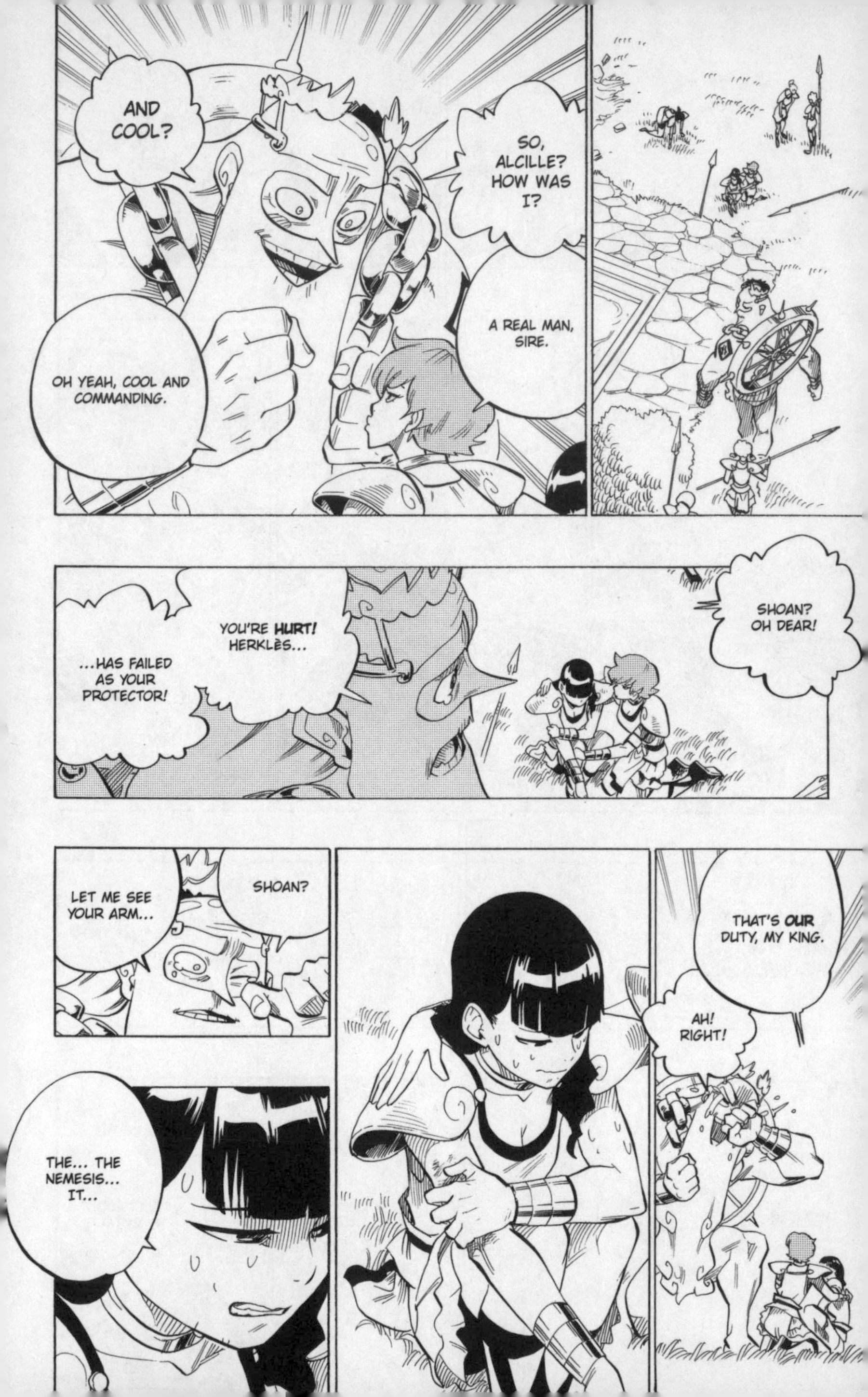
SO, ALCILLE? HOW WAS I?
A REAL MAN, SIRE.
AND COOL?
OH YEAH, COOL AND COMMANDING.
SHOAN? OH DEAR!
YOU'RE **HURT!** HERKLÈS...
...HAS FAILED AS YOUR PROTECTOR!
THAT'S **OUR** DUTY, MY KING.
AH! RIGHT!
SHOAN?
LET ME SEE YOUR ARM...
THE... THE NEMESIS... IT...

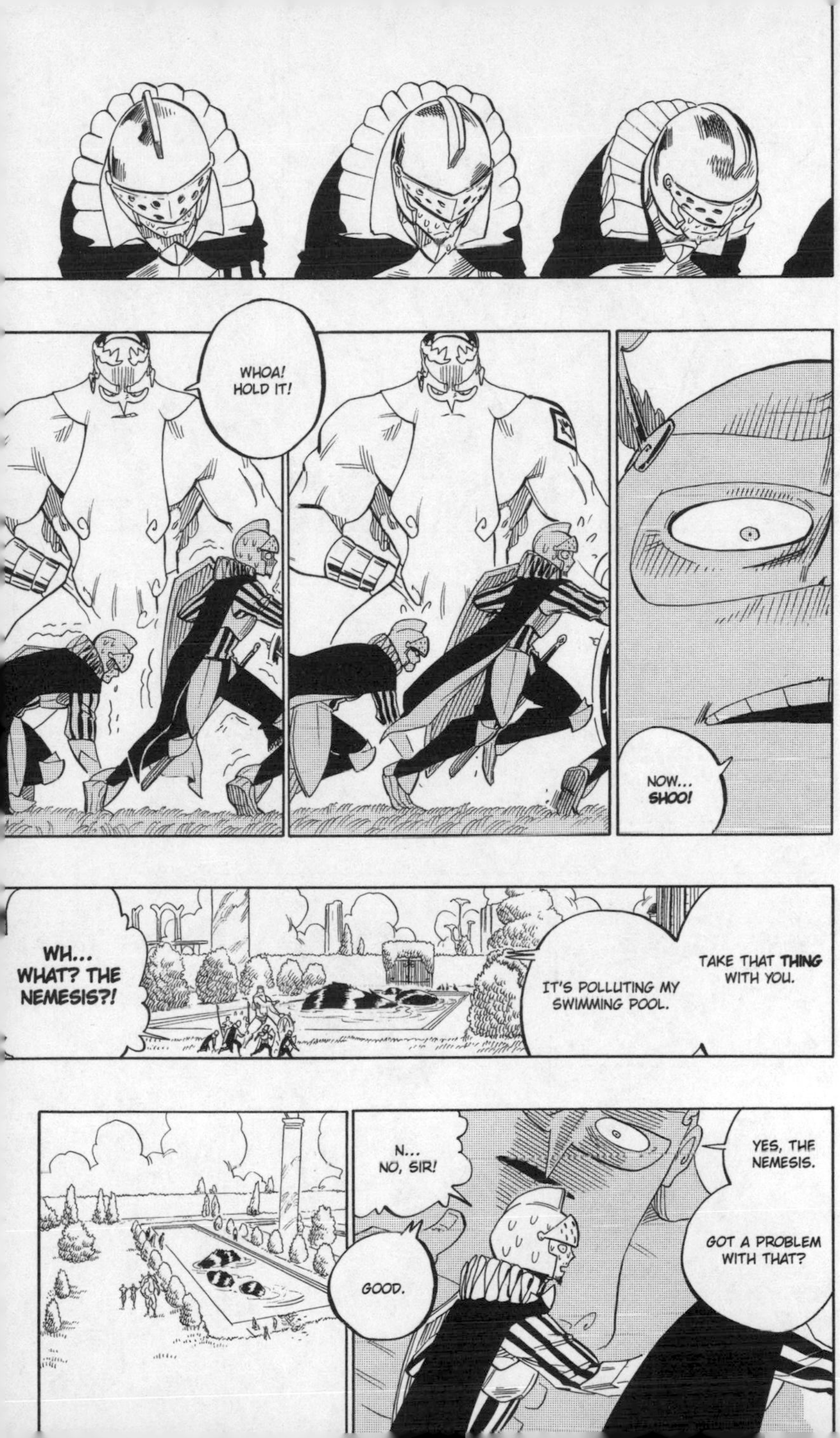
NOW... **SHOO!**
WHOA! HOLD IT!
TAKE THAT **THING** WITH YOU.
IT'S POLLUTING MY SWIMMING POOL.
WH... WHAT? THE NEMESIS?!
YES, THE NEMESIS.
GOT A PROBLEM WITH THAT?
N... NO, SIR!
GOOD.

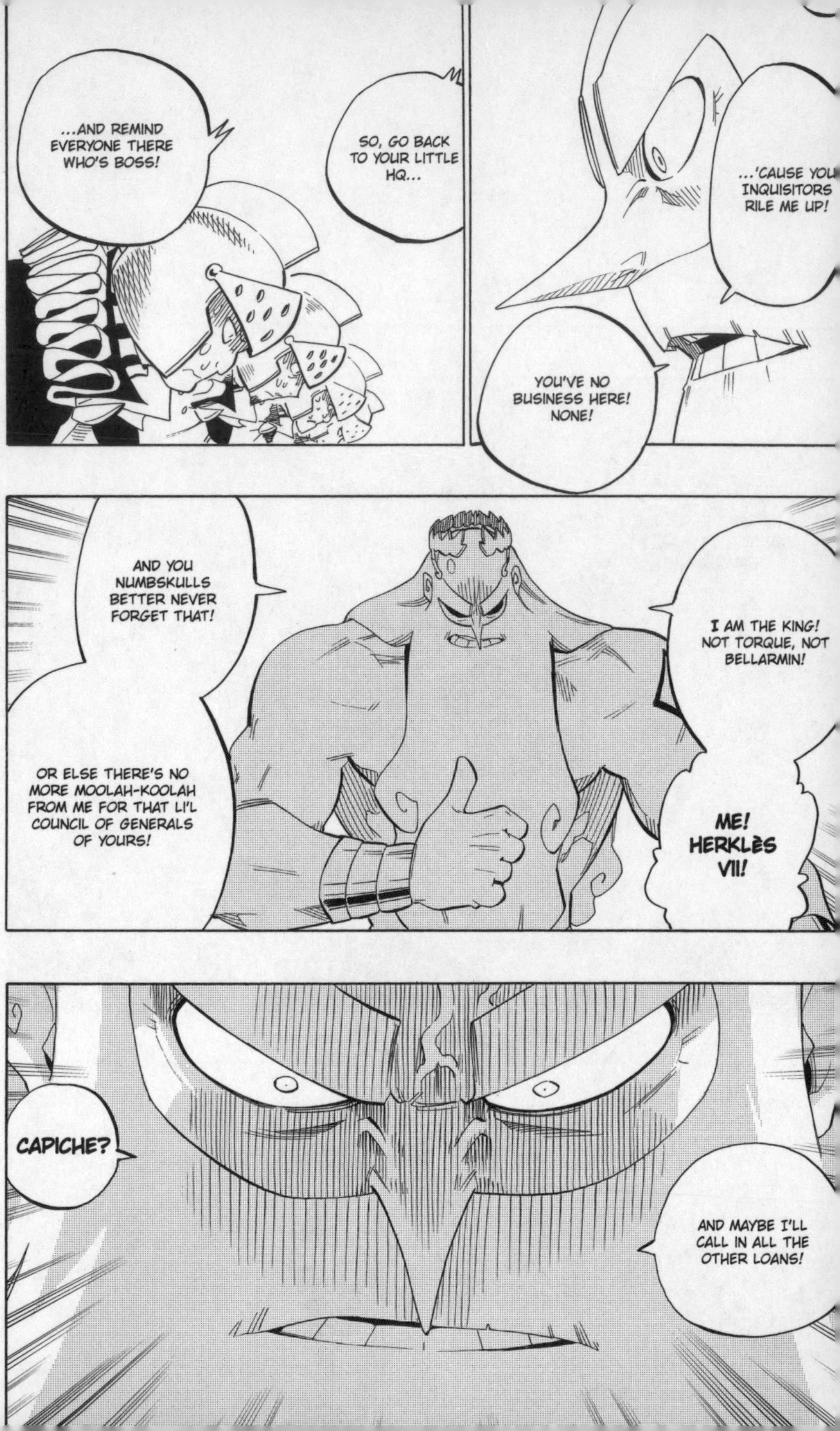
...'CAUSE YOU INQUISITORS RILE ME UP!
YOU'VE NO BUSINESS HERE! NONE!
SO, GO BACK TO YOUR LITTLE HQ...
...AND REMIND EVERYONE THERE WHO'S BOSS!
I AM THE KING! NOT TORQUE, NOT BELLARMIN!
ME! HERKLÈS VII!
AND YOU NUMBSKULLS BETTER NEVER FORGET THAT!
OR ELSE THERE'S NO MORE MOOLAH-KOOLAH FROM ME FOR THAT LI'L COUNCIL OF GENERALS OF YOURS!
AND MAYBE I'LL CALL IN ALL THE OTHER LOANS!
CAPICHE?

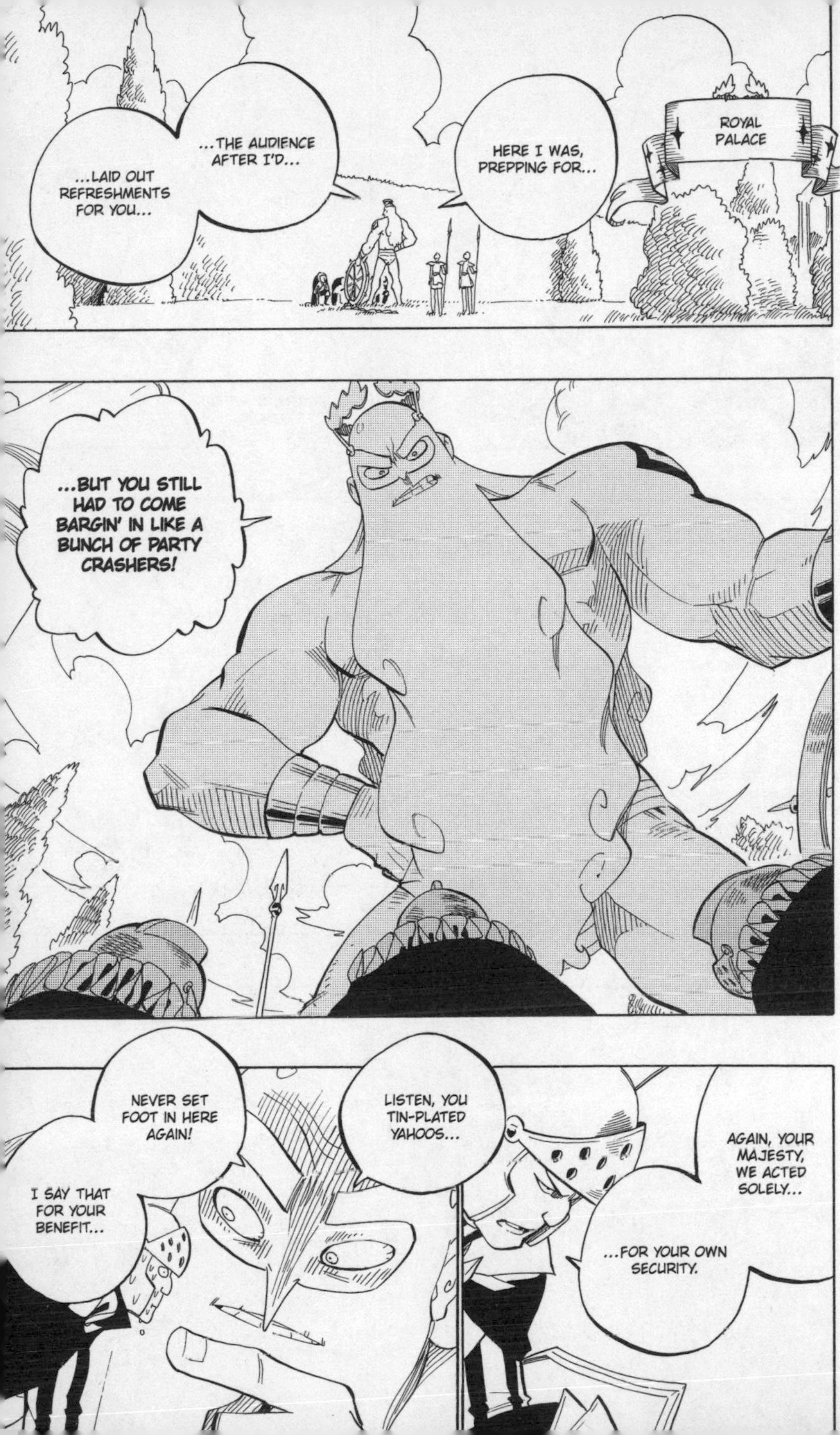
ROYAL PALACE
HERE I WAS, PREPPING FOR...
...THE AUDIENCE AFTER I'D...
...LAID OUT REFRESHMENTS FOR YOU...
...BUT YOU STILL HAD TO COME BARGIN' IN LIKE A BUNCH OF PARTY CRASHERS!
AGAIN, YOUR MAJESTY, WE ACTED SOLELY...
...FOR YOUR OWN SECURITY.
LISTEN, YOU TIN-PLATED YAHOOS...
NEVER SET FOOT IN HERE AGAIN!
I SAY THAT FOR YOUR BENEFIT...

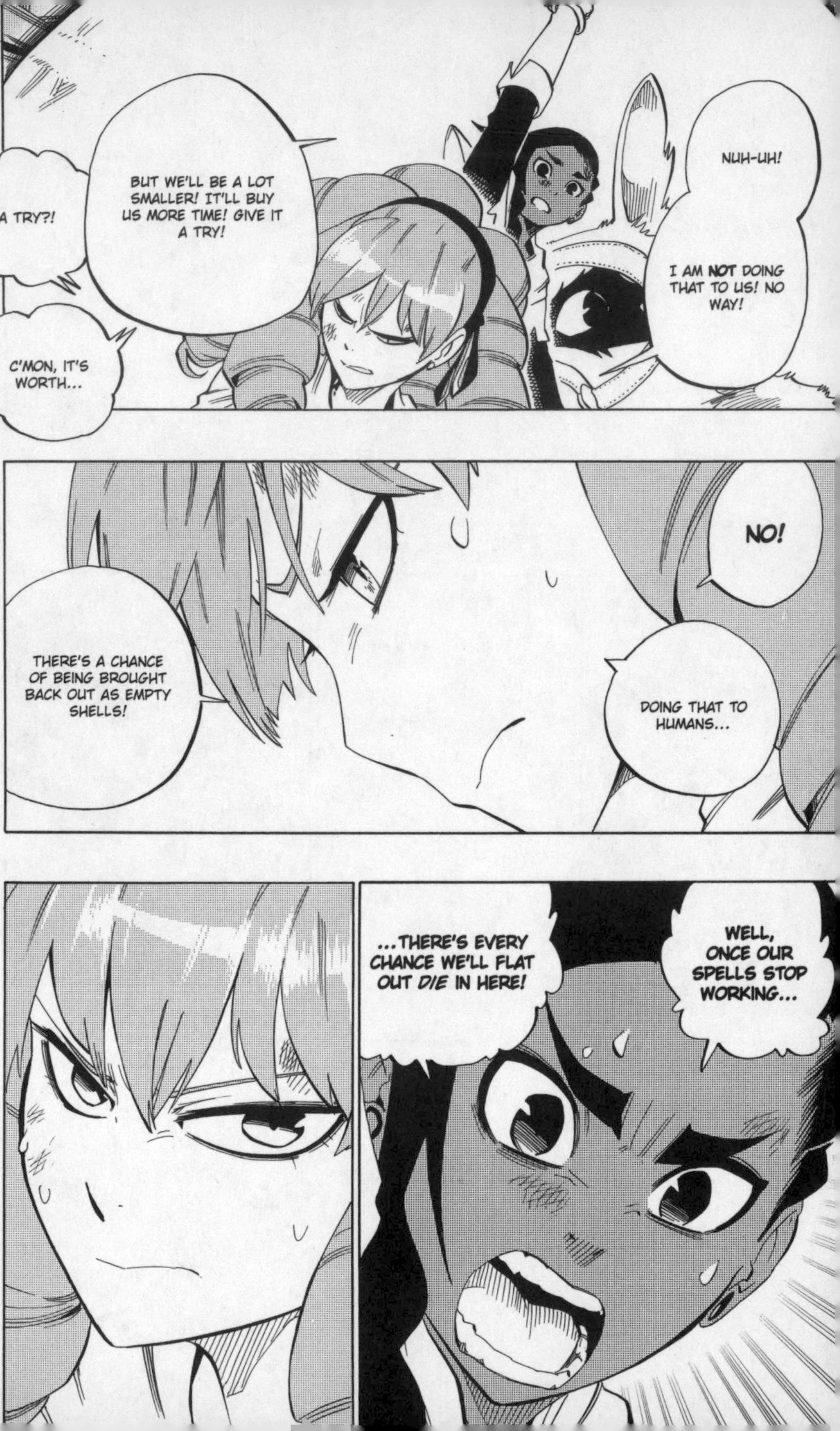
NUH-UH!
I AM **NOT** DOING THAT TO US! NO WAY!
BUT WE'LL BE A LOT SMALLER! IT'LL BUY US MORE TIME! GIVE IT A TRY!
C'MON, IT'S WORTH...
A TRY?!
NO!
DOING THAT TO HUMANS...
THERE'S A CHANCE OF BEING BROUGHT BACK OUT AS EMPTY SHELLS!
WELL, ONCE OUR SPELLS STOP WORKING...
...THERE'S EVERY CHANCE WE'LL FLAT OUT *DIE* IN HERE!

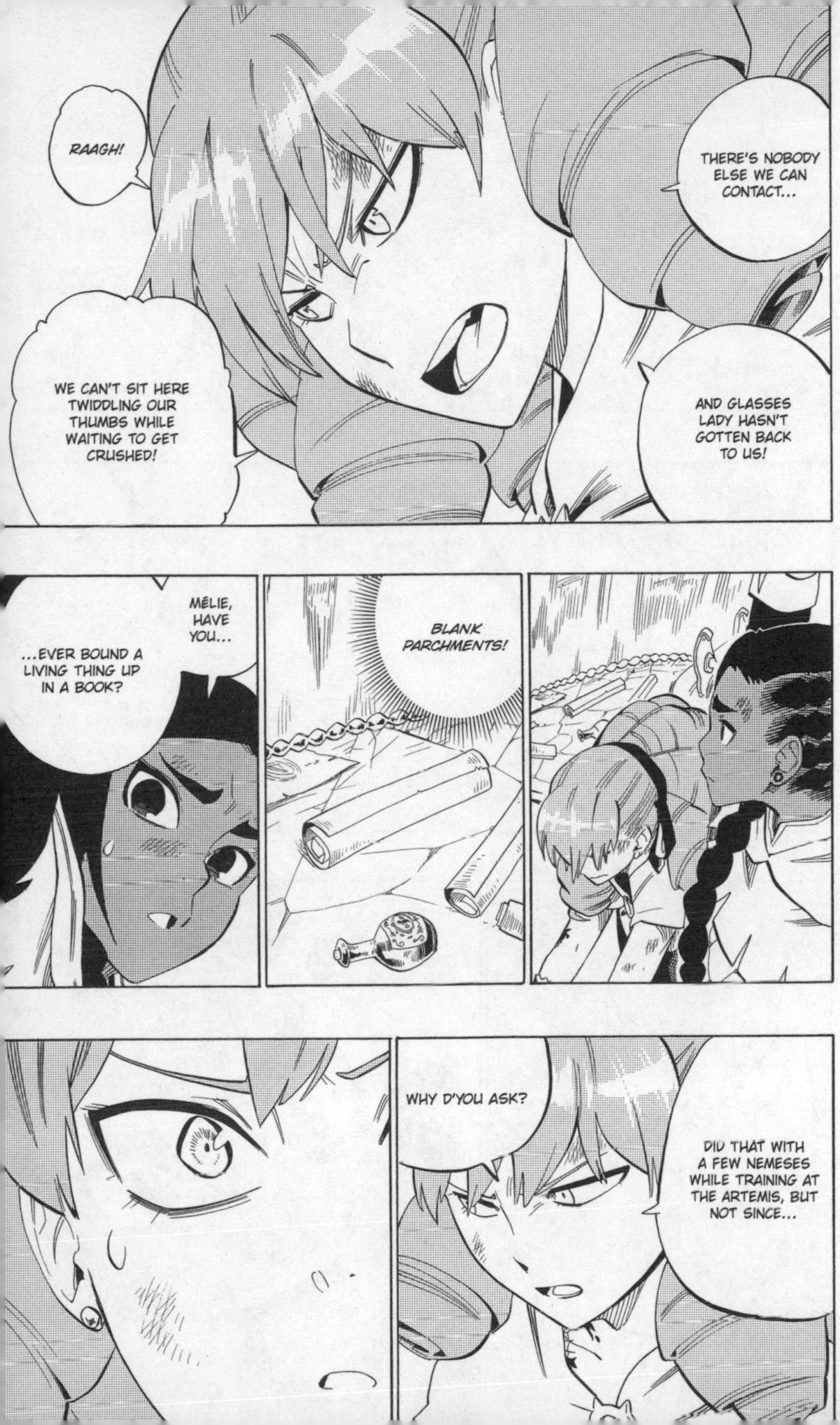
THERE'S NOBODY ELSE WE CAN CONTACT...
AND GLASSES LADY HASN'T GOTTEN BACK TO US!
RAAGH!
WE CAN'T SIT HERE TWIDDLING OUR THUMBS WHILE WAITING TO GET CRUSHED!
BLANK PARCHMENTS!
MÉLIE, HAVE YOU...
...EVER BOUND A LIVING THING UP IN A BOOK?
WHY D'YOU ASK?
DID THAT WITH A FEW NEMESES WHILE TRAINING AT THE ARTEMIS, BUT NOT SINCE...

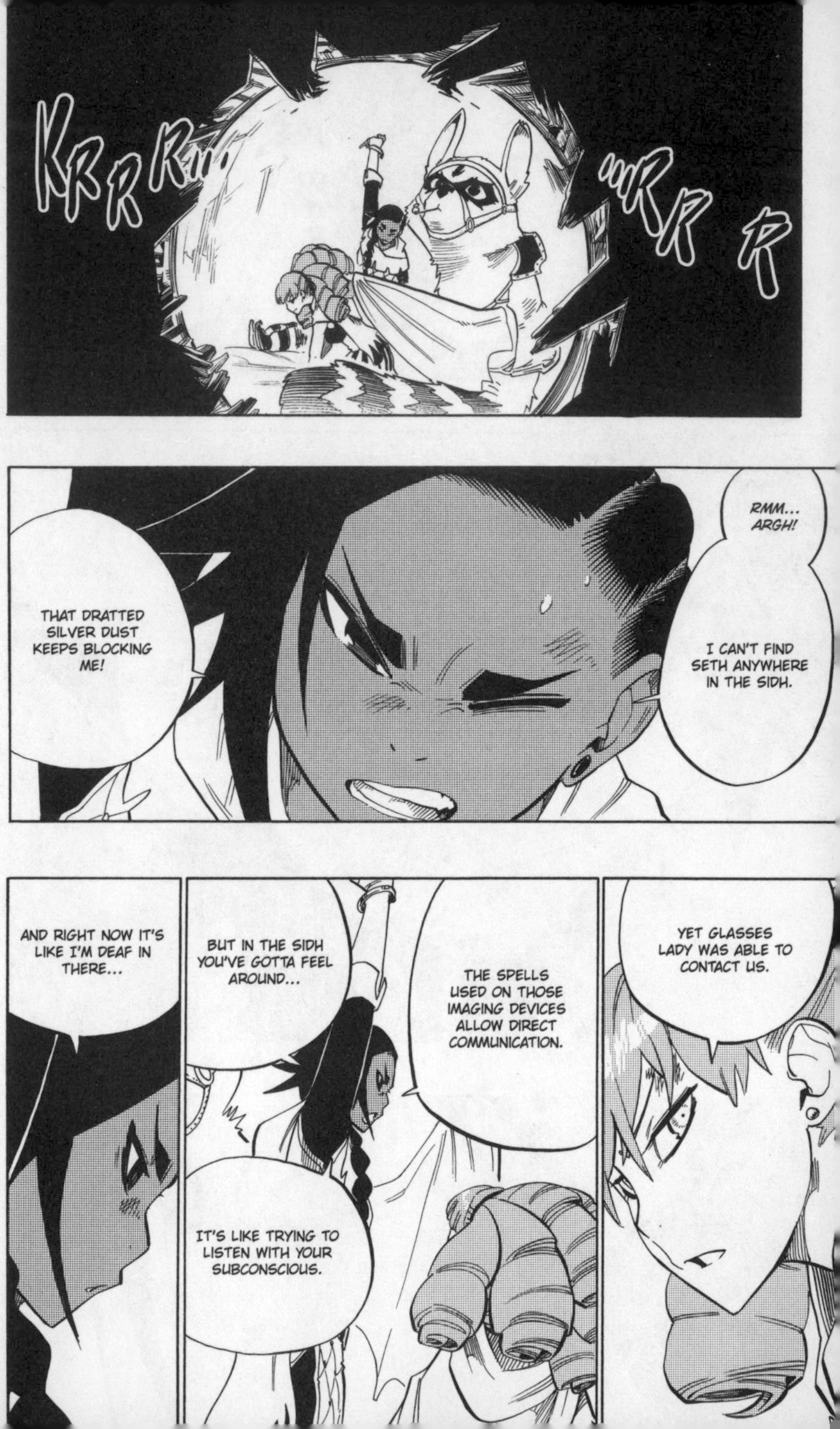
KRRR...
...RRR
RMM... ARGH!
I CAN'T FIND SETH ANYWHERE IN THE SIDH.
THAT DRATTED SILVER DUST KEEPS BLOCKING ME!
YET GLASSES LADY WAS ABLE TO CONTACT US.
THE SPELLS USED ON THOSE IMAGING DEVICES ALLOW DIRECT COMMUNICATION.
BUT IN THE SIDH YOU'VE GOTTA FEEL AROUND...
IT'S LIKE TRYING TO LISTEN WITH YOUR SUBCONSCIOUS.
AND RIGHT NOW IT'S LIKE I'M DEAF IN THERE...

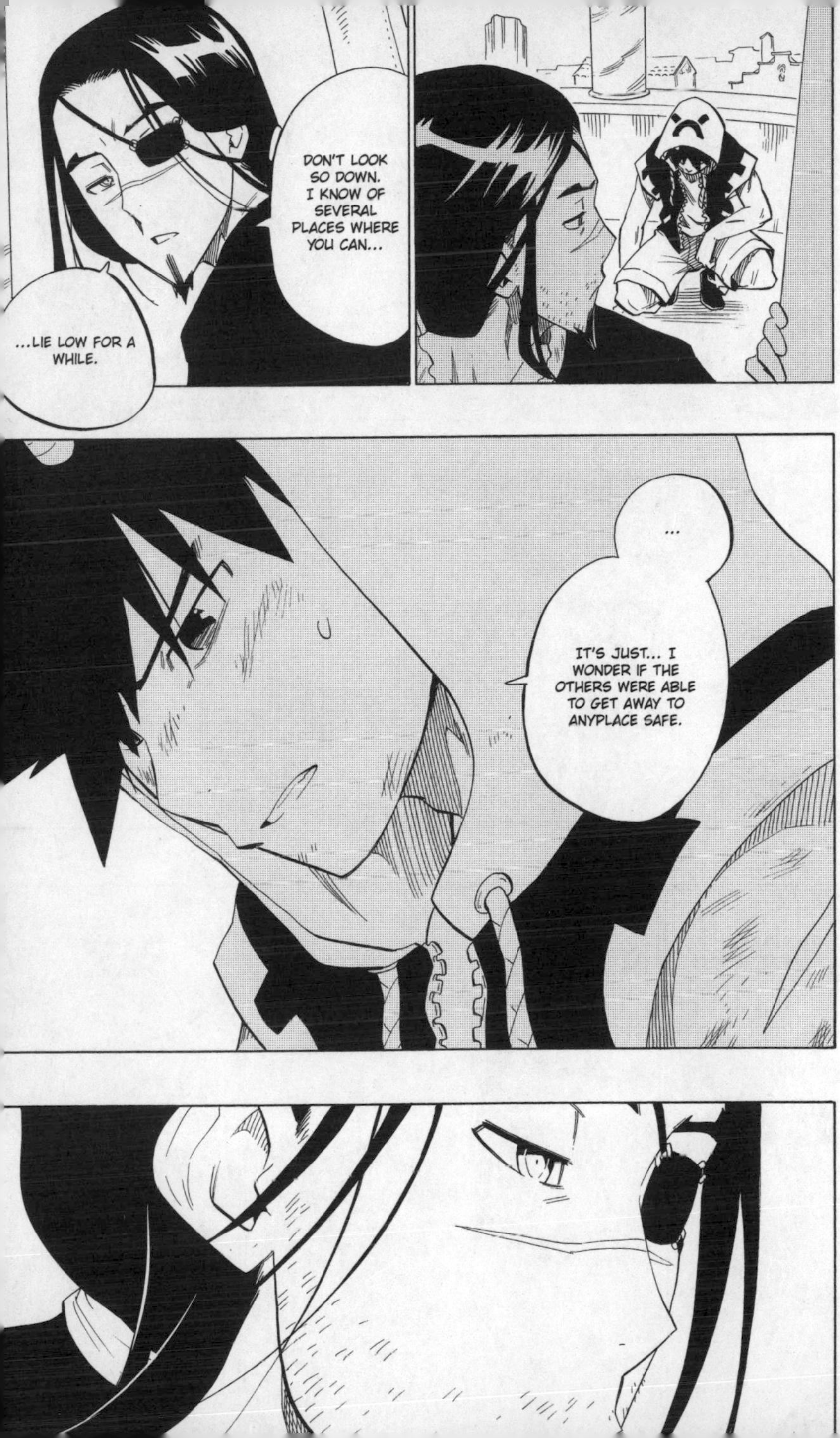
DON'T LOOK SO DOWN. I KNOW OF SEVERAL PLACES WHERE YOU CAN...
...LIE LOW FOR A WHILE.
...
IT'S JUST... I WONDER IF THE OTHERS WERE ABLE TO GET AWAY TO ANYPLACE SAFE.

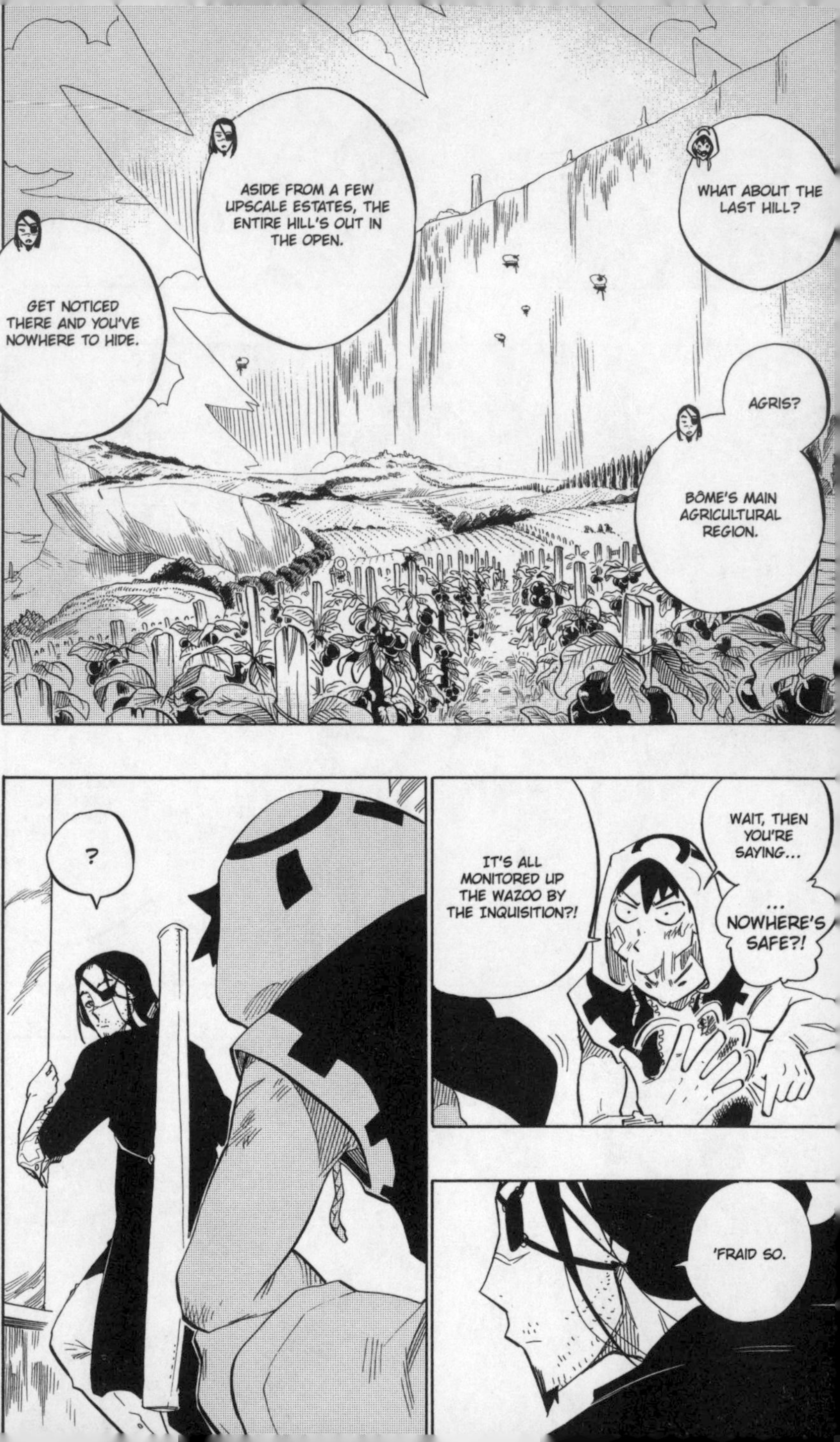
WHAT ABOUT THE LAST HILL?
AGRIS?
BÔME'S MAIN AGRICULTURAL REGION.
ASIDE FROM A FEW UPSCALE ESTATES, THE ENTIRE HILL'S OUT IN THE OPEN.
GET NOTICED THERE AND YOU'VE NOWHERE TO HIDE.
WAIT, THEN YOU'RE SAYING...
IT'S ALL MONITORED UP THE WAZOO BY THE INQUISITION?!
...NOWHERE'S SAFE?!
'FRAID SO.
?

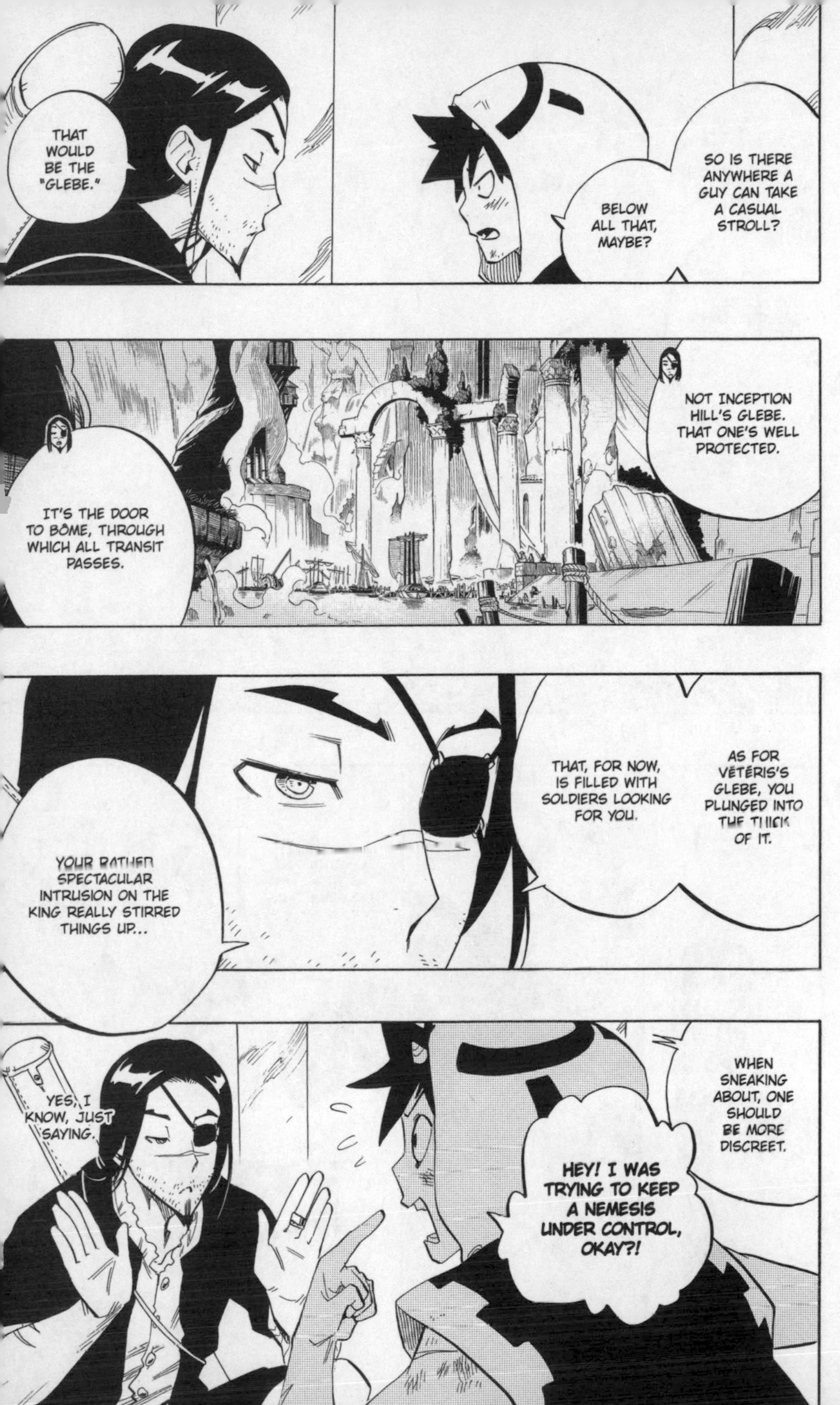
SO IS THERE ANYWHERE A GUY CAN TAKE A CASUAL STROLL?
BELOW ALL THAT, MAYBE?
THAT WOULD BE THE "GLEBE."
NOT INCEPTION HILL'S GLEBE. THAT ONE'S WELL PROTECTED.
IT'S THE DOOR TO BÔME, THROUGH WHICH ALL TRANSIT PASSES.
AS FOR VÉTÉRIS'S GLEBE, YOU PLUNGED INTO THE THICK OF IT.
THAT, FOR NOW, IS FILLED WITH SOLDIERS LOOKING FOR YOU.
YOUR RATHER SPECTACULAR INTRUSION ON THE KING REALLY STIRRED THINGS UP...
WHEN SNEAKING ABOUT, ONE SHOULD BE MORE DISCREET.
HEY! I WAS TRYING TO KEEP A NEMESIS UNDER CONTROL, OKAY?!
YES, I KNOW, JUST SAYING.

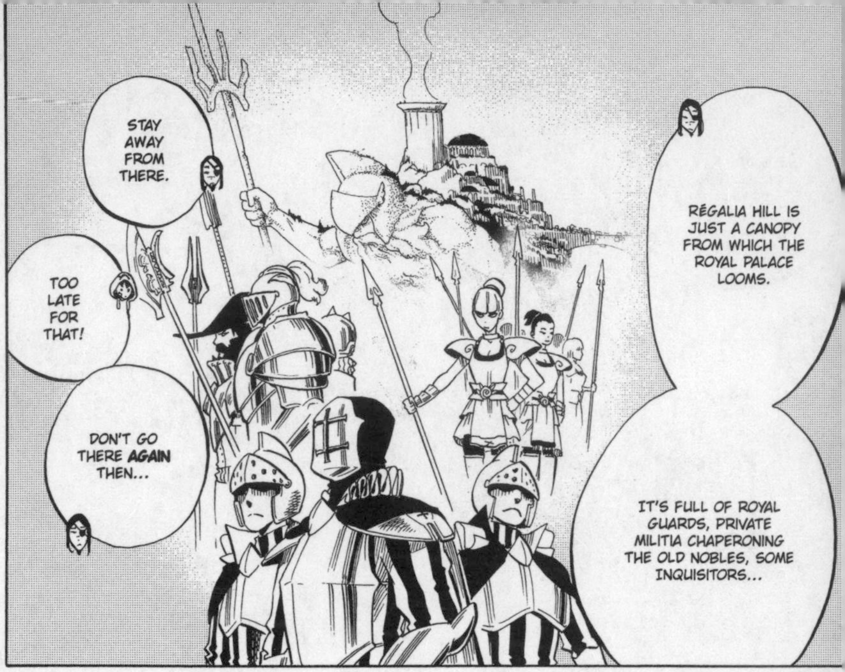
RÉGALIA HILL IS JUST A CANOPY FROM WHICH THE ROYAL PALACE LOOMS.
IT'S FULL OF ROYAL GUARDS, PRIVATE MILITIA CHAPERONING THE OLD NOBLES, SOME INQUISITORS...
STAY AWAY FROM THERE.
TOO LATE FOR THAT!
DON'T GO THERE **AGAIN** THEN...
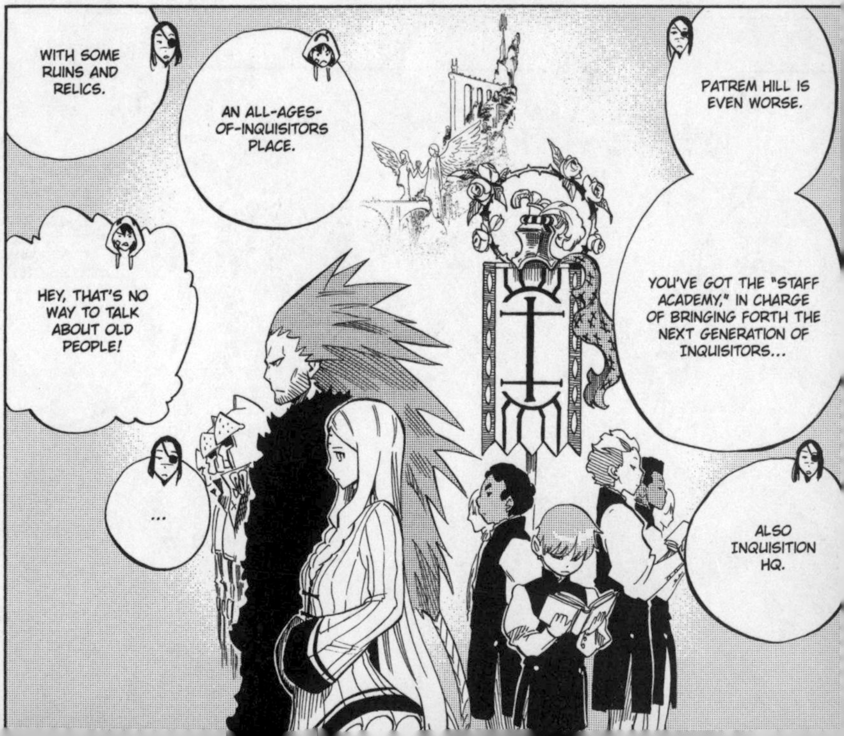
PATREM HILL IS EVEN WORSE.
YOU'VE GOT THE "STAFF ACADEMY," IN CHARGE OF BRINGING FORTH THE NEXT GENERATION OF INQUISITORS...
ALSO INQUISITION HQ.
AN ALL-AGES-OF-INQUISITORS PLACE.
WITH SOME RUINS AND RELICS.
HEY, THAT'S NO WAY TO TALK ABOUT OLD PEOPLE!
...

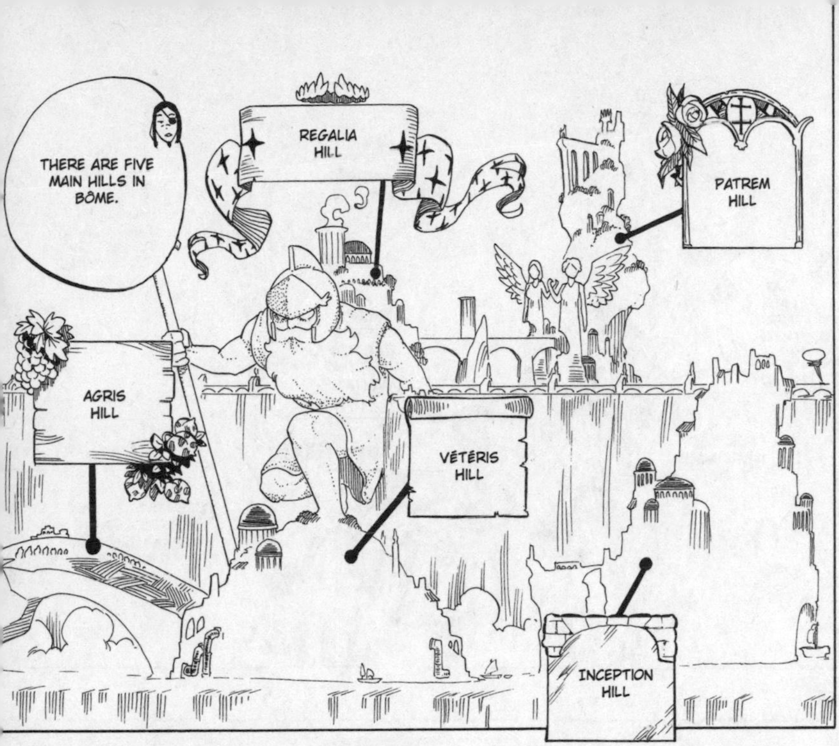
PATREM HILL
REGALIA HILL
THERE ARE FIVE MAIN HILLS IN BÔME.
VÉTÉRIS HILL
AGRIS HILL
INCEPTION HILL

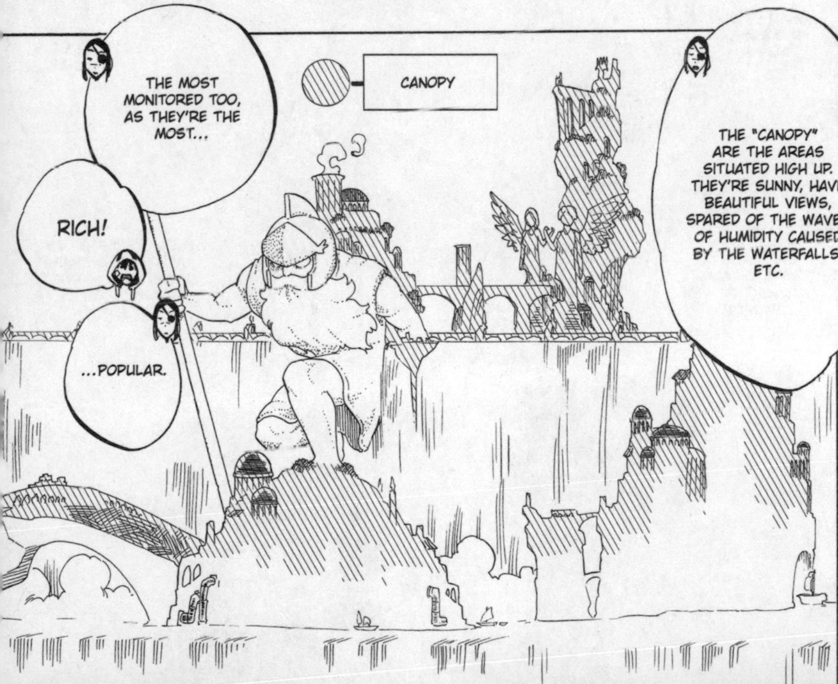
THE "CANOPY" ARE THE AREAS SITUATED HIGH UP. THEY'RE SUNNY, HAVE BEAUTIFUL VIEWS, SPARED OF THE WAVES OF HUMIDITY CAUSED BY THE WATERFALLS, ETC.
CANOPY
THE MOST MONITORED TOO, AS THEY'RE THE MOST...
RICH!
...POPULAR.

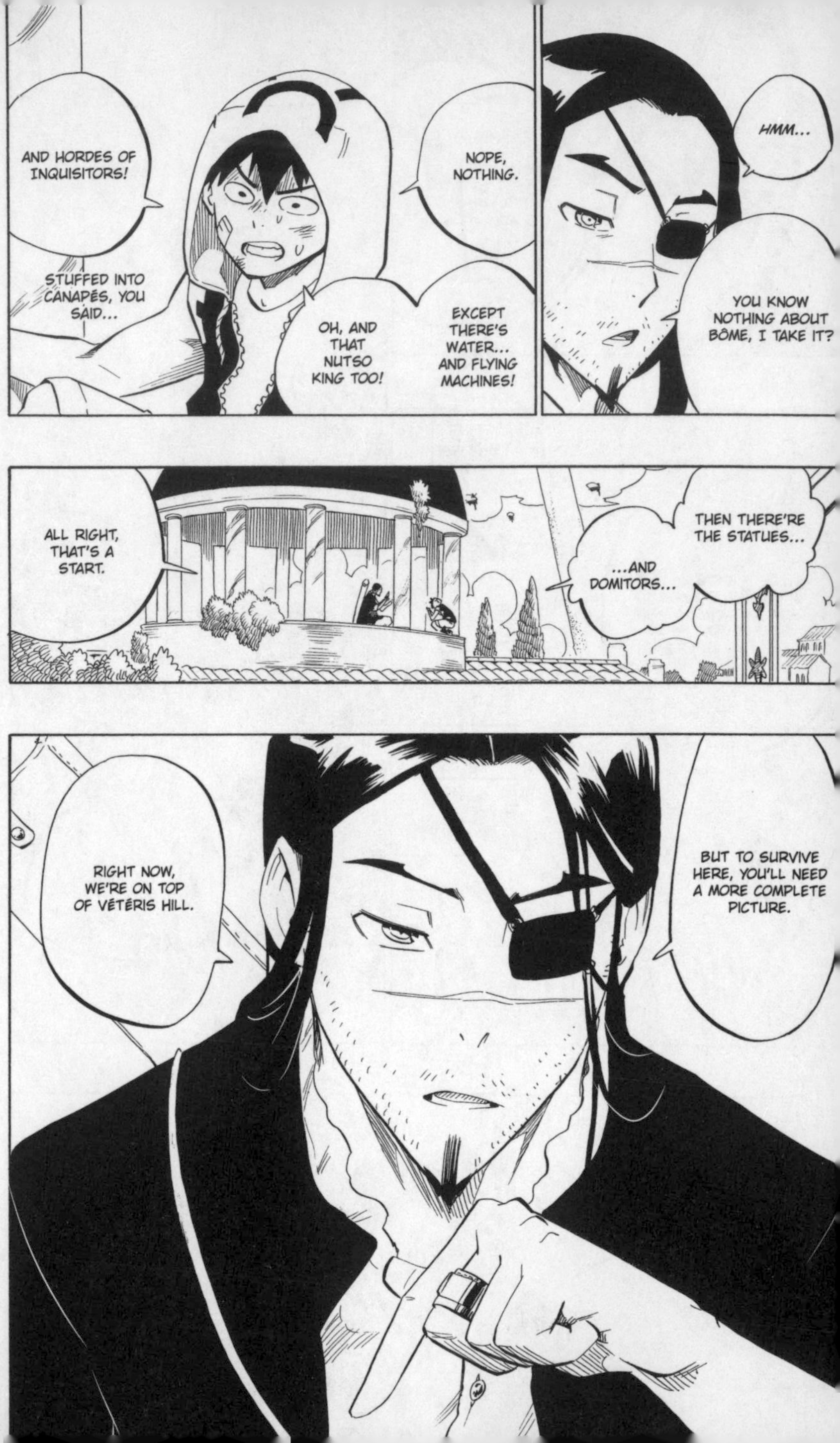
HMM...
YOU KNOW NOTHING ABOUT BÔME, I TAKE IT?
NOPE, NOTHING.
EXCEPT THERE'S WATER... AND FLYING MACHINES!
OH, AND THAT NUTSO KING TOO!
AND HORDES OF INQUISITORS!
STUFFED INTO CANAPÉS, YOU SAID...
THEN THERE'RE THE STATUES...
...AND DOMITORS...
ALL RIGHT, THAT'S A START.
BUT TO SURVIVE HERE, YOU'LL NEED A MORE COMPLETE PICTURE.
RIGHT NOW, WE'RE ON TOP OF VÉTERIS HILL.

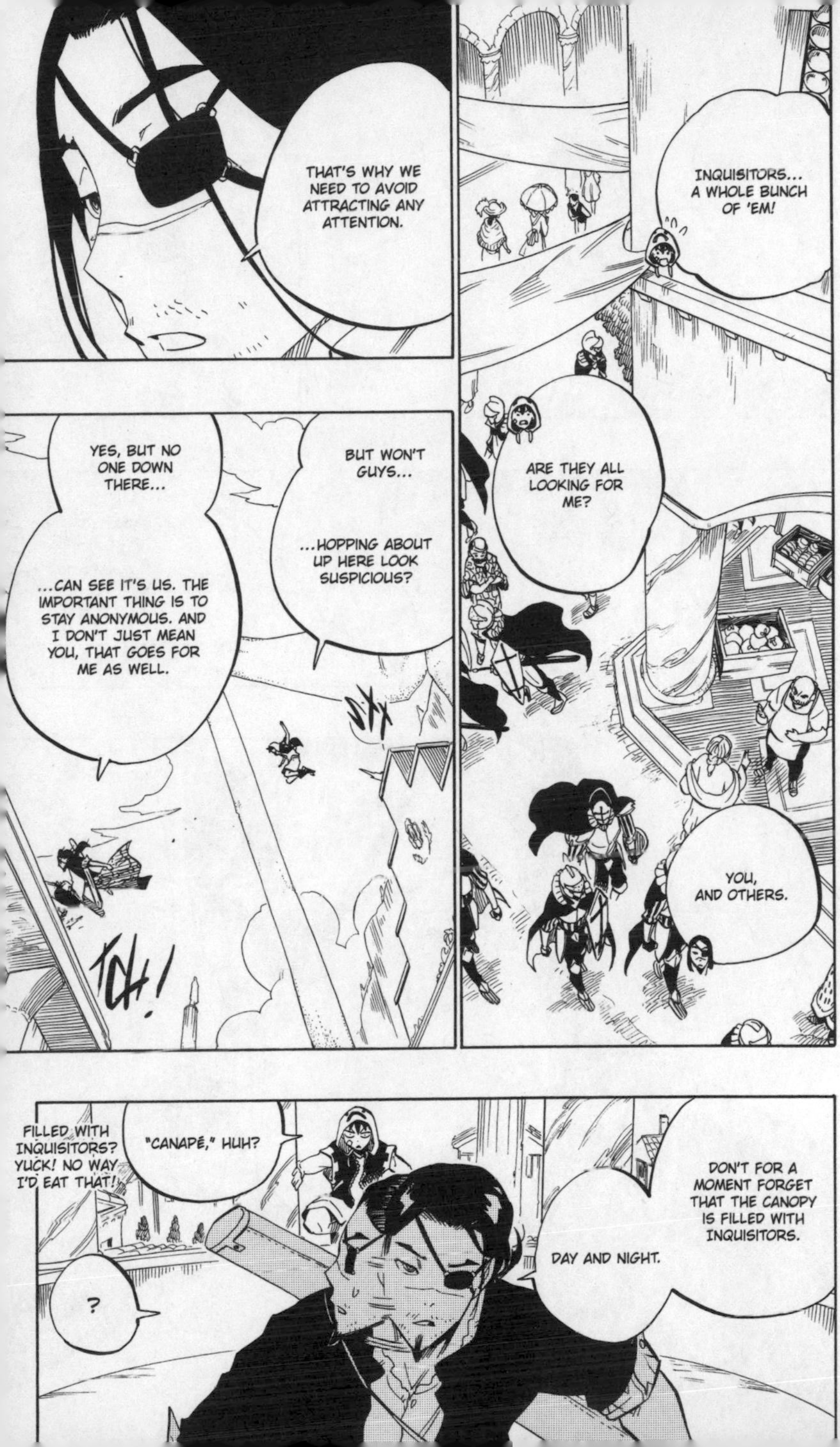
INQUISITORS... A WHOLE BUNCH OF 'EM!
ARE THEY ALL LOOKING FOR ME?
YOU, AND OTHERS.
THAT'S WHY WE NEED TO AVOID ATTRACTING ANY ATTENTION.
BUT WON'T GUYS...
...HOPPING ABOUT UP HERE LOOK SUSPICIOUS?
YES, BUT NO ONE DOWN THERE...
...CAN SEE IT'S US. THE IMPORTANT THING IS TO STAY ANONYMOUS. AND I DON'T JUST MEAN YOU, THAT GOES FOR ME AS WELL.
TCH!
DON'T FOR A MOMENT FORGET THAT THE CANOPY IS FILLED WITH INQUISITORS.
DAY AND NIGHT.
"CANAPÉ," HUH?
FILLED WITH INQUISITORS? YUCK! NO WAY I'D EAT THAT!
?

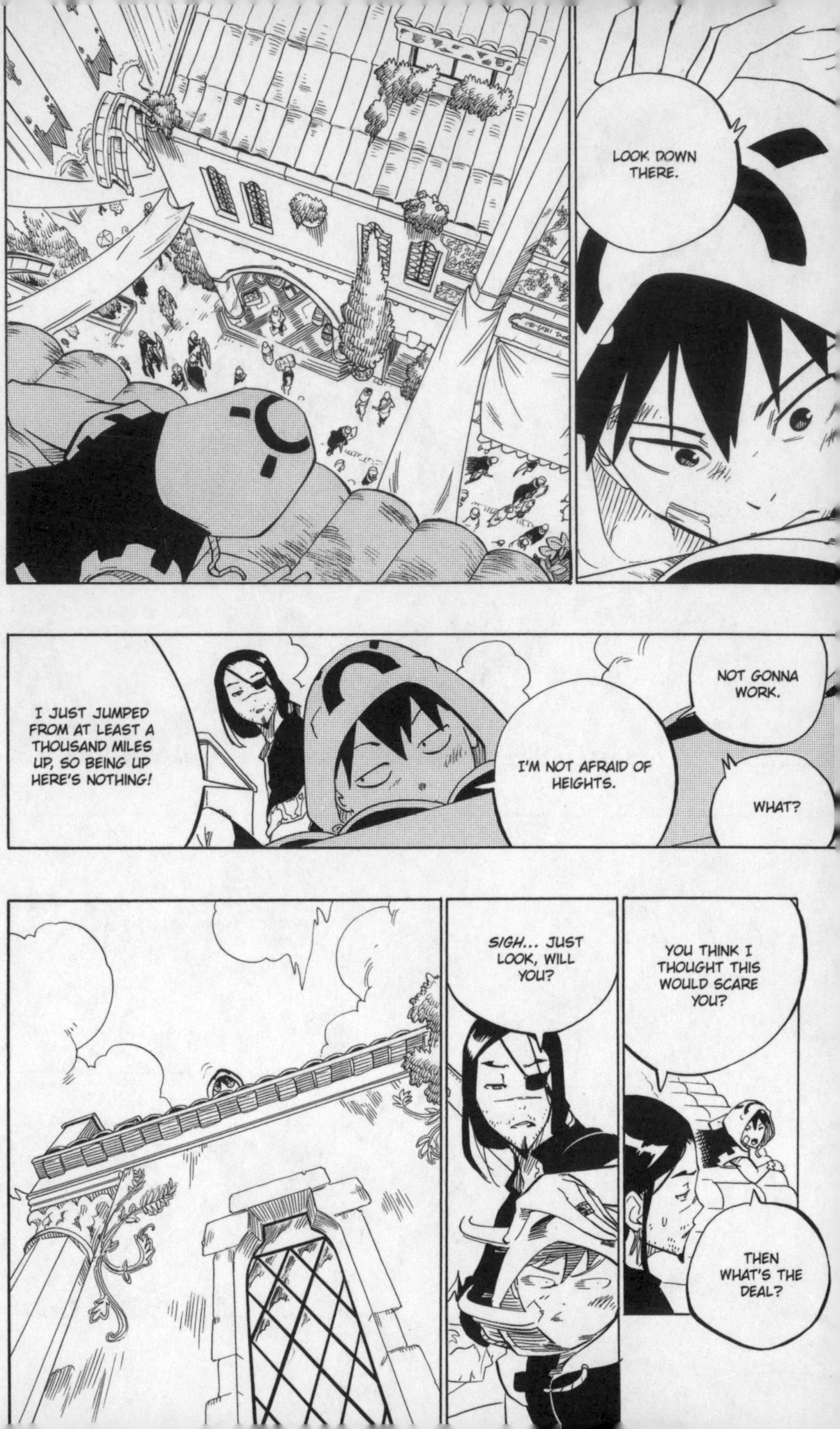
LOOK DOWN THERE.
NOT GONNA WORK.
WHAT?
I'M NOT AFRAID OF HEIGHTS.
I JUST JUMPED FROM AT LEAST A THOUSAND MILES UP, SO BEING UP HERE'S NOTHING!
YOU THINK I THOUGHT THIS WOULD SCARE YOU?
THEN WHAT'S THE DEAL?
SIGH... JUST LOOK, WILL YOU?

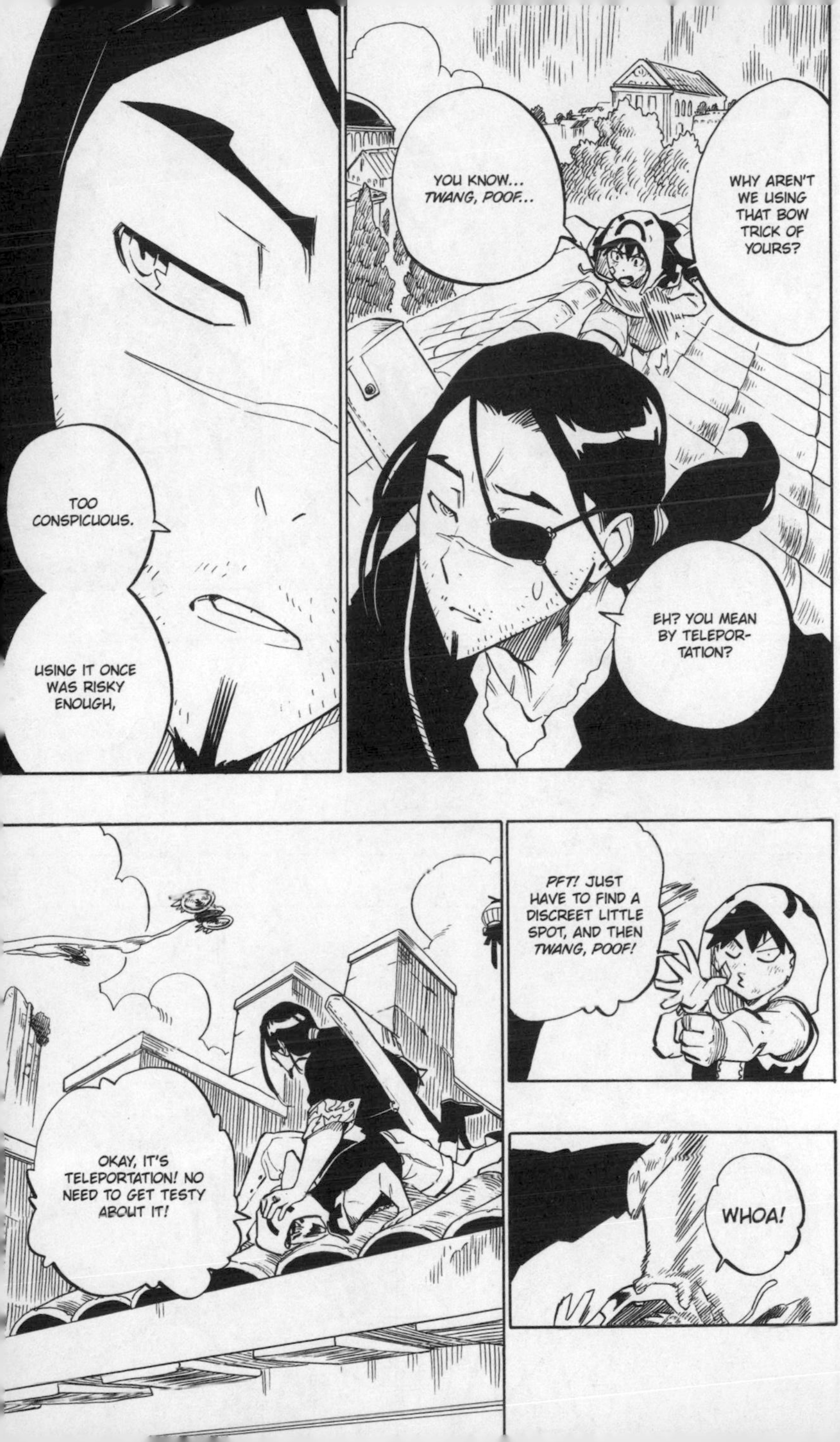
WHY AREN'T WE USING THAT BOW TRICK OF YOURS?
YOU KNOW... *TWANG, POOF...*
EH? YOU MEAN BY TELEPORTATION?
TOO CONSPICUOUS.
USING IT ONCE WAS RISKY ENOUGH,
PFT! JUST HAVE TO FIND A DISCREET LITTLE SPOT, AND THEN *TWANG, POOF!*
WHOA!
OKAY, IT'S TELEPORTATION! NO NEED TO GET TESTY ABOUT IT!

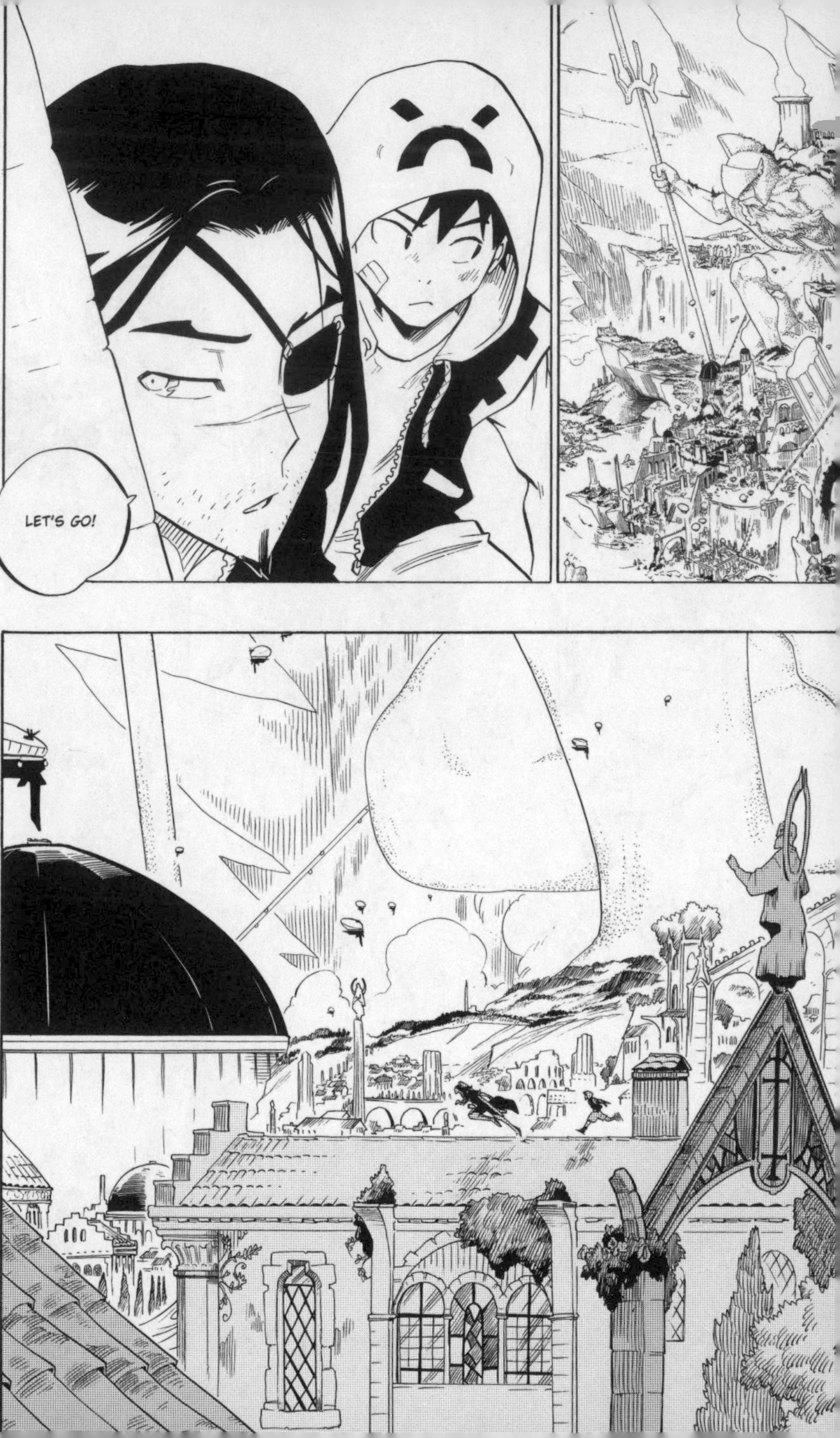
LET'S GO!

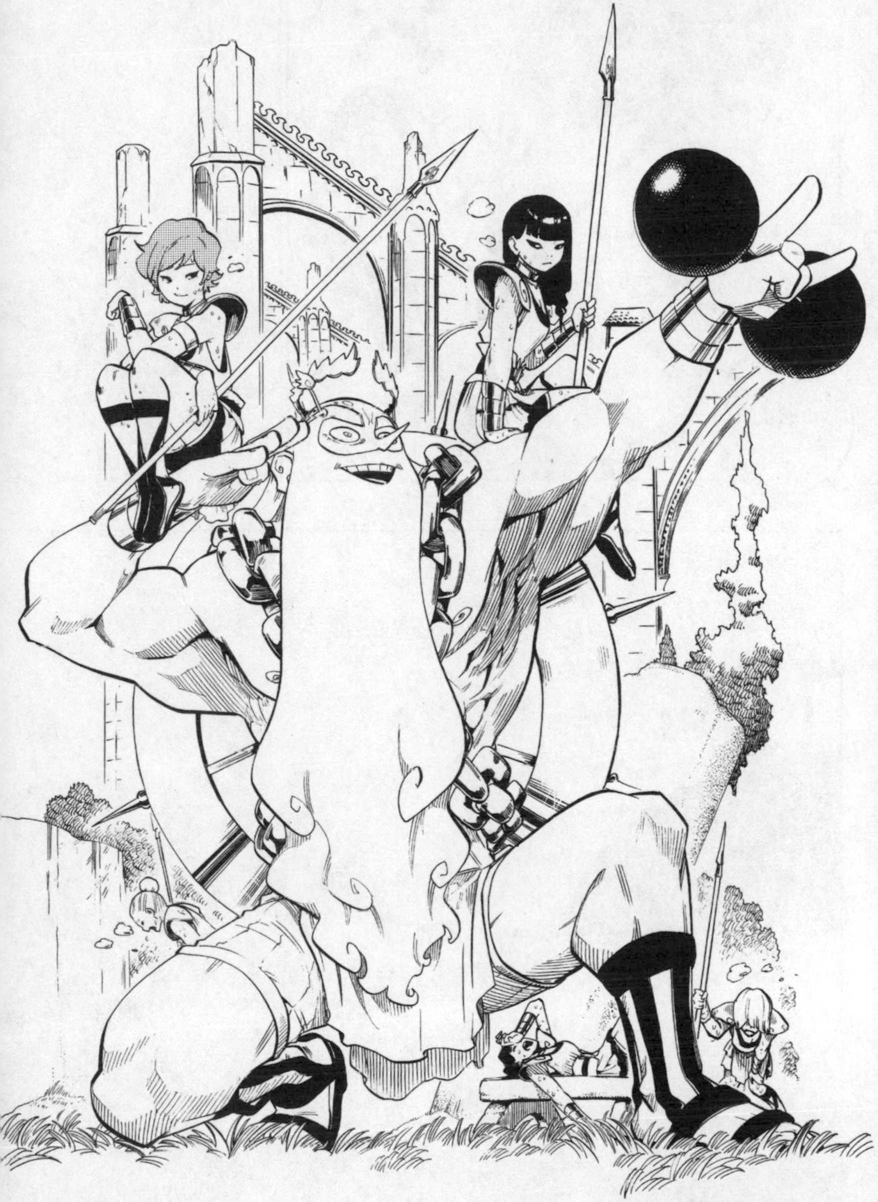

Chapter 95

The Hills of Bôme

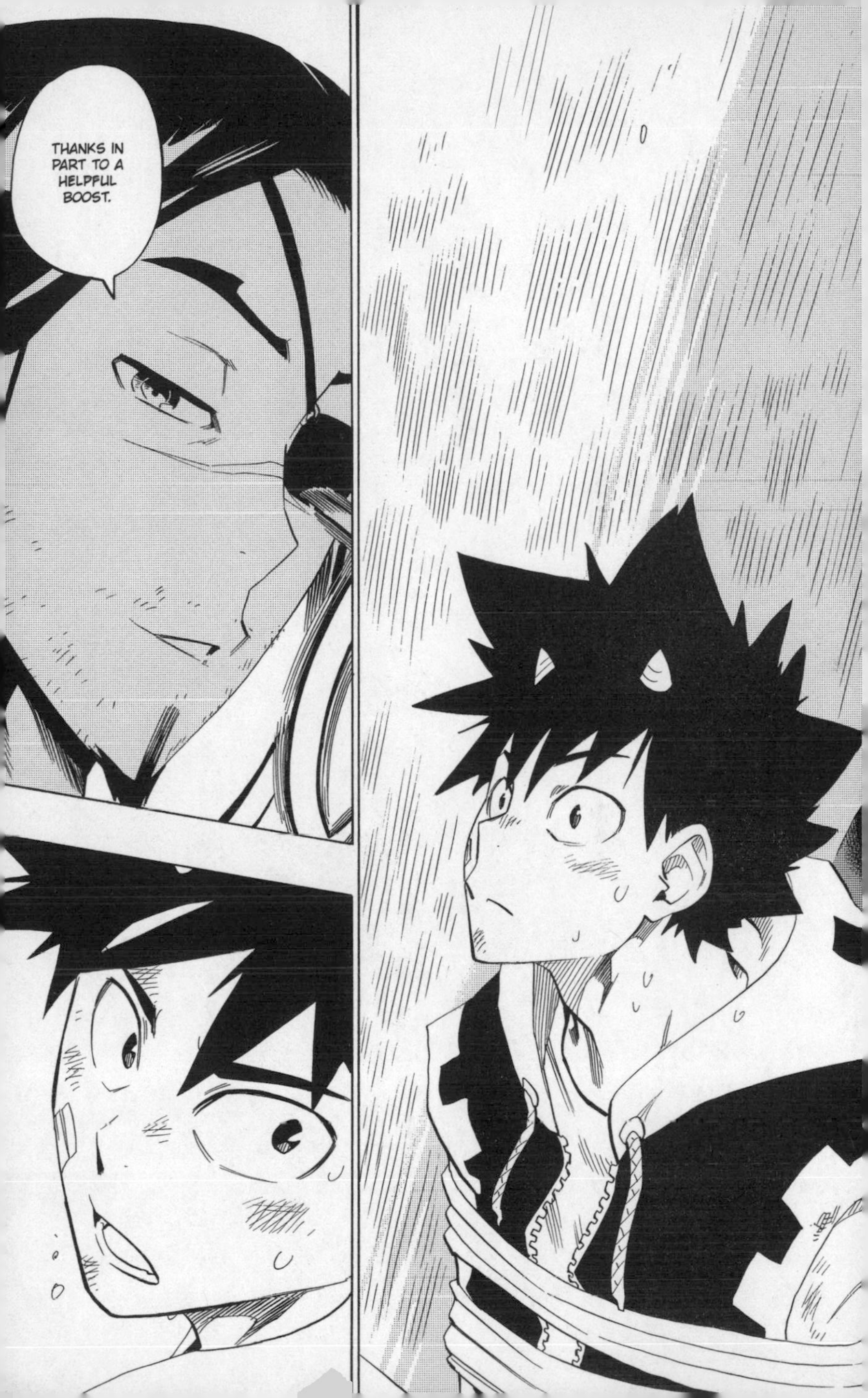
THANKS IN PART TO A HELPFUL BOOST.

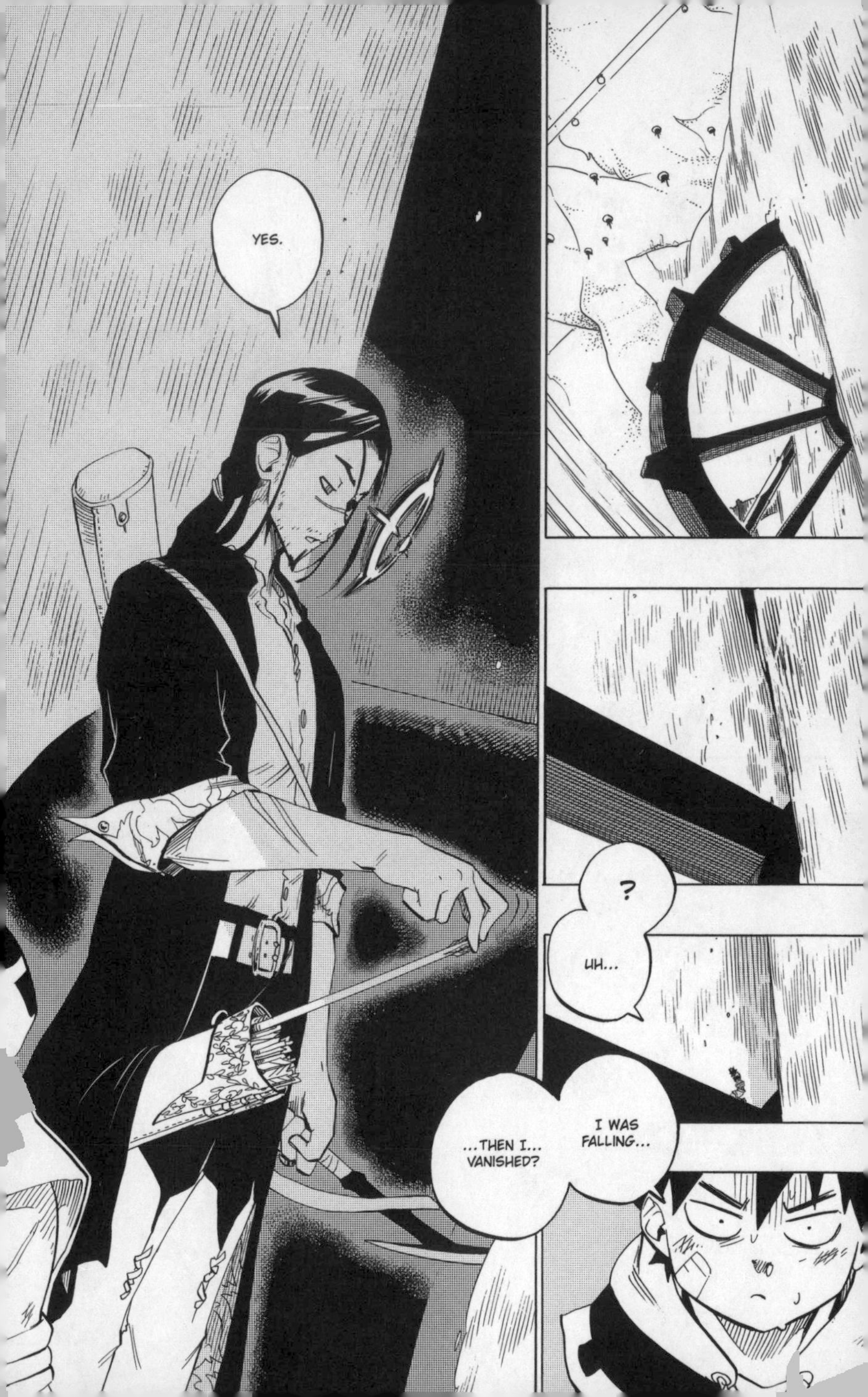
?
UH...
I WAS FALLING...
...THEN I... VANISHED?
YES.

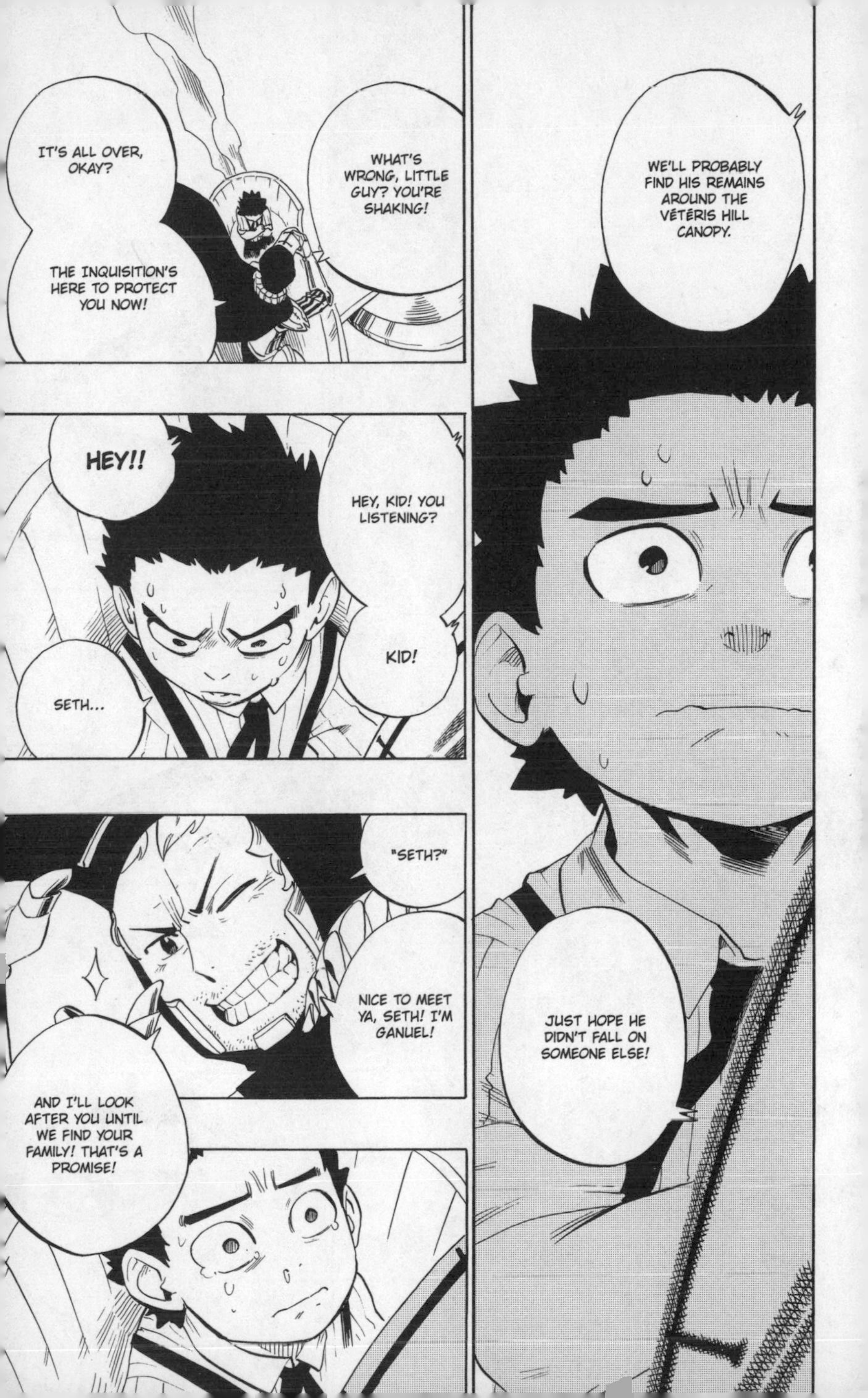

WE'LL PROBABLY FIND HIS REMAINS AROUND THE VÉTÉRIS HILL CANOPY.
JUST HOPE HE DIDN'T FALL ON SOMEONE ELSE!
WHAT'S WRONG, LITTLE GUY? YOU'RE SHAKING!
IT'S ALL OVER, OKAY?
THE INQUISITION'S HERE TO PROTECT YOU NOW!
HEY!!
HEY, KID! YOU LISTENING?
KID!
SETH...
"SETH?"
NICE TO MEET YA, SETH! I'M GANUEL!
AND I'LL LOOK AFTER YOU UNTIL WE FIND YOUR FAMILY! THAT'S A PROMISE!

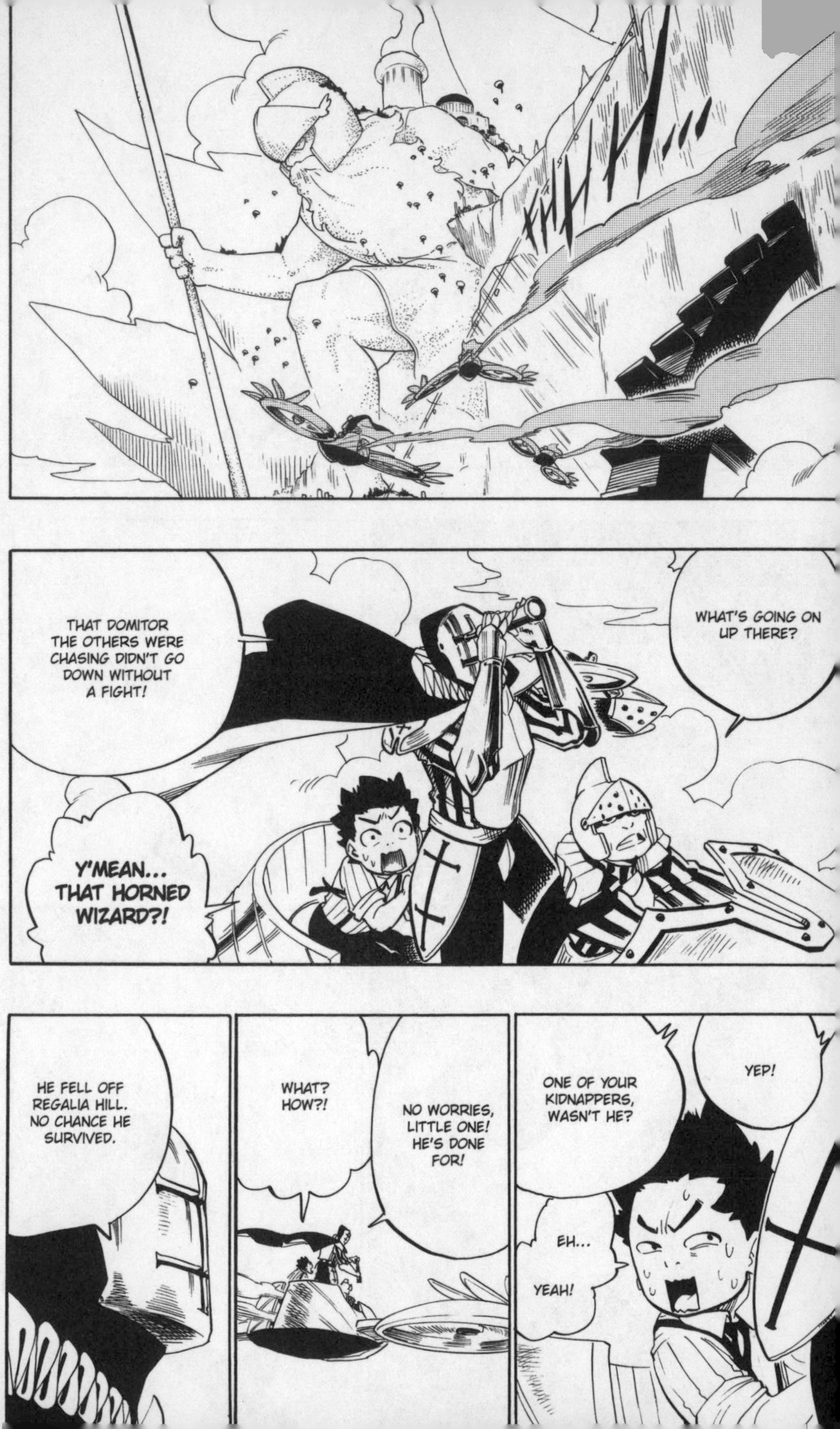
FHHH...
WHAT'S GOING ON UP THERE?
THAT DOMITOR THE OTHERS WERE CHASING DIDN'T GO DOWN WITHOUT A FIGHT!
Y'MEAN... THAT HORNED WIZARD?!
YEP!
ONE OF YOUR KIDNAPPERS, WASN'T HE?
EH...
YEAH!
NO WORRIES, LITTLE ONE! HE'S DONE FOR!
WHAT? HOW?!
HE FELL OFF REGALIA HILL. NO CHANCE HE SURVIVED.

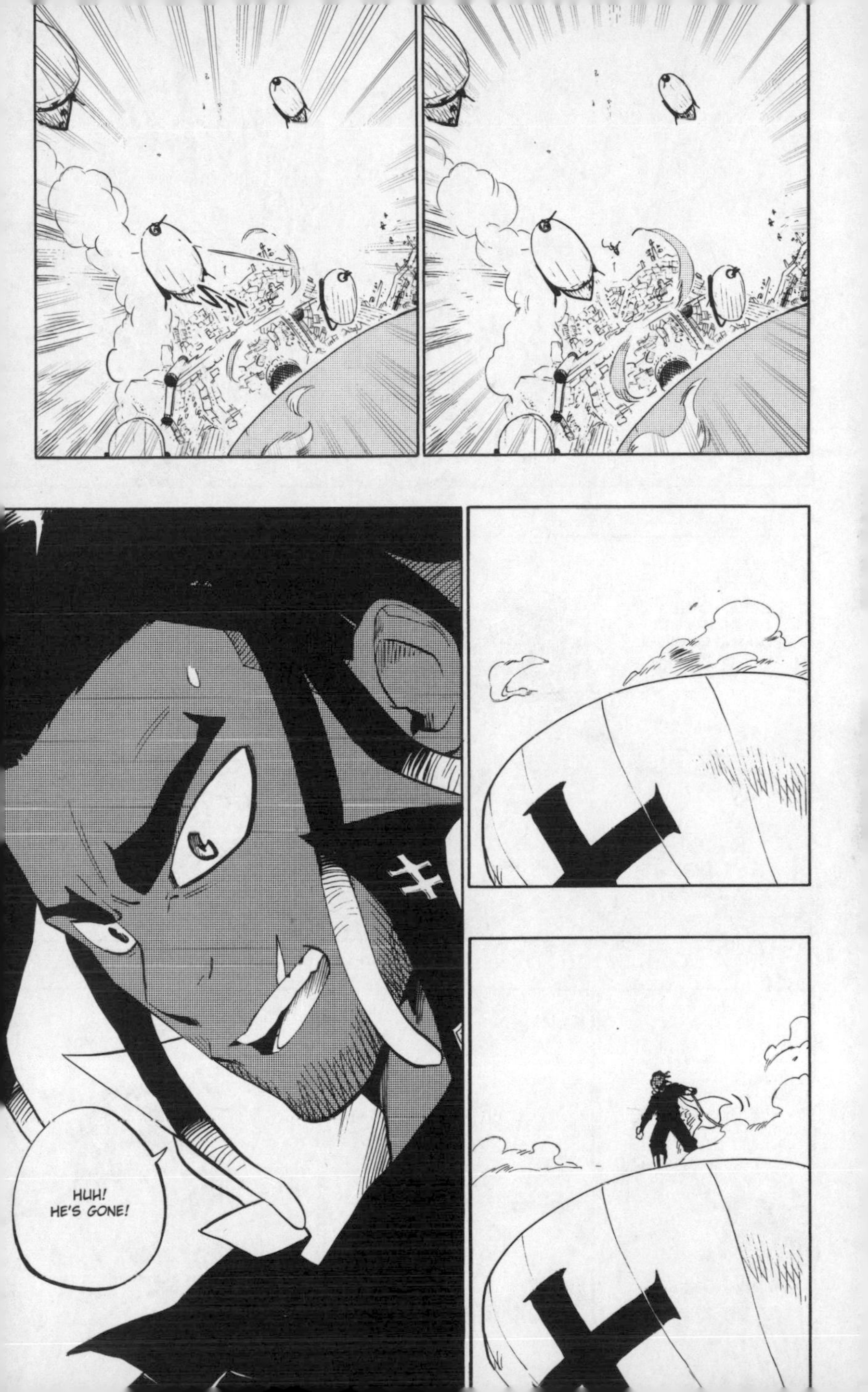
HUH! HE'S GONE!

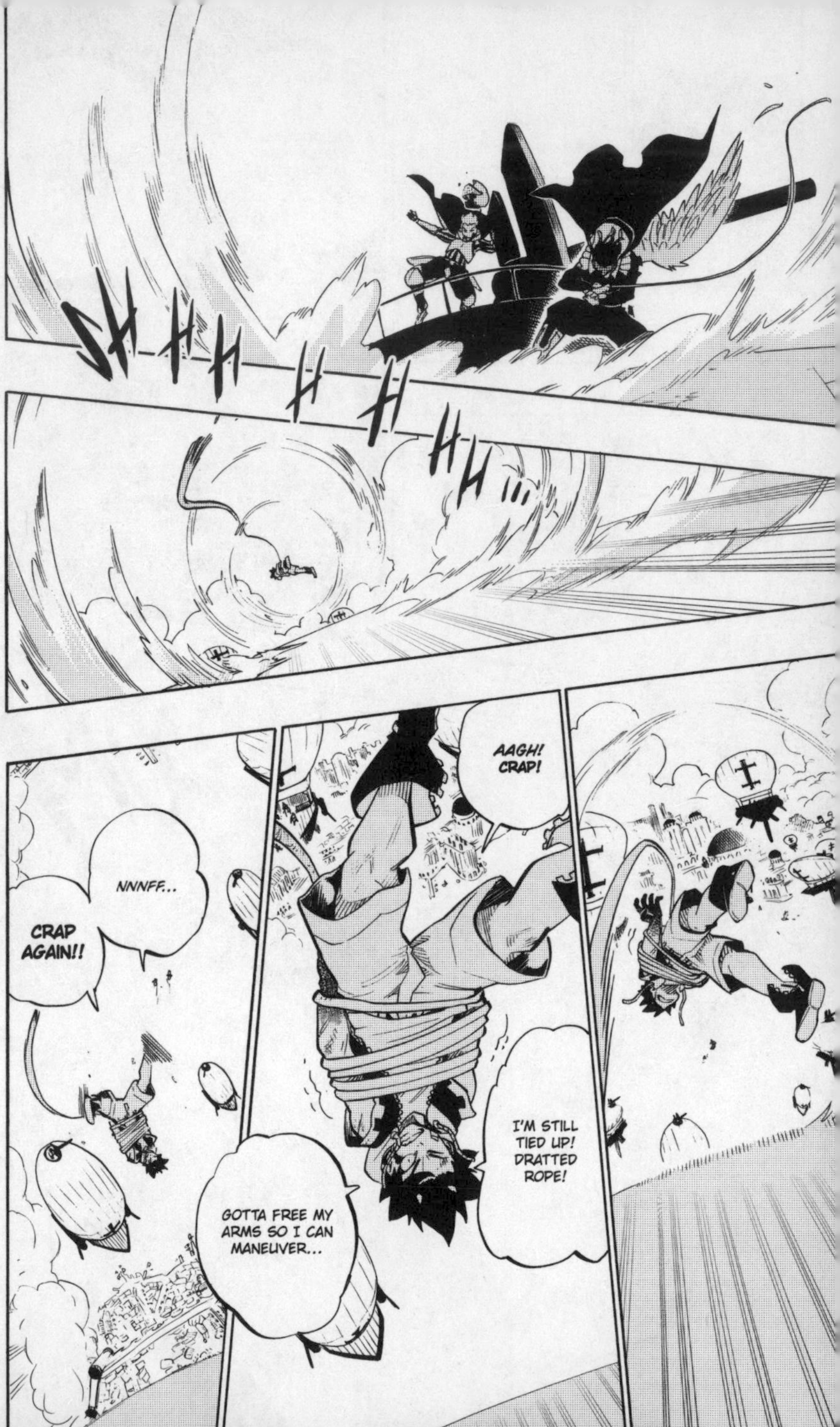
SHHHHHHH...
AAGH! CRAP!
I'M STILL TIED UP! DRATTED ROPE!
GOTTA FREE MY ARMS SO I CAN MANEUVER...
NNNFF...
CRAP AGAIN!!

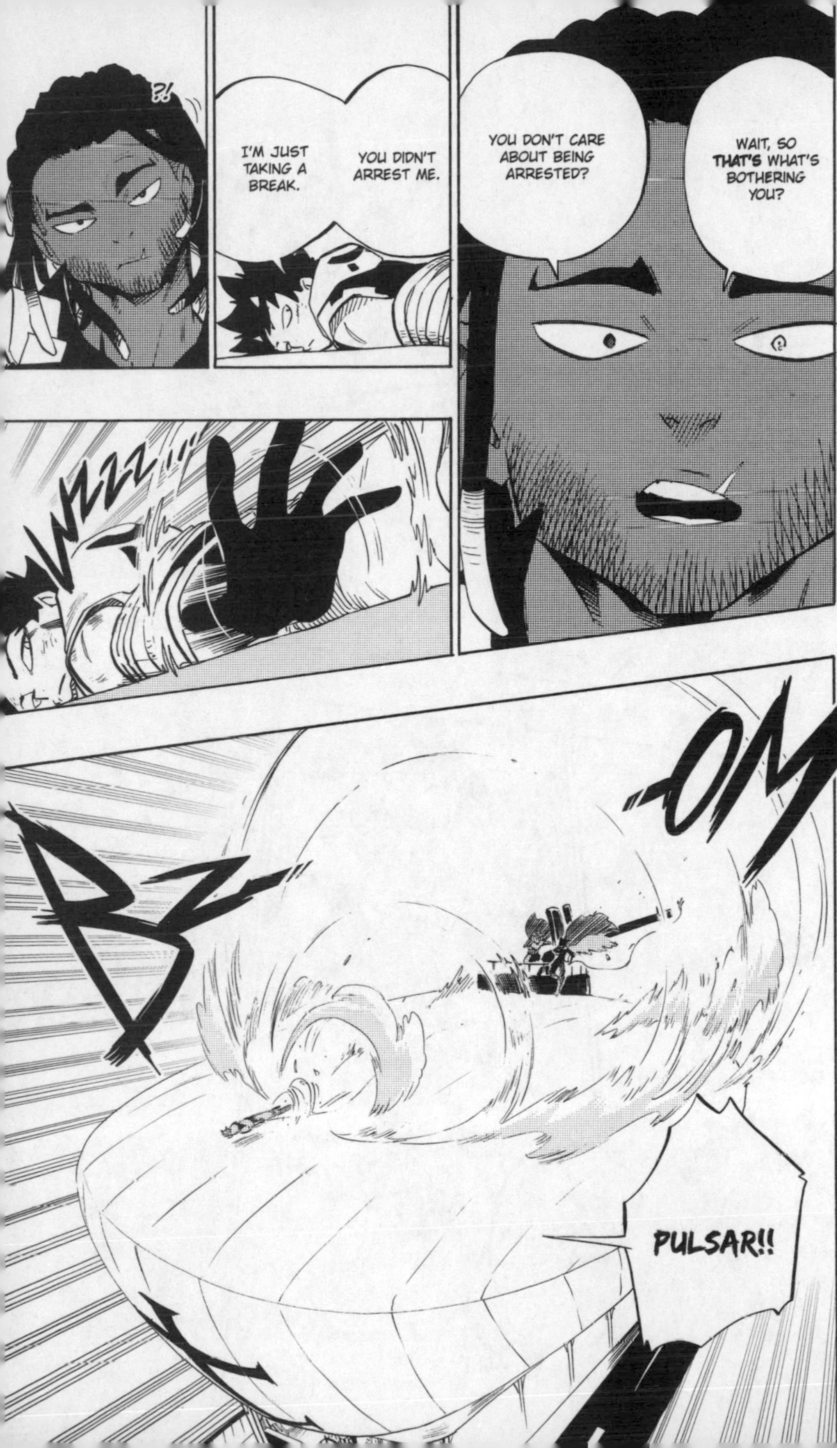
WAIT, SO **THAT'S** WHAT'S BOTHERING YOU?
YOU DON'T CARE ABOUT BEING ARRESTED?
YOU DIDN'T ARREST ME.
I'M JUST TAKING A BREAK.
?!
WZZZ
PULSAR!!

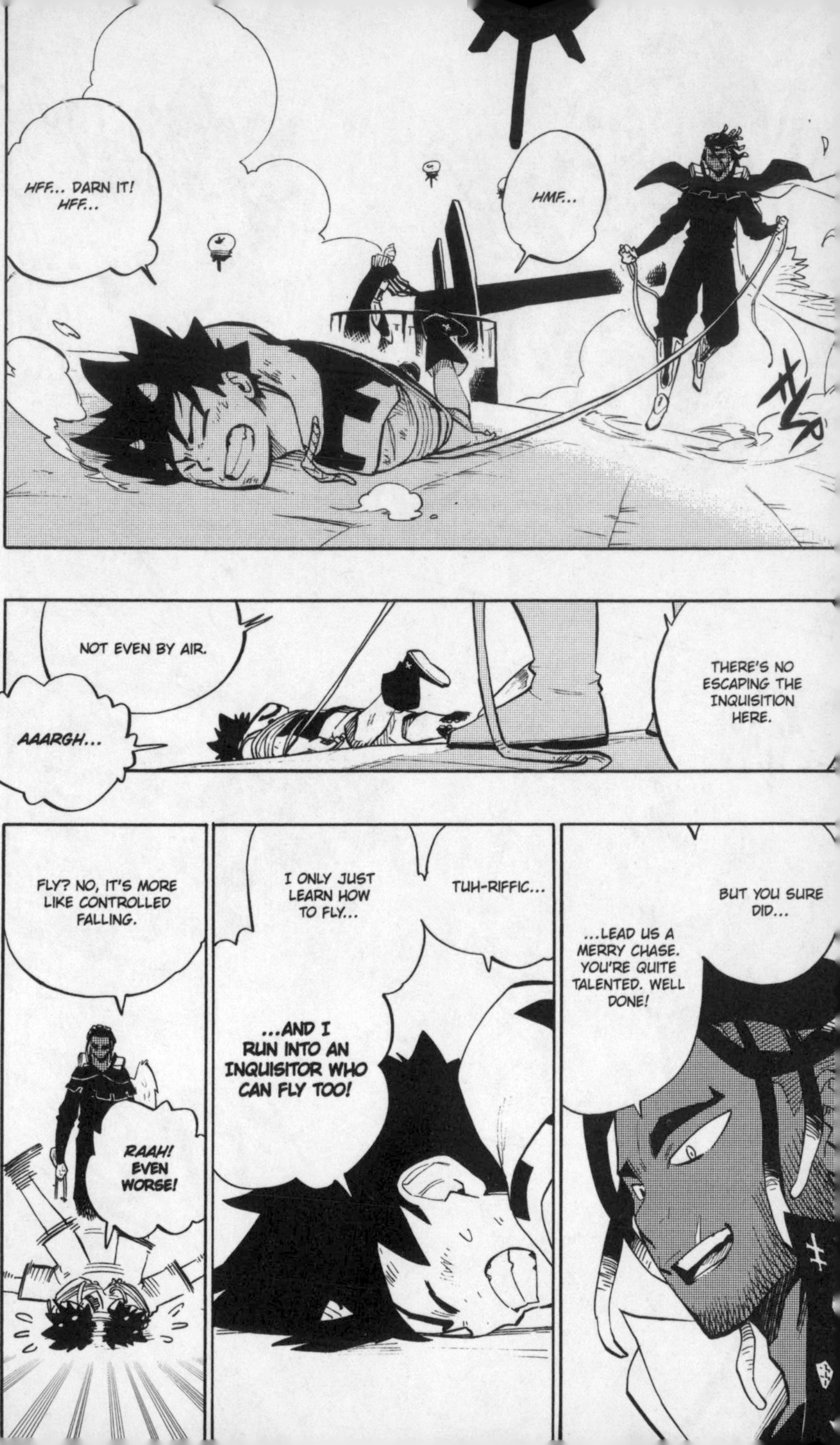
HMF...
HFF... DARN IT! HFF...
THERE'S NO ESCAPING THE INQUISITION HERE.
NOT EVEN BY AIR.
AAARGH...
BUT YOU SURE DID...
...LEAD US A MERRY CHASE. YOU'RE QUITE TALENTED. WELL DONE!
TUH-RIFFIC...
I ONLY JUST LEARN HOW TO FLY...
...AND I RUN INTO AN INQUISITOR WHO CAN FLY TOO!
FLY? NO, IT'S MORE LIKE CONTROLLED FALLING.
RAAH! EVEN WORSE!

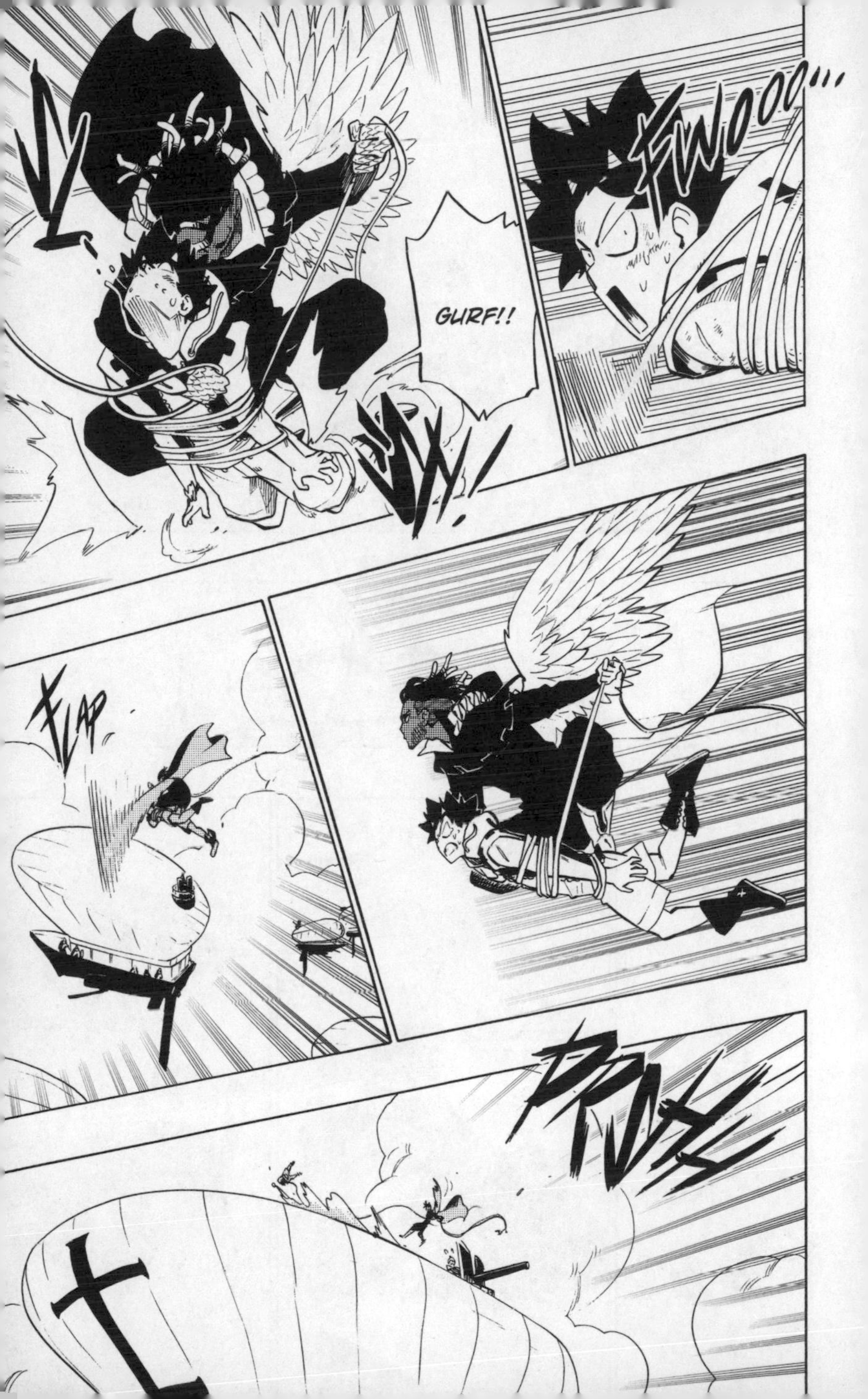

FWOOO...
GURF!!
FLAP

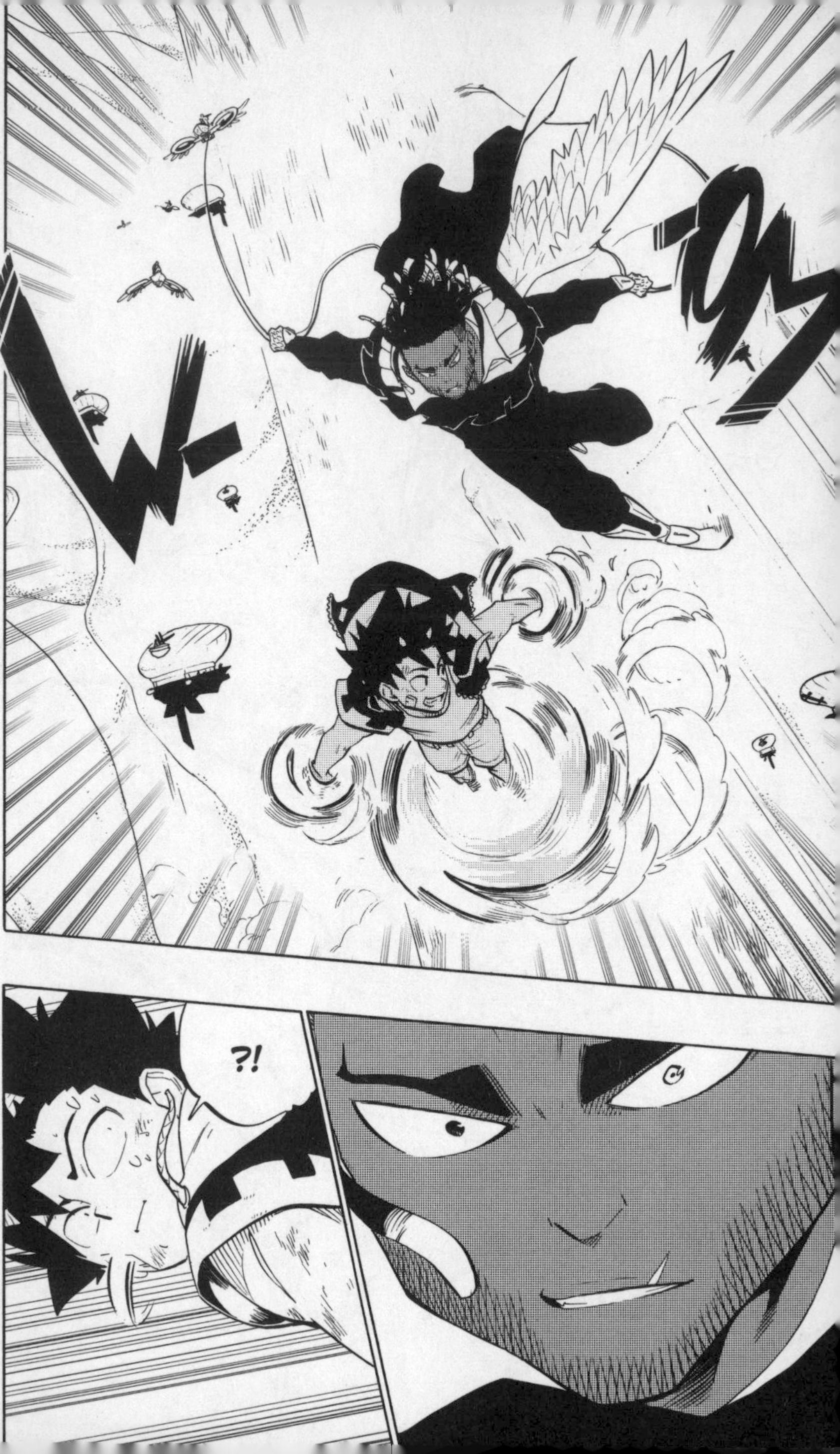
W-
-OM
?!

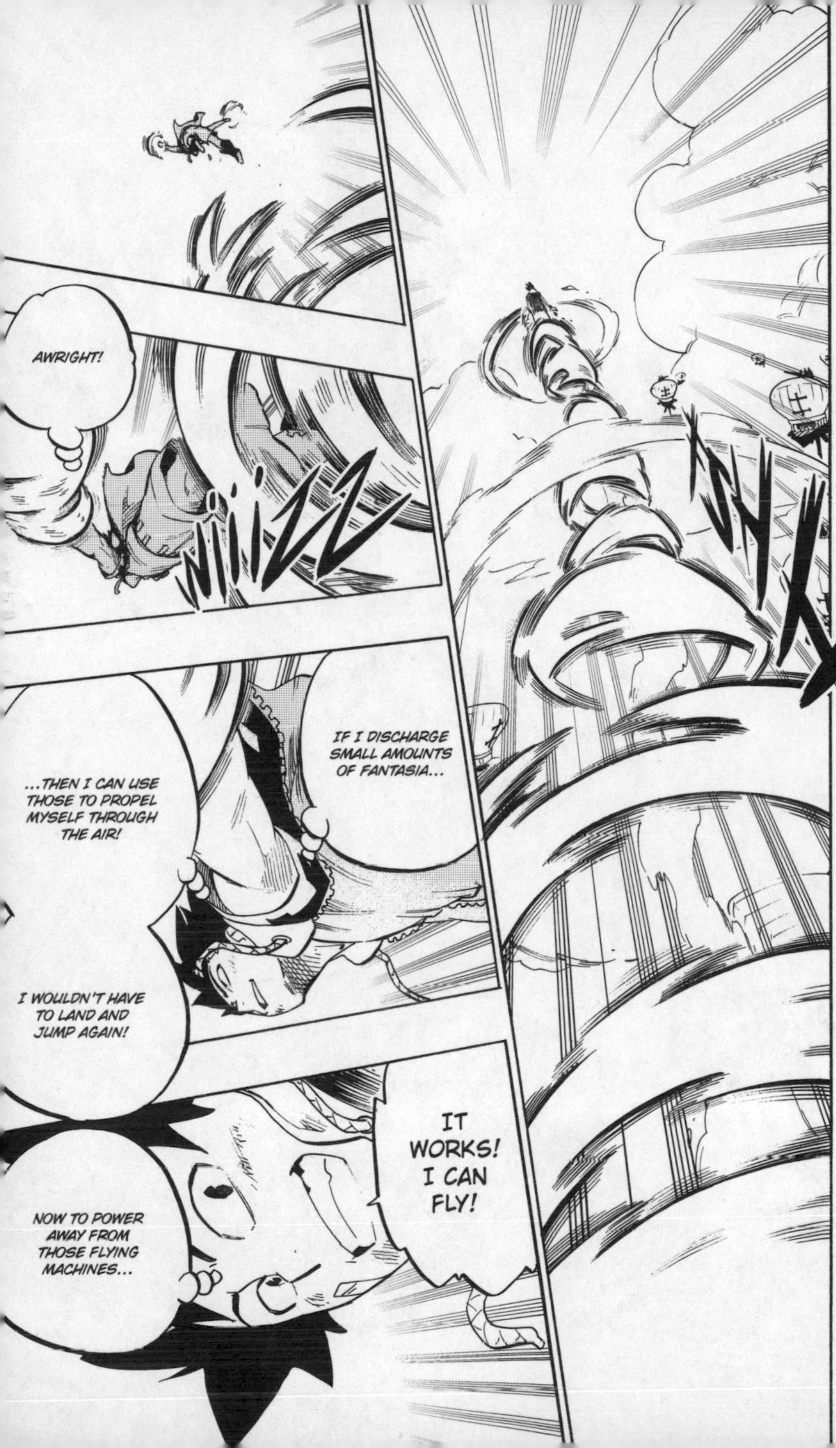
AWRIGHT!
WHIZZ
IF I DISCHARGE SMALL AMOUNTS OF FANTASIA...
...THEN I CAN USE THOSE TO PROPEL MYSELF THROUGH THE AIR!
I WOULDN'T HAVE TO LAND AND JUMP AGAIN!
IT WORKS! I CAN FLY!
NOW TO POWER AWAY FROM THOSE FLYING MACHINES...

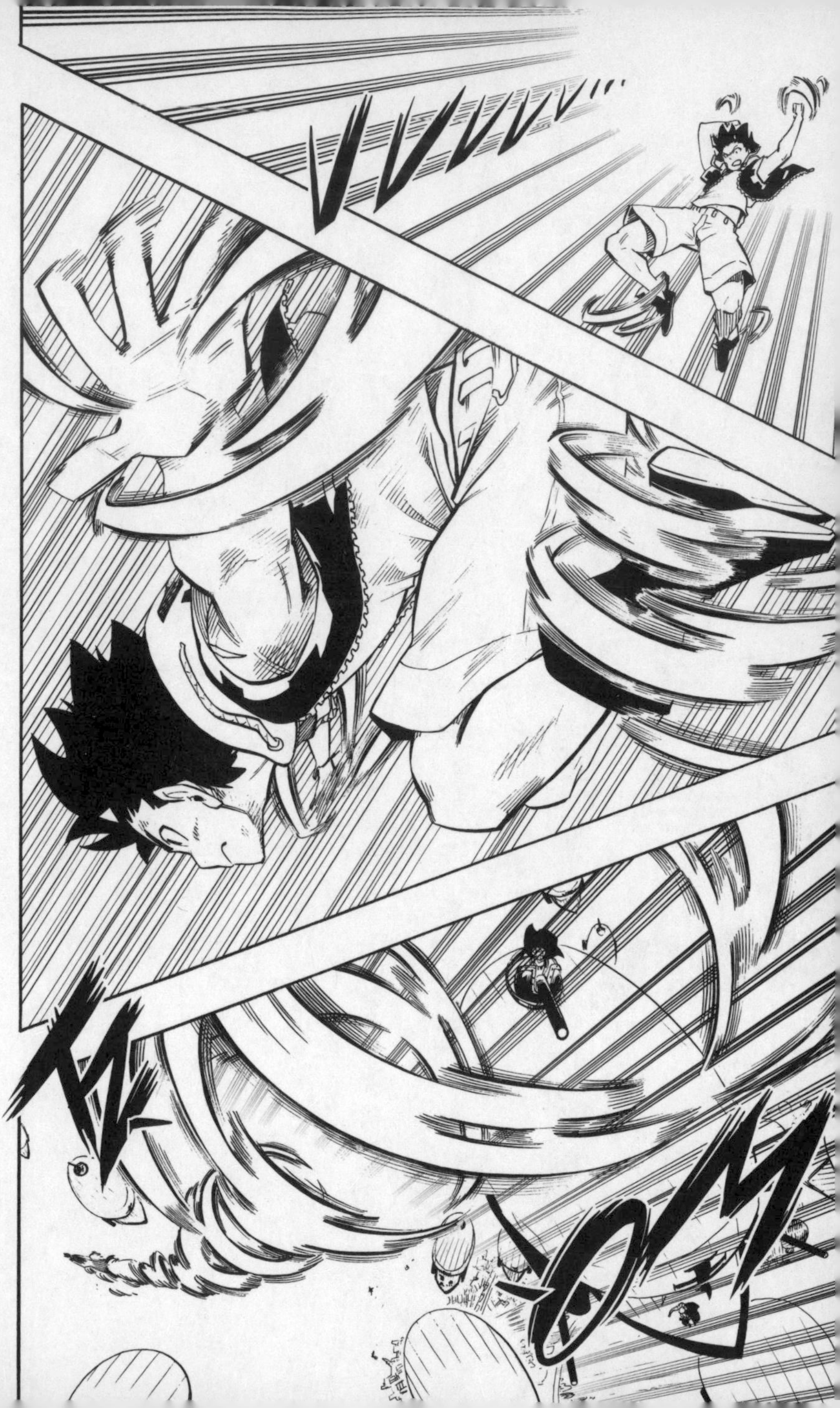

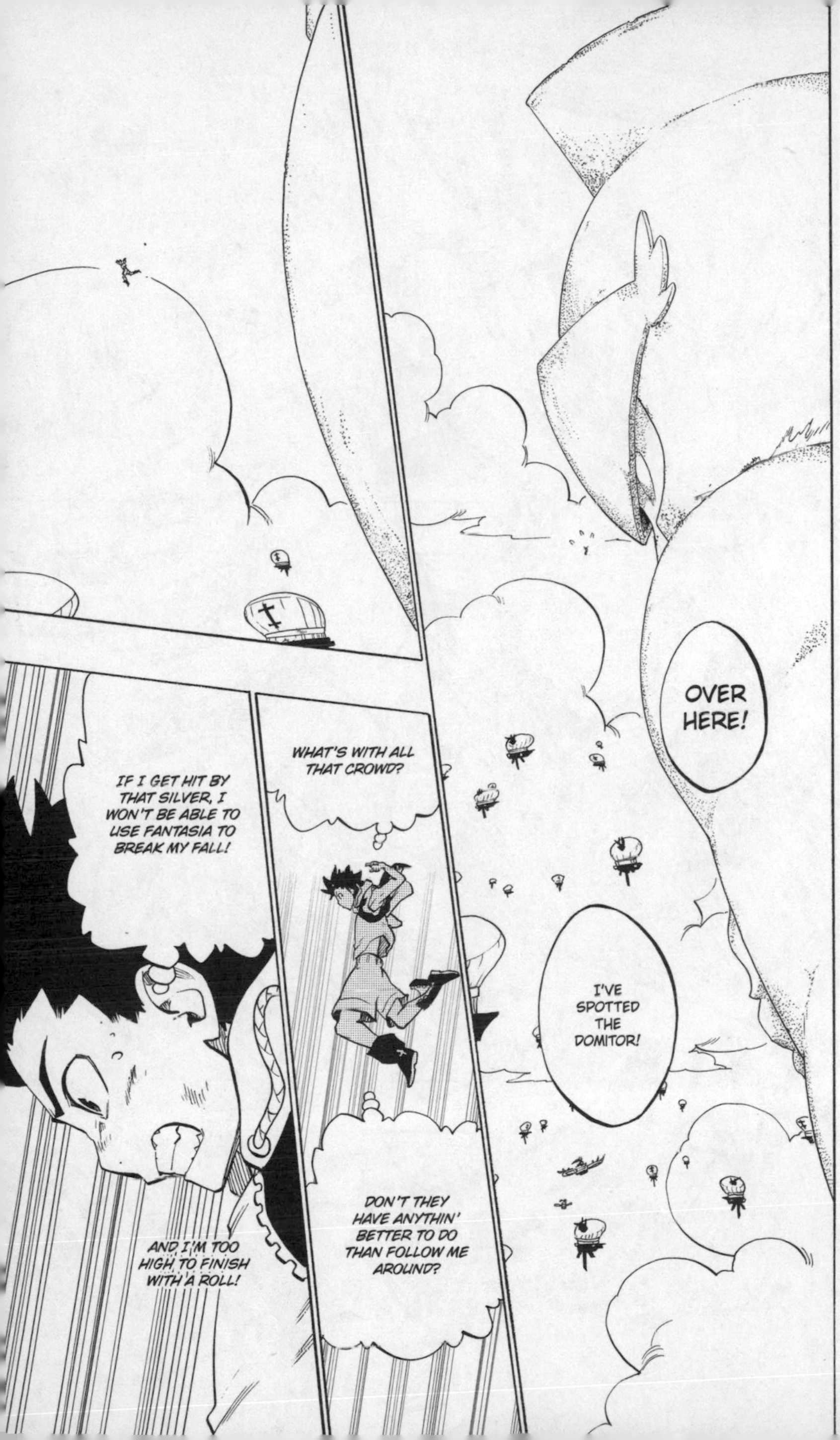
OVER HERE!
I'VE SPOTTED THE DOMITOR!
WHAT'S WITH ALL THAT CROWD?
DON'T THEY HAVE ANYTHIN' BETTER TO DO THAN FOLLOW ME AROUND?
IF I GET HIT BY THAT SILVER, I WON'T BE ABLE TO USE FANTASIA TO BREAK MY FALL!
AND I'M TOO HIGH TO FINISH WITH A ROLL!

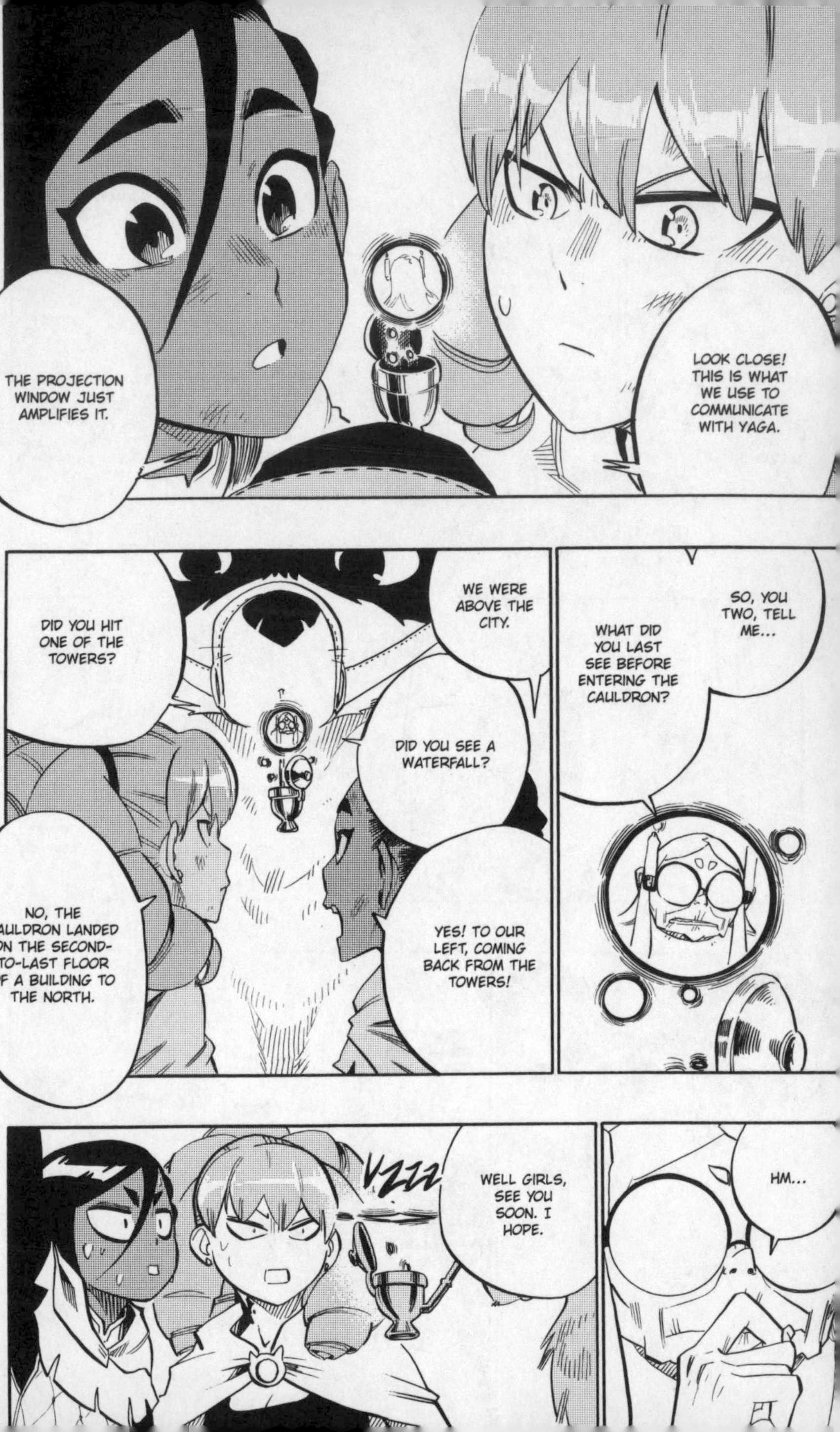
LOOK CLOSE! THIS IS WHAT WE USE TO COMMUNICATE WITH YAGA.
THE PROJECTION WINDOW JUST AMPLIFIES IT.
SO, YOU TWO, TELL ME...
WHAT DID YOU LAST SEE BEFORE ENTERING THE CAULDRON?
WE WERE ABOVE THE CITY.
DID YOU HIT ONE OF THE TOWERS?
DID YOU SEE A WATERFALL?
YES! TO OUR LEFT, COMING BACK FROM THE TOWERS!
NO, THE CAULDRON LANDED ON THE SECOND-TO-LAST FLOOR OF A BUILDING TO THE NORTH.
HM...
WELL GIRLS, SEE YOU SOON. I HOPE.
VZZZ

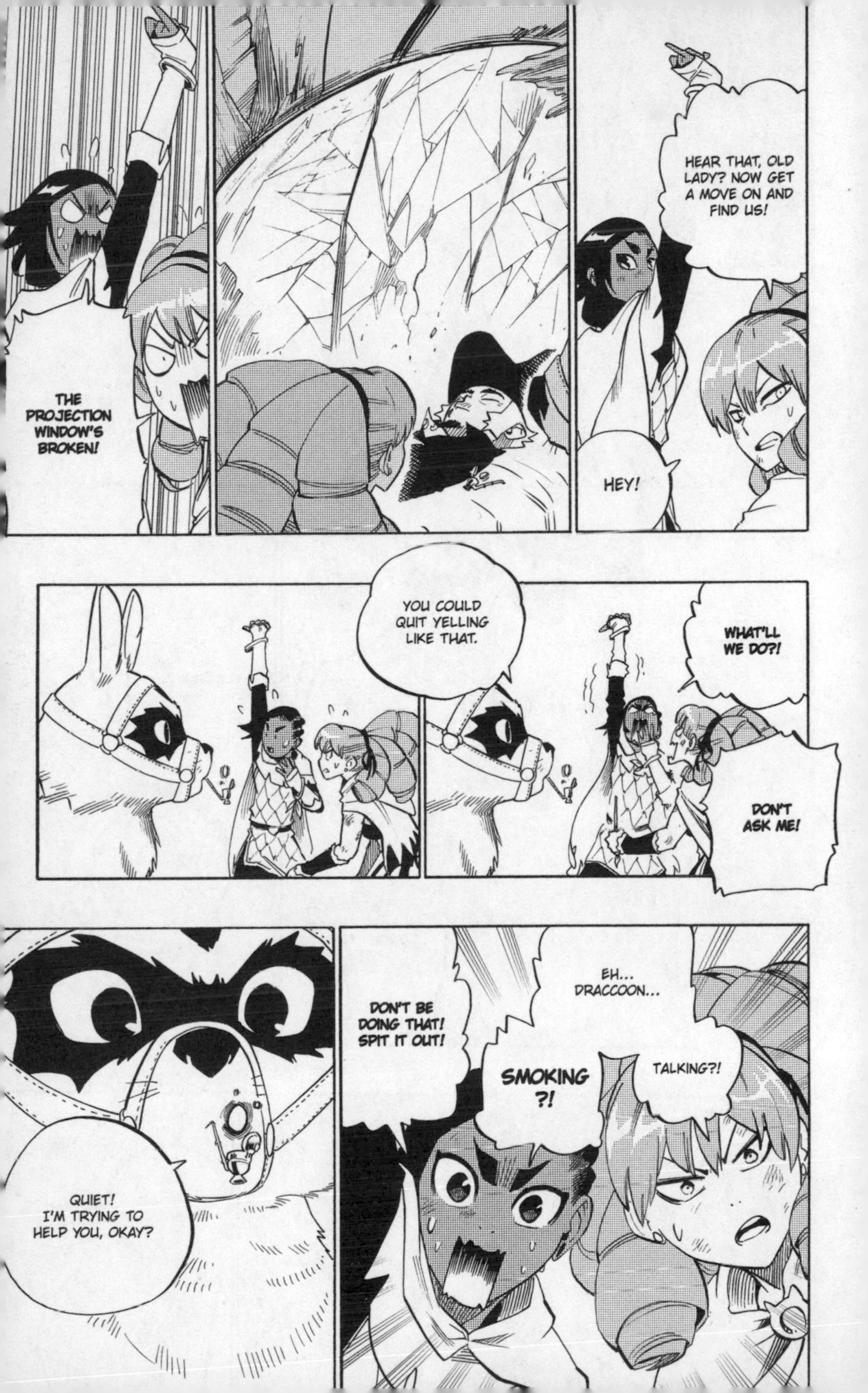
HEAR THAT, OLD LADY? NOW GET A MOVE ON AND FIND US!
HEY!
THE PROJECTION WINDOW'S BROKEN!
WHAT'LL WE DO?!
DON'T ASK ME!
YOU COULD QUIT YELLING LIKE THAT.
EH... DRACCOON...
TALKING?!
SMOKING ?!
DON'T BE DOING THAT! SPIT IT OUT!
QUIET! I'M TRYING TO HELP YOU, OKAY?

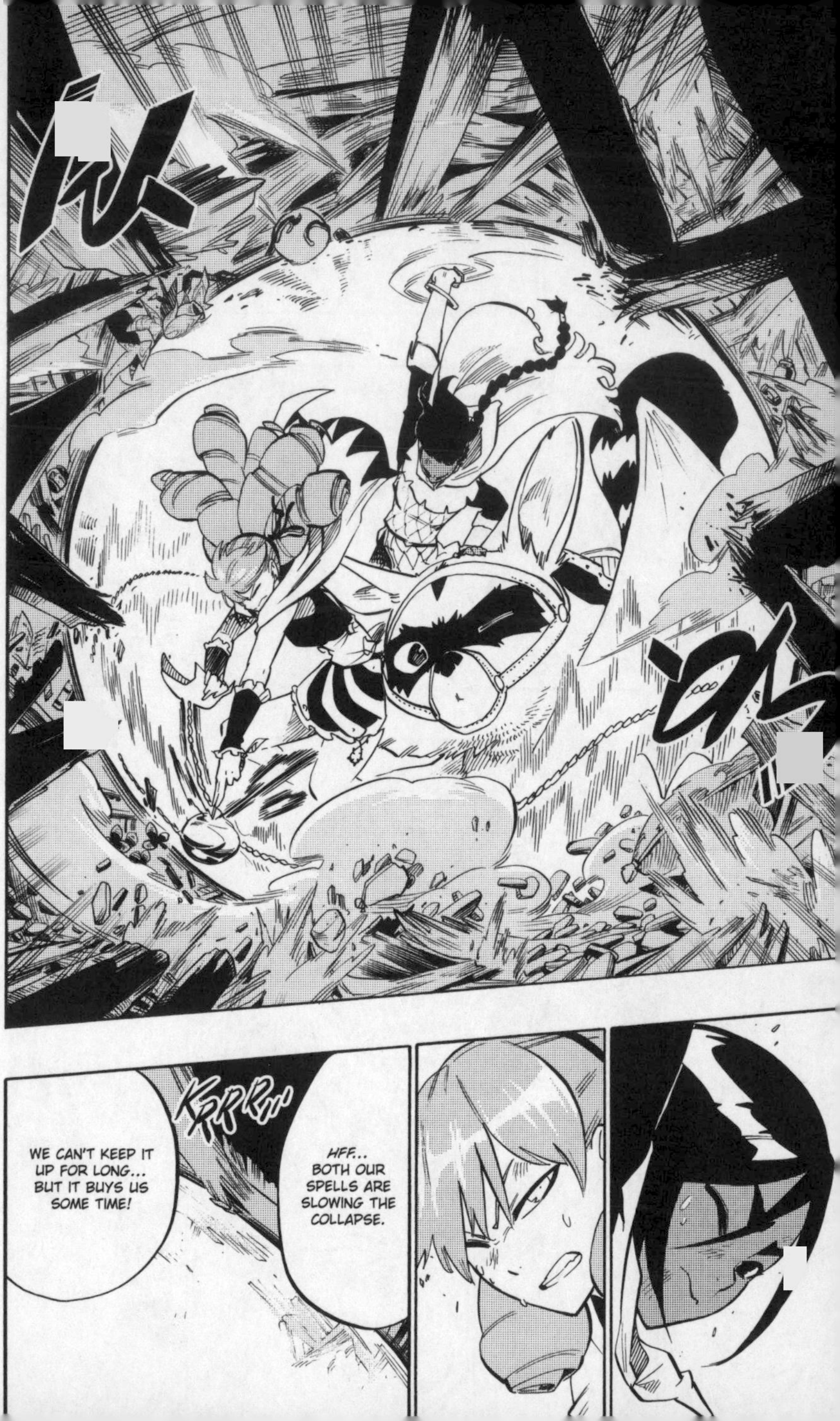
HFF... BOTH OUR SPELLS ARE SLOWING THE COLLAPSE.
KRRR...
WE CAN'T KEEP IT UP FOR LONG... BUT IT BUYS US SOME TIME!

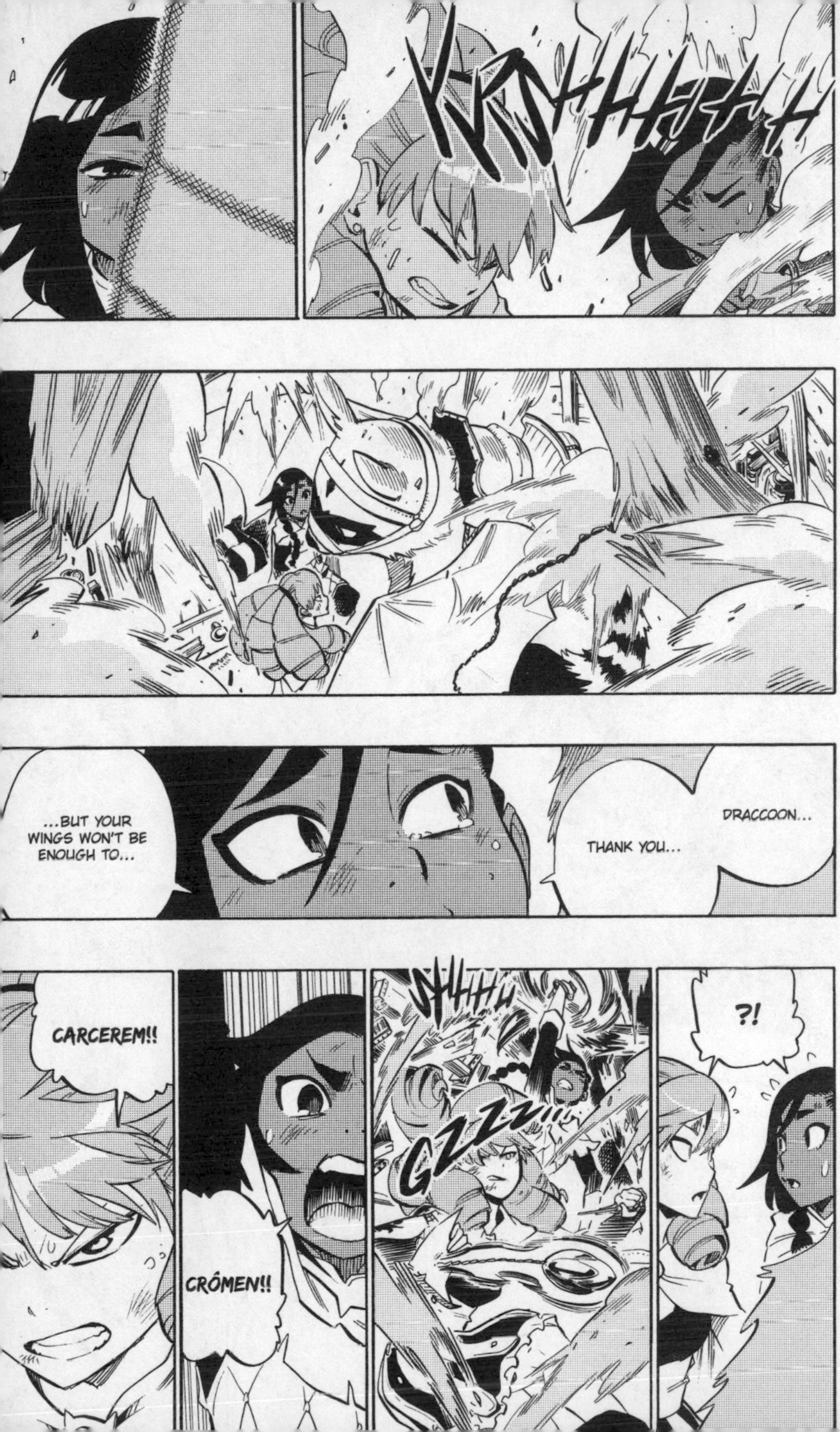
DRACCOON...
THANK YOU...
...BUT YOUR WINGS WON'T BE ENOUGH TO...
?!
CRÔMEN!!
CARCEREM!!

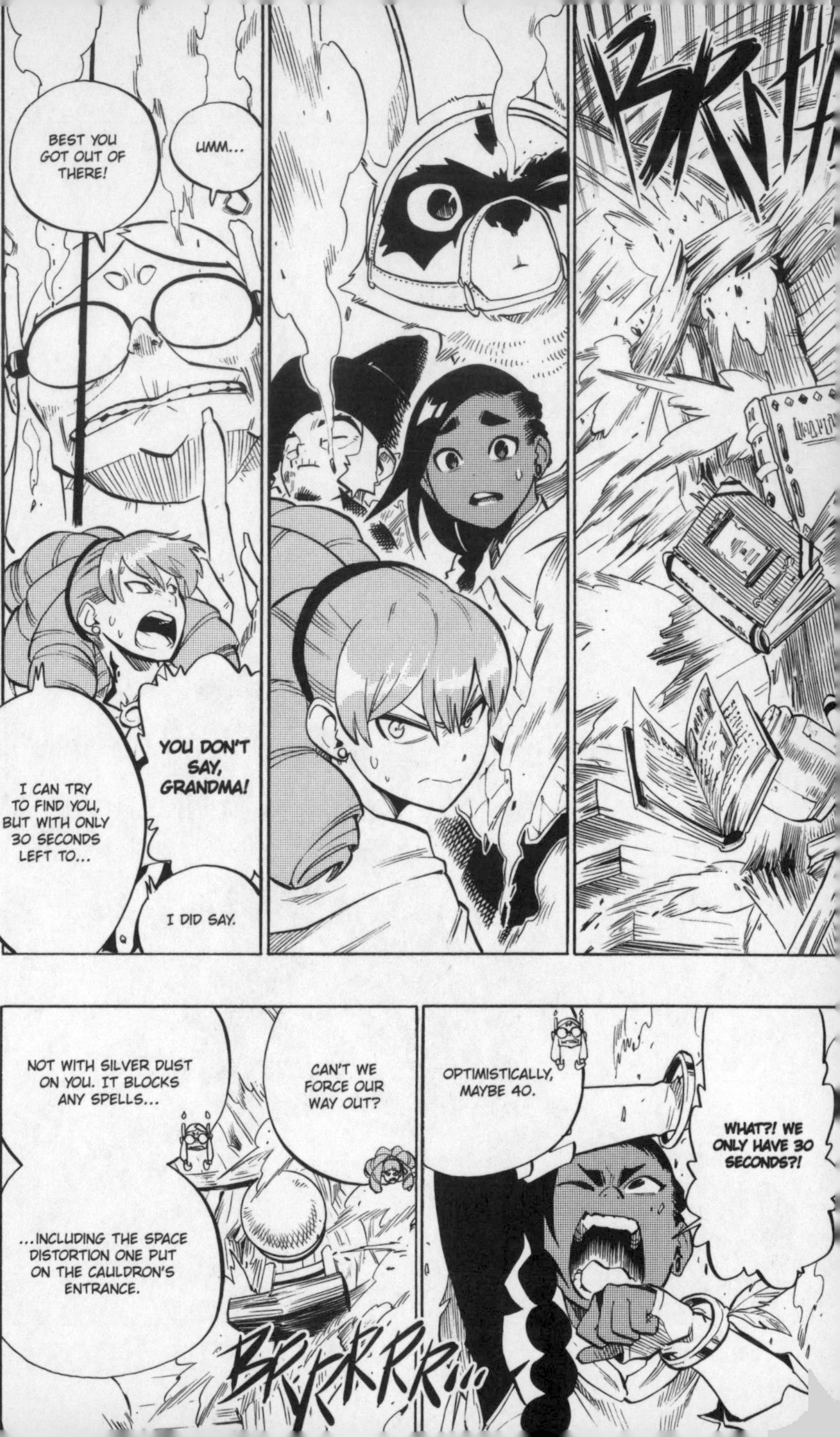
UMM...
BEST YOU GOT OUT OF THERE!
YOU DON'T SAY, GRANDMA!
I CAN TRY TO FIND YOU, BUT WITH ONLY 30 SECONDS LEFT TO...
I DID SAY.
WHAT?! WE ONLY HAVE 30 SECONDS?!
OPTIMISTICALLY, MAYBE 40.
CAN'T WE FORCE OUR WAY OUT?
NOT WITH SILVER DUST ON YOU. IT BLOCKS ANY SPELLS...
...INCLUDING THE SPACE DISTORTION ONE PUT ON THE CAULDRON'S ENTRANCE.

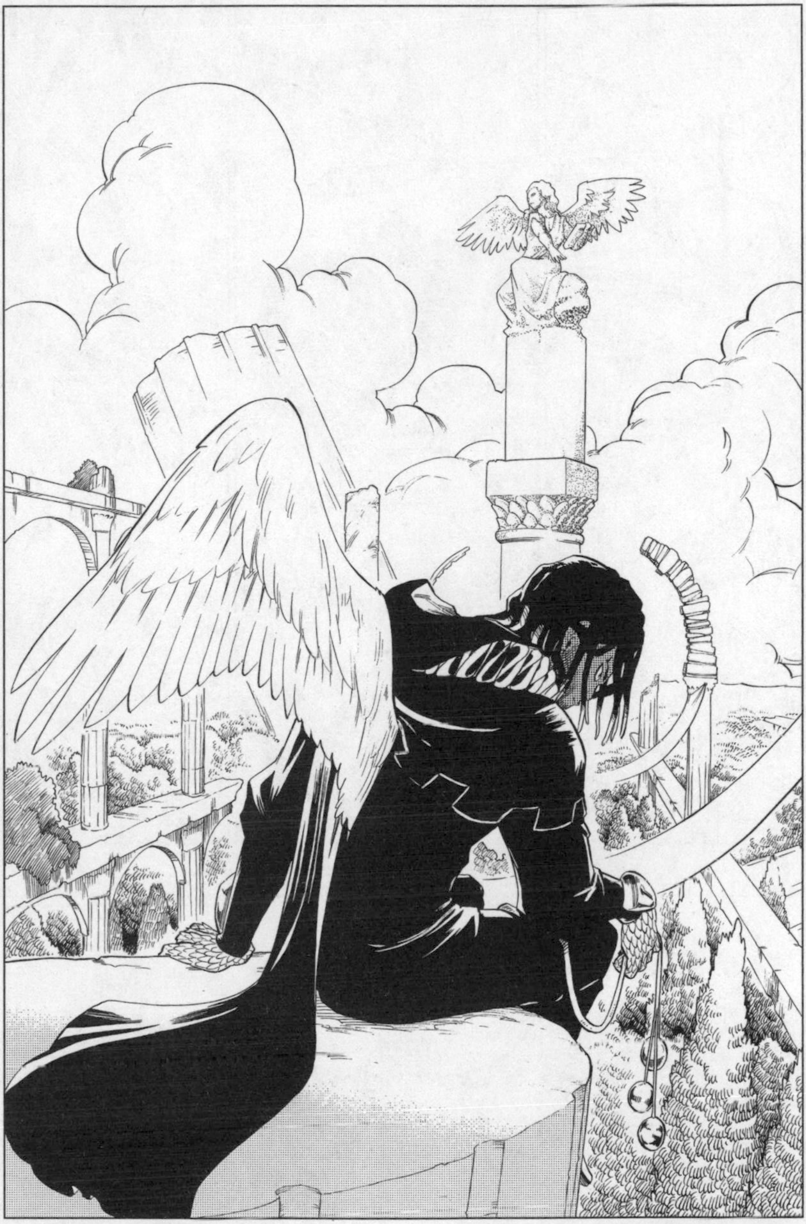

Chapter 94

Helpful Boost

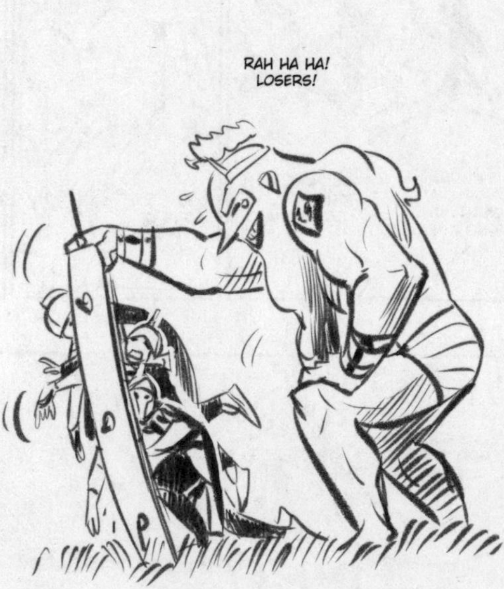
RAH HA HA!
LOSERS!

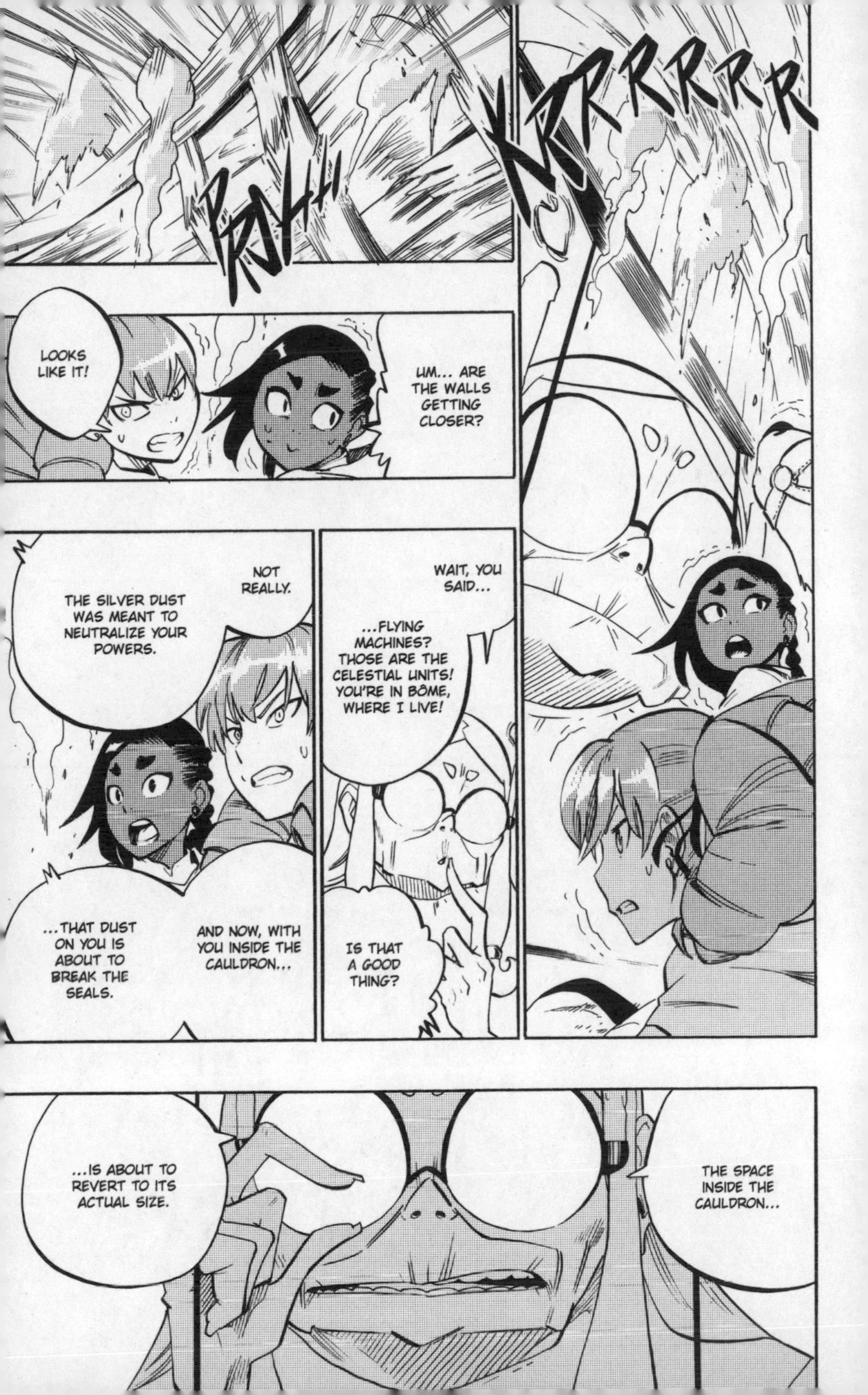
KRRRRRRR
PRSHH
UM... ARE THE WALLS GETTING CLOSER?
LOOKS LIKE IT!
WAIT, YOU SAID...
...FLYING MACHINES? THOSE ARE THE CELESTIAL UNITS! YOU'RE IN BÔME, WHERE I LIVE!
IS THAT A GOOD THING?
NOT REALLY.
THE SILVER DUST WAS MEANT TO NEUTRALIZE YOUR POWERS.
AND NOW, WITH YOU INSIDE THE CAULDRON...
...THAT DUST ON YOU IS ABOUT TO BREAK THE SEALS.
THE SPACE INSIDE THE CAULDRON...
...IS ABOUT TO REVERT TO ITS ACTUAL SIZE.

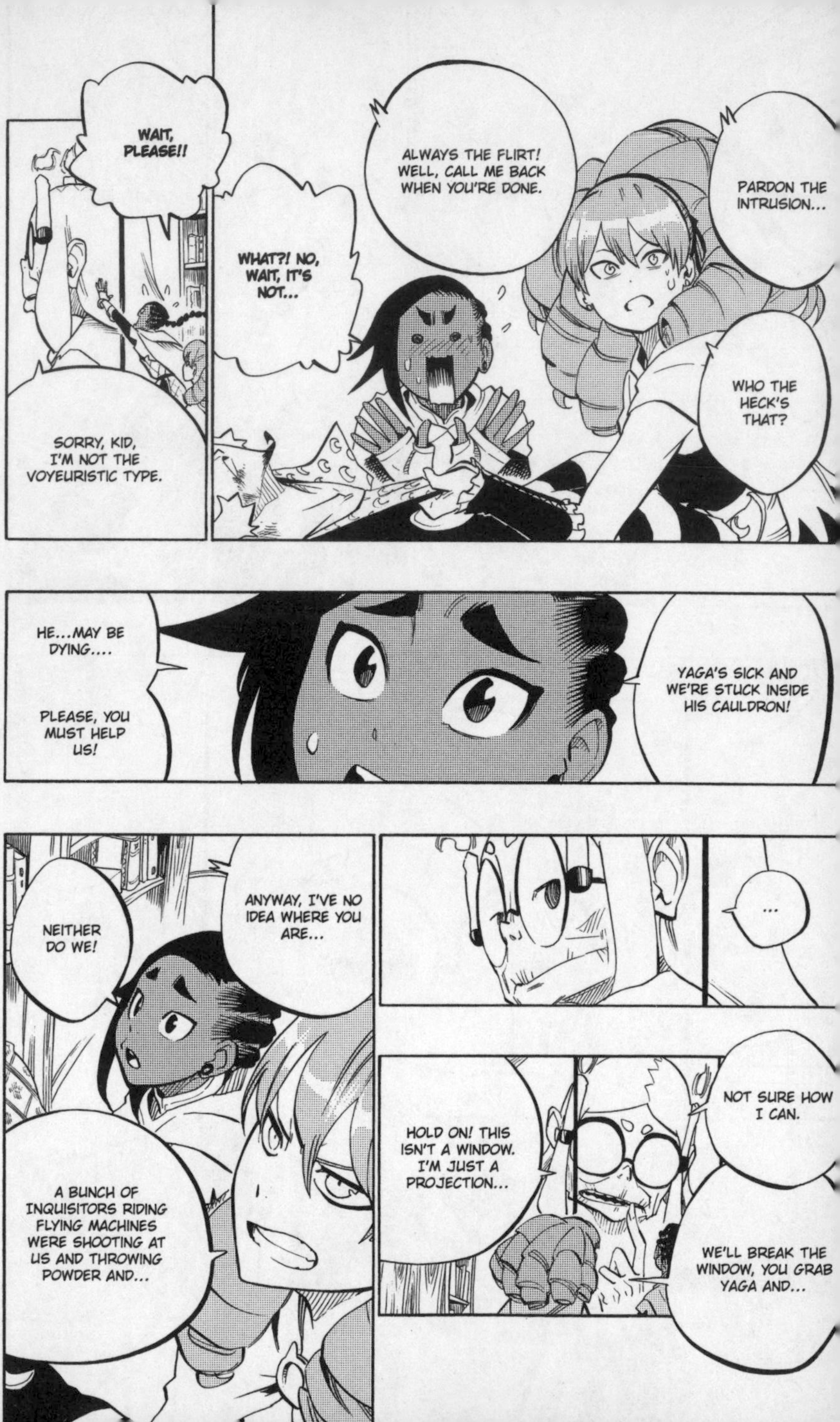
PARDON THE INTRUSION...
ALWAYS THE FLIRT! WELL, CALL ME BACK WHEN YOU'RE DONE.
WHO THE HECK'S THAT?
WHAT?! NO, WAIT, IT'S NOT...
WAIT, PLEASE!!
SORRY, KID, I'M NOT THE VOYEURISTIC TYPE.
YAGA'S SICK AND WE'RE STUCK INSIDE HIS CAULDRON!
HE...MAY BE DYING....
PLEASE, YOU MUST HELP US!
...
NOT SURE HOW I CAN.
HOLD ON! THIS ISN'T A WINDOW. I'M JUST A PROJECTION...
WE'LL BREAK THE WINDOW, YOU GRAB YAGA AND...
ANYWAY, I'VE NO IDEA WHERE YOU ARE...
NEITHER DO WE!
A BUNCH OF INQUISITORS RIDING FLYING MACHINES WERE SHOOTING AT US AND THROWING POWDER AND...

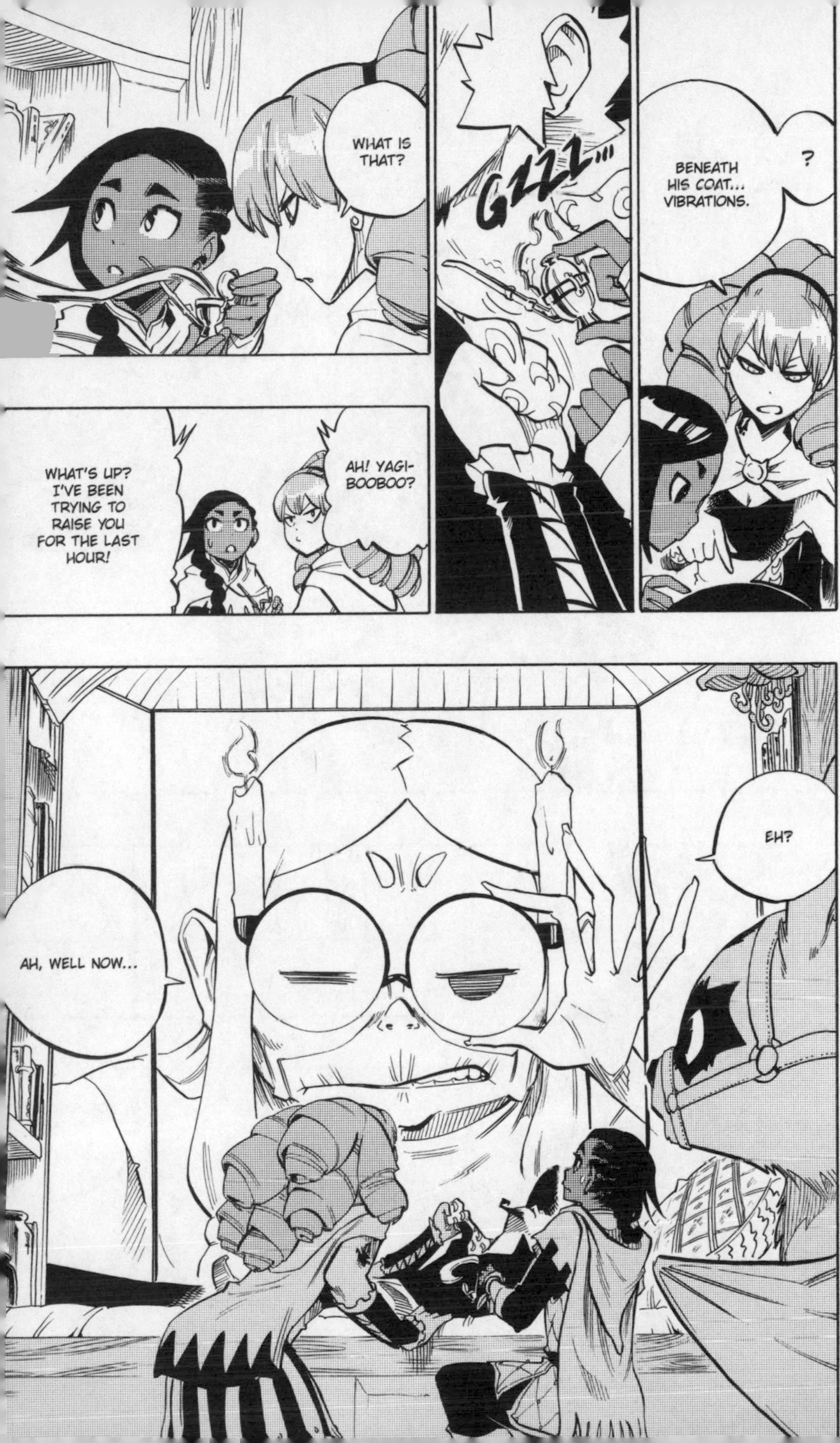
?
BENEATH HIS COAT... VIBRATIONS.
GZZZ...
WHAT IS THAT?
AH! YAGI-BOOBOO?
WHAT'S UP? I'VE BEEN TRYING TO RAISE YOU FOR THE LAST HOUR!
EH?
AH, WELL NOW...

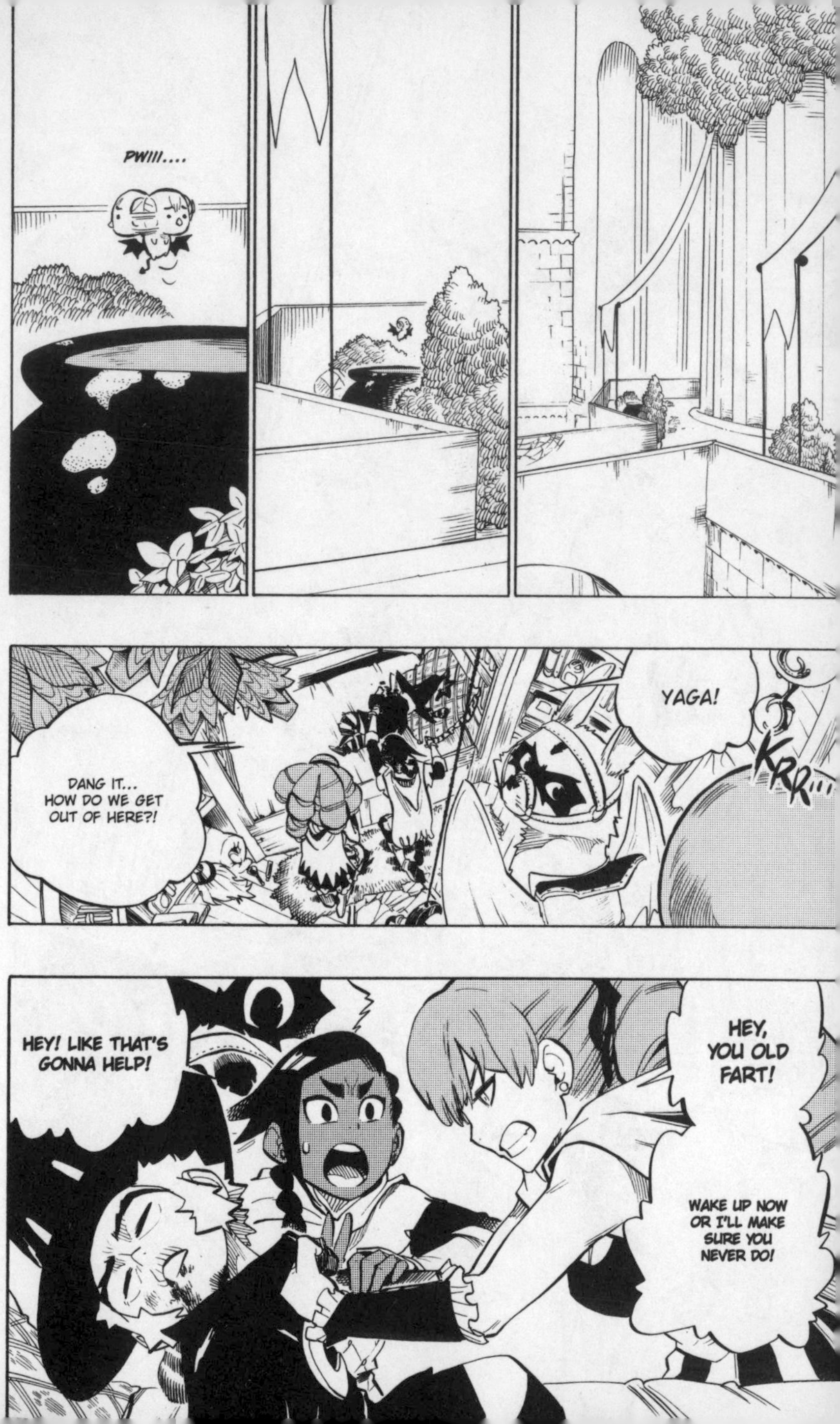
PWIII....
YAGA!
KRR...
DANG IT... HOW DO WE GET OUT OF HERE?!
HEY, YOU OLD FART!
WAKE UP NOW OR I'LL MAKE SURE YOU NEVER DO!
HEY! LIKE THAT'S GONNA HELP!

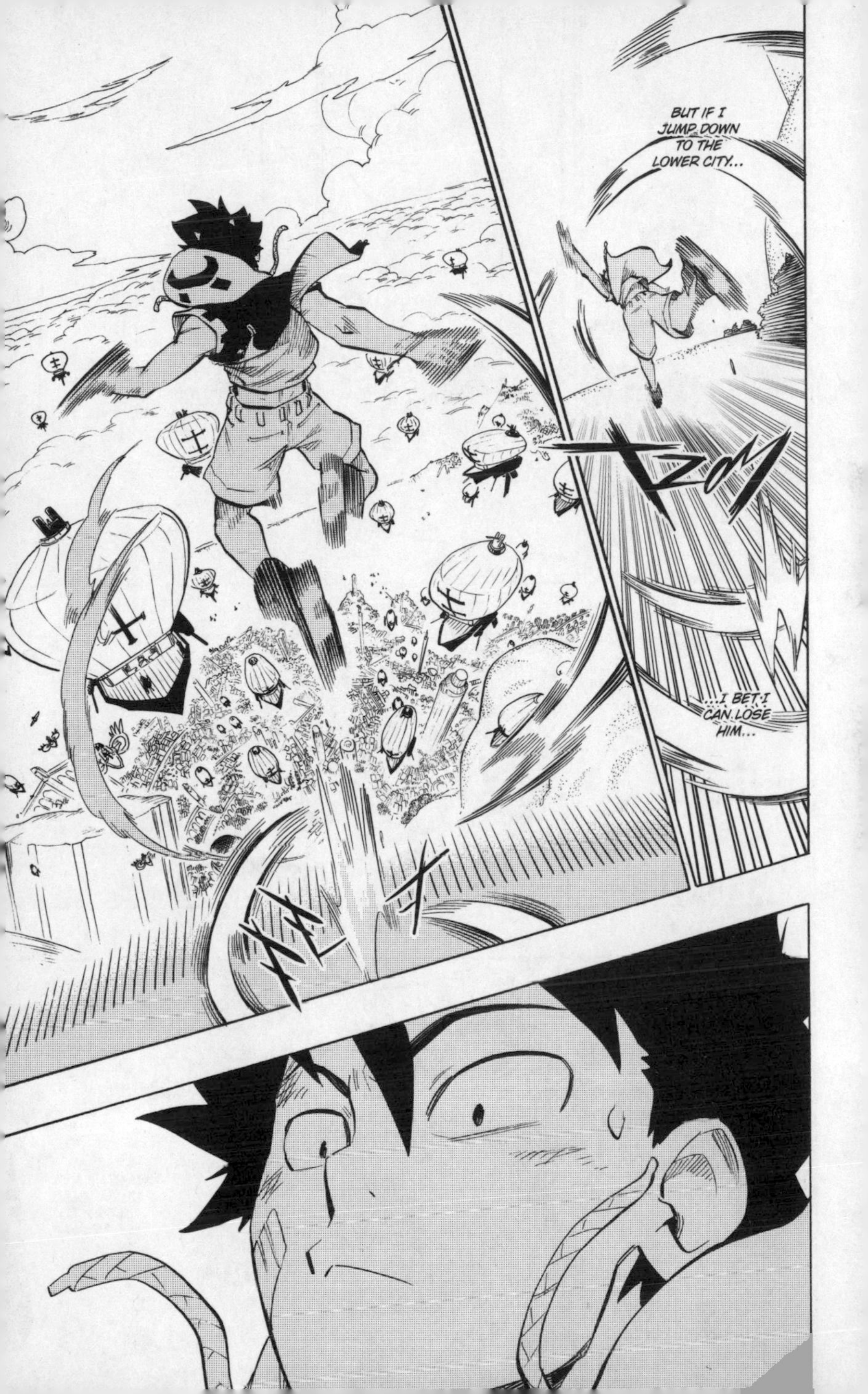
BUT IF I JUMP DOWN TO THE LOWER CITY...
FZOOM
...I BET I CAN LOSE HIM...
HMM

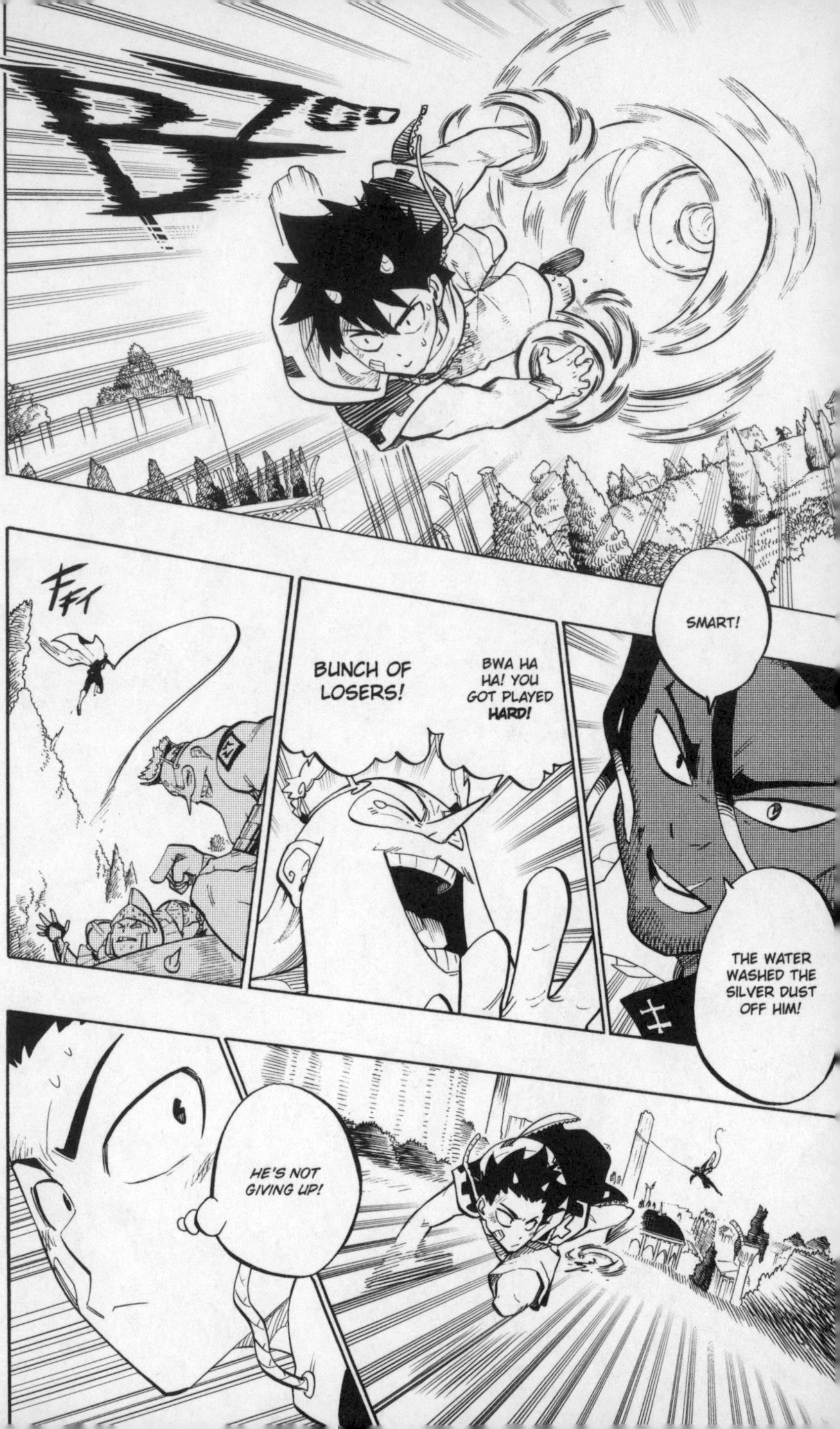
BWOOP
SMART!
THE WATER WASHED THE SILVER DUST OFF HIM!
BWA HA HA! YOU GOT PLAYED HARD!
BUNCH OF LOSERS!
FFT
HE'S NOT GIVING UP!

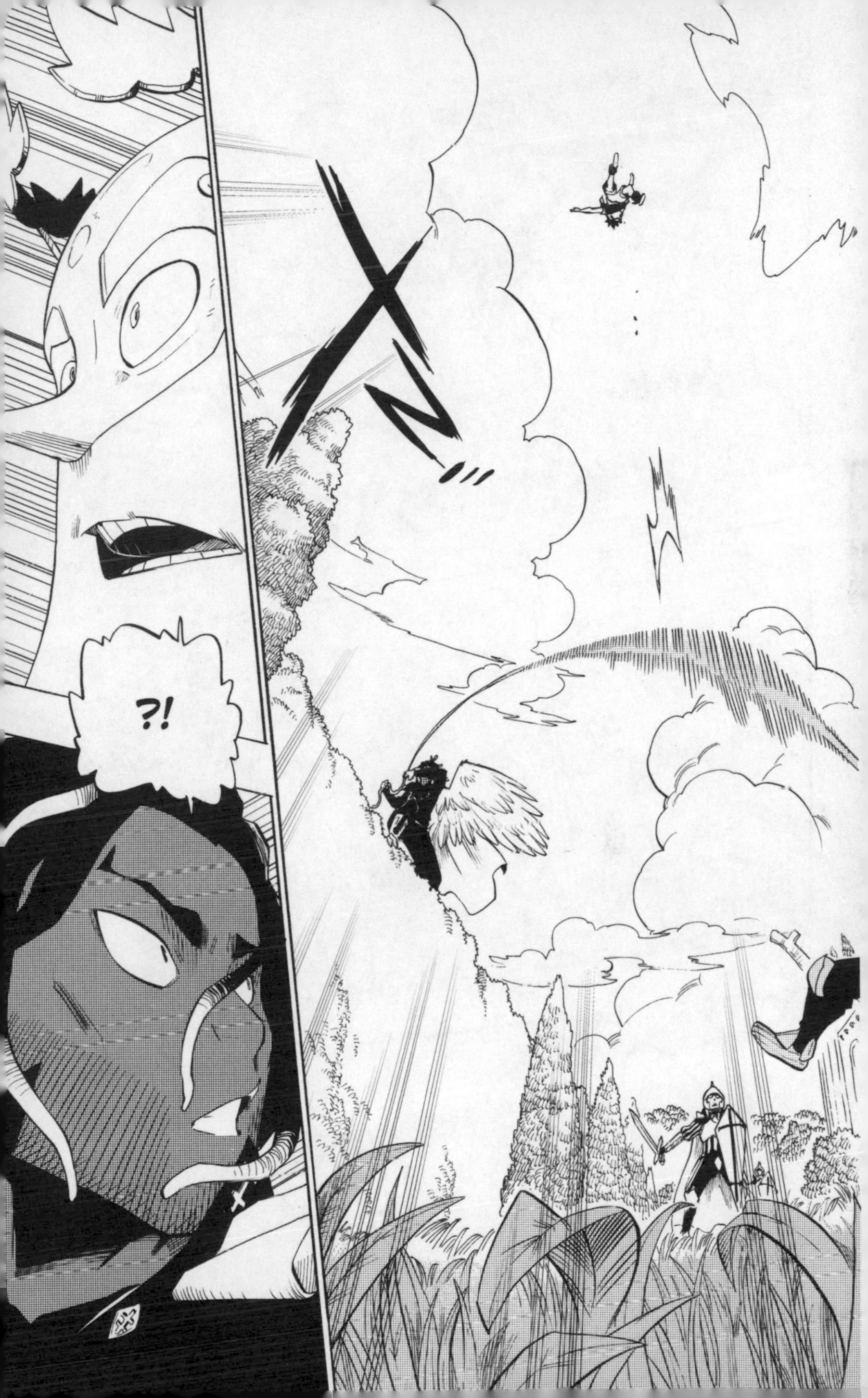
?!

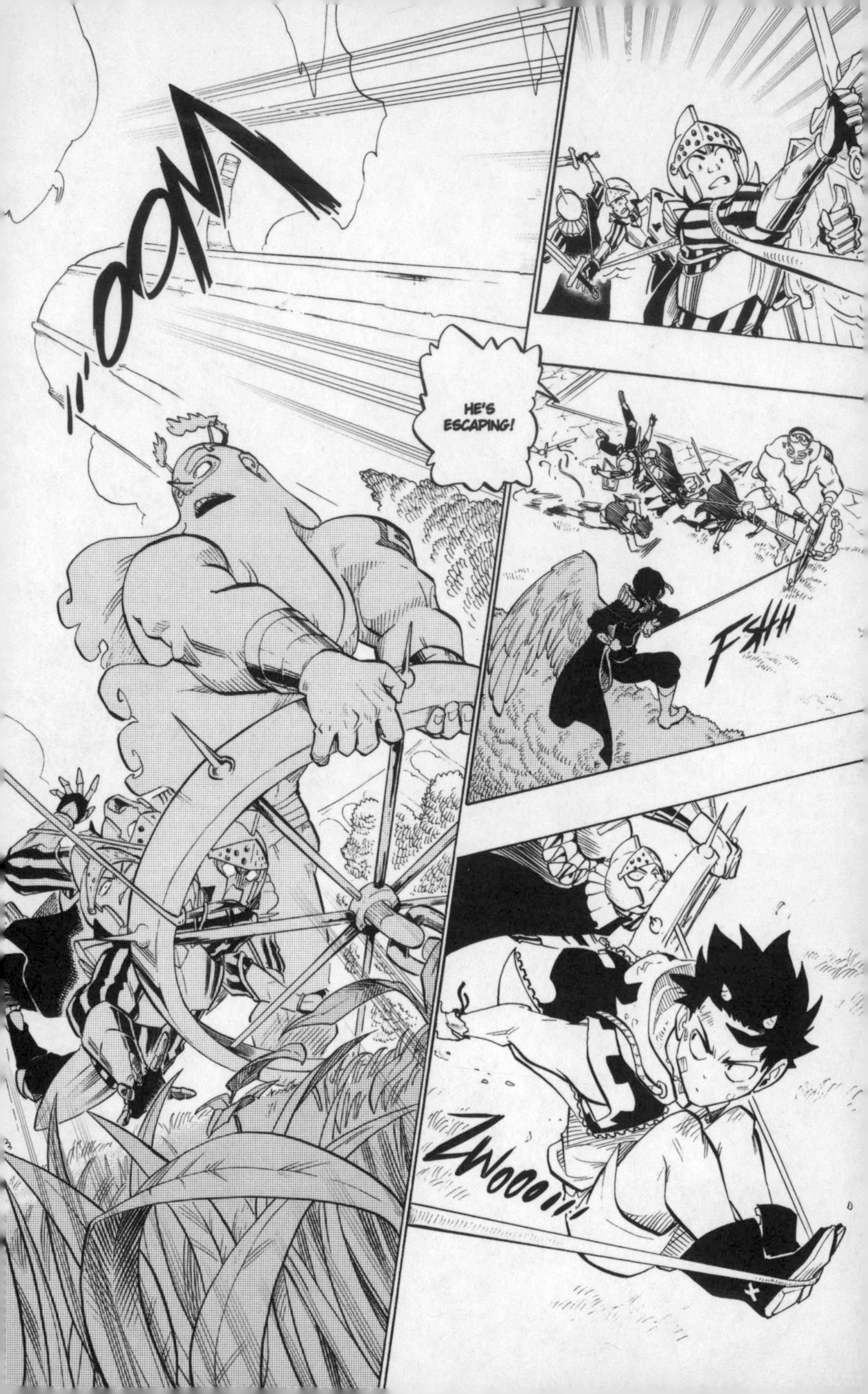
HE'S ESCAPING!
FSHH
ZWOOO!!
WOOO!!

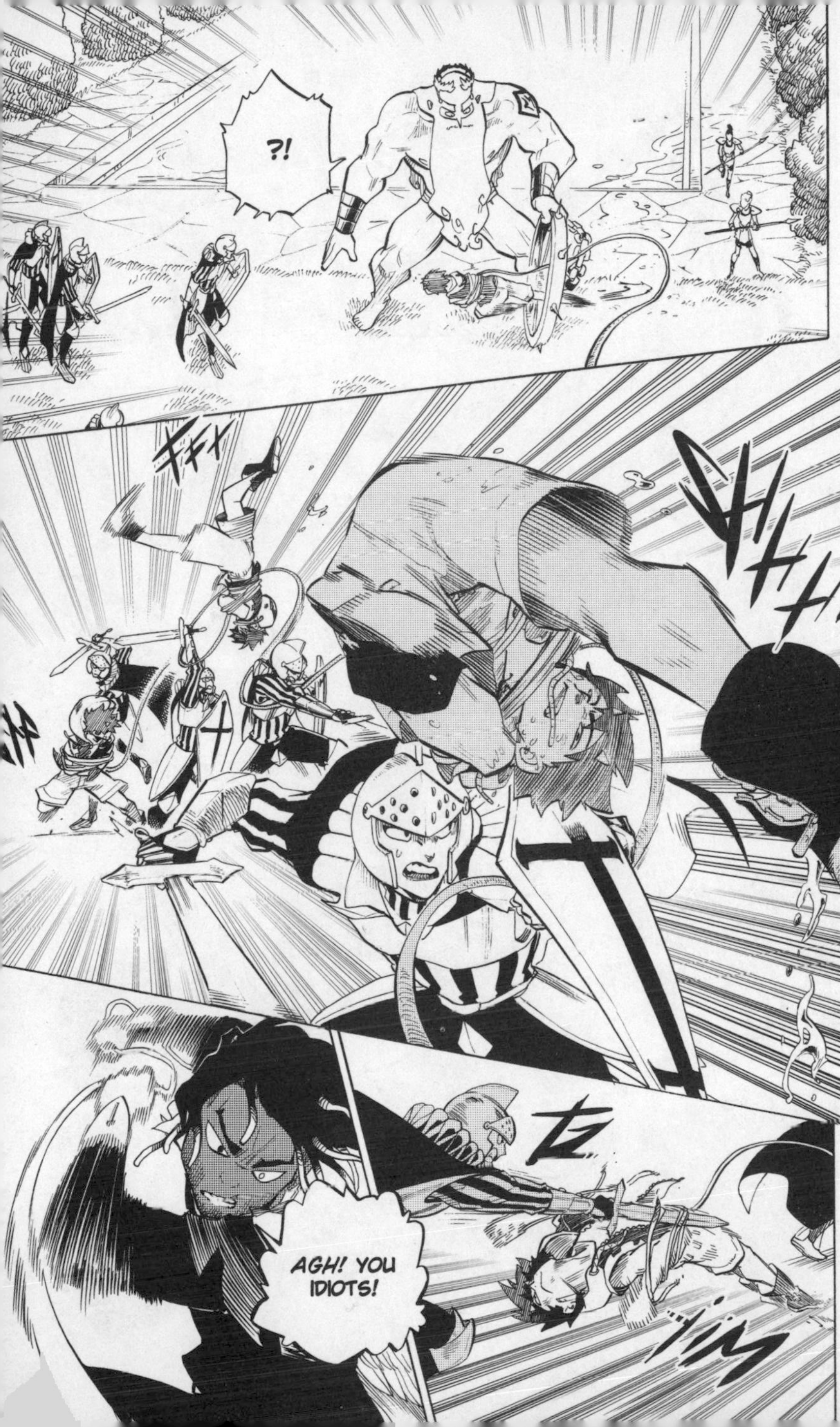
?!
AGH! YOU IDIOTS!

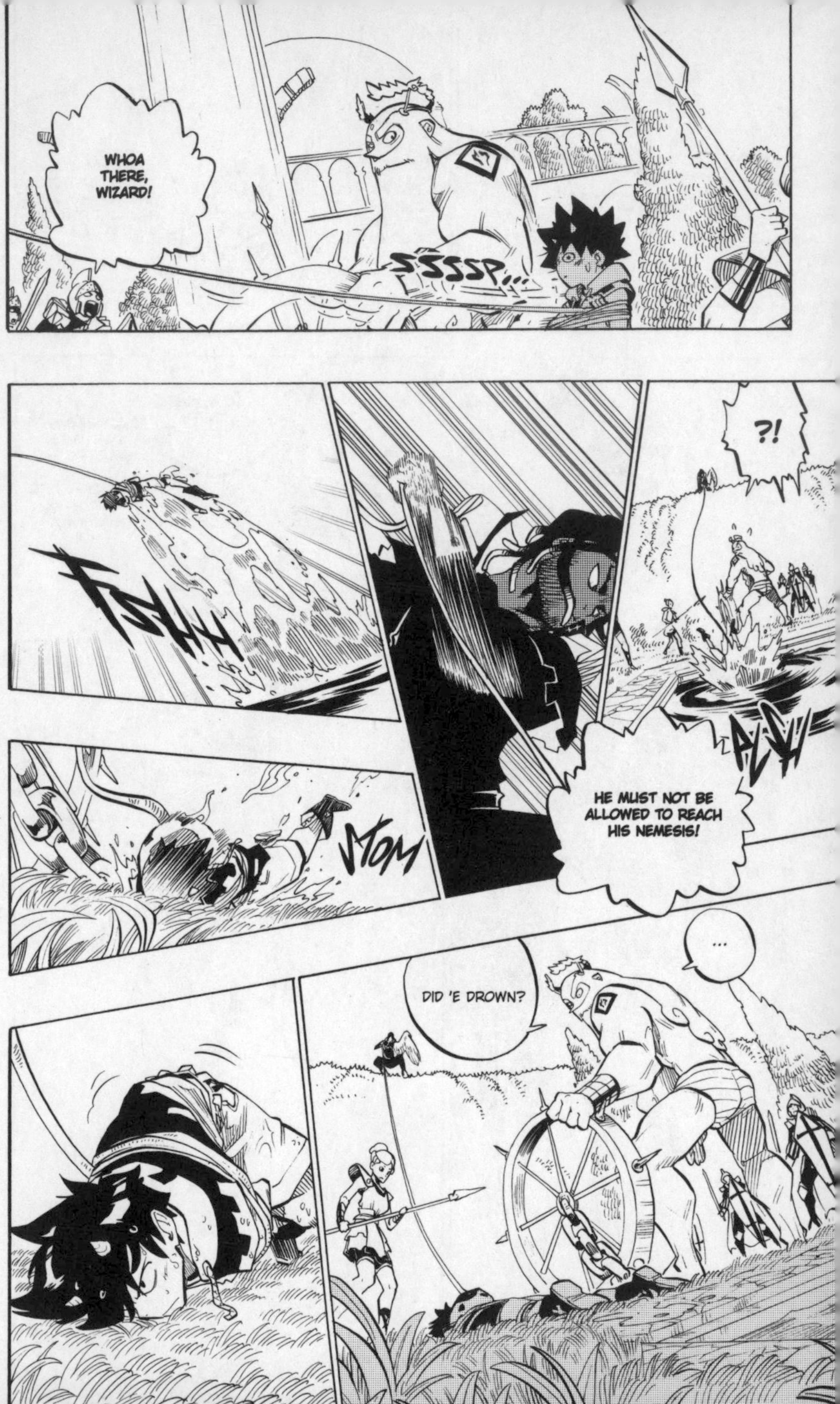
WHOA THERE, WIZARD!
SSSSP...
?!
HE MUST NOT BE ALLOWED TO REACH HIS NEMESIS!
...
DID 'E DROWN?

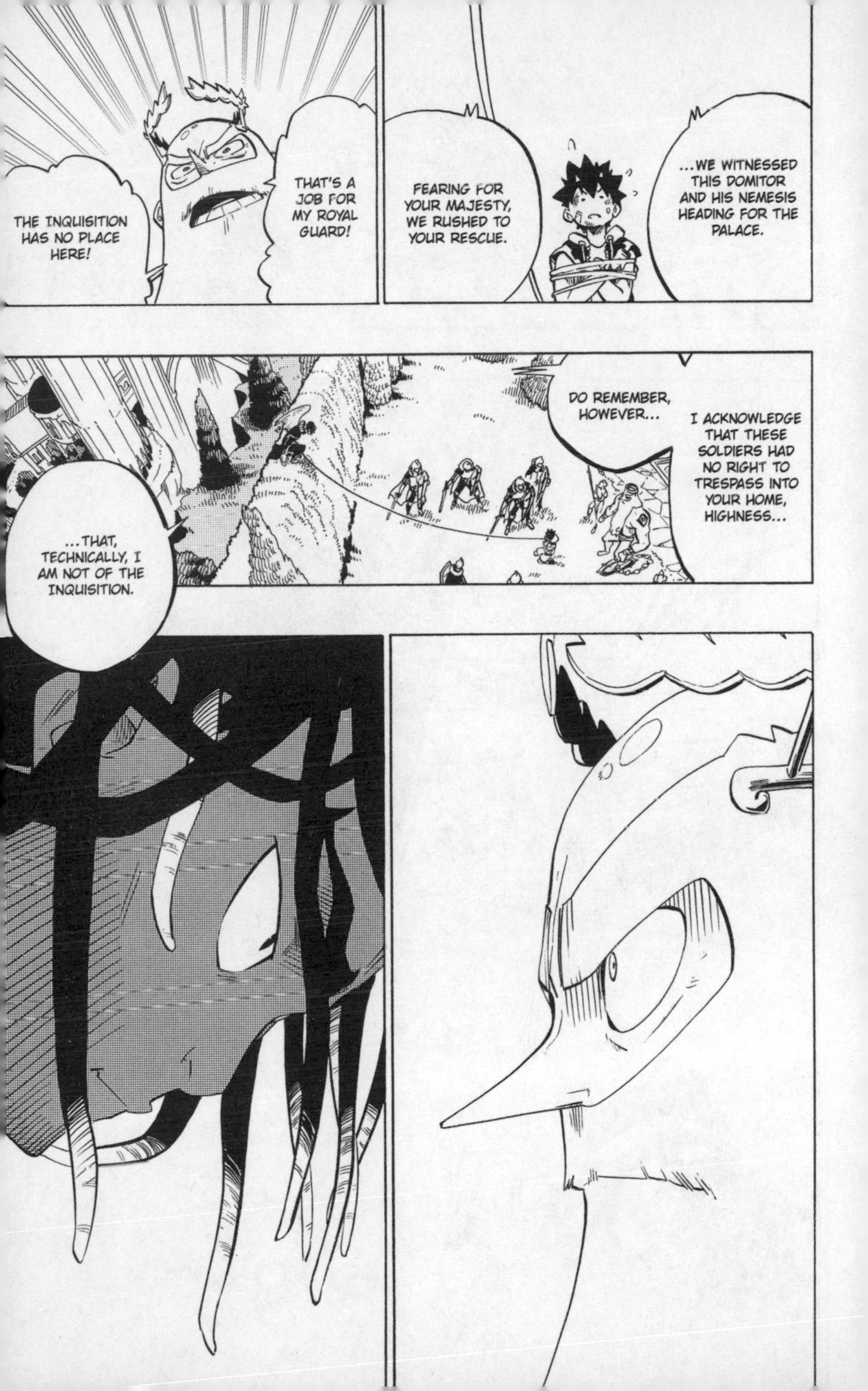
...WE WITNESSED THIS DOMITOR AND HIS NEMESIS HEADING FOR THE PALACE.
FEARING FOR YOUR MAJESTY, WE RUSHED TO YOUR RESCUE.
THAT'S A JOB FOR MY ROYAL GUARD!
THE INQUISITION HAS NO PLACE HERE!
I ACKNOWLEDGE THAT THESE SOLDIERS HAD NO RIGHT TO TRESPASS INTO YOUR HOME, HIGHNESS...
DO REMEMBER, HOWEVER...
...THAT, TECHNICALLY, I AM NOT OF THE INQUISITION.

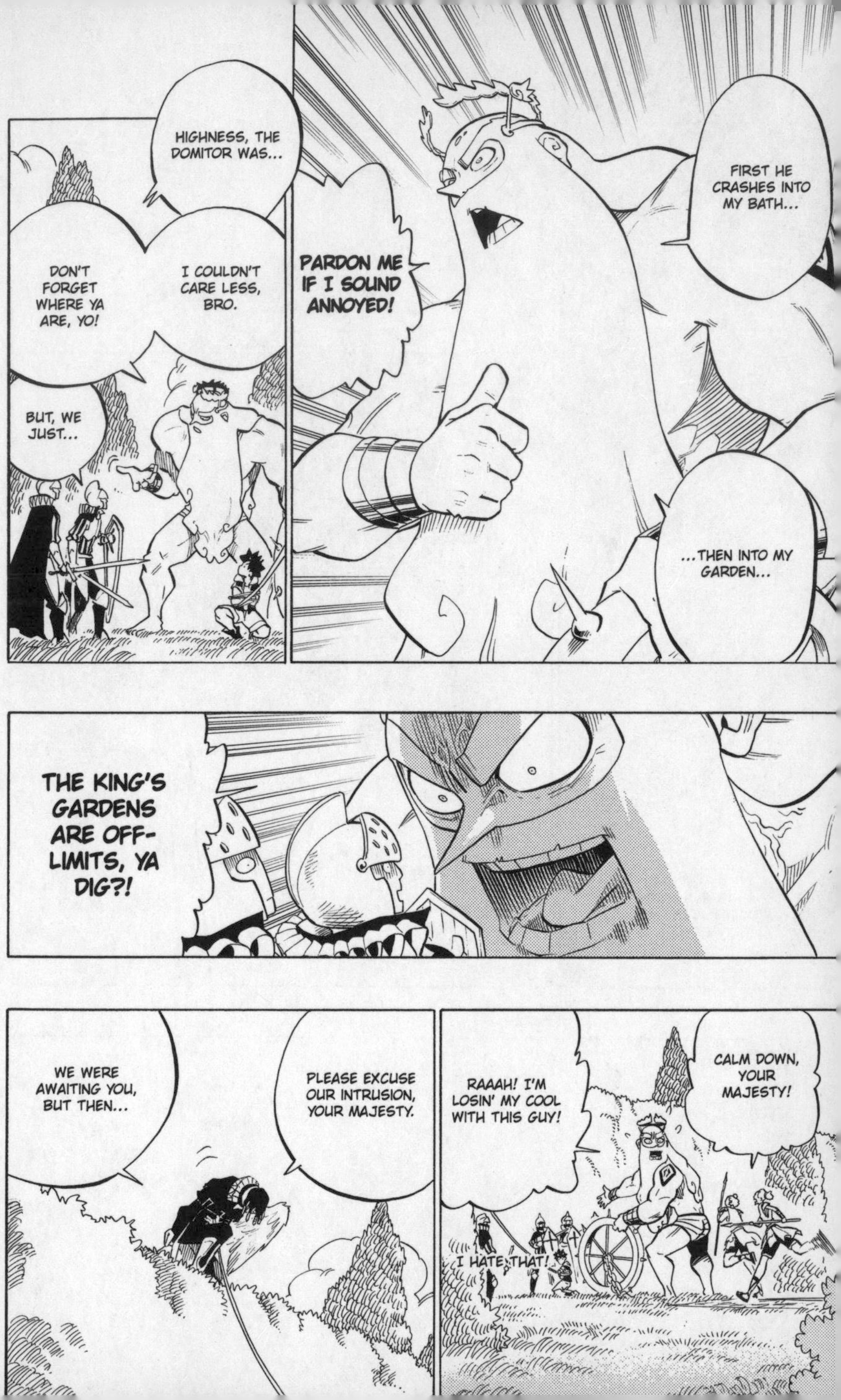
FIRST HE CRASHES INTO MY BATH...
PARDON ME IF I SOUND ANNOYED!
...THEN INTO MY GARDEN...
HIGHNESS, THE DOMITOR WAS...
I COULDN'T CARE LESS, BRO.
DON'T FORGET WHERE YA ARE, YO!
BUT, WE JUST...
THE KING'S GARDENS ARE OFF-LIMITS, YA DIG?!
CALM DOWN, YOUR MAJESTY!
RAAAH! I'M LOSIN' MY COOL WITH THIS GUY!
I HATE THAT!
PLEASE EXCUSE OUR INTRUSION, YOUR MAJESTY.
WE WERE AWAITING YOU, BUT THEN...

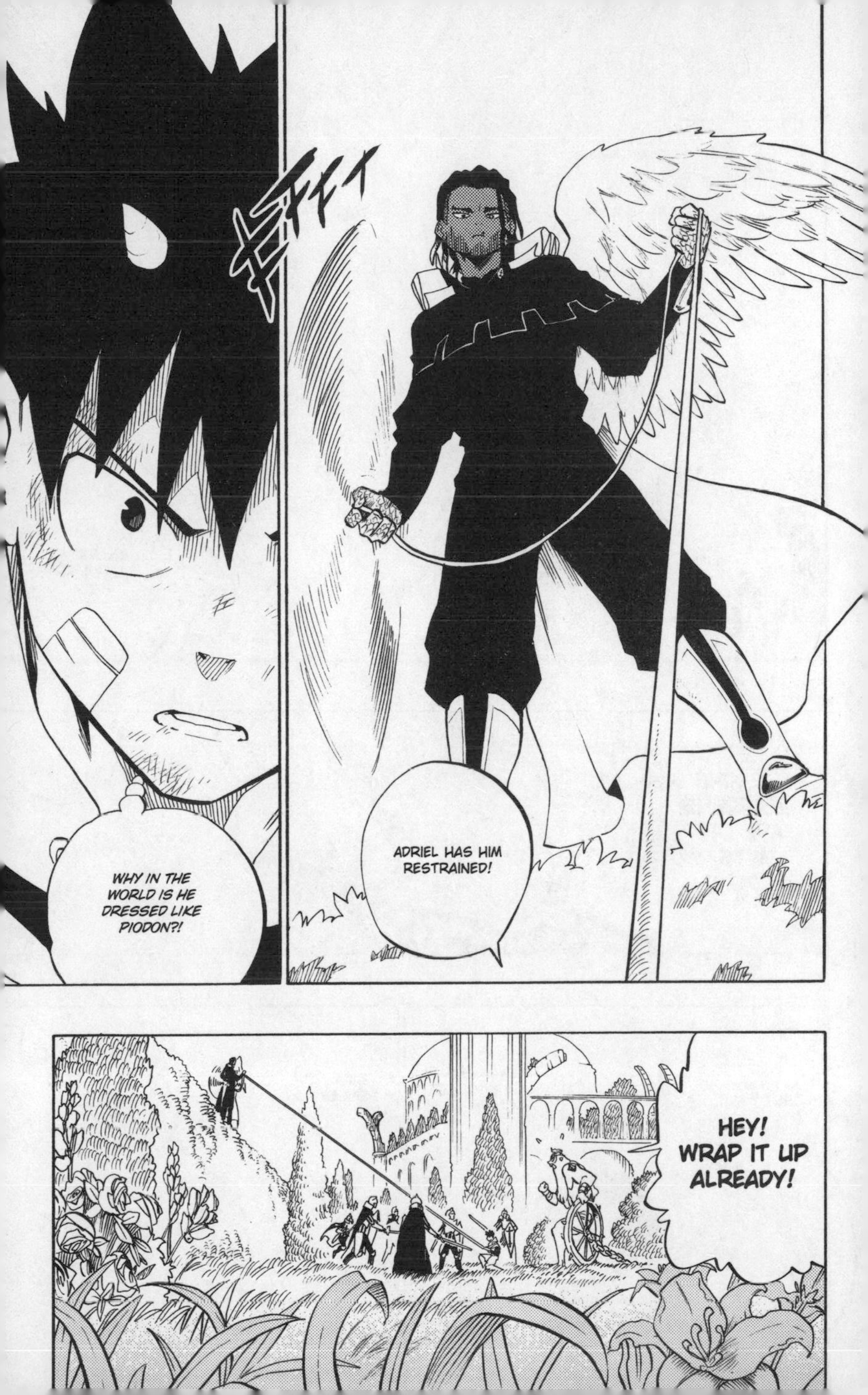
ADRIEL HAS HIM RESTRAINED!
WHY IN THE WORLD IS HE DRESSED LIKE PIODON?!
HEY! WRAP IT UP ALREADY!

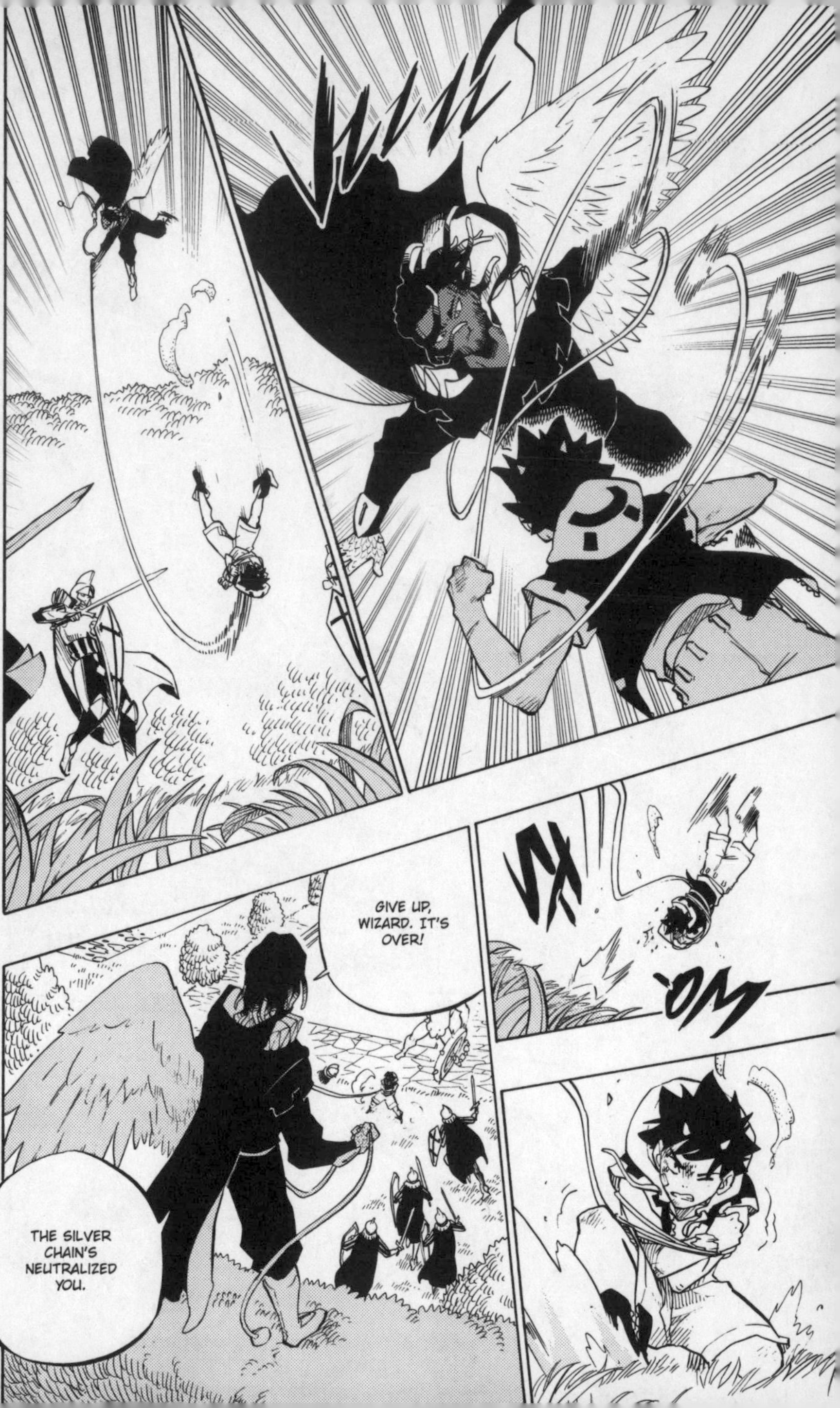
GIVE UP, WIZARD. IT'S OVER!
THE SILVER CHAIN'S NEUTRALIZED YOU.

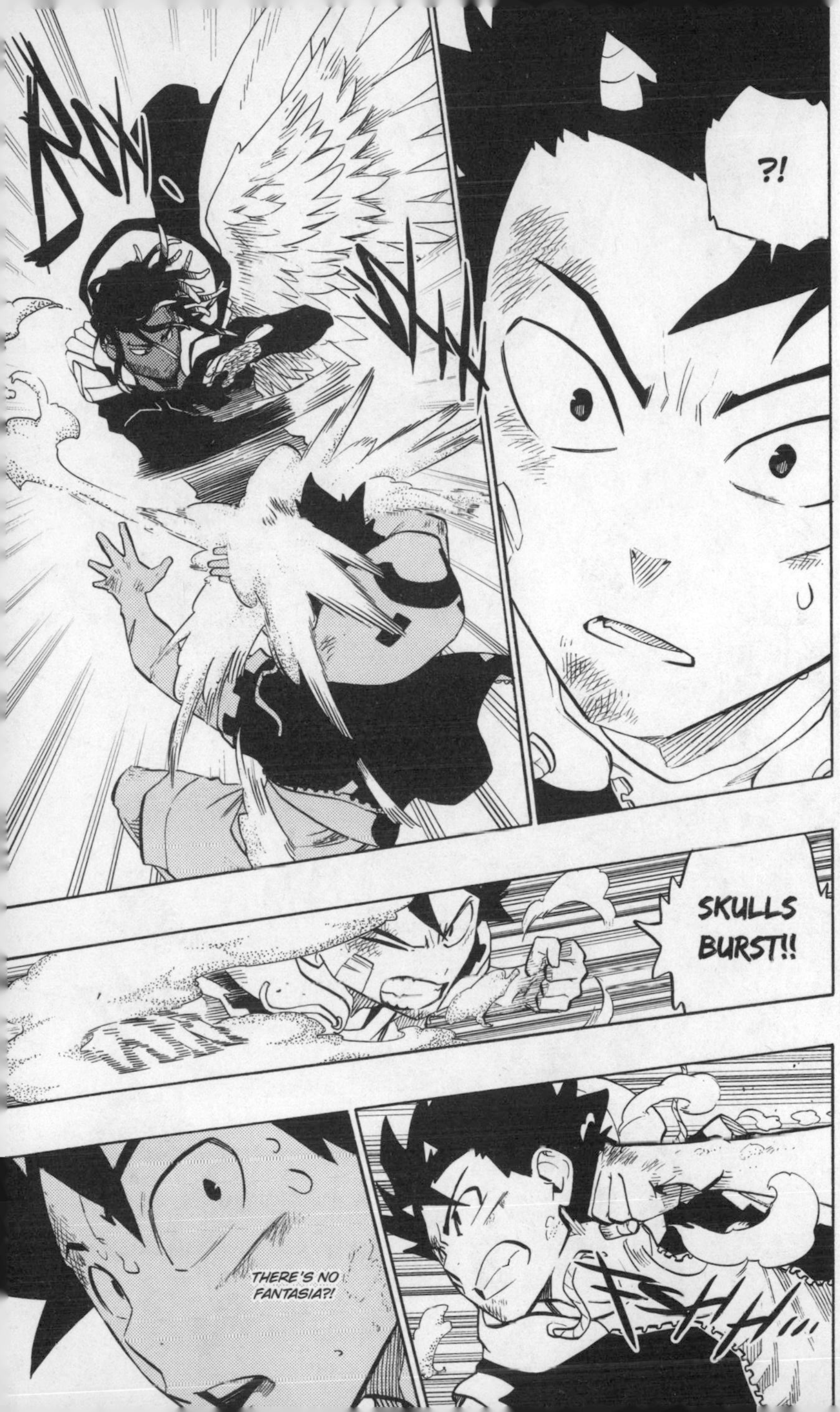
?!
SKULLS BURST!!
THERE'S NO FANTASIA?!

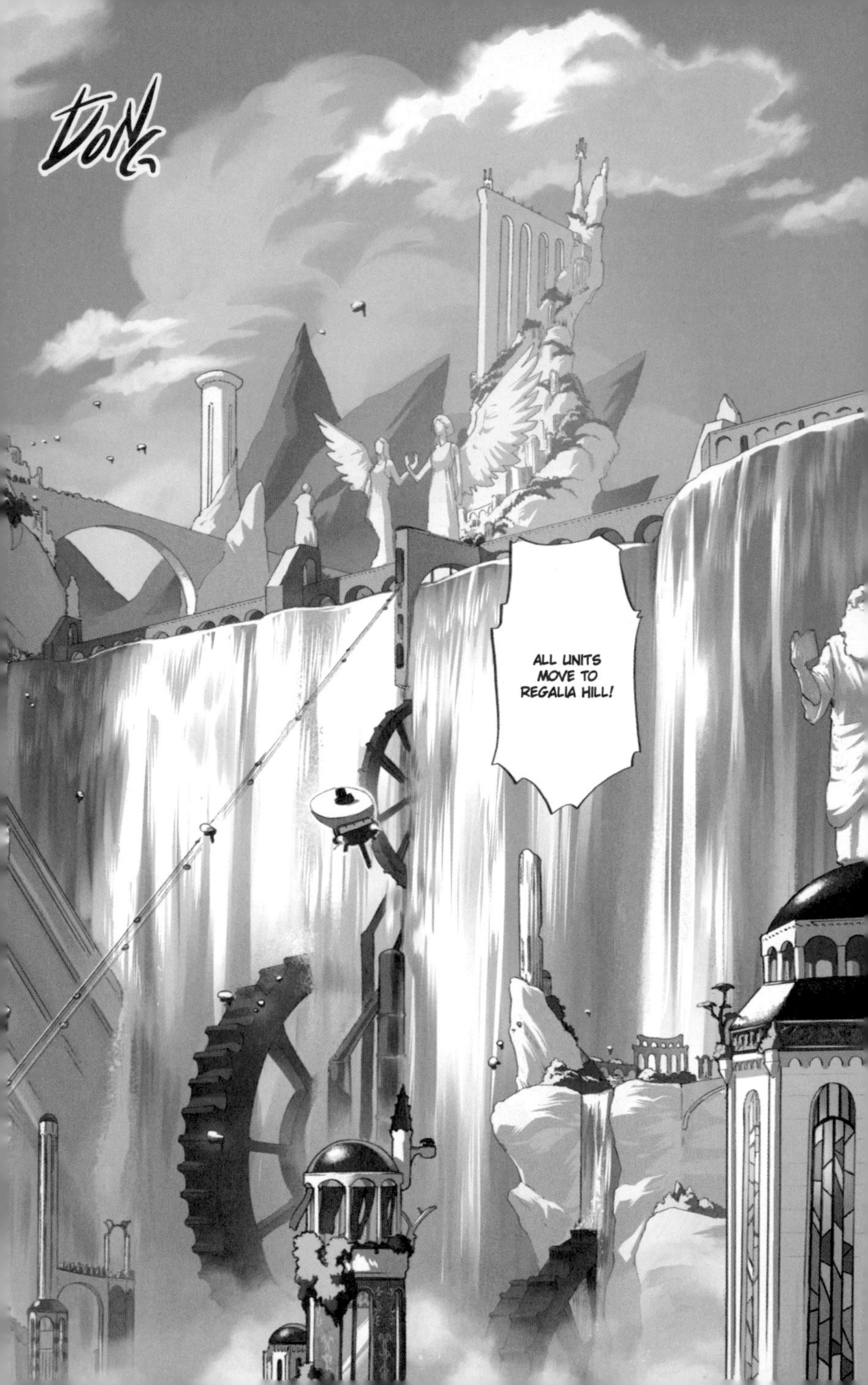
DON
ALL UNITS MOVE TO REGALIA HILL!

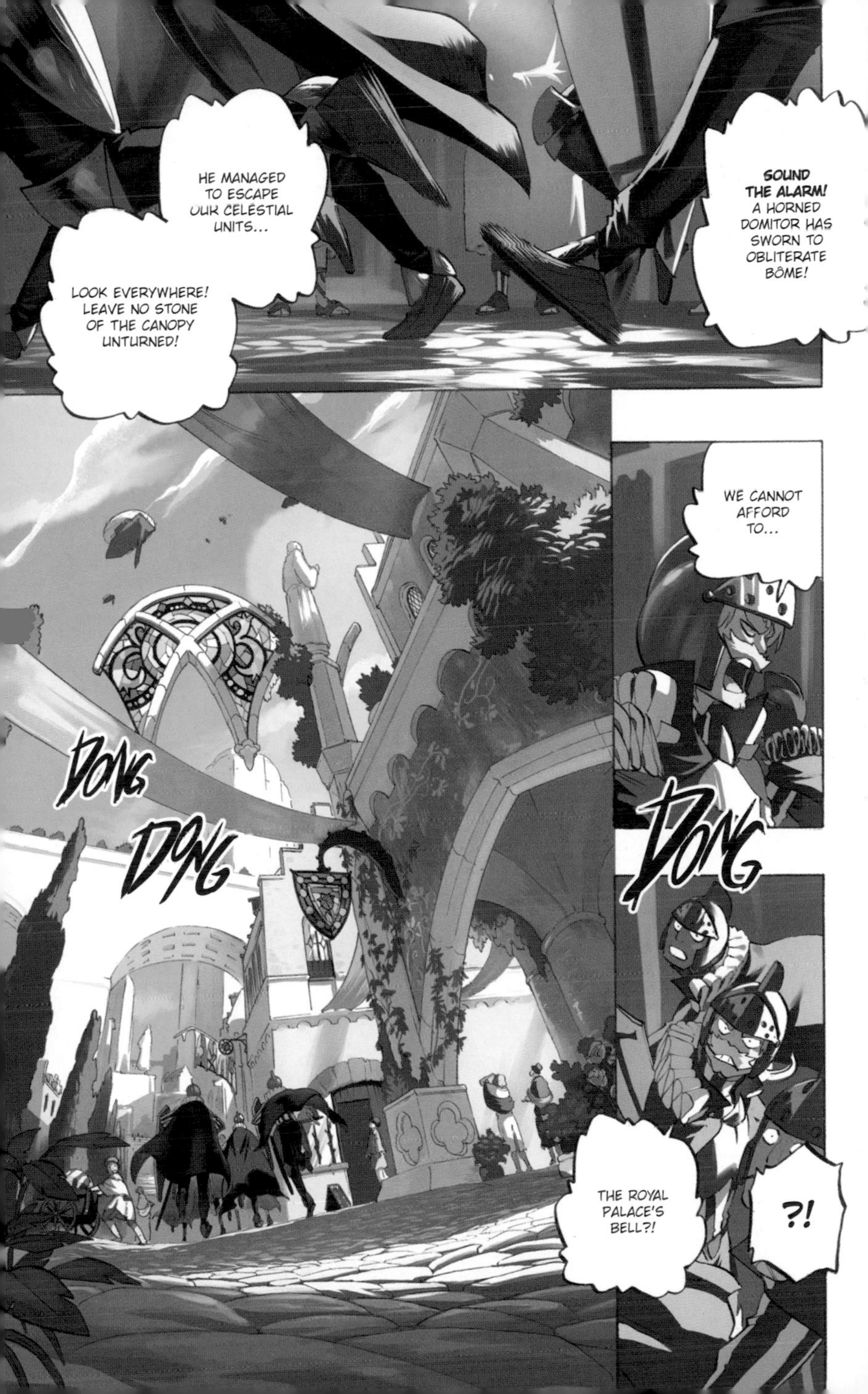
SOUND THE ALARM! A HORNED DOMITOR HAS SWORN TO OBLITERATE BÔME!
HE MANAGED TO ESCAPE OUR CELESTIAL UNITS...
LOOK EVERYWHERE! LEAVE NO STONE OF THE CANOPY UNTURNED!
WE CANNOT AFFORD TO...
DONG
?!
THE ROYAL PALACE'S BELL?!
DONG
DONG

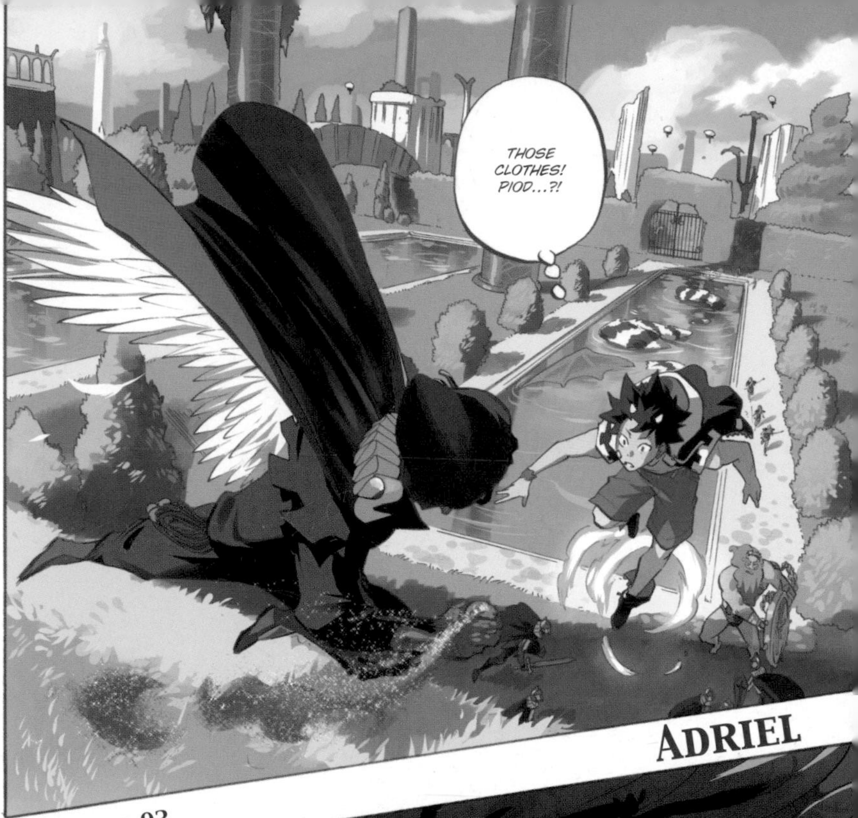
THOSE CLOTHES! PIOD...?!

Chapter 93
Adriel

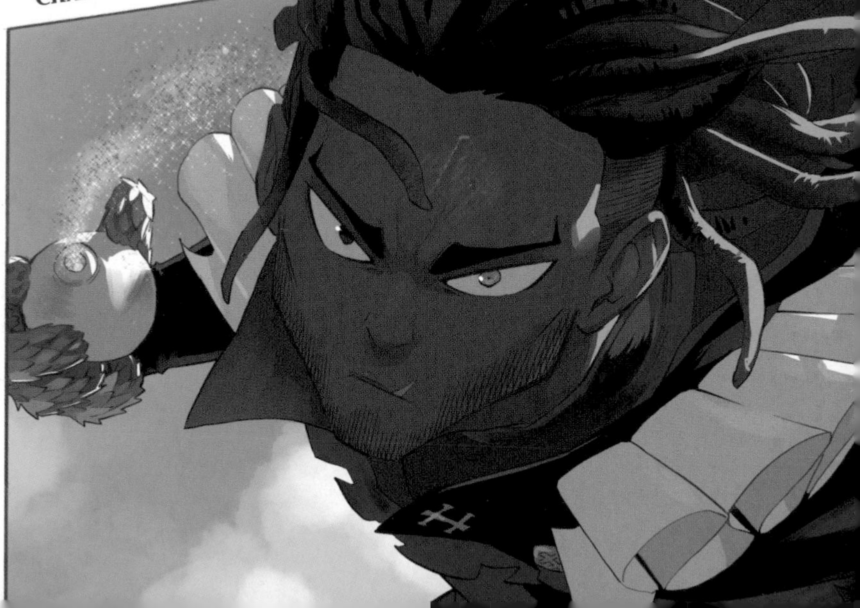

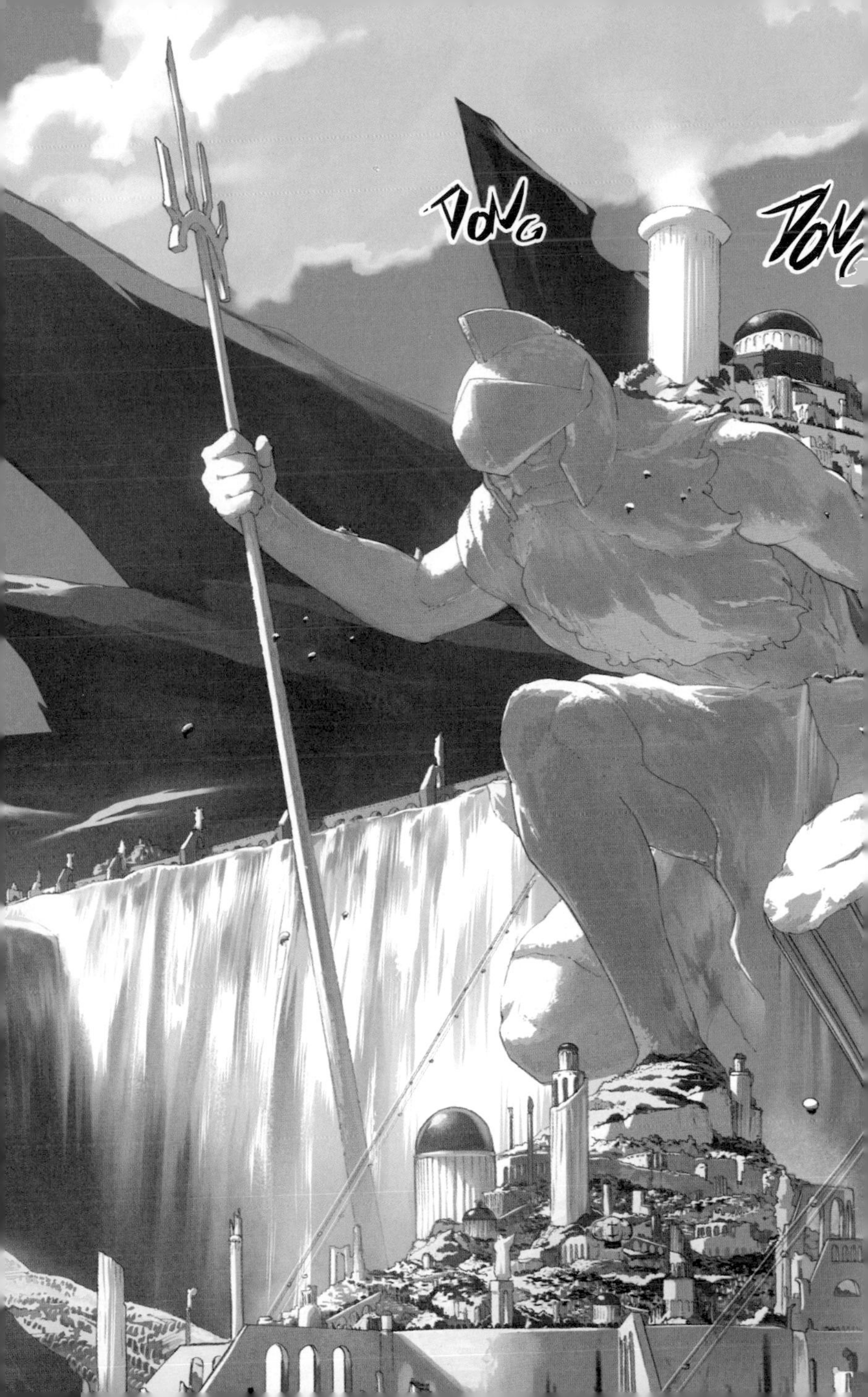
DONG
DONG

Synopsis of the previous volume:

After taking on Capula and Engti Nocti, two sisters belonging to an evil coven known as the Mesnie, Doc and Yaga arrive in Bôme, guided by Draccoon and Mr. Boobrie, in order to save Seth, Ocoho and Mélie. Thanks to his outward appearance of an old infant, Doc succeeds in swiping the book of Lupa Lycco, a Domitor, and freeing both his friends and the Nemesis the Domitor captured. While Seth is trying to subdue the Nemesis in an attempt to save the city, he comes face-to-face with Herklès VII, king of Bôme, and with Adriel, an Inquisition Converso.

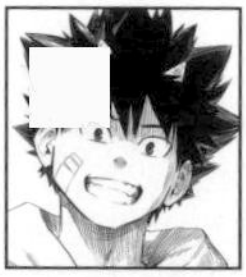

- SETH -
Apprentice Wizard.
His Infection manifests as horns growing from his head. Dreams of finding the Radiant, the place from which Nemeses arise, in order to destroy it.

- MÉLIE -
Trapper Wizard. Her Infection changes her usual sweet personality into one that's bossy and hotheaded.

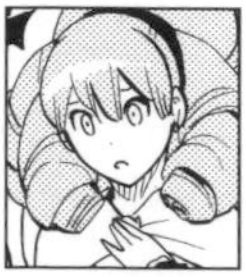

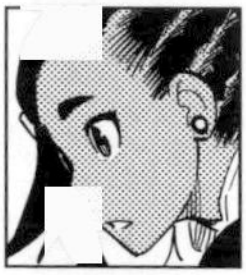

- OCOHO -
Crown princess of Cyfandir.
Her unfortunate Infection allows anyone to control her by pressing on a spot underneath her right ear.

- DOC -
Research Wizard.
His Infection allows him to regenerate back into a newborn.

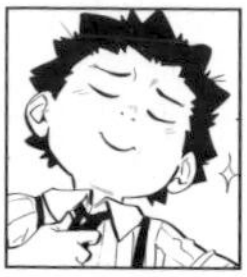

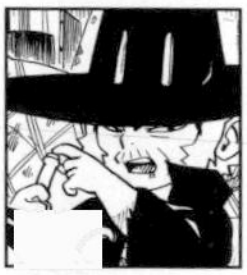

- YAGA -
Retired Artemis wizard.
Member of the Coven of Thirteen.

- DRAGUNOV -
Captain Inquisitor.
New member of the Thaumaturge congregation.

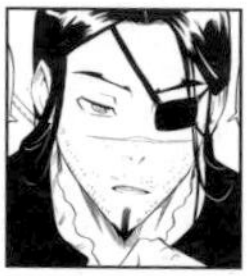

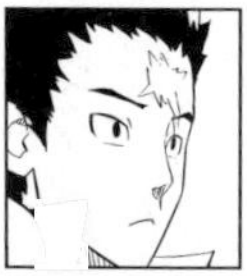

- PIODON -
Seth's mysterious big brother.
Inquisition Converso.

- ADRIEL -
Inquisition Converso.

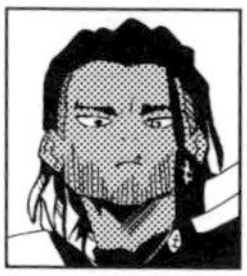

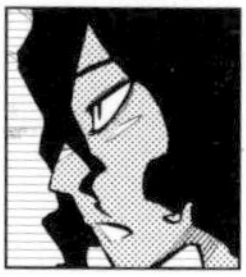

- ININNA -
Colonel Inquisitor from the region of Kumhère.

- SARGON -
General Inquisitor from the region of Kumhère.

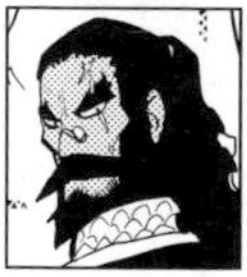

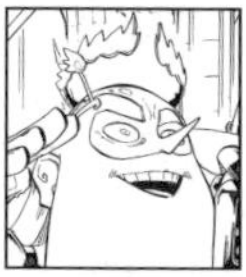

- HERKLÈS VII -
King of Bôme.

- LUPA LYCCO -
Domitor Wizard.

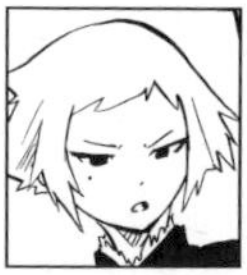

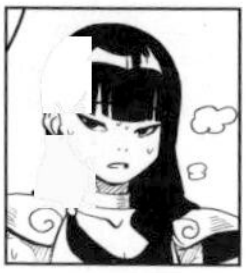

- SHOAN -
Royal guard.

- ALCILLE -
Royal guard, right-hand woman of King Herklès VII.

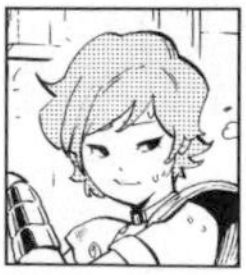

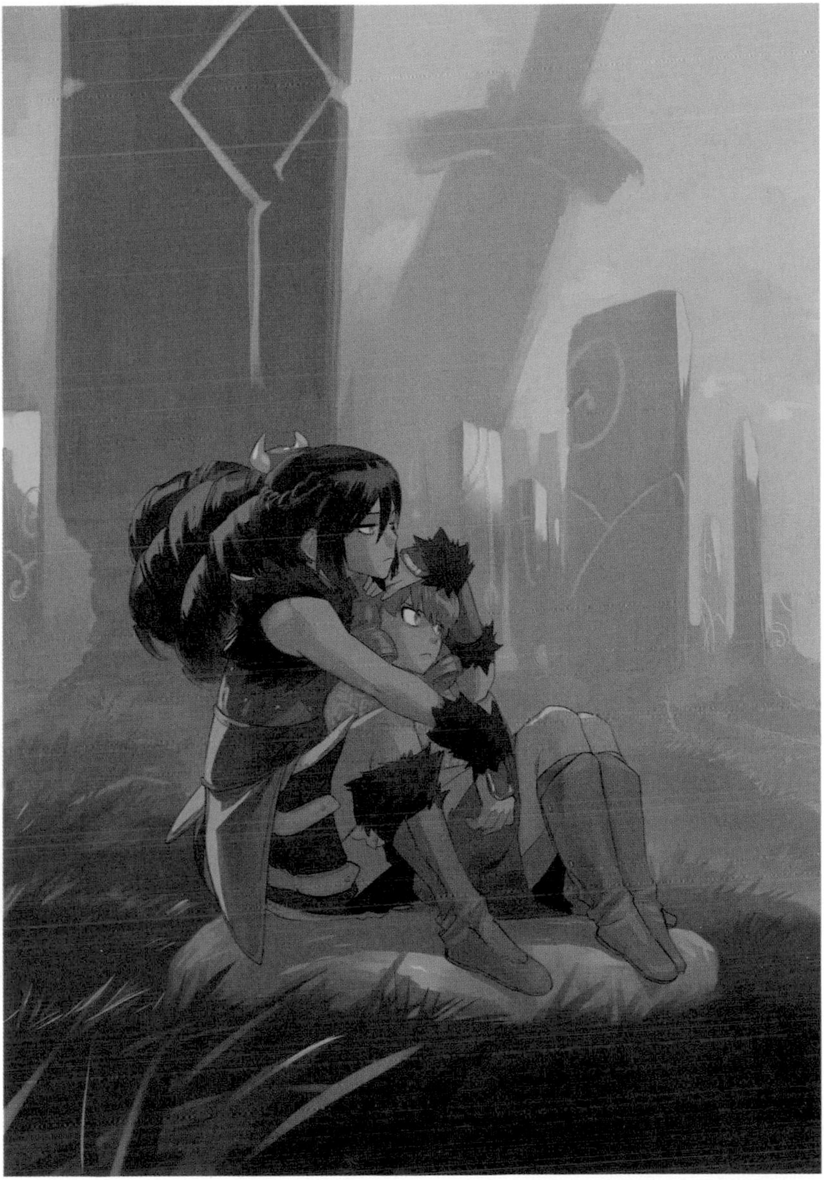

CHAPTER 96

I WON'T LET YOU GO

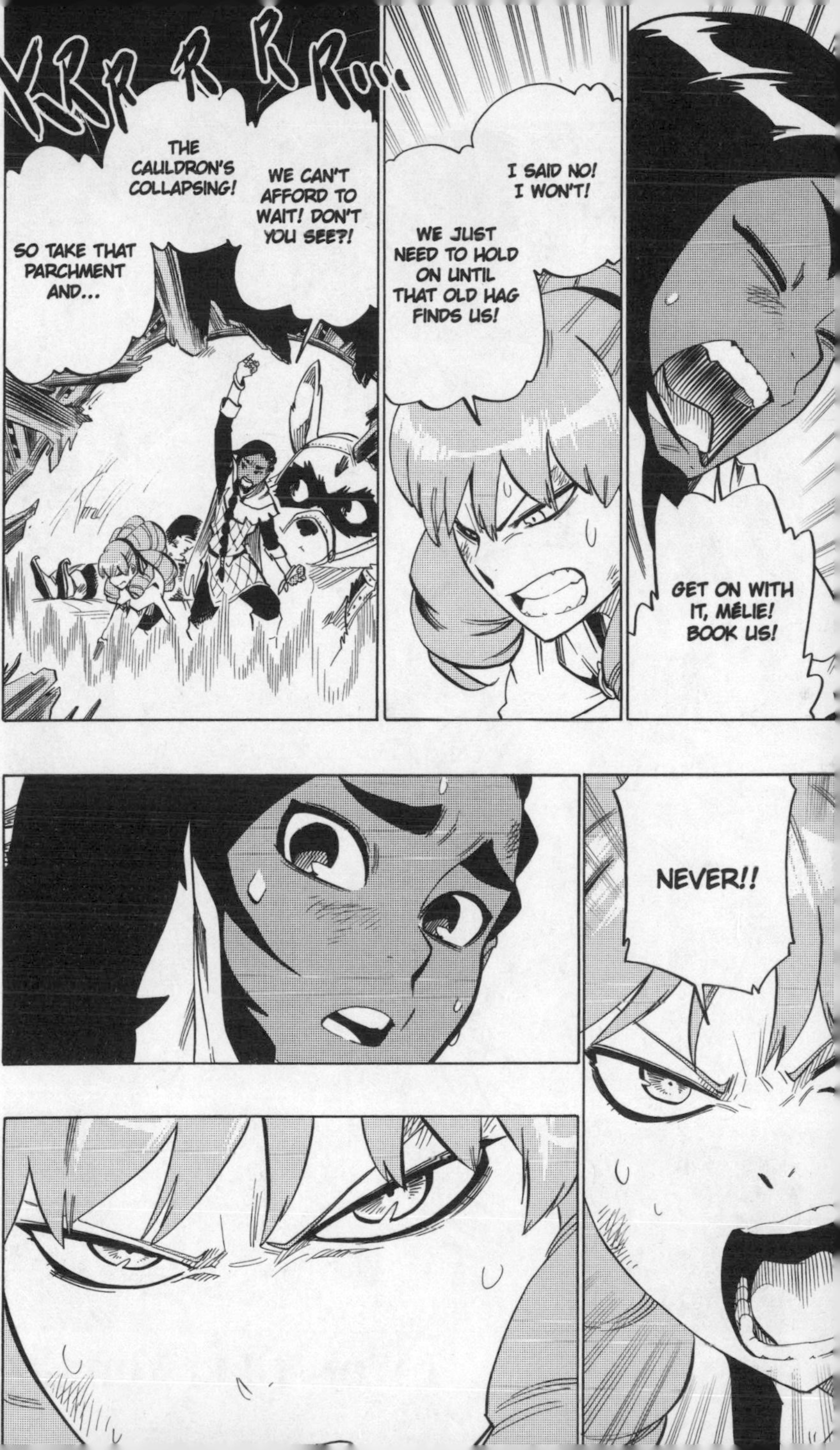
GET ON WITH IT, MÉLIE! BOOK US!
I SAID NO! I WON'T!
WE JUST NEED TO HOLD ON UNTIL THAT OLD HAG FINDS US!
KRRRRR...
THE CAULDRON'S COLLAPSING!
WE CAN'T AFFORD TO WAIT! DON'T YOU SEE?!
SO TAKE THAT PARCHMENT AND...
NEVER!!

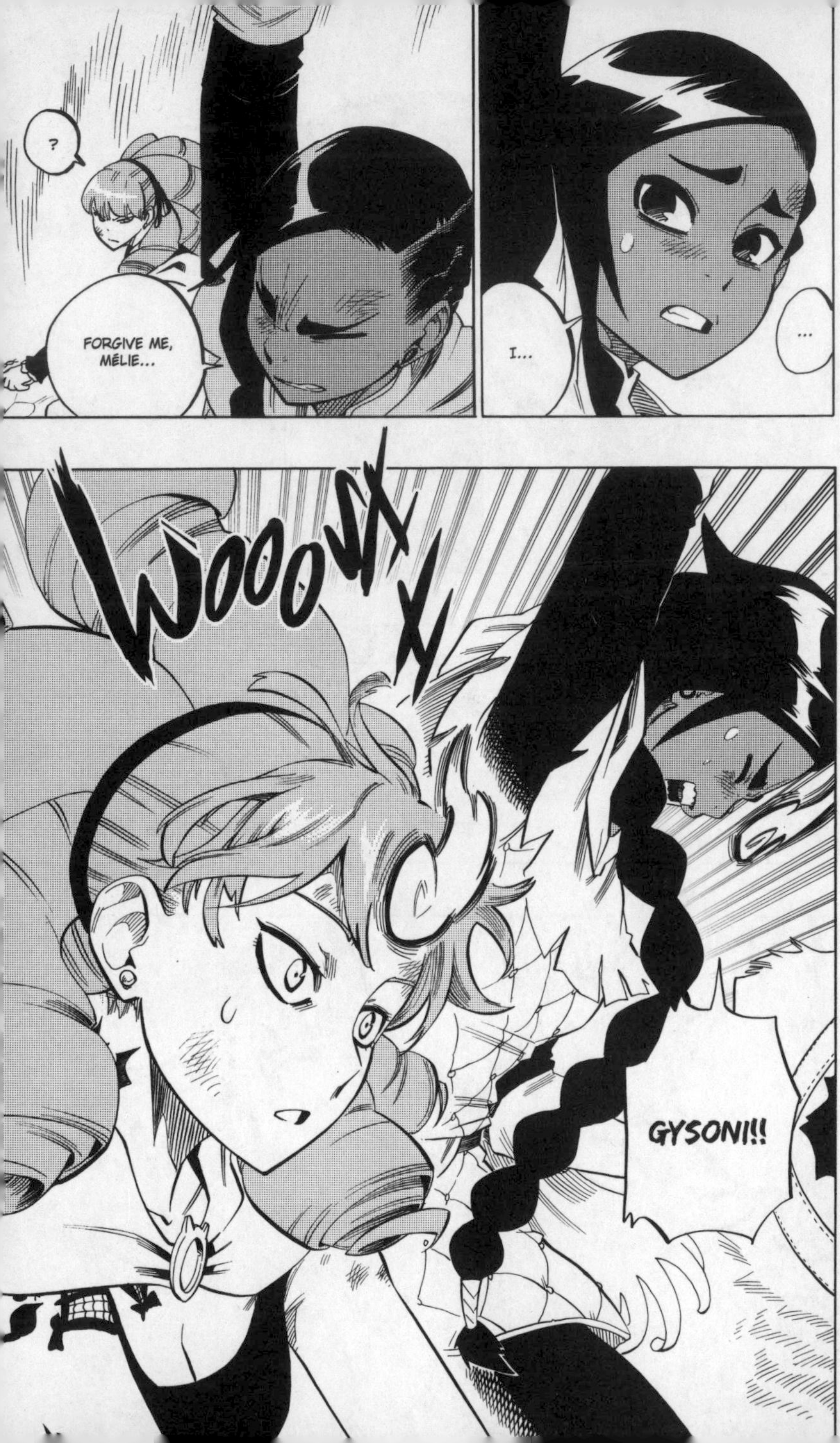
...
I...
?
FORGIVE ME, MÉLIE...
GYSONI!!
WOOOSH

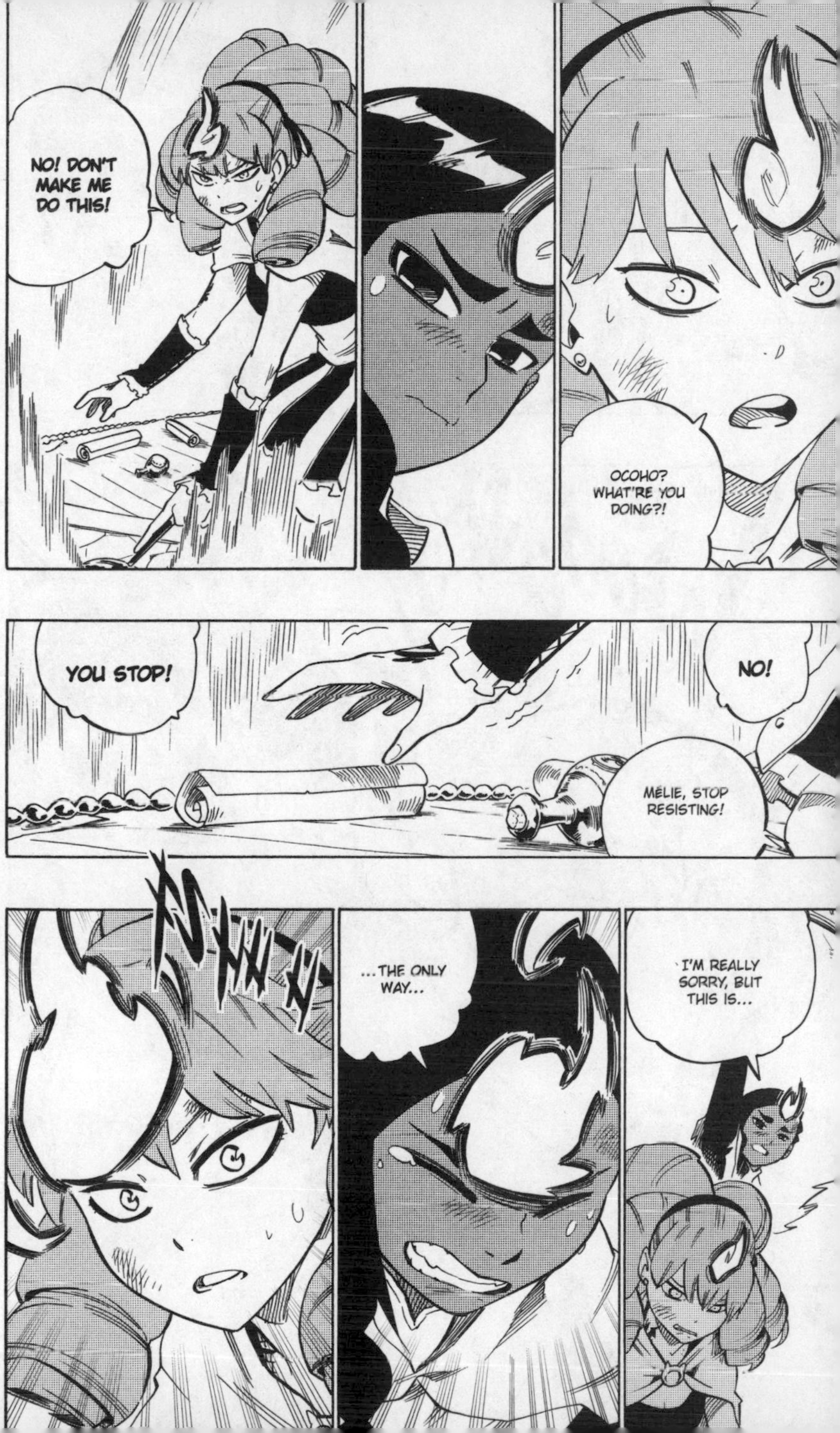
OCOHO? WHAT'RE YOU DOING?!
NO! DON'T MAKE ME DO THIS!
NO!
MÉLIE, STOP RESISTING!
YOU STOP!
I'M REALLY SORRY, BUT THIS IS...
...THE ONLY WAY...

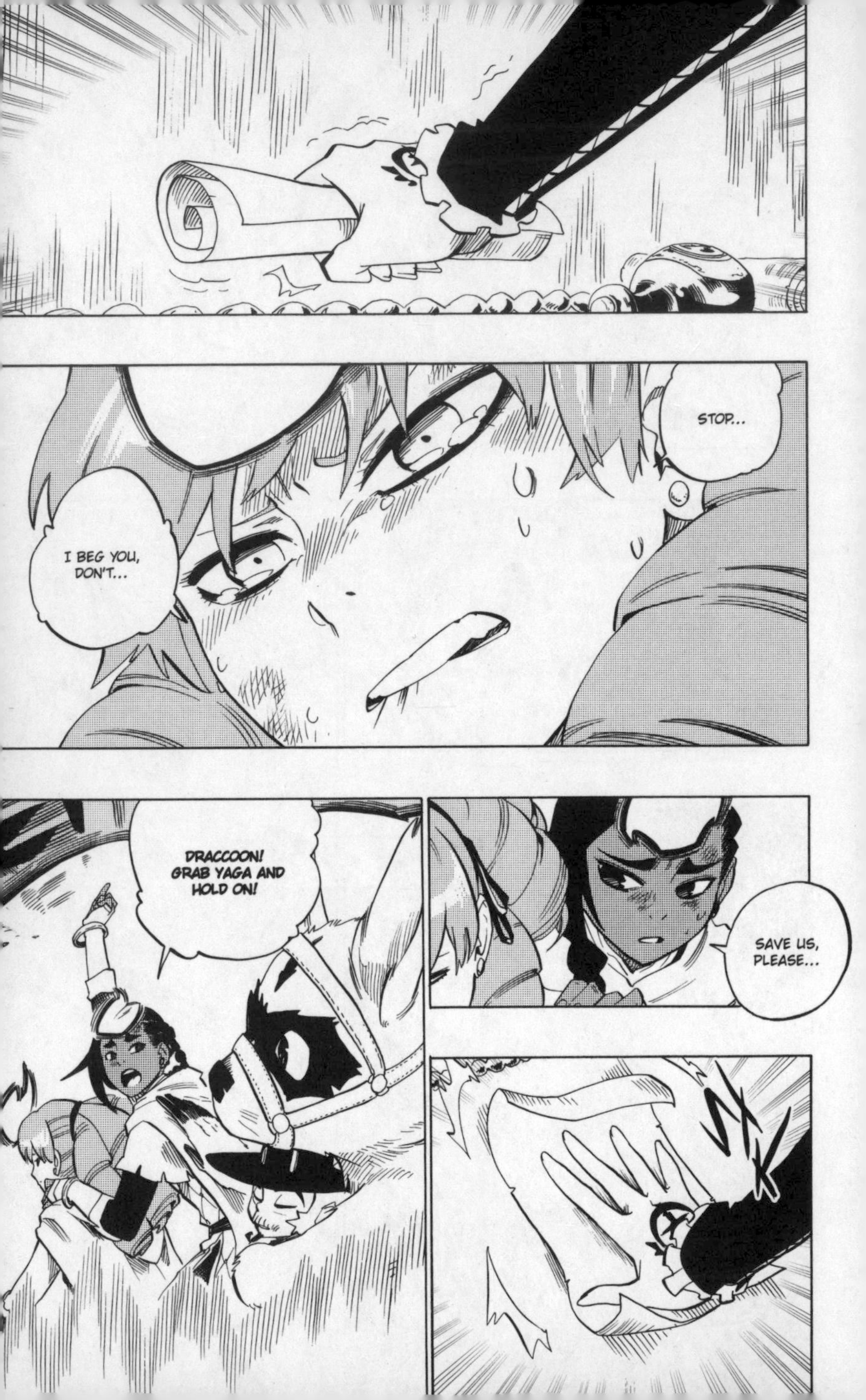
STOP...
I BEG YOU, DON'T...
SAVE US, PLEASE...
DRACCOON! GRAB YAGA AND HOLD ON!

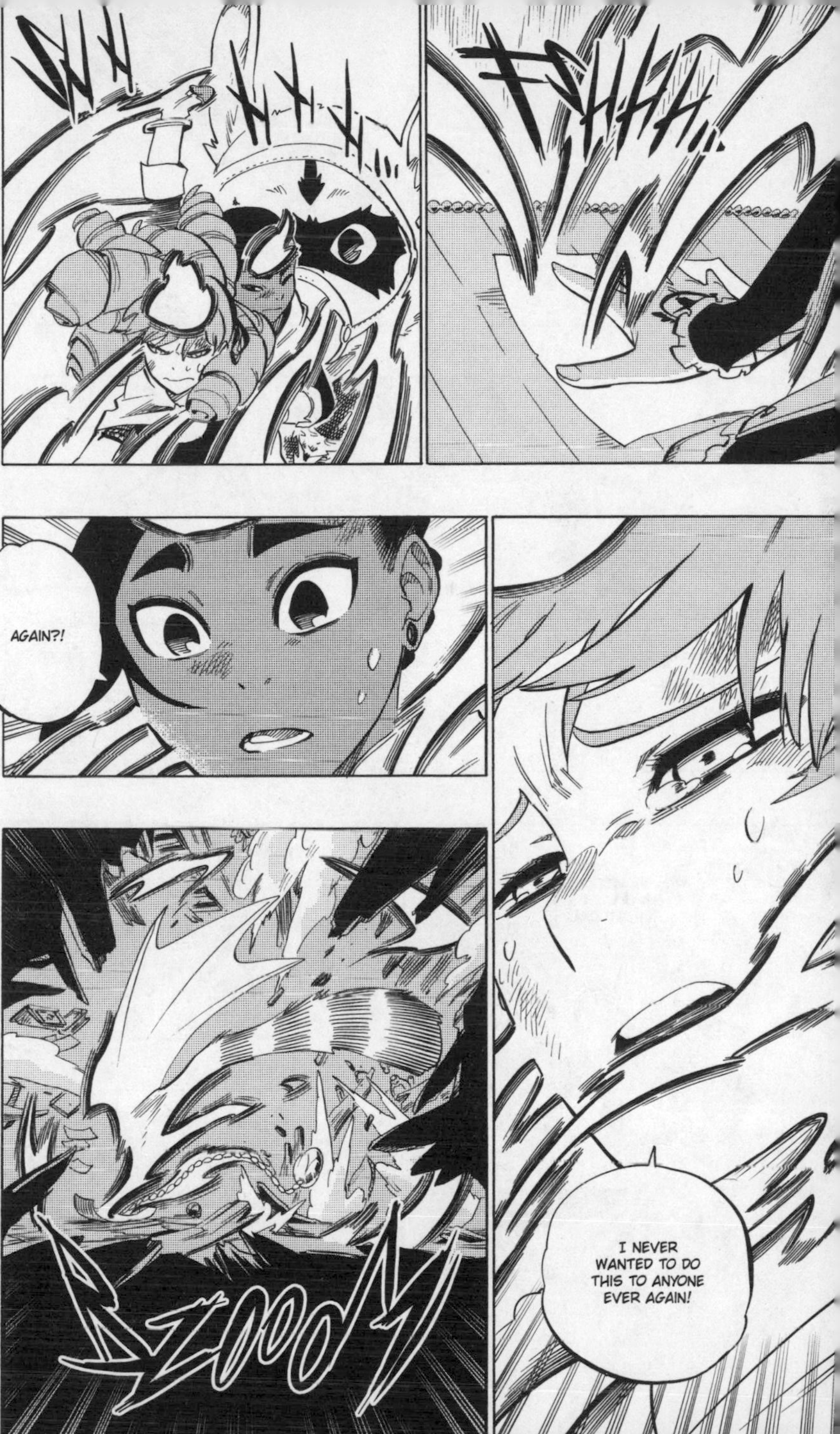
FSHHH..
I NEVER WANTED TO DO THIS TO ANYONE EVER AGAIN!
AGAIN?!
ZOOOM

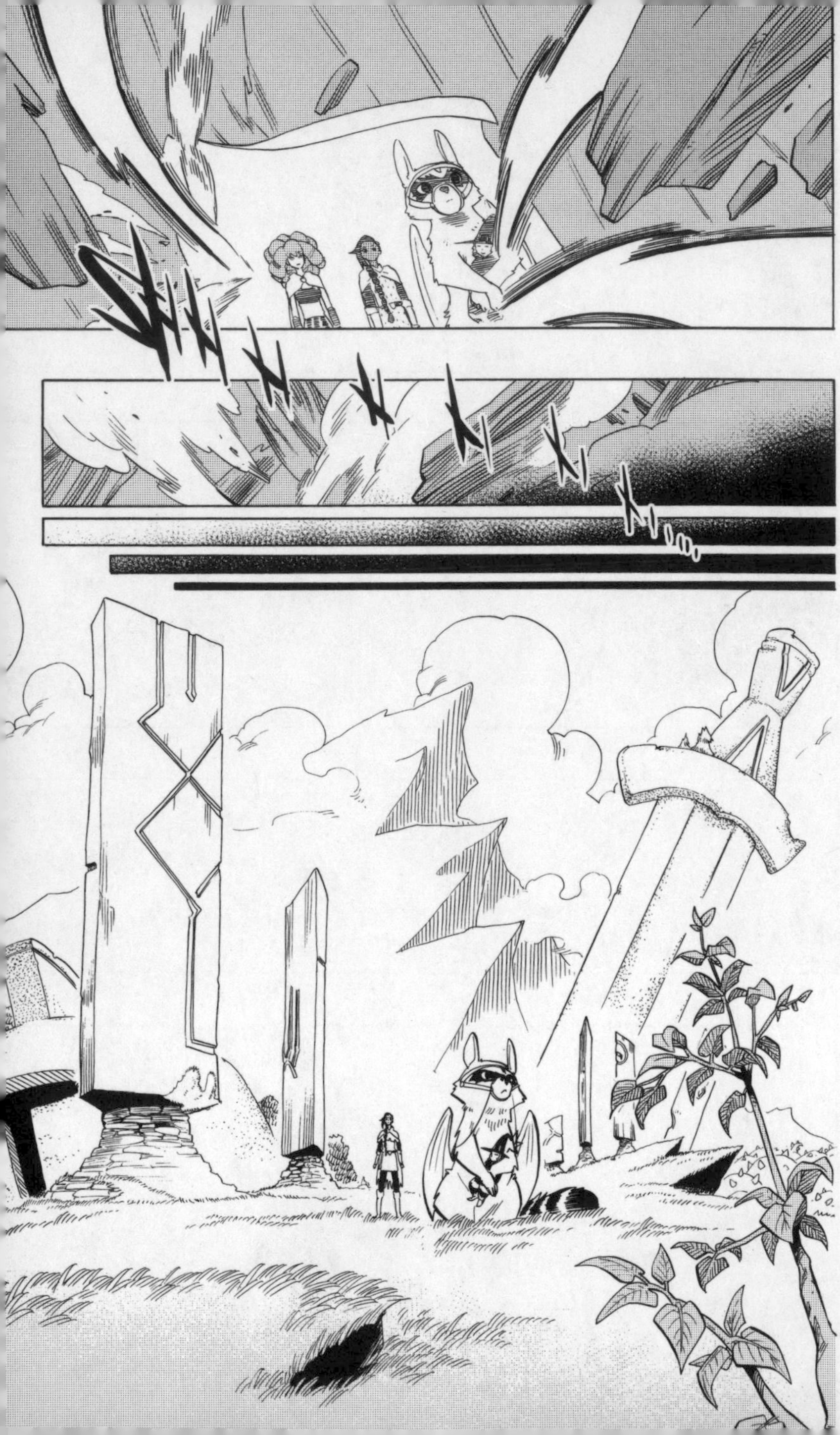
SHHHHHH...

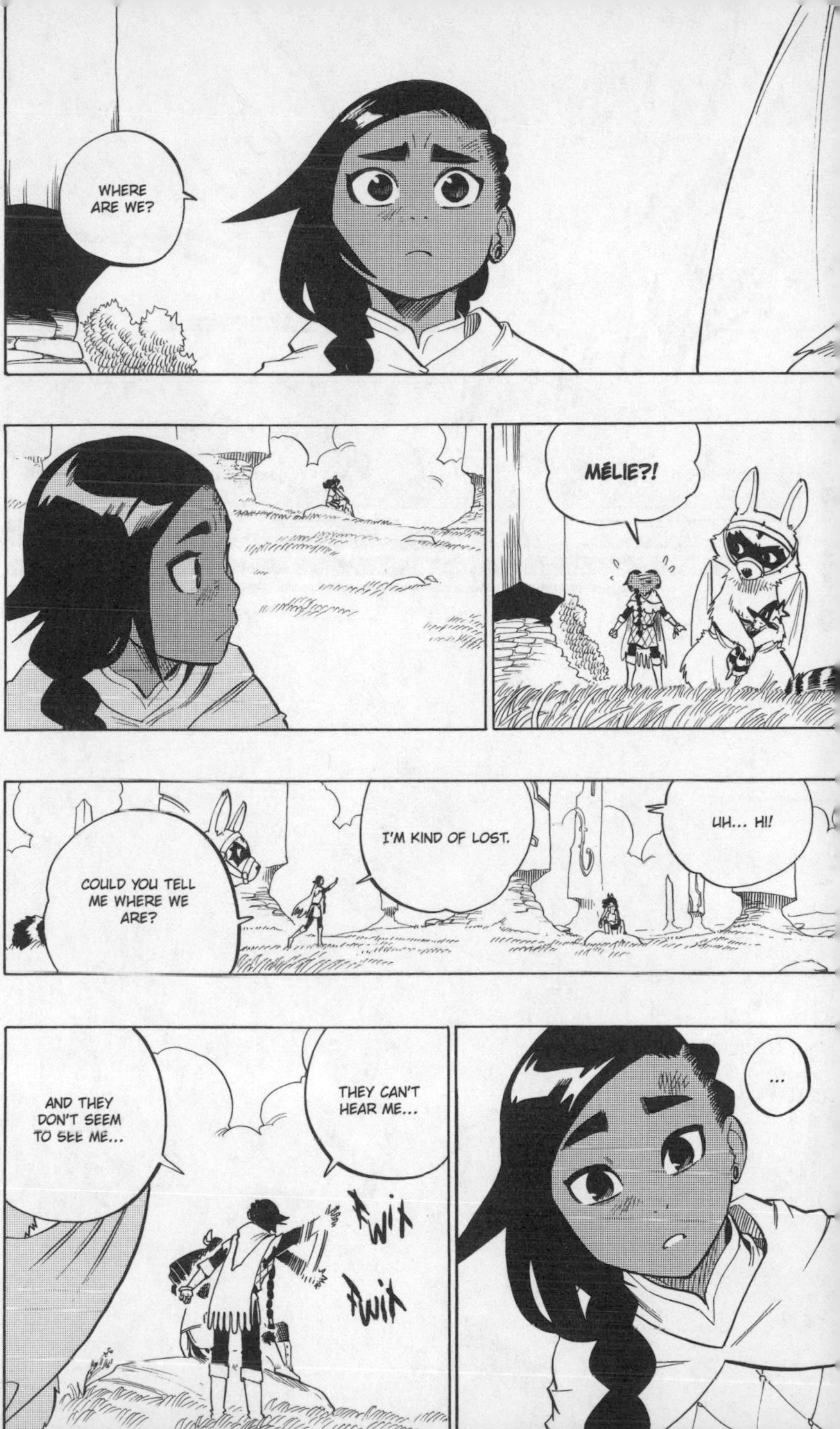
WHERE ARE WE?
MÉLIE?!
UH... HI!
I'M KIND OF LOST.
COULD YOU TELL ME WHERE WE ARE?
...
THEY CAN'T HEAR ME...
AND THEY DON'T SEEM TO SEE ME...
FWIT
FWIT

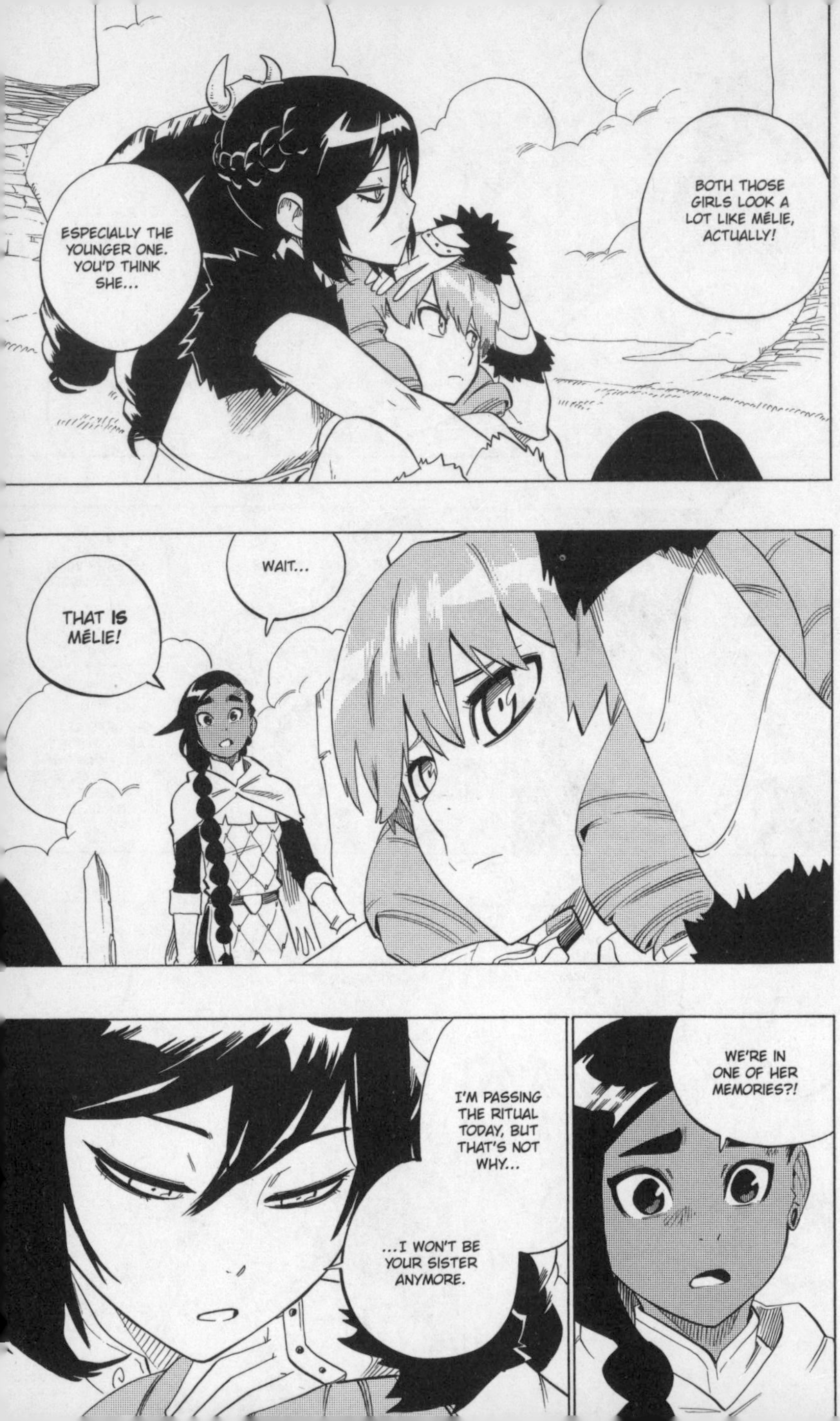
BOTH THOSE GIRLS LOOK A LOT LIKE MÉLIE, ACTUALLY!
ESPECIALLY THE YOUNGER ONE. YOU'D THINK SHE...
WAIT...
THAT IS MÉLIE!
WE'RE IN ONE OF HER MEMORIES?!
I'M PASSING THE RITUAL TODAY, BUT THAT'S NOT WHY...
...I WON'T BE YOUR SISTER ANYMORE.

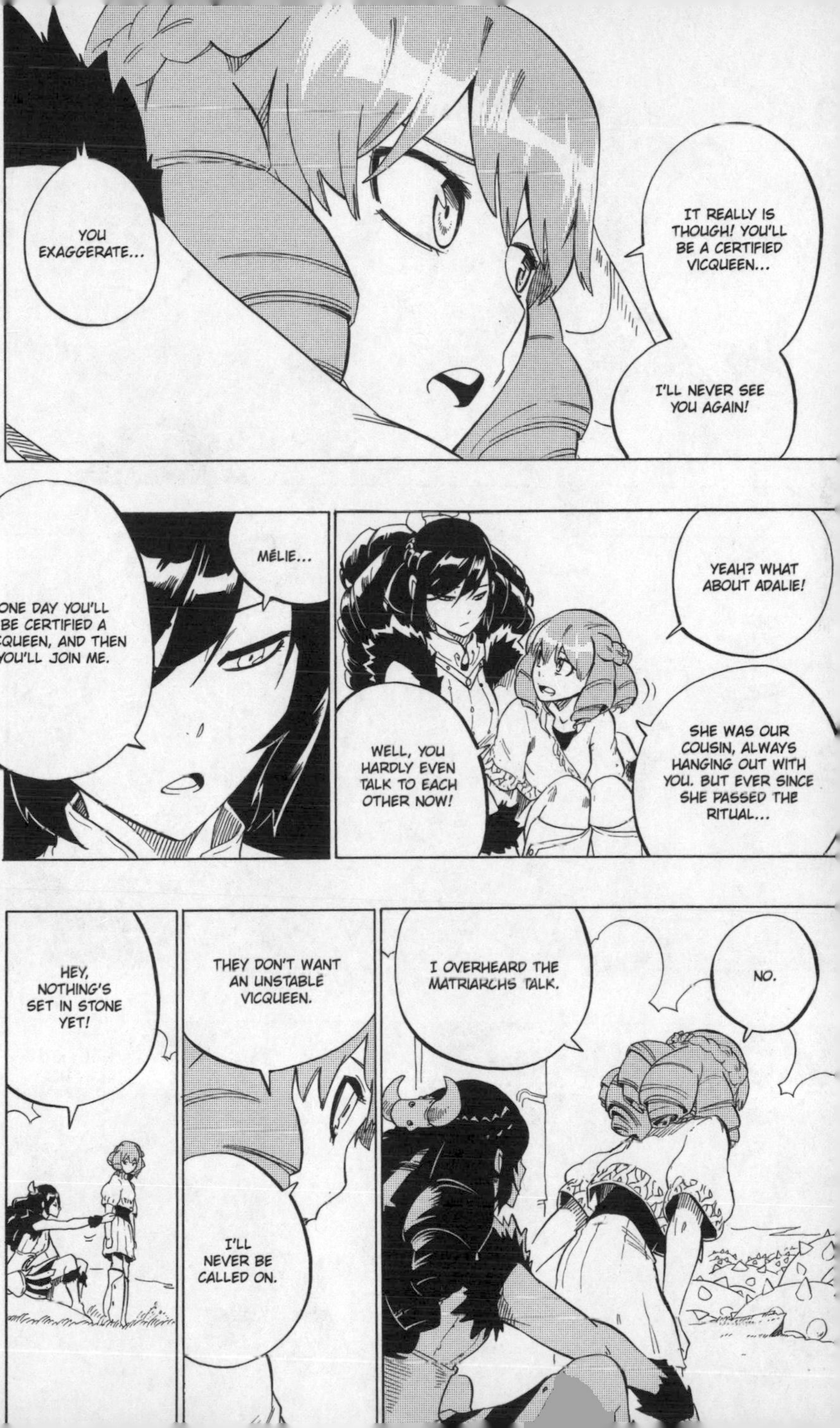
IT REALLY IS THOUGH! YOU'LL BE A CERTIFIED VICQUEEN...
I'LL NEVER SEE YOU AGAIN!
YOU EXAGGERATE...
YEAH? WHAT ABOUT ADALIE!
SHE WAS OUR COUSIN, ALWAYS HANGING OUT WITH YOU. BUT EVER SINCE SHE PASSED THE RITUAL...
WELL, YOU HARDLY EVEN TALK TO EACH OTHER NOW!
MÉLIE...
ONE DAY YOU'LL BE CERTIFIED A VICQUEEN, AND THEN YOU'LL JOIN ME.
NO.
I OVERHEARD THE MATRIARCHS TALK.
THEY DON'T WANT AN UNSTABLE VICQUEEN.
I'LL NEVER BE CALLED ON.
HEY, NOTHING'S SET IN STONE YET!

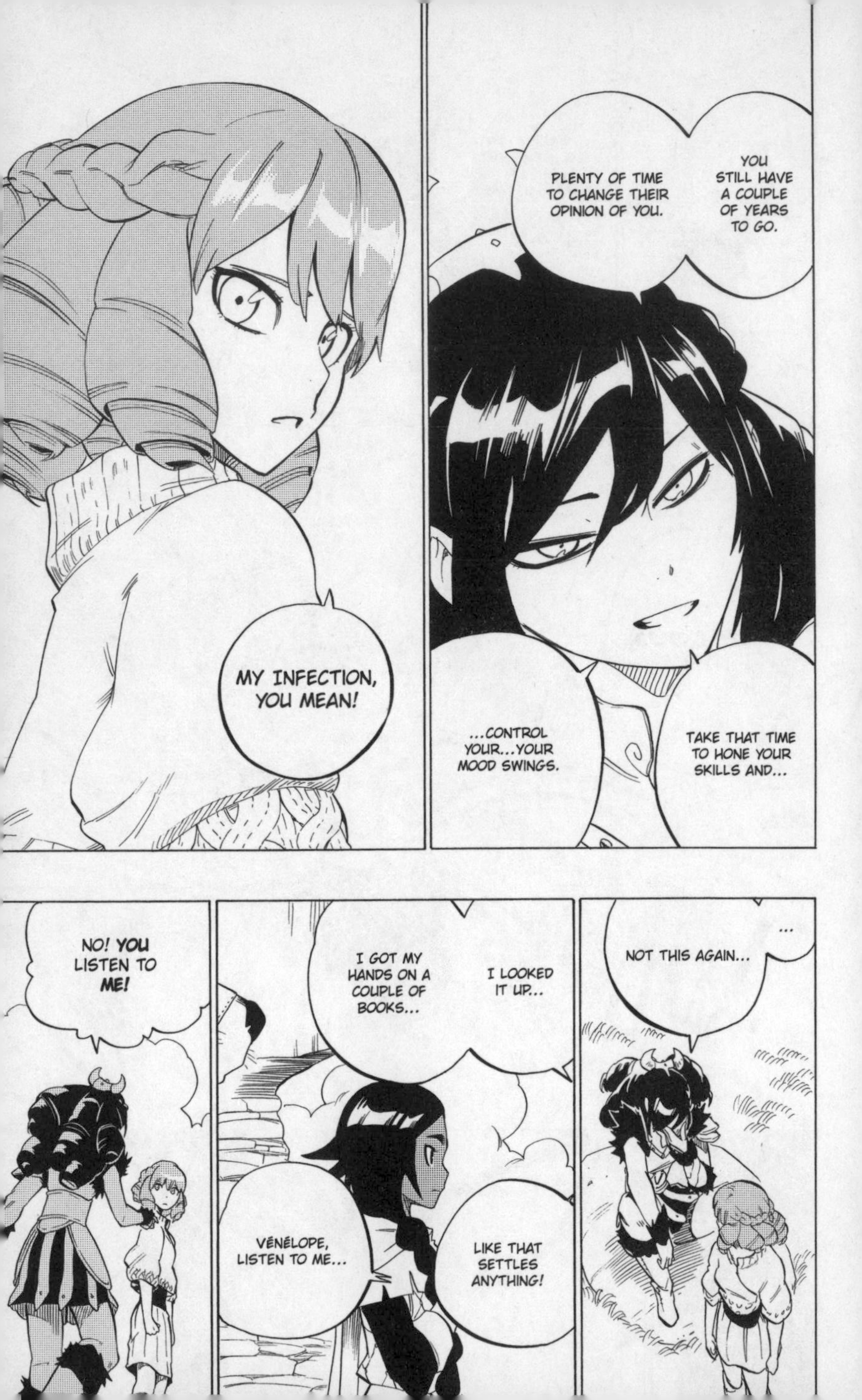
YOU STILL HAVE A COUPLE OF YEARS TO GO.
PLENTY OF TIME TO CHANGE THEIR OPINION OF YOU.
TAKE THAT TIME TO HONE YOUR SKILLS AND...
...CONTROL YOUR...YOUR MOOD SWINGS.
MY INFECTION, YOU MEAN!
...
NOT THIS AGAIN...
I LOOKED IT UP...
I GOT MY HANDS ON A COUPLE OF BOOKS...
LIKE THAT SETTLES ANYTHING!
VÉNÉLOPE, LISTEN TO ME...
NO! YOU LISTEN TO ME!

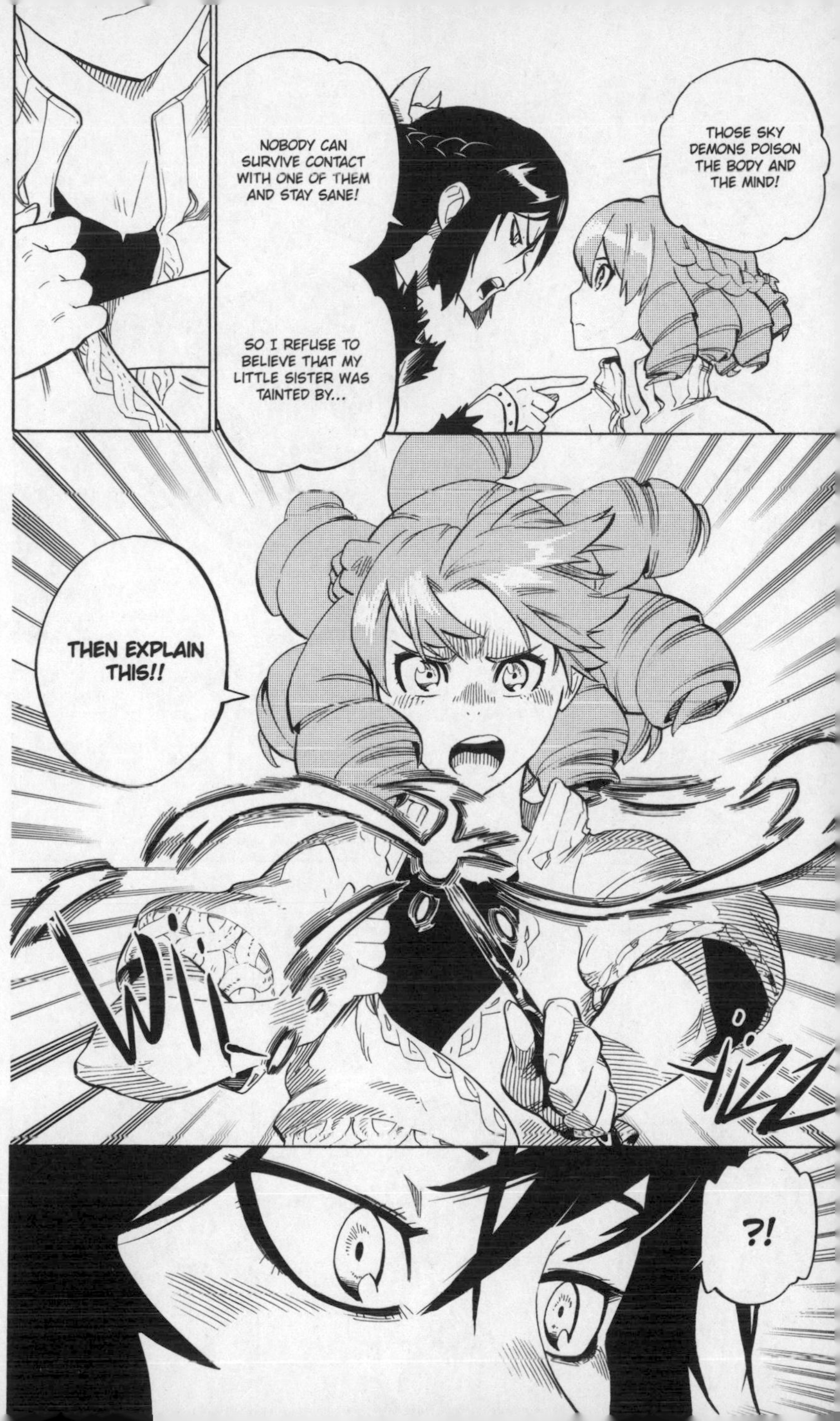
THOSE SKY DEMONS POISON THE BODY AND THE MIND!
NOBODY CAN SURVIVE CONTACT WITH ONE OF THEM AND STAY SANE!
SO I REFUSE TO BELIEVE THAT MY LITTLE SISTER WAS TAINTED BY...
THEN EXPLAIN THIS!!
?!

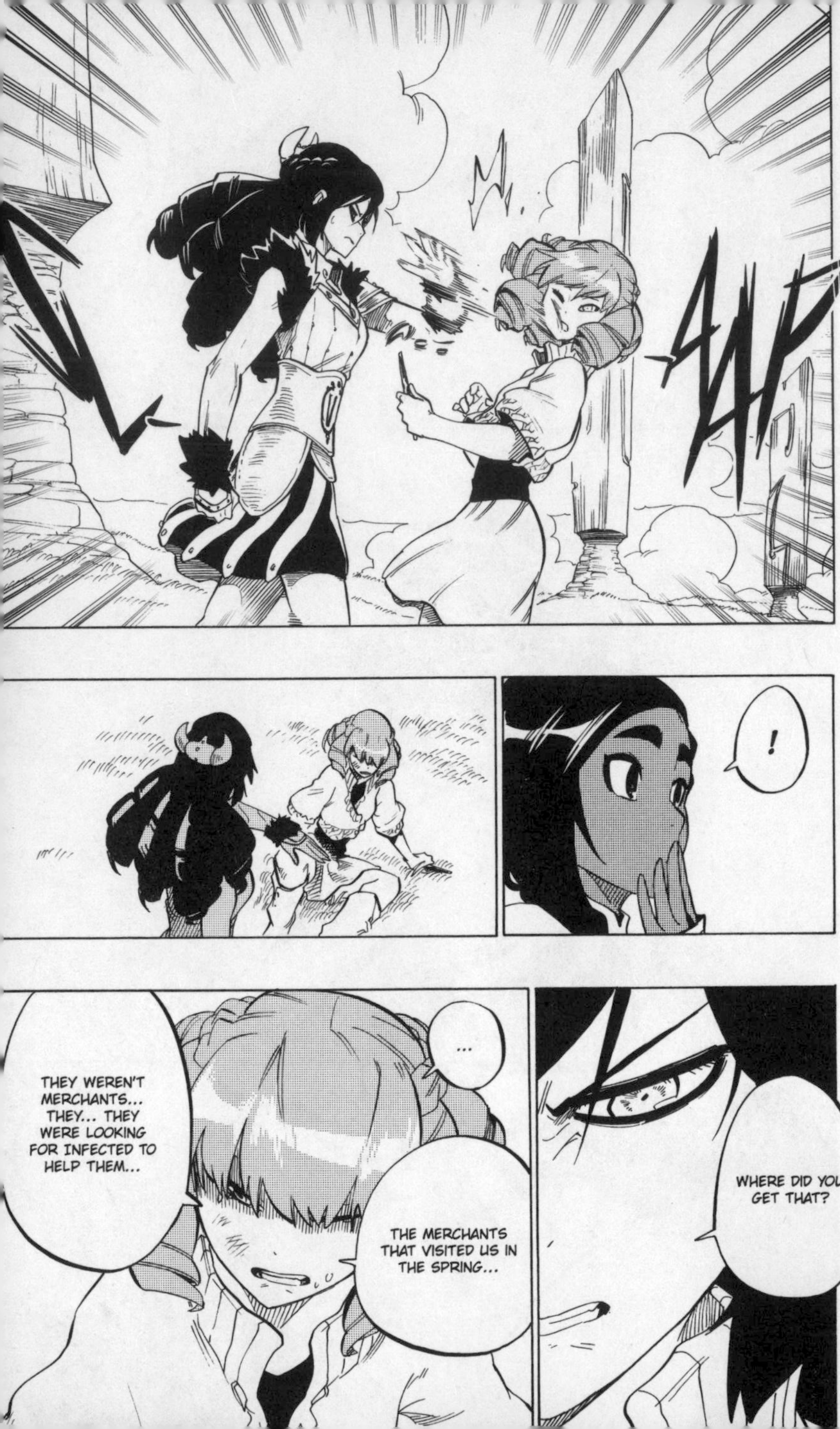
!
WHERE DID YOU GET THAT?
...
THE MERCHANTS THAT VISITED US IN THE SPRING...
THEY WEREN'T MERCHANTS... THEY... THEY WERE LOOKING FOR INFECTED TO HELP THEM...

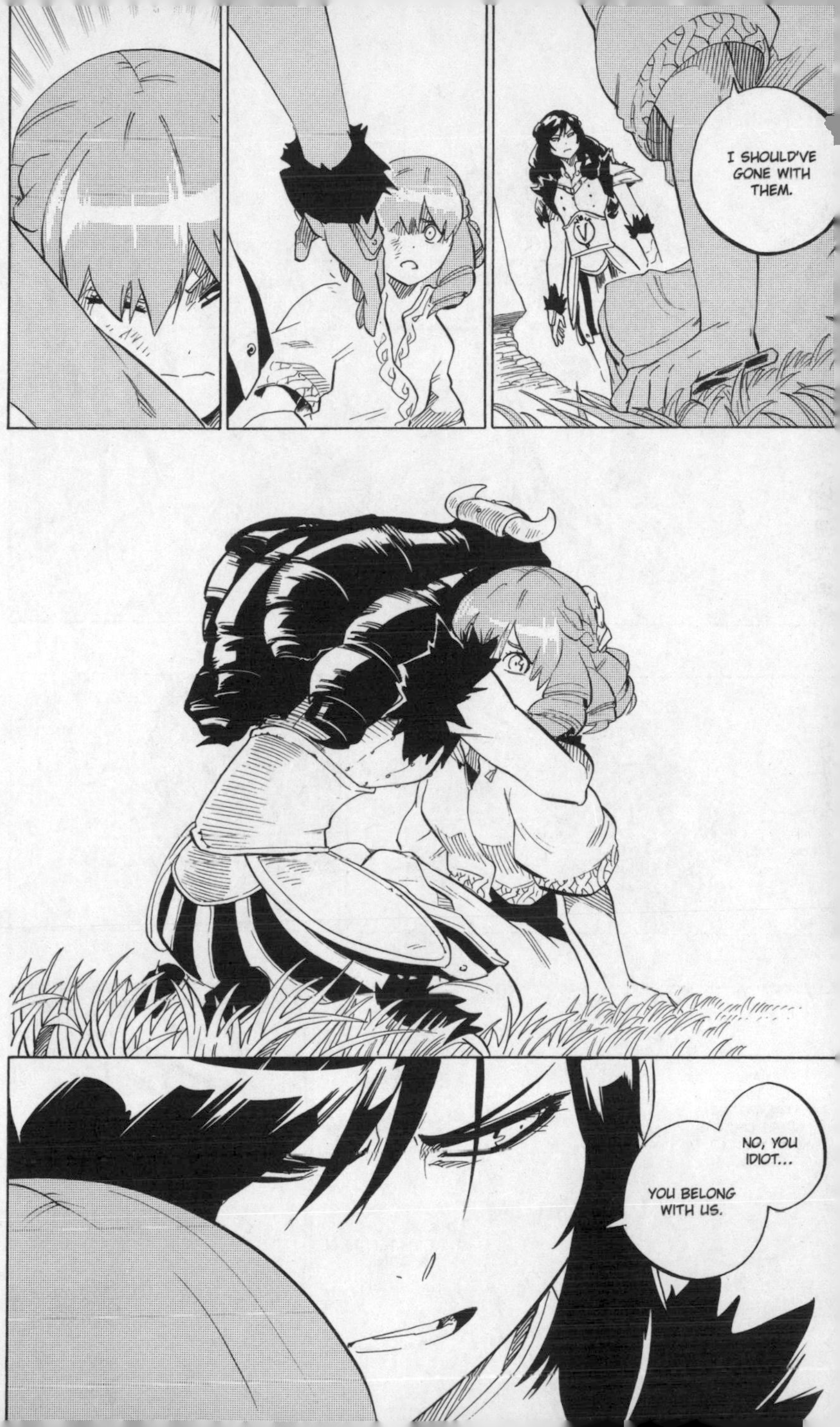
I SHOULD'VE GONE WITH THEM.
NO, YOU IDIOT...
YOU BELONG WITH US.

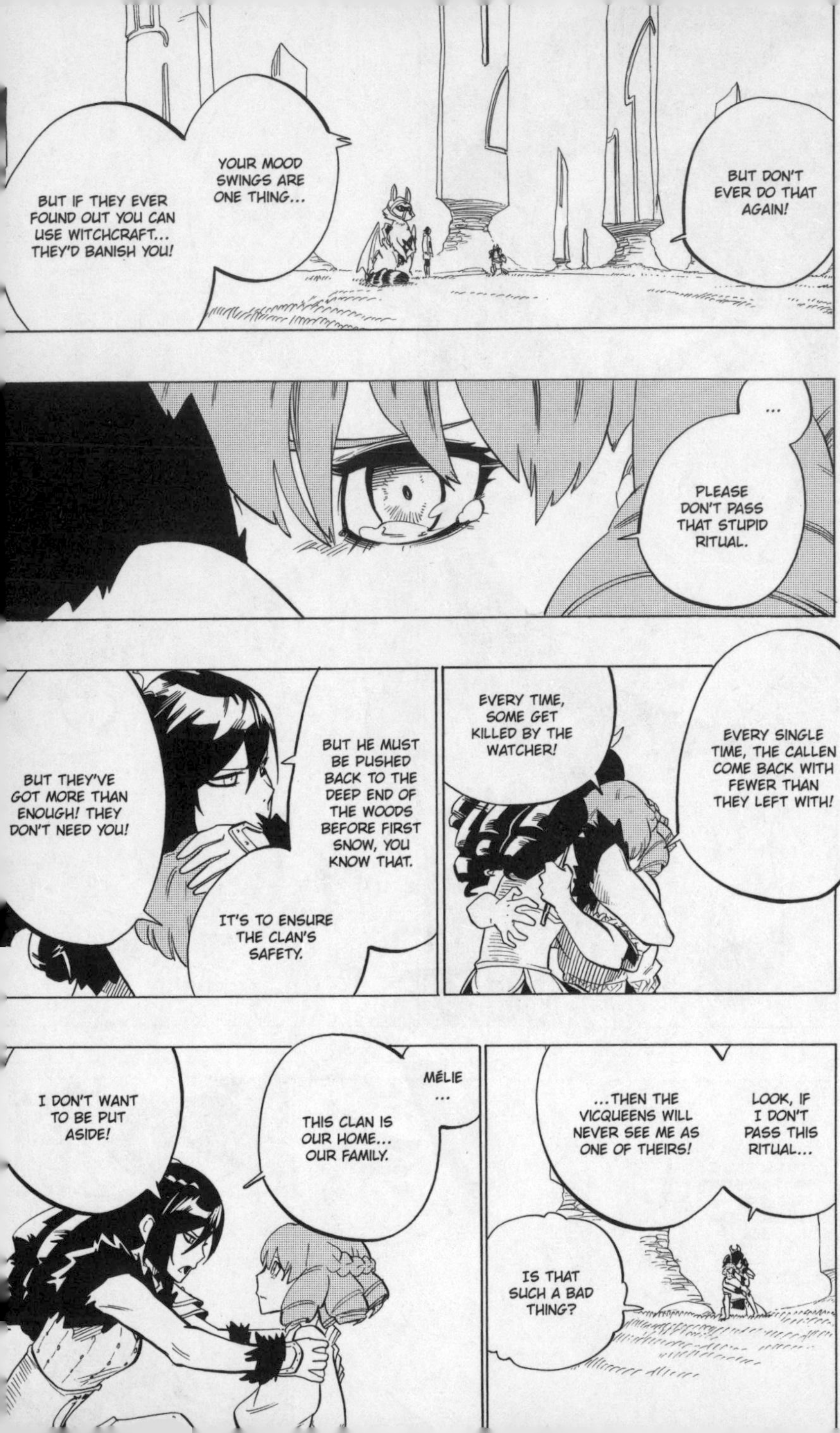
BUT DON'T EVER DO THAT AGAIN!
YOUR MOOD SWINGS ARE ONE THING...
BUT IF THEY EVER FOUND OUT YOU CAN USE WITCHCRAFT... THEY'D BANISH YOU!
...
PLEASE DON'T PASS THAT STUPID RITUAL.
EVERY SINGLE TIME, THE CALLEN COME BACK WITH FEWER THAN THEY LEFT WITH!
EVERY TIME, SOME GET KILLED BY THE WATCHER!
BUT HE MUST BE PUSHED BACK TO THE DEEP END OF THE WOODS BEFORE FIRST SNOW, YOU KNOW THAT.
IT'S TO ENSURE THE CLAN'S SAFETY.
BUT THEY'VE GOT MORE THAN ENOUGH! THEY DON'T NEED YOU!
LOOK, IF I DON'T PASS THIS RITUAL...
...THEN THE VICQUEENS WILL NEVER SEE ME AS ONE OF THEIRS!
IS THAT SUCH A BAD THING?
MÉLIE ...
THIS CLAN IS OUR HOME... OUR FAMILY.
I DON'T WANT TO BE PUT ASIDE!

WELL, I DON'T WANT TO BE PUT ASIDE EITHER!
...
IT'S GETTING LATE.
THE RITUAL'S GOING TO START SOON, SO WE SHOULD HEAD BACK.

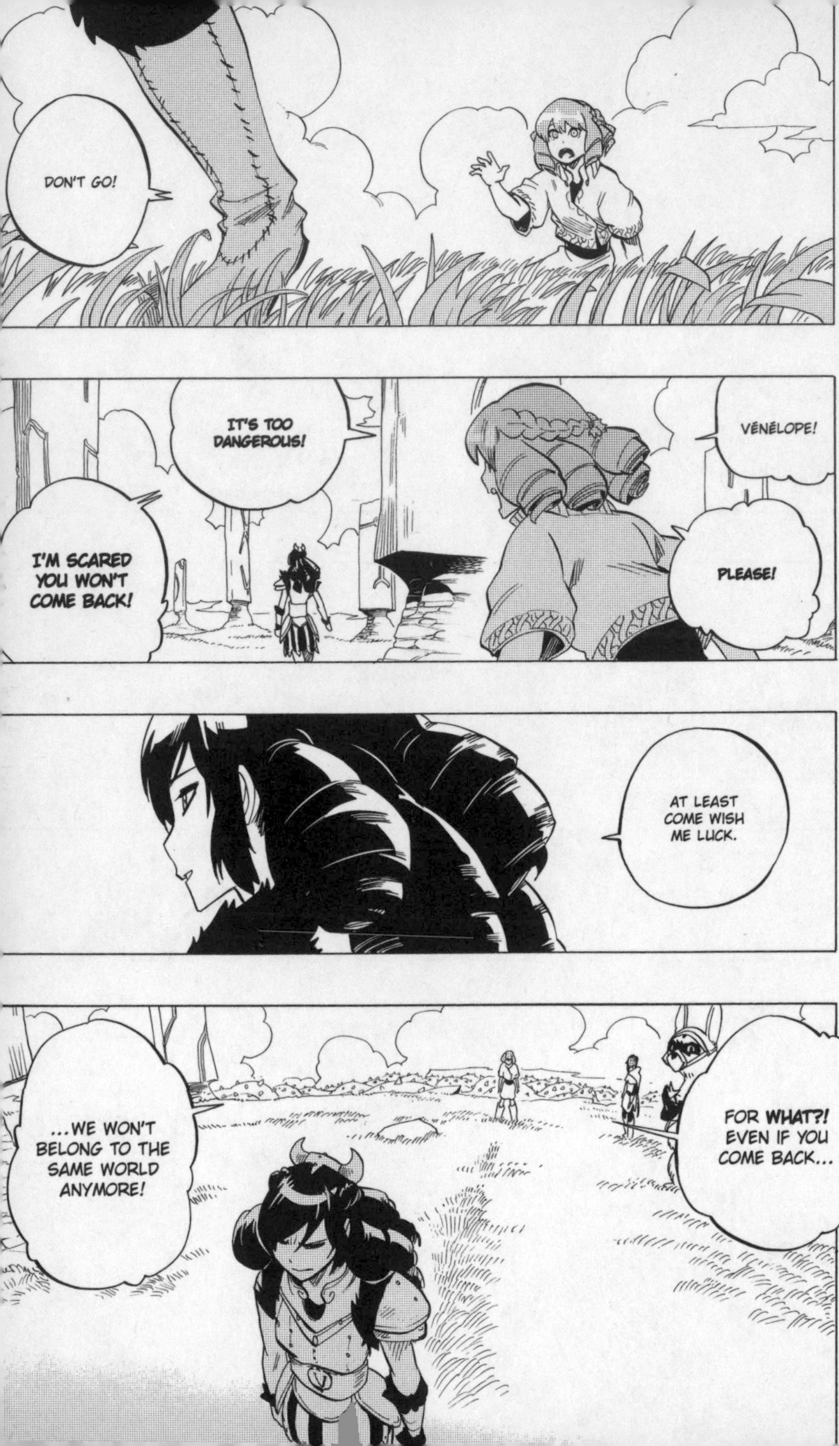
DON'T GO!
VÉNELOPE!
PLEASE!
IT'S TOO DANGEROUS!
I'M SCARED YOU WON'T COME BACK!
AT LEAST COME WISH ME LUCK.
FOR WHAT?! EVEN IF YOU COME BACK...
...WE WON'T BELONG TO THE SAME WORLD ANYMORE!

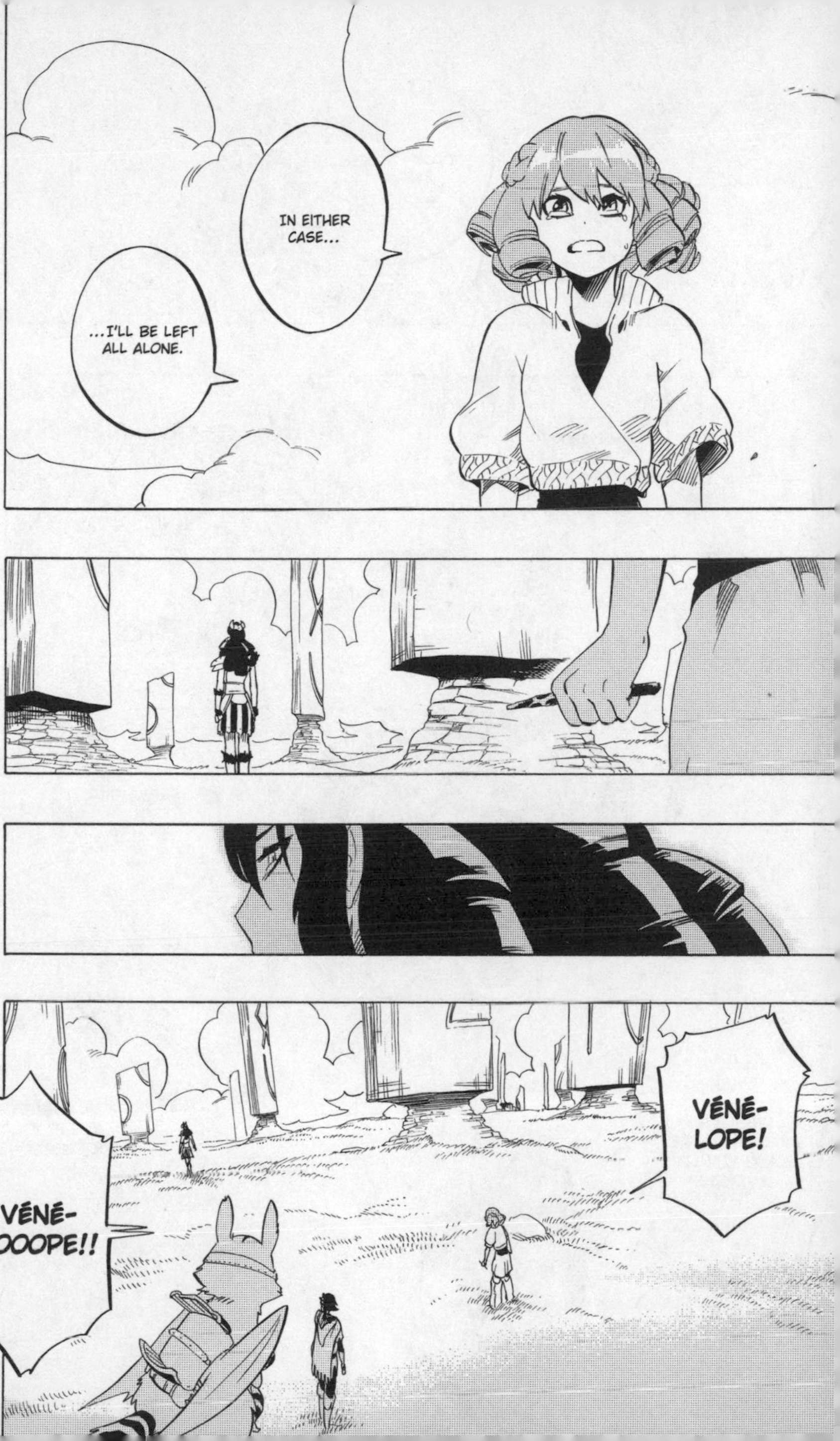
IN EITHER CASE...
...I'LL BE LEFT ALL ALONE.
VÉNÉ-LOPE!
VÉNÉ-LOOOPE!!

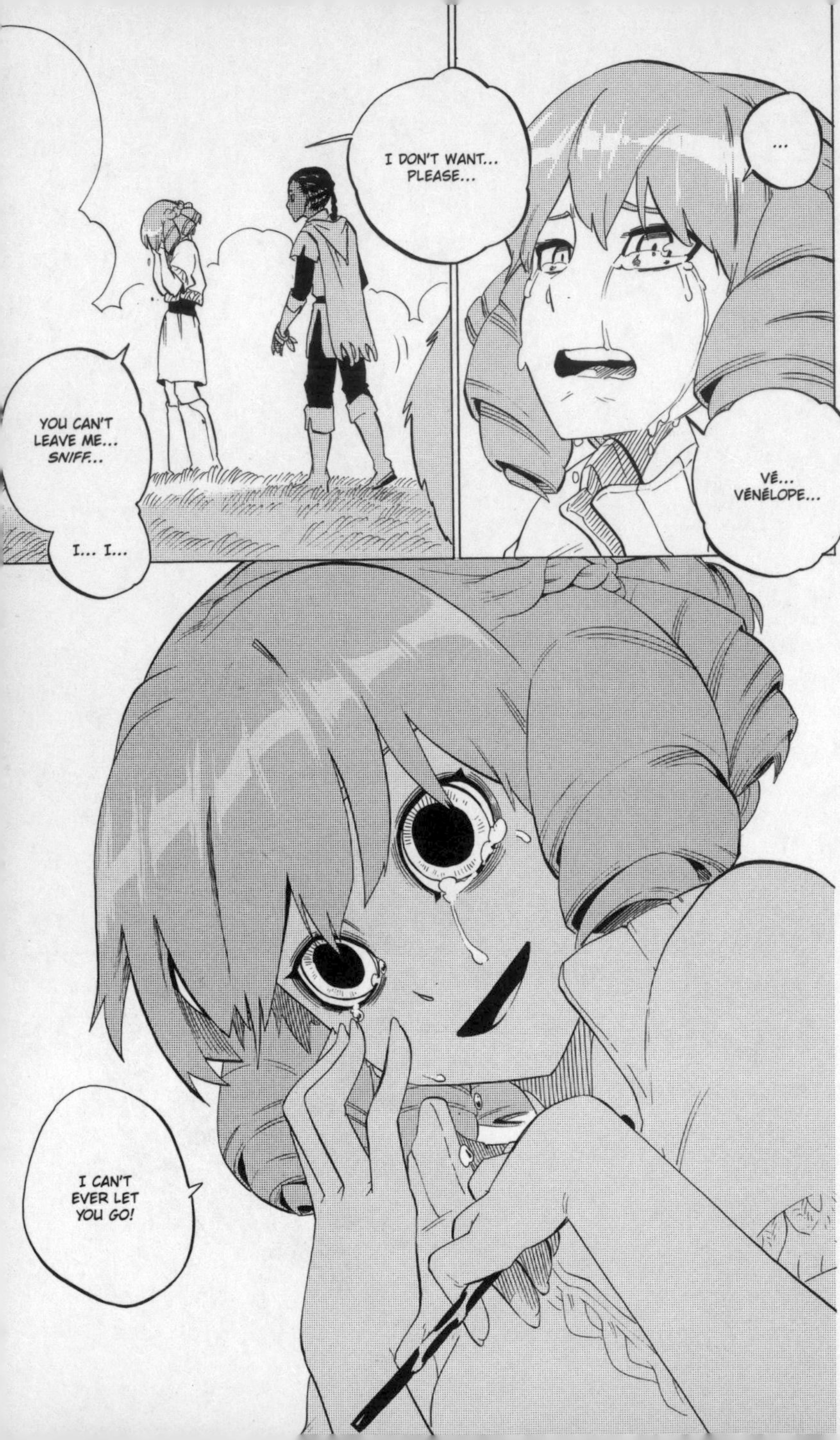
...
I DON'T WANT... PLEASE...
VÉ... VÉNÉLOPE...
YOU CAN'T LEAVE ME... SNIFF...
I... I...
I CAN'T EVER LET YOU GO!

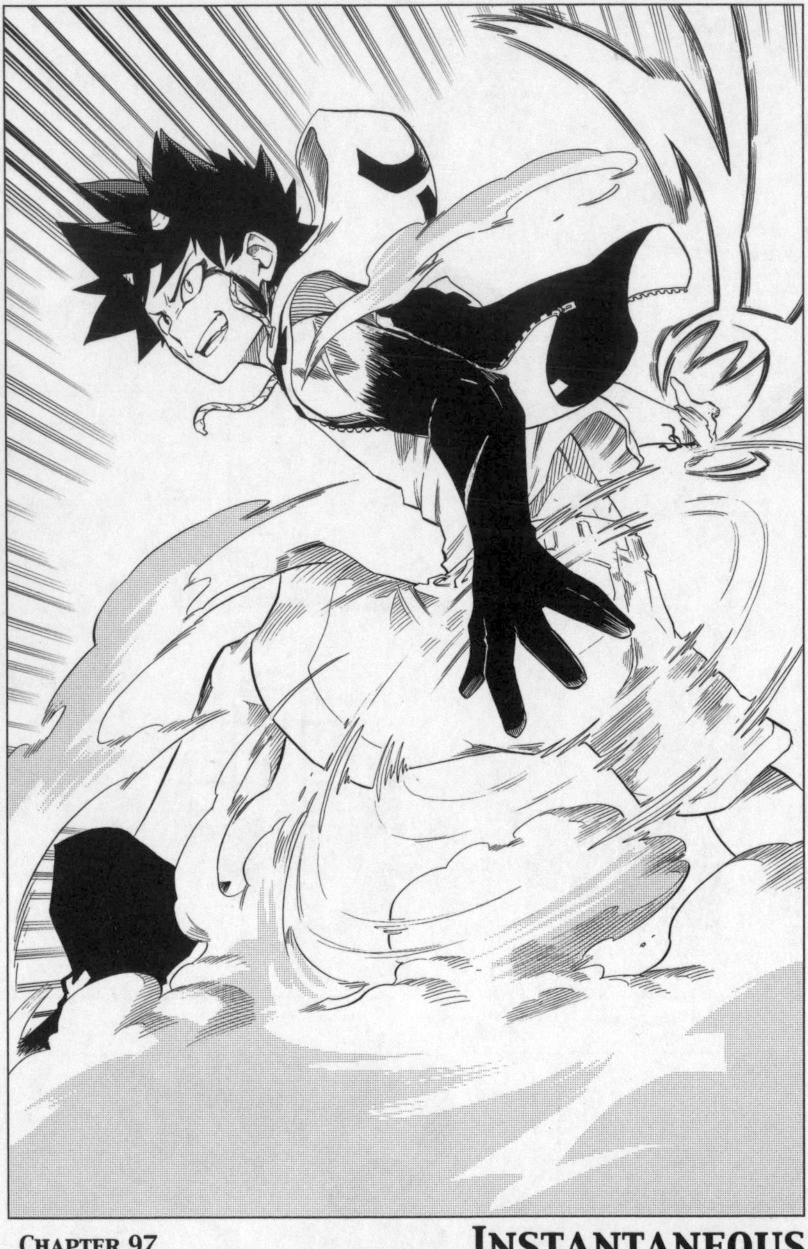

Chapter 97

Instantaneous

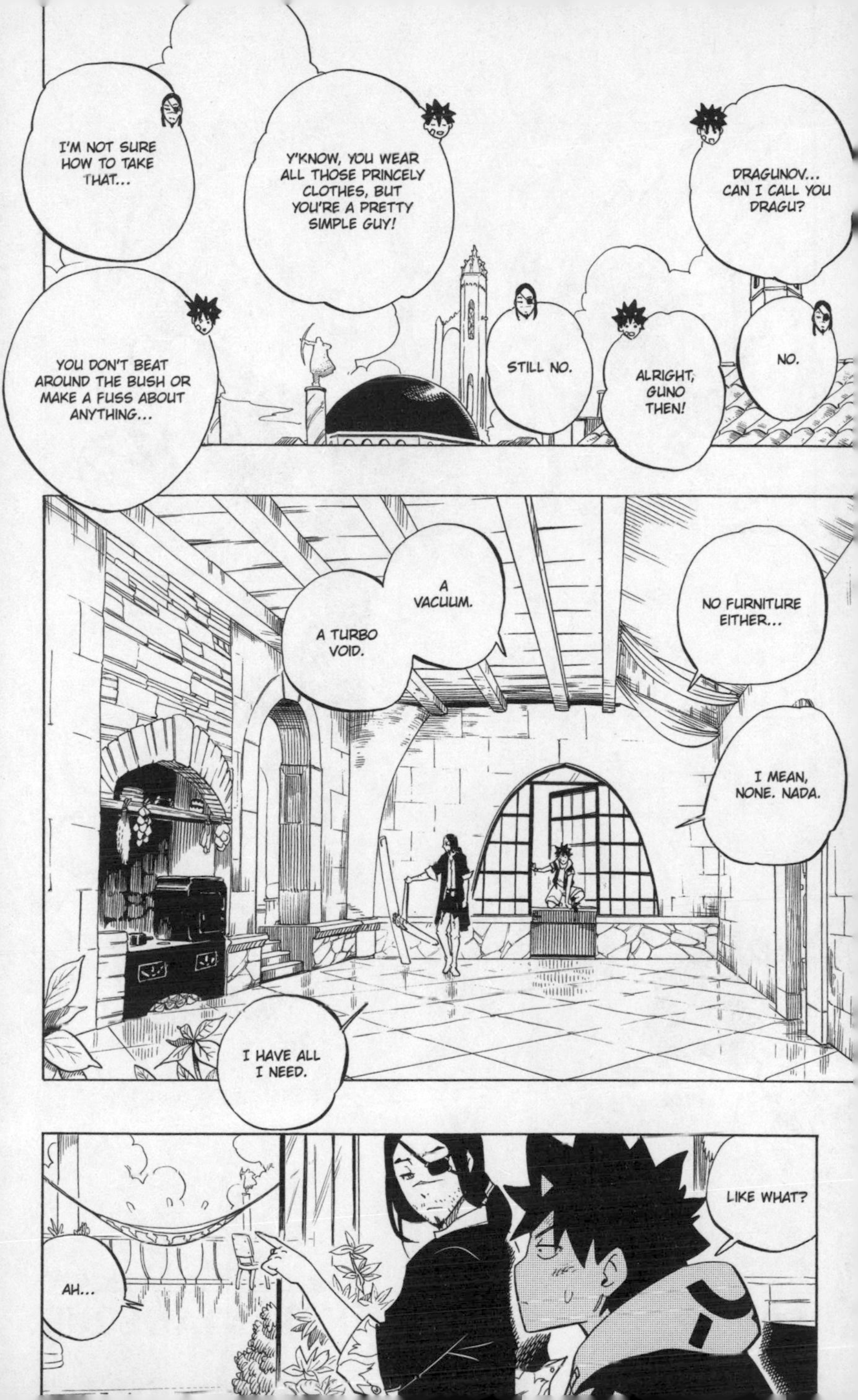
DRAGUNOV... CAN I CALL YOU DRAGU?
NO.
ALRIGHT, GUNO THEN!
STILL NO.
Y'KNOW, YOU WEAR ALL THOSE PRINCELY CLOTHES, BUT YOU'RE A PRETTY SIMPLE GUY!
YOU DON'T BEAT AROUND THE BUSH OR MAKE A FUSS ABOUT ANYTHING...
I'M NOT SURE HOW TO TAKE THAT...
NO FURNITURE EITHER...
I MEAN, NONE. NADA.
A VACUUM.
A TURBO VOID.
I HAVE ALL I NEED.
LIKE WHAT?
AH...

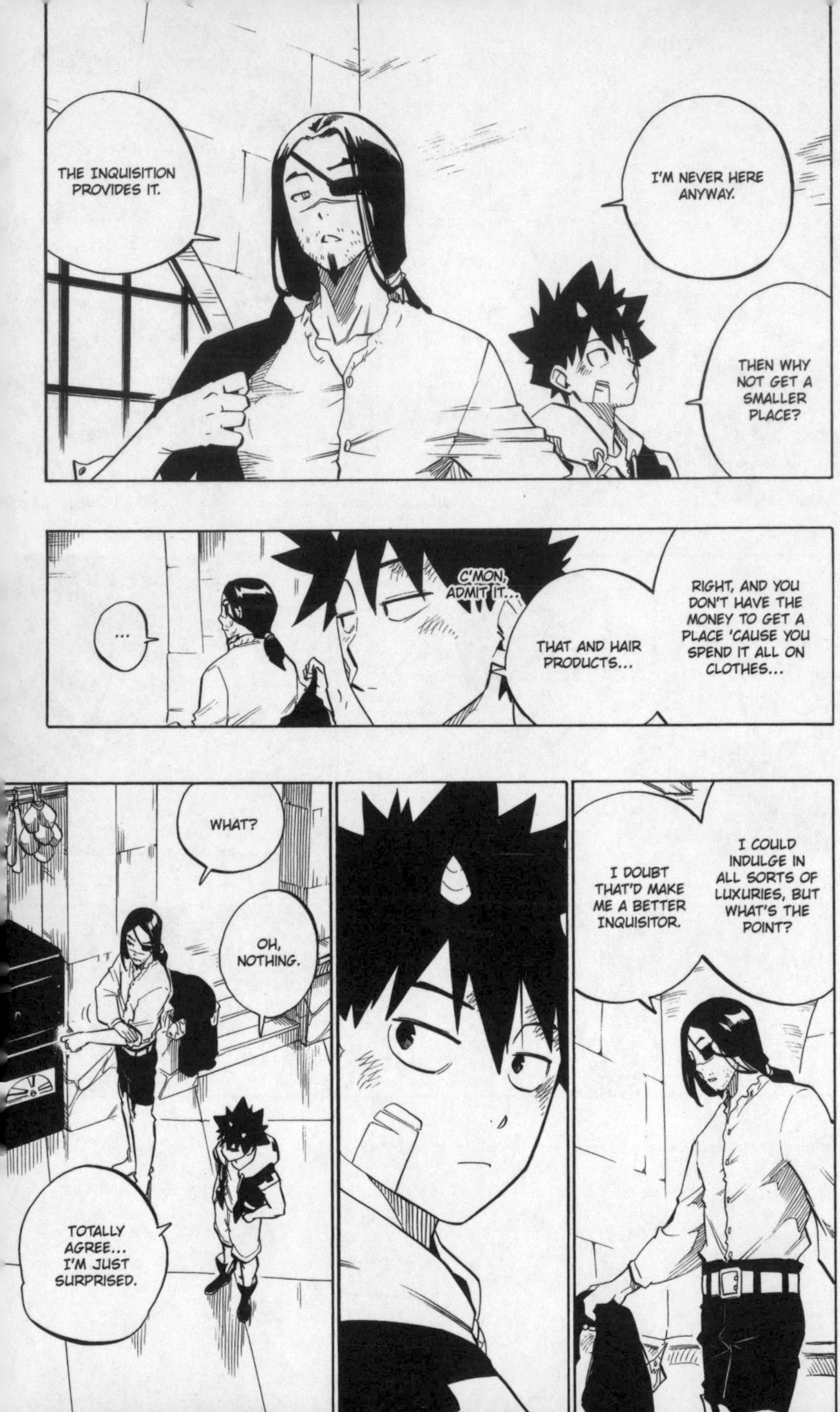
I'M NEVER HERE ANYWAY.
THE INQUISITION PROVIDES IT.
THEN WHY NOT GET A SMALLER PLACE?
RIGHT, AND YOU DON'T HAVE THE MONEY TO GET A PLACE 'CAUSE YOU SPEND IT ALL ON CLOTHES...
THAT AND HAIR PRODUCTS...
C'MON, ADMIT IT...
...
I COULD INDULGE IN ALL SORTS OF LUXURIES, BUT WHAT'S THE POINT?
I DOUBT THAT'D MAKE ME A BETTER INQUISITOR.
WHAT?
OH, NOTHING.
TOTALLY AGREE... I'M JUST SURPRISED.

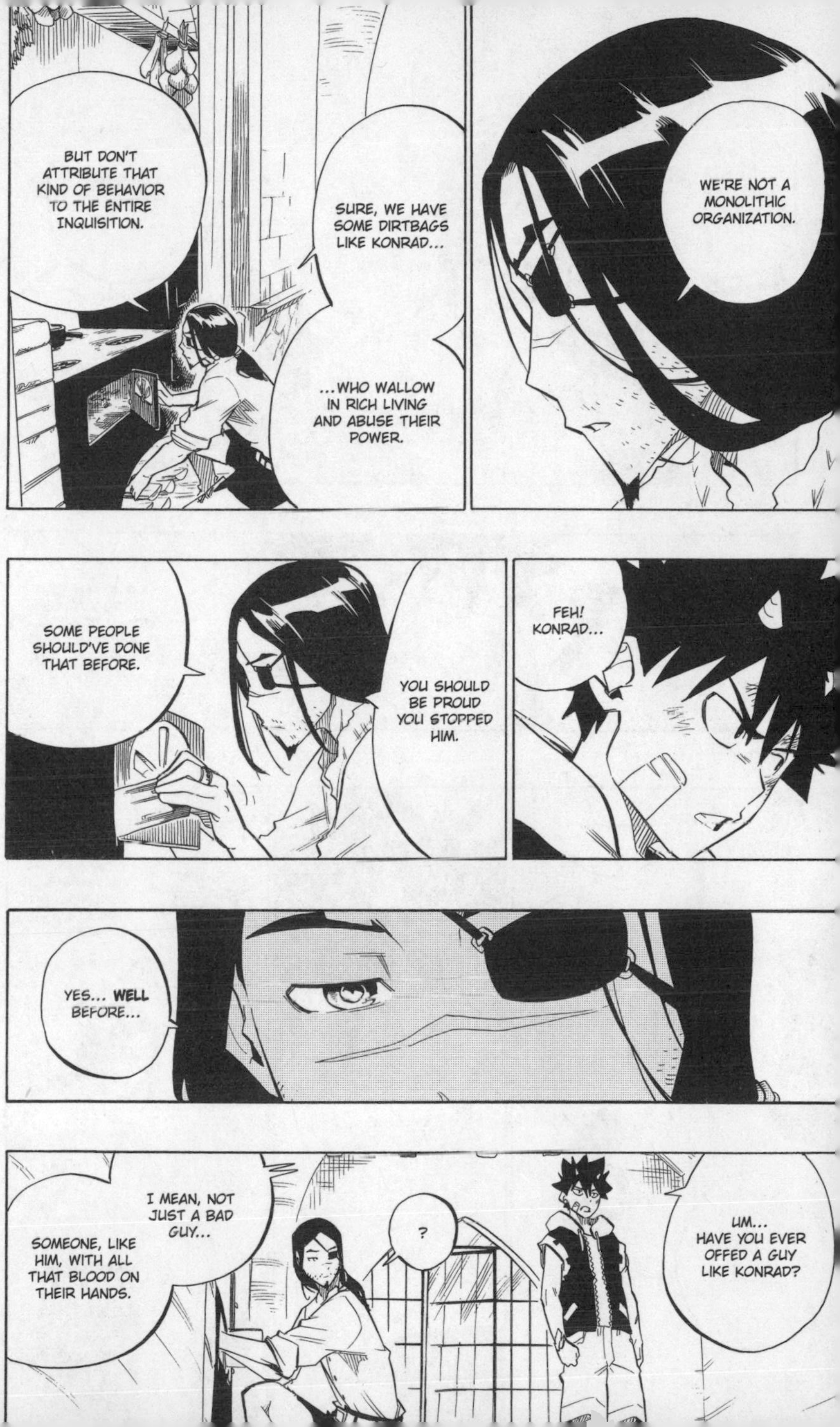
WE'RE NOT A MONOLITHIC ORGANIZATION.
SURE, WE HAVE SOME DIRTBAGS LIKE KONRAD...
...WHO WALLOW IN RICH LIVING AND ABUSE THEIR POWER.
BUT DON'T ATTRIBUTE THAT KIND OF BEHAVIOR TO THE ENTIRE INQUISITION.
FEH! KONRAD...
YOU SHOULD BE PROUD YOU STOPPED HIM.
SOME PEOPLE SHOULD'VE DONE THAT BEFORE.
YES... **WELL** BEFORE...
UM... HAVE YOU EVER OFFED A GUY LIKE KONRAD?
?
I MEAN, NOT JUST A BAD GUY...
SOMEONE, LIKE HIM, WITH ALL THAT BLOOD ON THEIR HANDS.

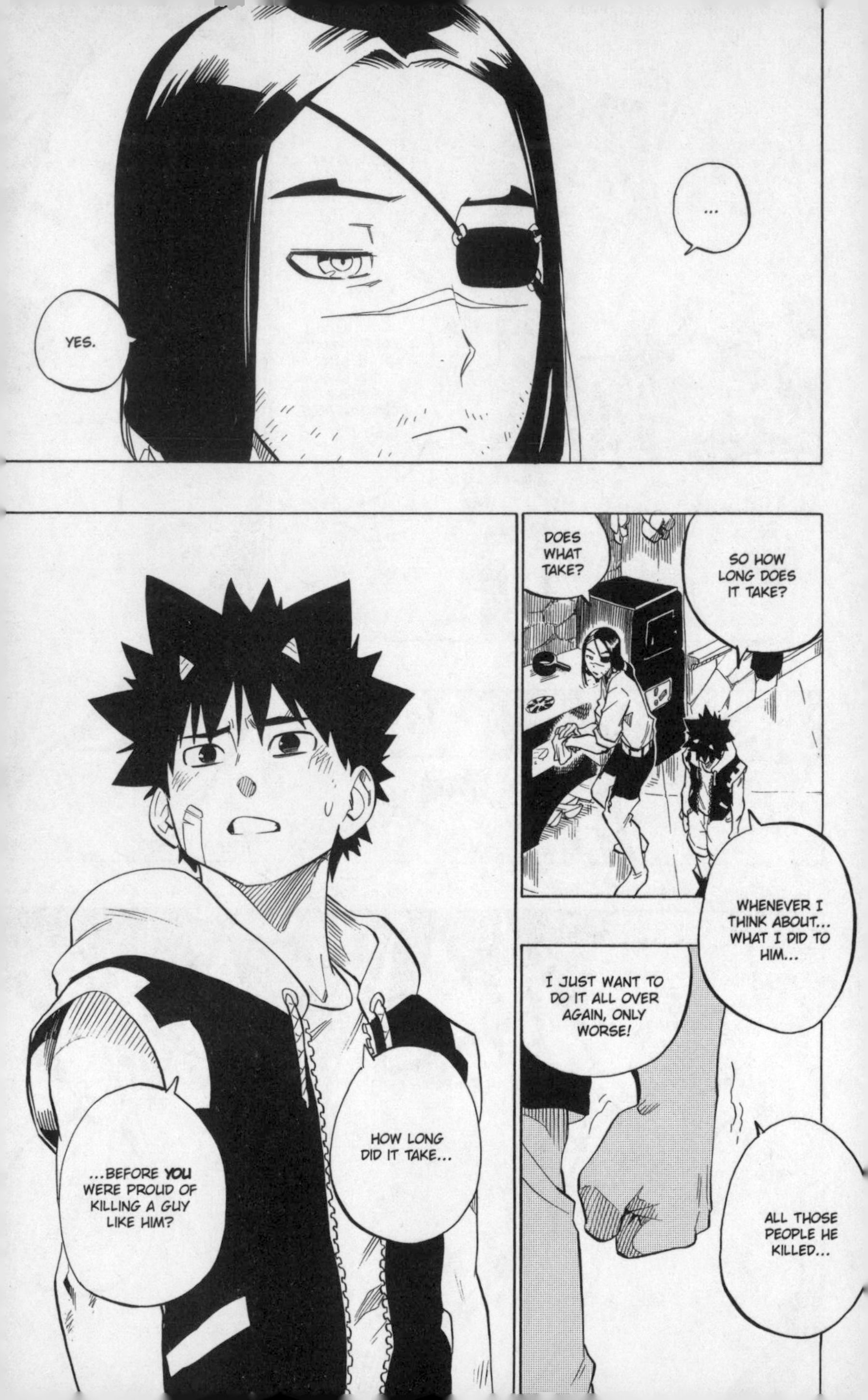
...
YES.
SO HOW LONG DOES IT TAKE?
DOES WHAT TAKE?
WHENEVER I THINK ABOUT... WHAT I DID TO HIM...
ALL THOSE PEOPLE HE KILLED...
I JUST WANT TO DO IT ALL OVER AGAIN, ONLY WORSE!
HOW LONG DID IT TAKE...
...BEFORE **YOU** WERE PROUD OF KILLING A GUY LIKE HIM?

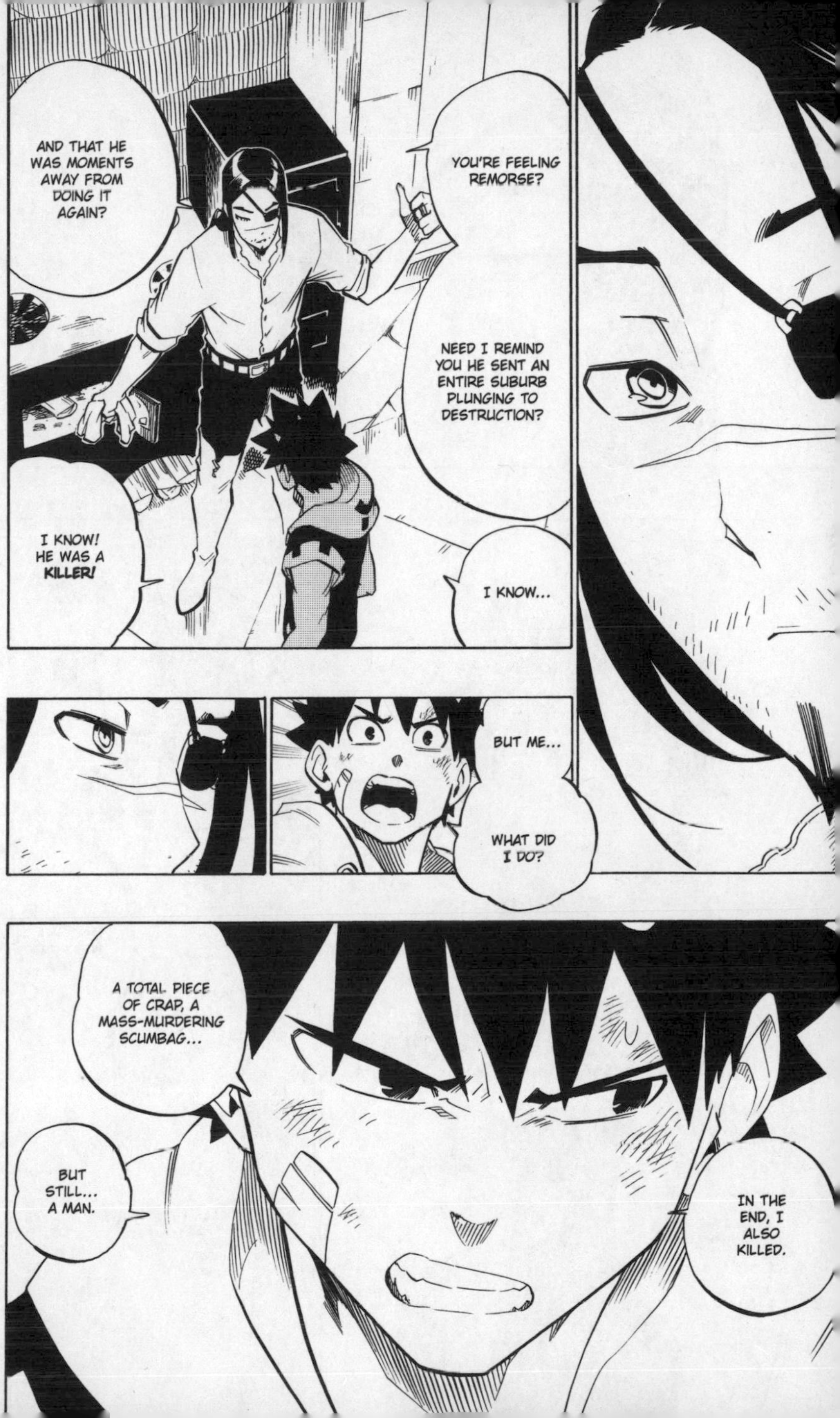
YOU'RE FEELING REMORSE?
NEED I REMIND YOU HE SENT AN ENTIRE SUBURB PLUNGING TO DESTRUCTION?
AND THAT HE WAS MOMENTS AWAY FROM DOING IT AGAIN?
I KNOW...
I KNOW! HE WAS A **KILLER!**
BUT ME...
WHAT DID I DO?
IN THE END, I ALSO KILLED.
A TOTAL PIECE OF CRAP, A MASS-MURDERING SCUMBAG...
BUT STILL... A MAN.

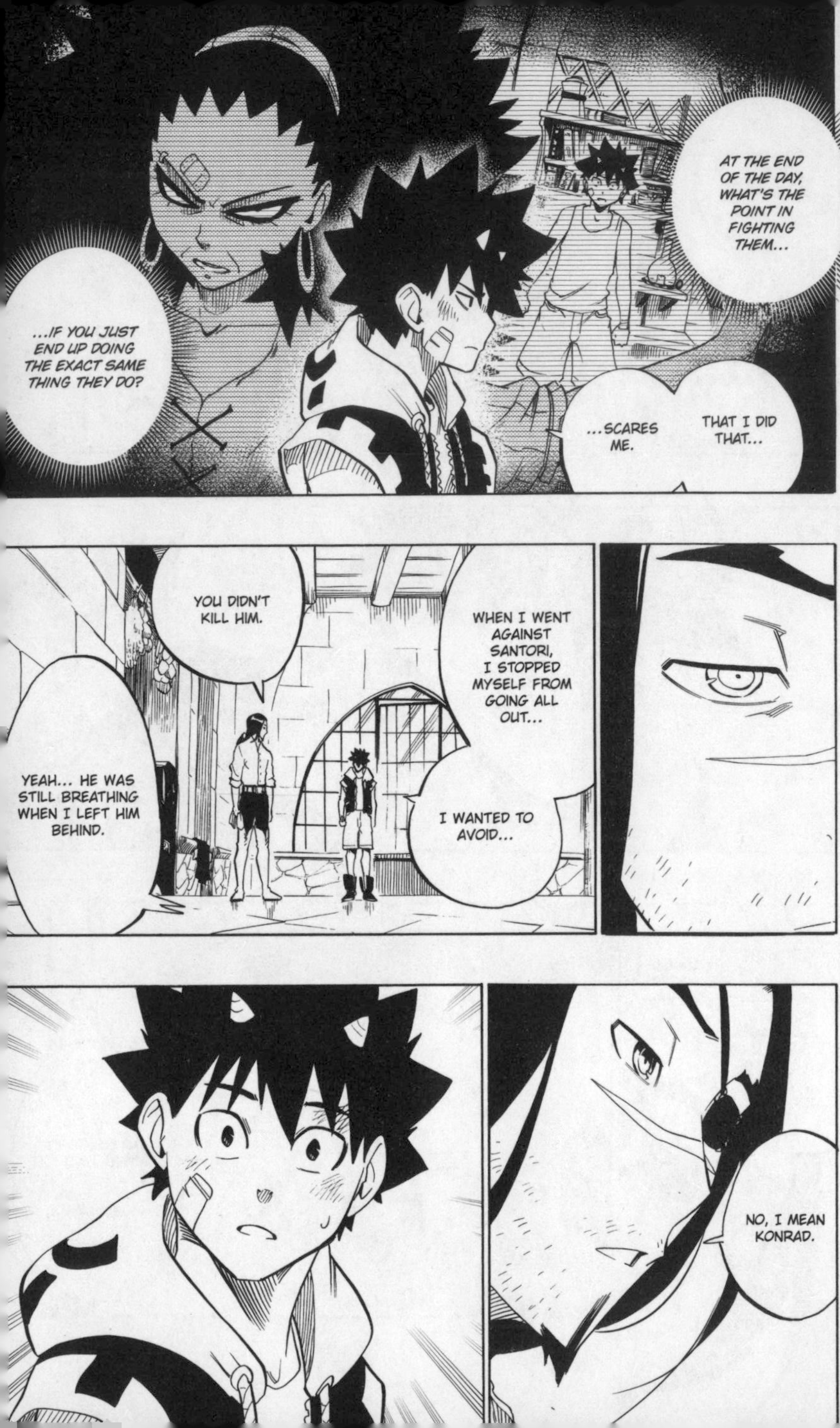
AT THE END OF THE DAY, WHAT'S THE POINT IN FIGHTING THEM...
...IF YOU JUST END UP DOING THE EXACT SAME THING THEY DO?
THAT I DID THAT...
...SCARES ME.
WHEN I WENT AGAINST SANTORI, I STOPPED MYSELF FROM GOING ALL OUT...
I WANTED TO AVOID...
YOU DIDN'T KILL HIM.
YEAH... HE WAS STILL BREATHING WHEN I LEFT HIM BEHIND.
NO, I MEAN KONRAD.

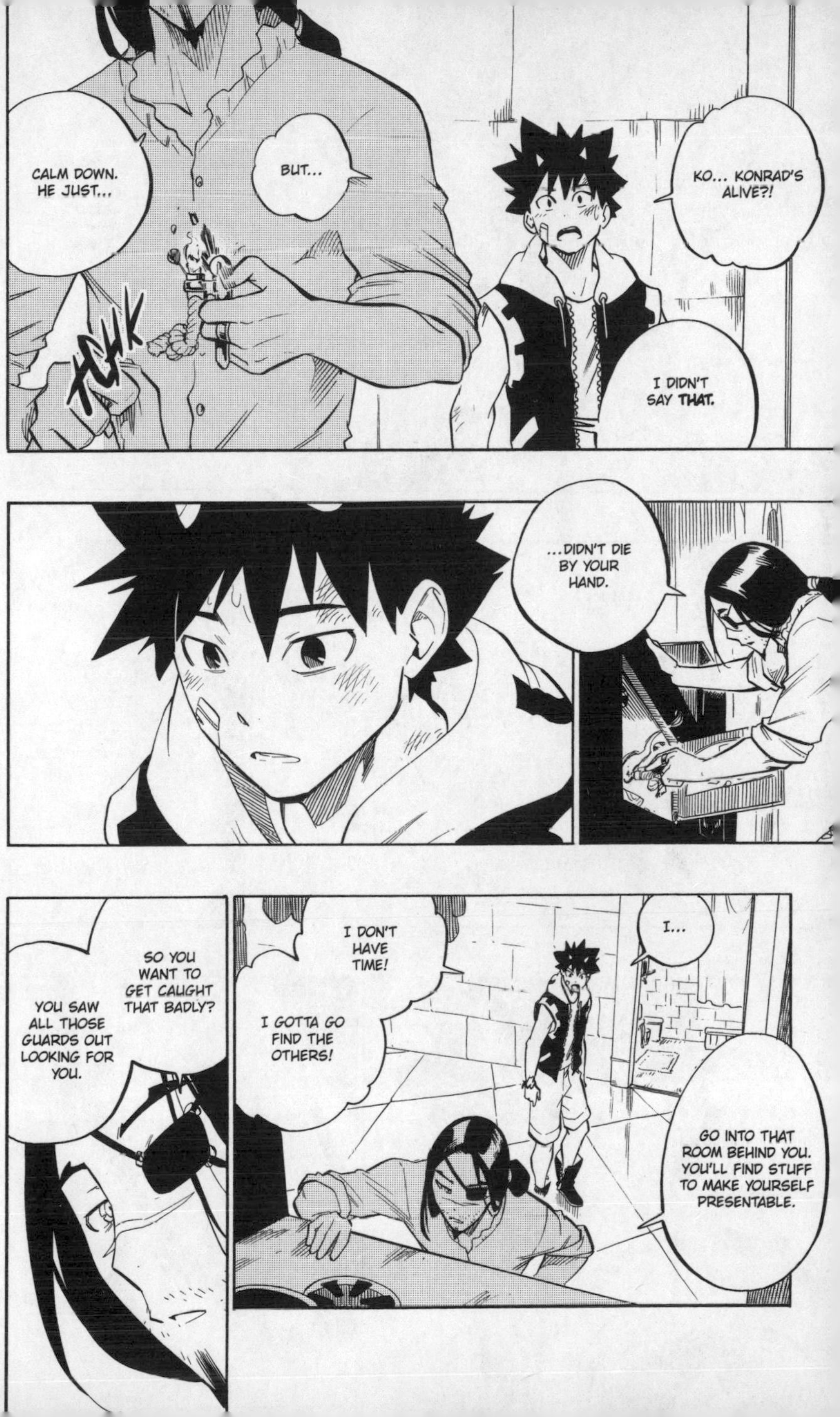
KO... KONRAD'S ALIVE?!
I DIDN'T SAY THAT.
BUT...
CALM DOWN. HE JUST...
...DIDN'T DIE BY YOUR HAND.
I...
GO INTO THAT ROOM BEHIND YOU. YOU'LL FIND STUFF TO MAKE YOURSELF PRESENTABLE.
I DON'T HAVE TIME!
I GOTTA GO FIND THE OTHERS!
SO YOU WANT TO GET CAUGHT THAT BADLY?
YOU SAW ALL THOSE GUARDS OUT LOOKING FOR YOU.

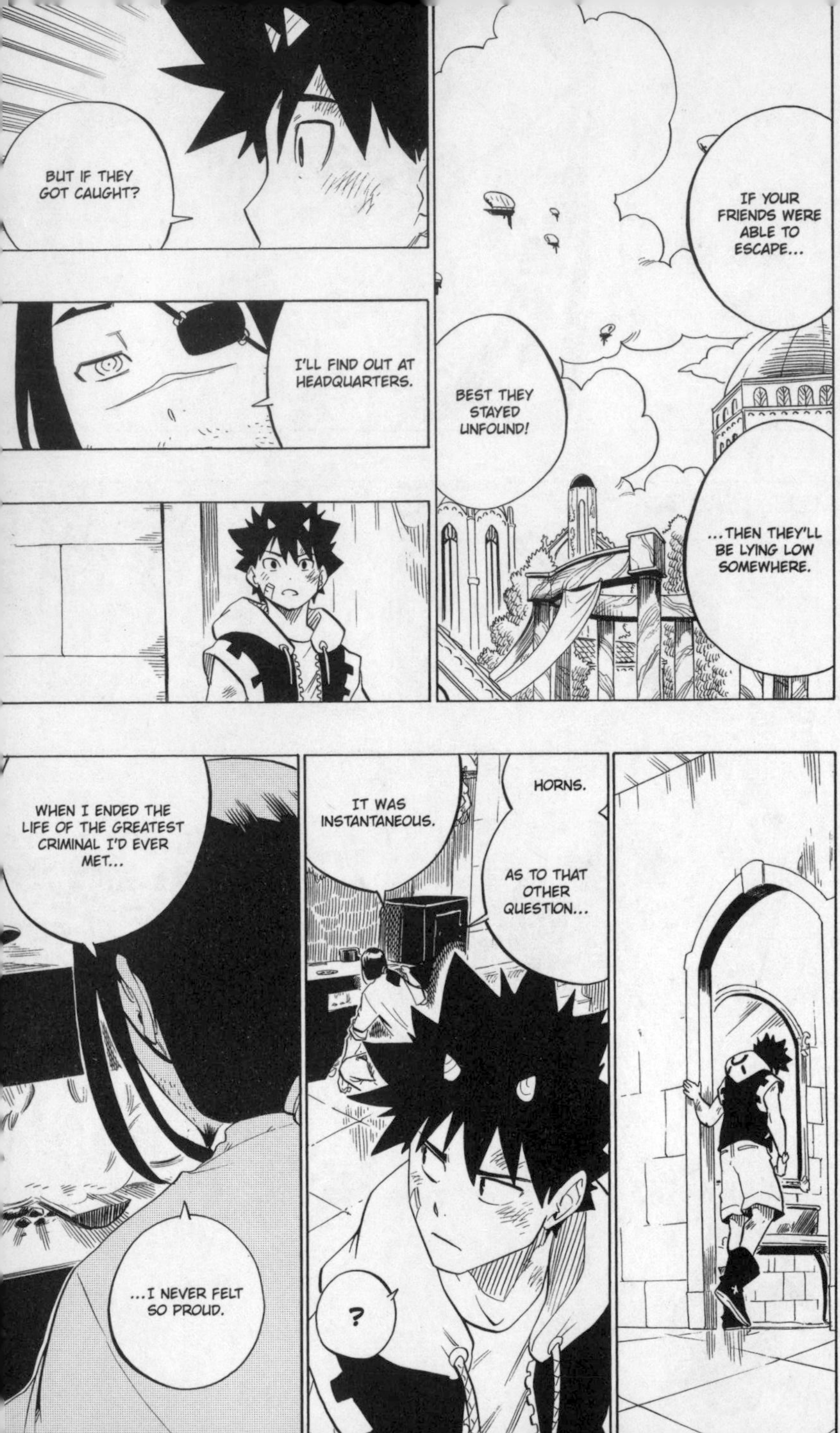
IF YOUR FRIENDS WERE ABLE TO ESCAPE...
...THEN THEY'LL BE LYING LOW SOMEWHERE.
BEST THEY STAYED UNFOUND!
BUT IF THEY GOT CAUGHT?
I'LL FIND OUT AT HEADQUARTERS.
HORNS.
AS TO THAT OTHER QUESTION...
IT WAS INSTANTANEOUS.
?
WHEN I ENDED THE LIFE OF THE GREATEST CRIMINAL I'D EVER MET...
...I NEVER FELT SO PROUD.

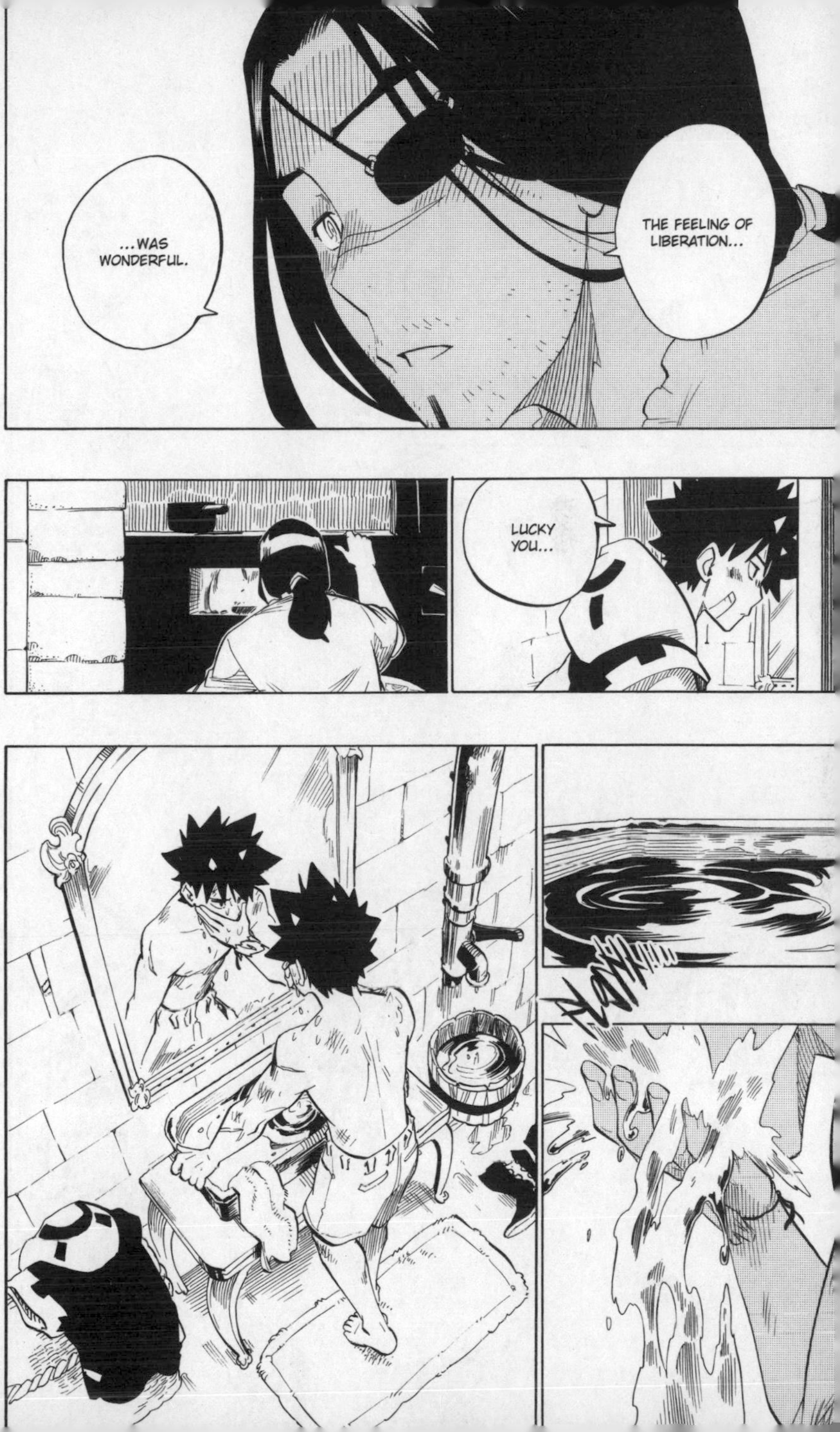
THE FEELING OF LIBERATION...
...WAS WONDERFUL.
LUCKY YOU...

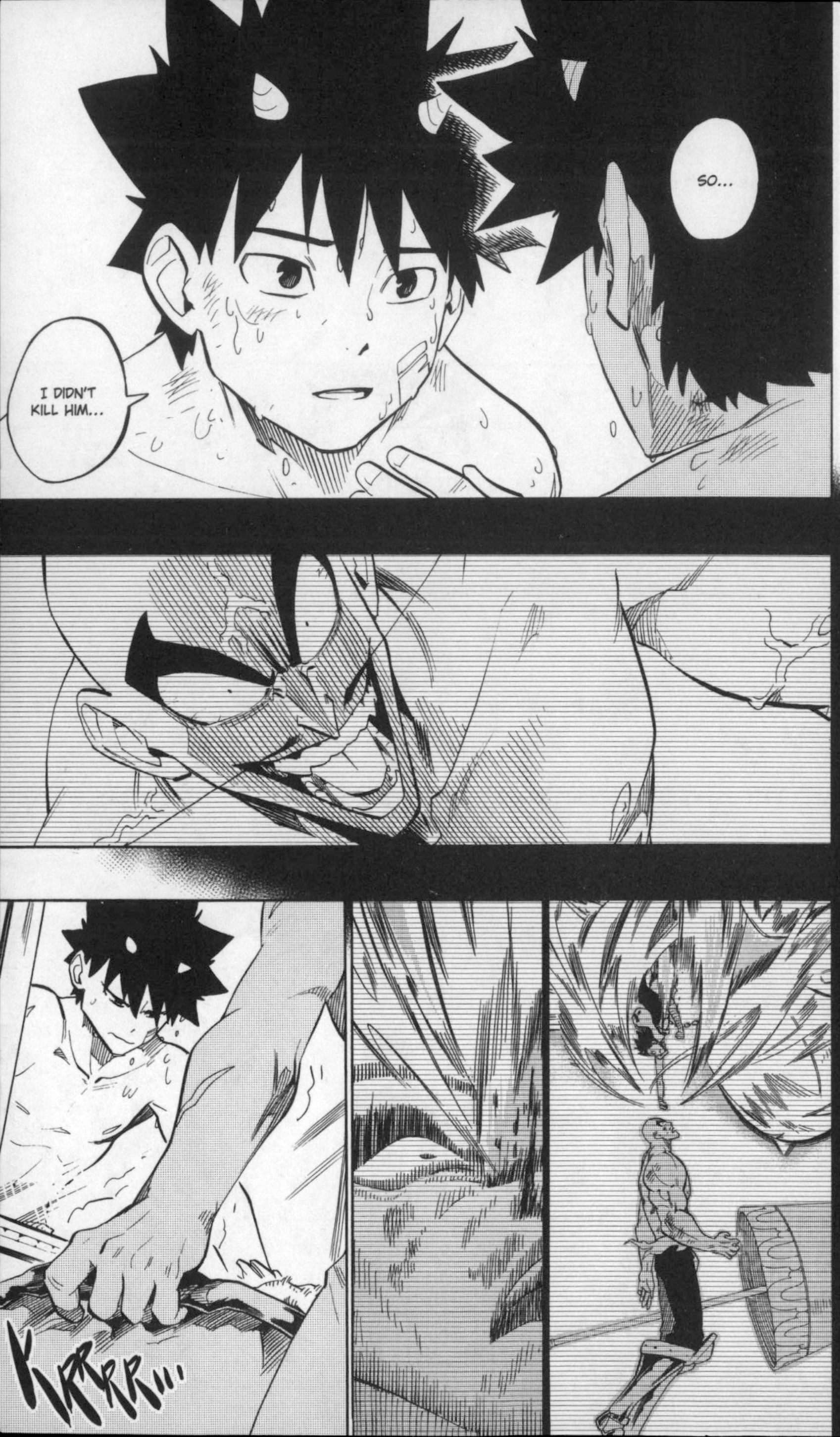
SO...
I DIDN'T KILL HIM...
KRRRR!!

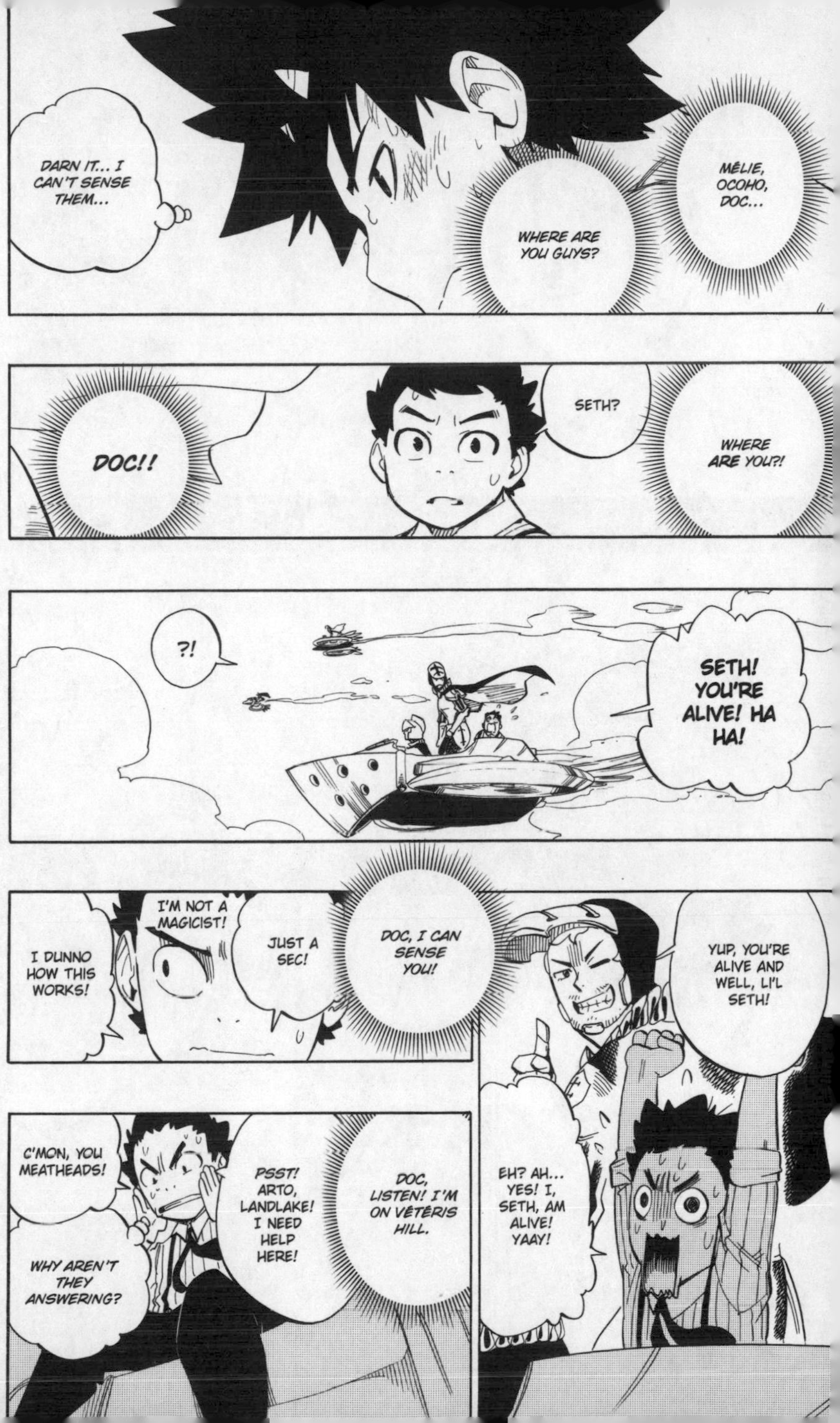
MÊLIE, OCOHO, DOC...
WHERE ARE YOU GUYS?
DARN IT... I CAN'T SENSE THEM...
WHERE ARE YOU?!
SETH?
DOC!!
SETH! YOU'RE ALIVE! HA HA!
?!
YUP, YOU'RE ALIVE AND WELL, LI'L SETH!
EH? AH... YES! I, SETH, AM ALIVE! YAAY!
DOC, I CAN SENSE YOU!
JUST A SEC!
I'M NOT A MAGICIST!
I DUNNO HOW THIS WORKS!
DOC, LISTEN! I'M ON VÊTERIS HILL.
PSST! ARTO, LANDLAKE! I NEED HELP HERE!
C'MON, YOU MEATHEADS!
WHY AREN'T THEY ANSWERING?

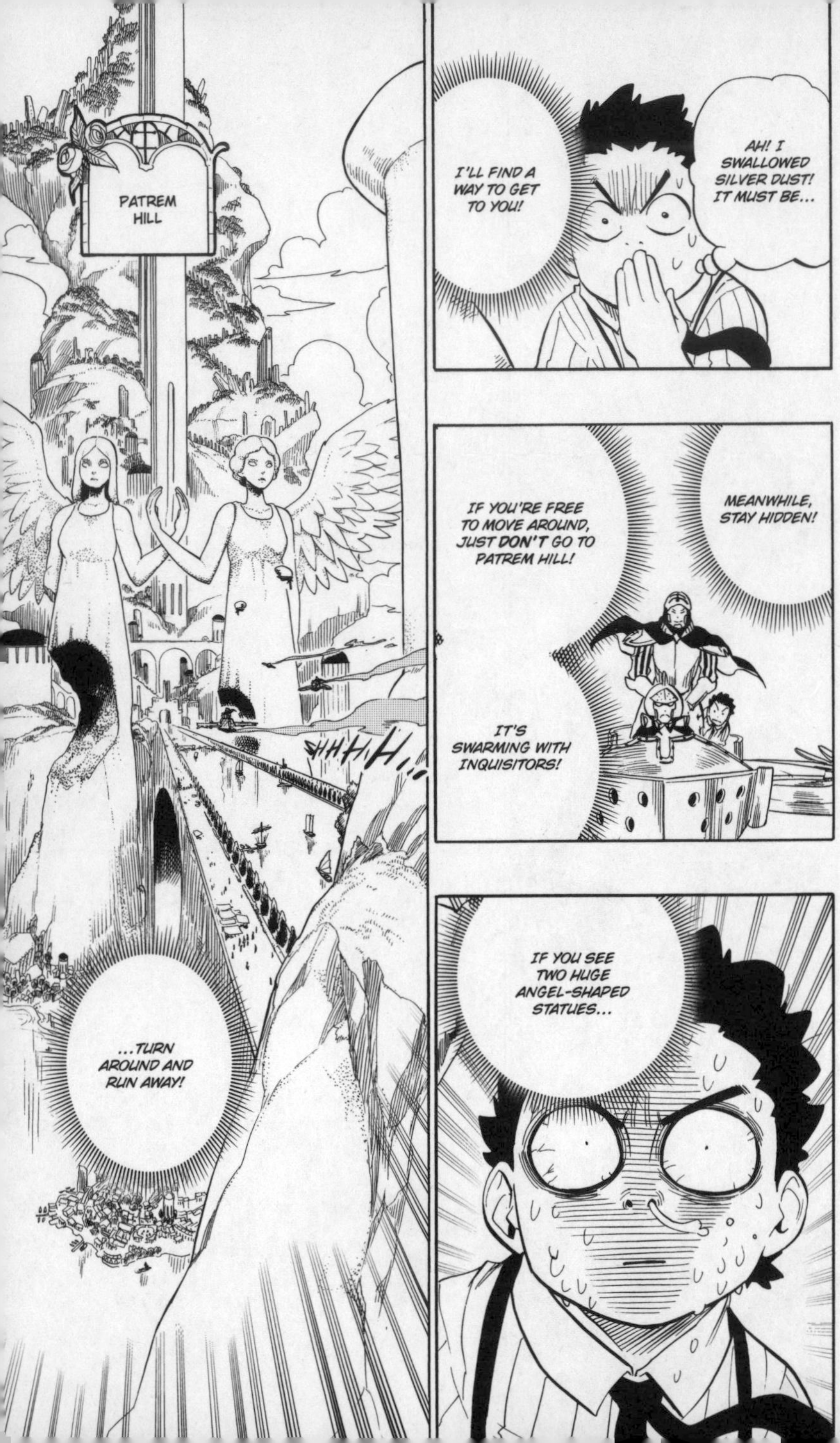
AH! I SWALLOWED SILVER DUST! IT MUST BE...
I'LL FIND A WAY TO GET TO YOU!
MEANWHILE, STAY HIDDEN!
IF YOU'RE FREE TO MOVE AROUND, JUST DON'T GO TO PATREM HILL!
IT'S SWARMING WITH INQUISITORS!
IF YOU SEE TWO HUGE ANGEL-SHAPED STATUES...
PATREM HILL
SHHHH...
...TURN AROUND AND RUN AWAY!

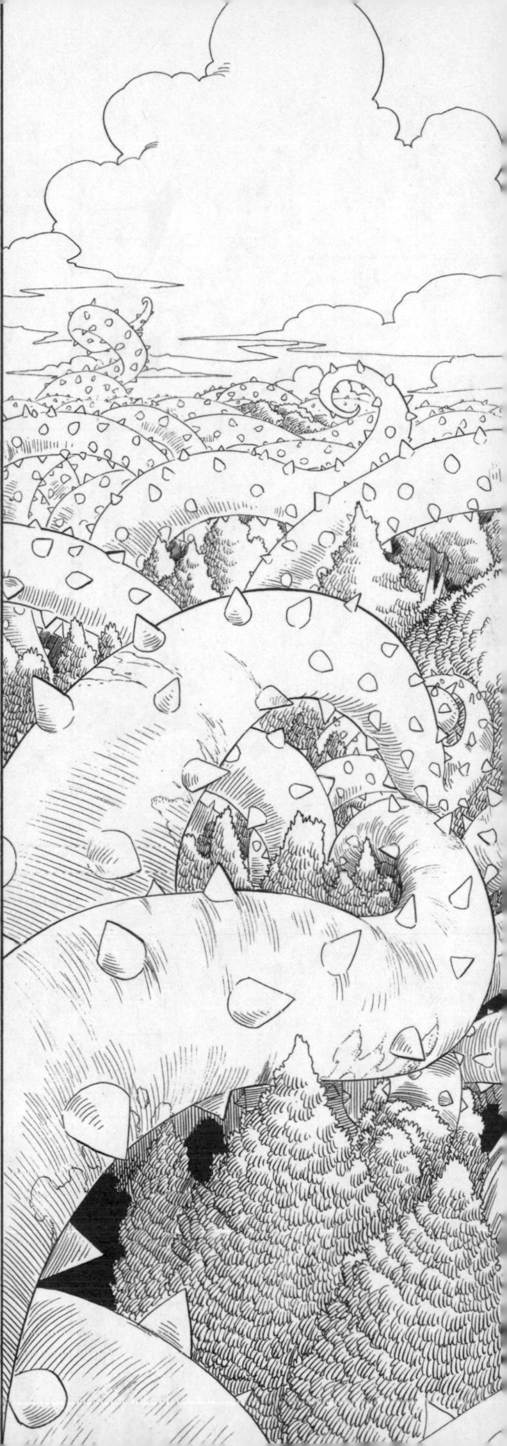

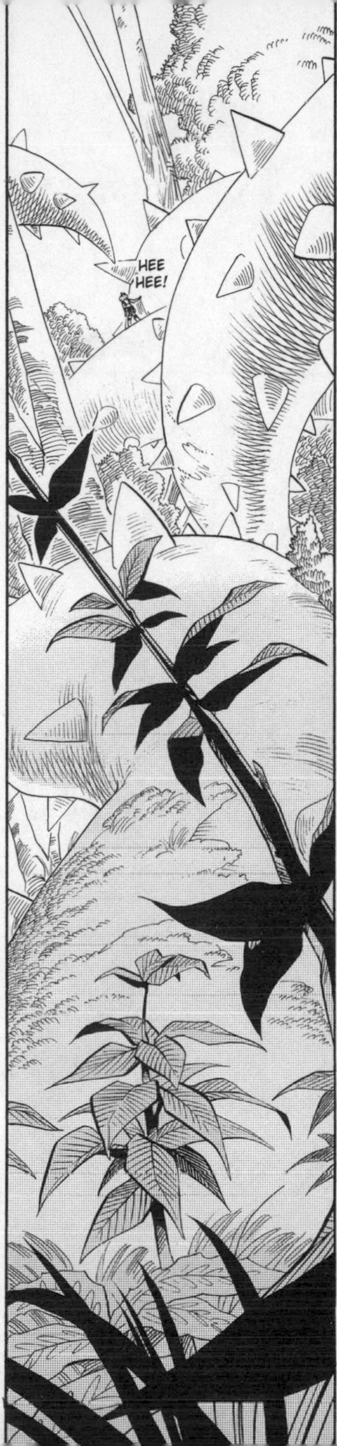
HEE HEE!

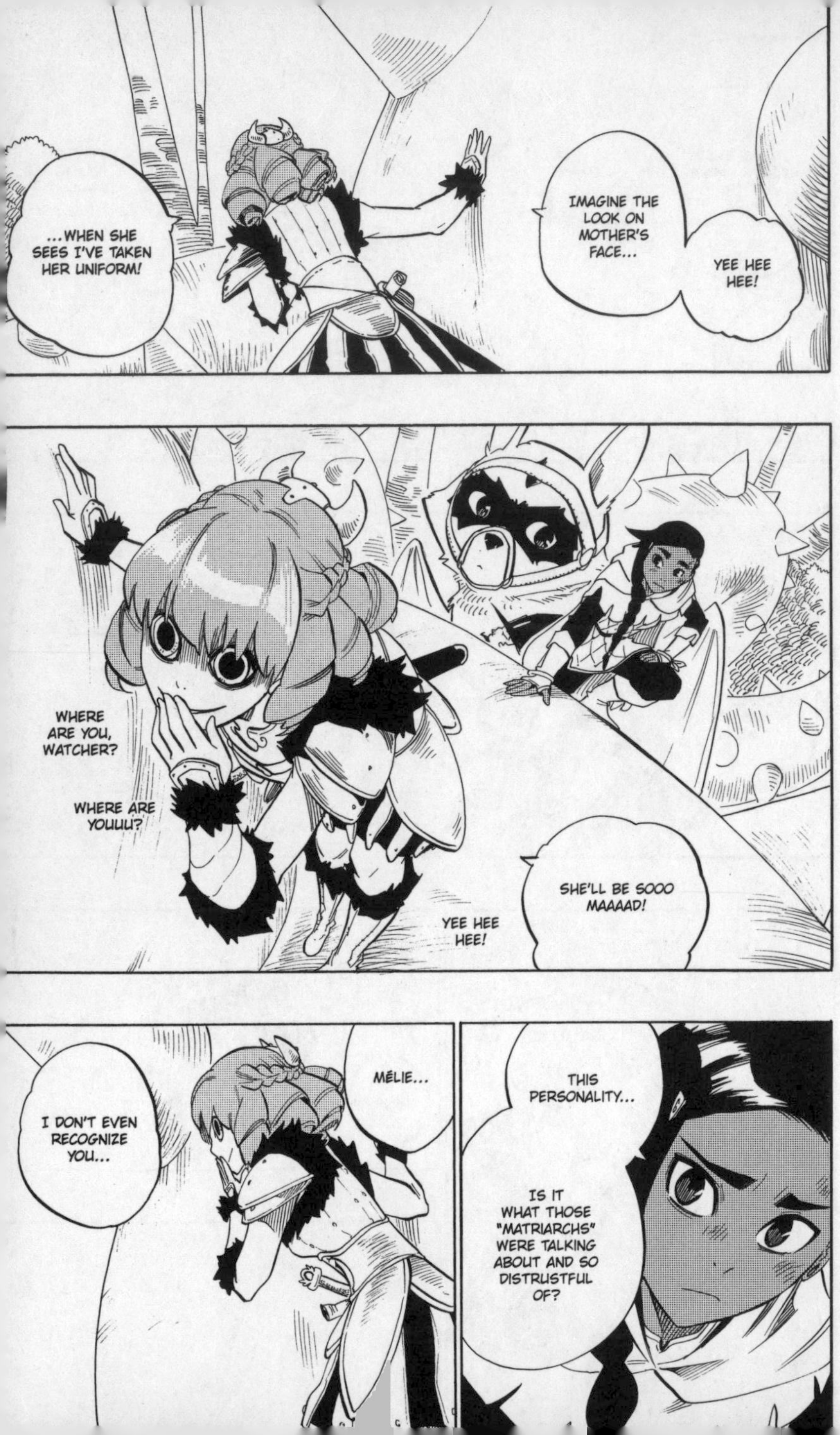
IMAGINE THE LOOK ON MOTHER'S FACE...
YEE HEE HEE!
...WHEN SHE SEES I'VE TAKEN HER UNIFORM!
SHE'LL BE SOOO MAAAAD!
YEE HEE HEE!
WHERE ARE YOU, WATCHER?
WHERE ARE YOUUU?
THIS PERSONALITY...
IS IT WHAT THOSE "MATRIARCHS" WERE TALKING ABOUT AND SO DISTRUSTFUL OF?
MÉLIE...
I DON'T EVEN RECOGNIZE YOU...

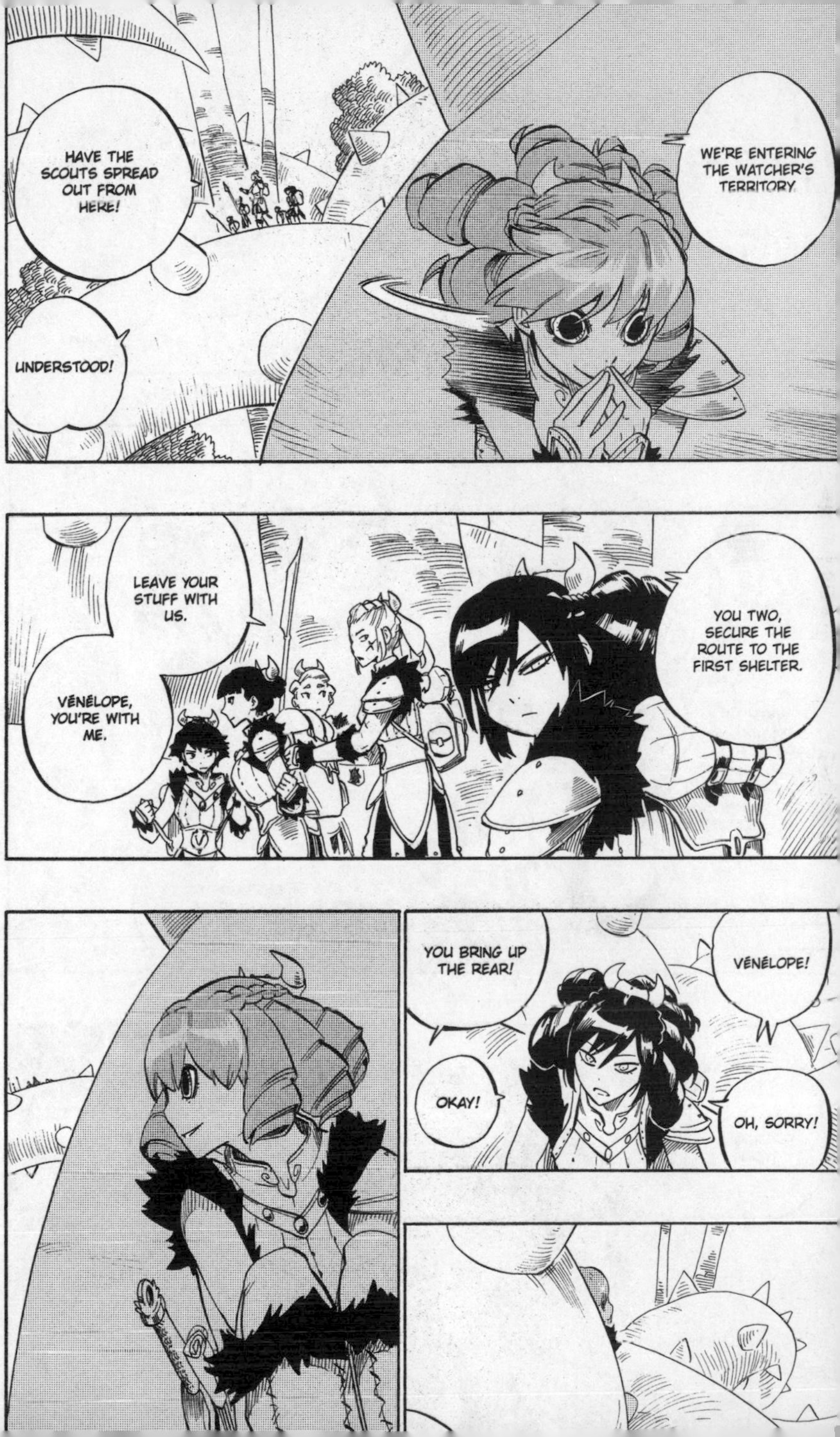
WE'RE ENTERING THE WATCHER'S TERRITORY.
HAVE THE SCOUTS SPREAD OUT FROM HERE!
UNDERSTOOD!
YOU TWO, SECURE THE ROUTE TO THE FIRST SHELTER.
LEAVE YOUR STUFF WITH US.
VÉNÉLOPE, YOU'RE WITH ME.
VÉNÉLOPE!
YOU BRING UP THE REAR!
OH, SORRY!
OKAY!

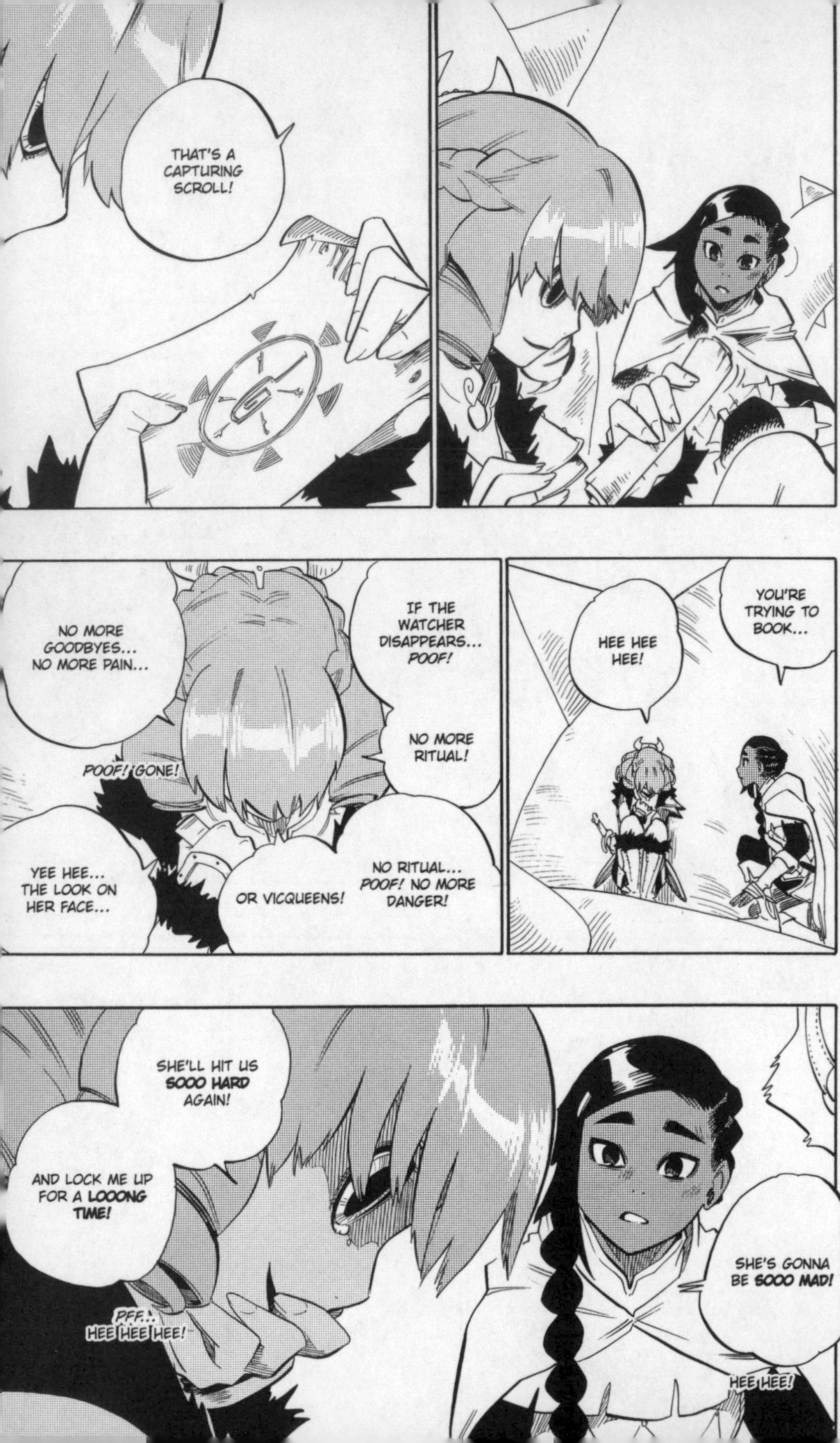
THAT'S A CAPTURING SCROLL!
YOU'RE TRYING TO BOOK...
HEE HEE HEE!
IF THE WATCHER DISAPPEARS... *POOF!*
NO MORE GOODBYES... NO MORE PAIN...
NO MORE RITUAL!
POOF! GONE!
NO RITUAL... *POOF!* NO MORE DANGER!
OR VICQUEENS!
YEE HEE... THE LOOK ON HER FACE...
SHE'S GONNA BE **SOOO MAD!**
SHE'LL HIT US **SOOO HARD** AGAIN!
AND LOCK ME UP FOR A **LOOONG TIME!**
HEE HEE!
PFF... HEE HEE HEE!

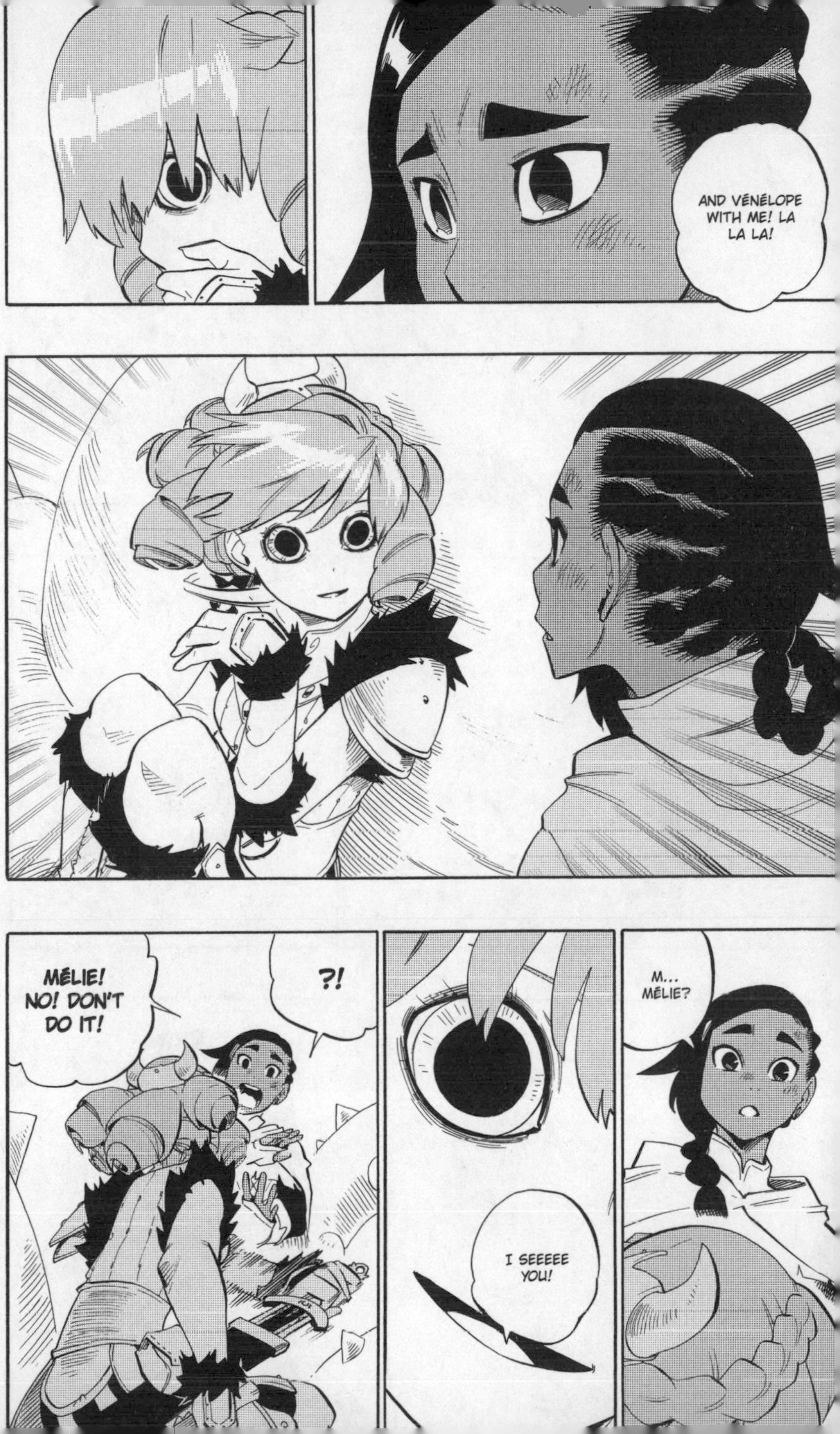
AND VÉNÉLOPE WITH ME! LA LA LA!
M... MÉLIE?
I SEEEEE YOU!
?!
MÉLIE! NO! DON'T DO IT!

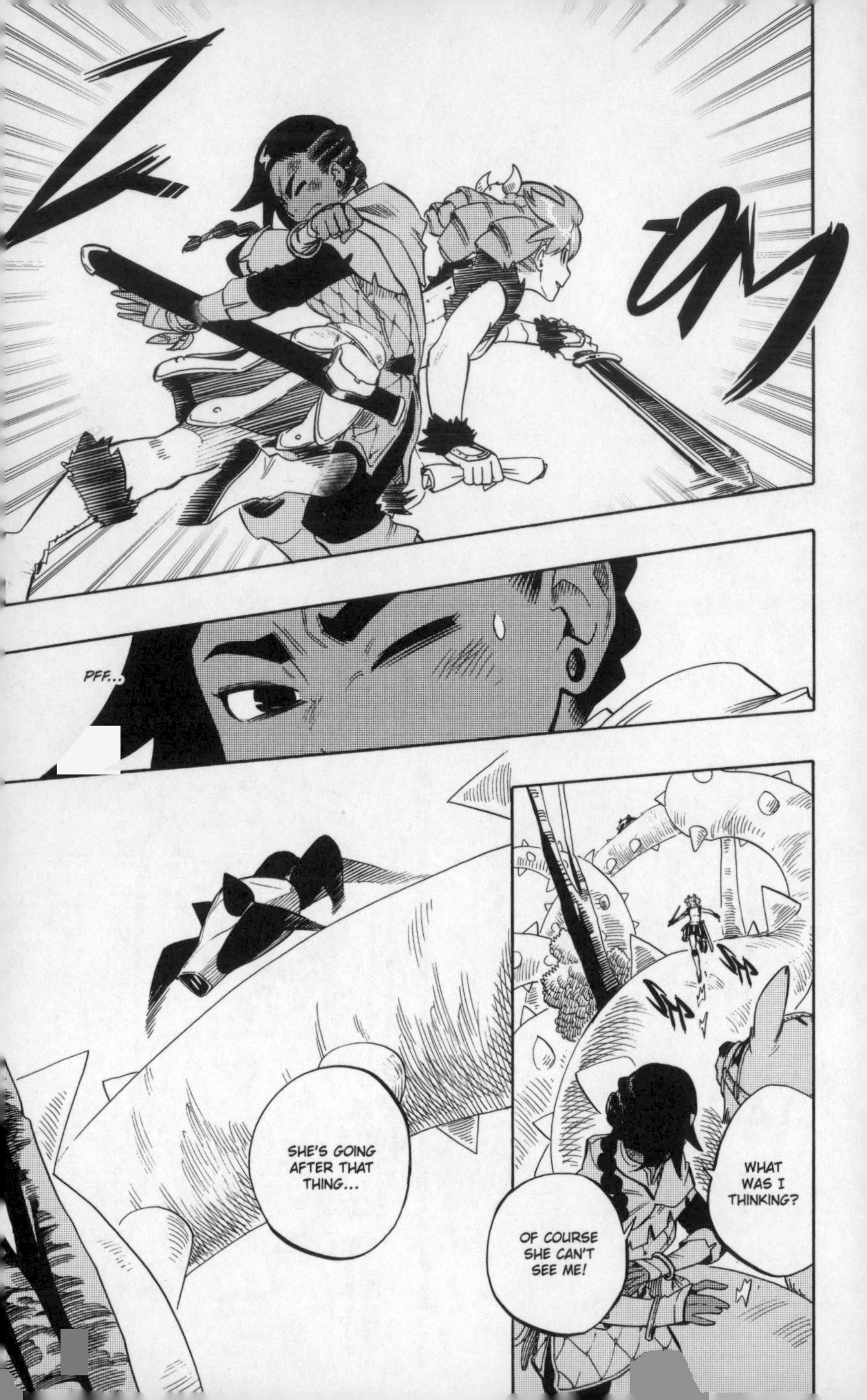
PFF...
WHAT WAS I THINKING?
OF COURSE SHE CAN'T SEE ME!
SHE'S GOING AFTER THAT THING...

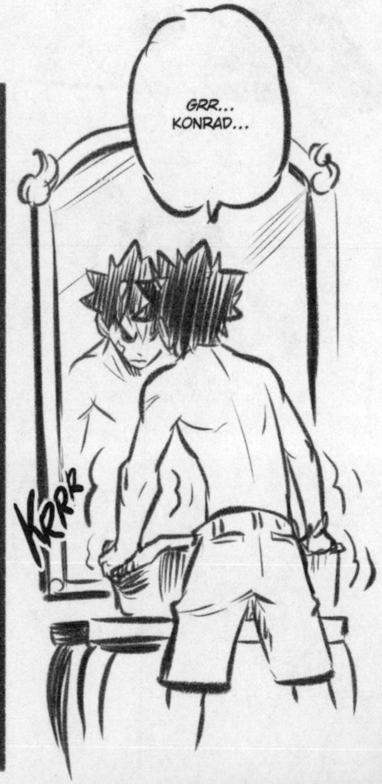
GRR...
KONRAD...
KRRR

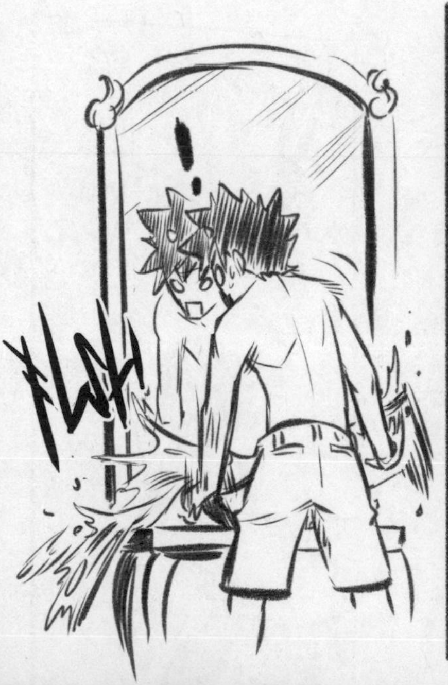

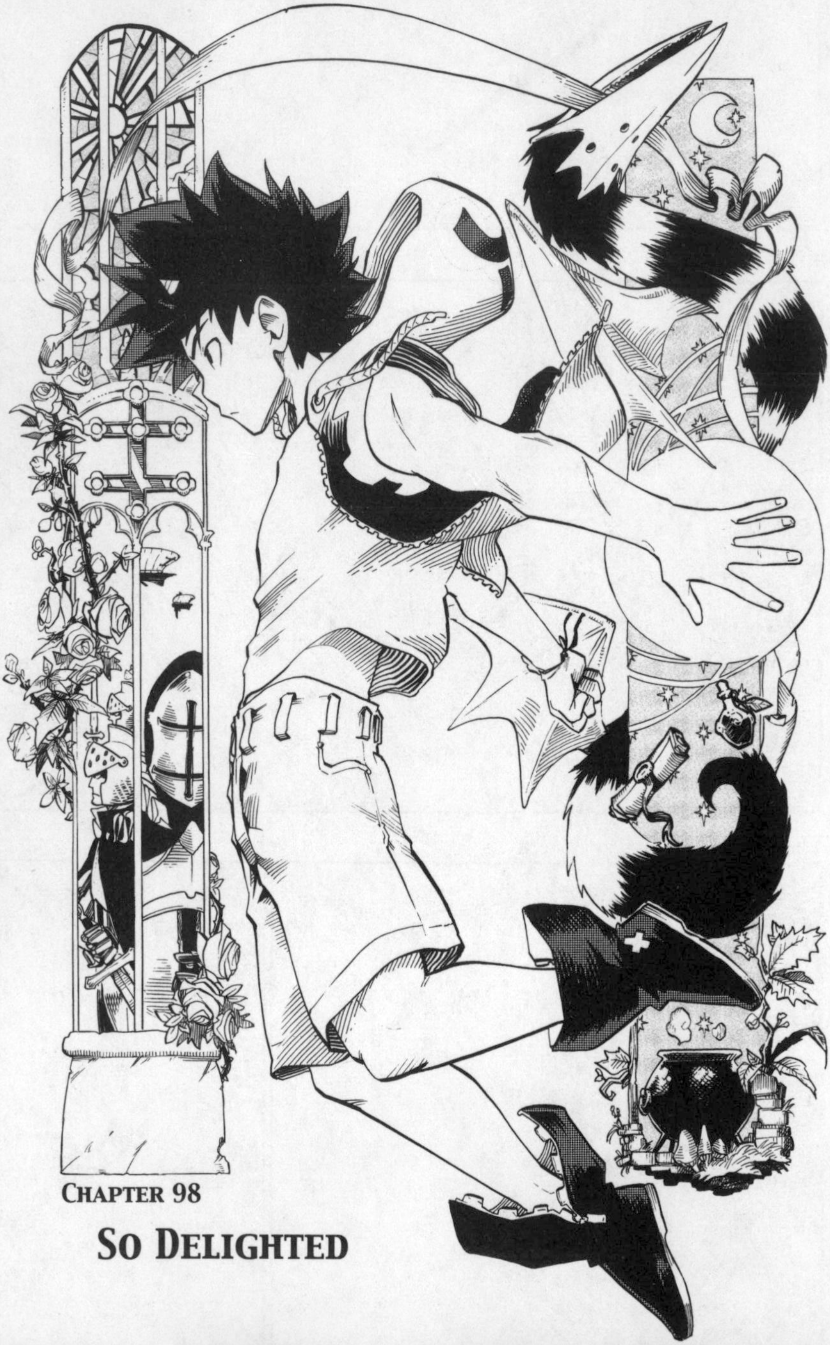

Chapter 98

So Delighted

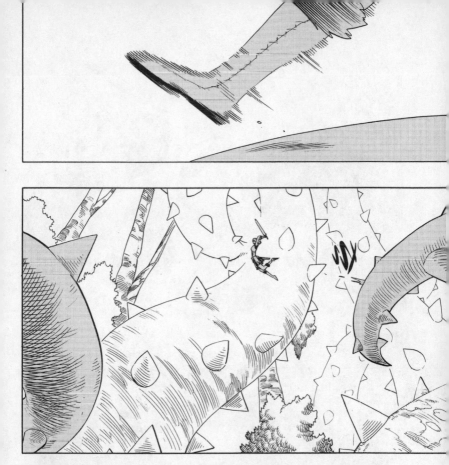

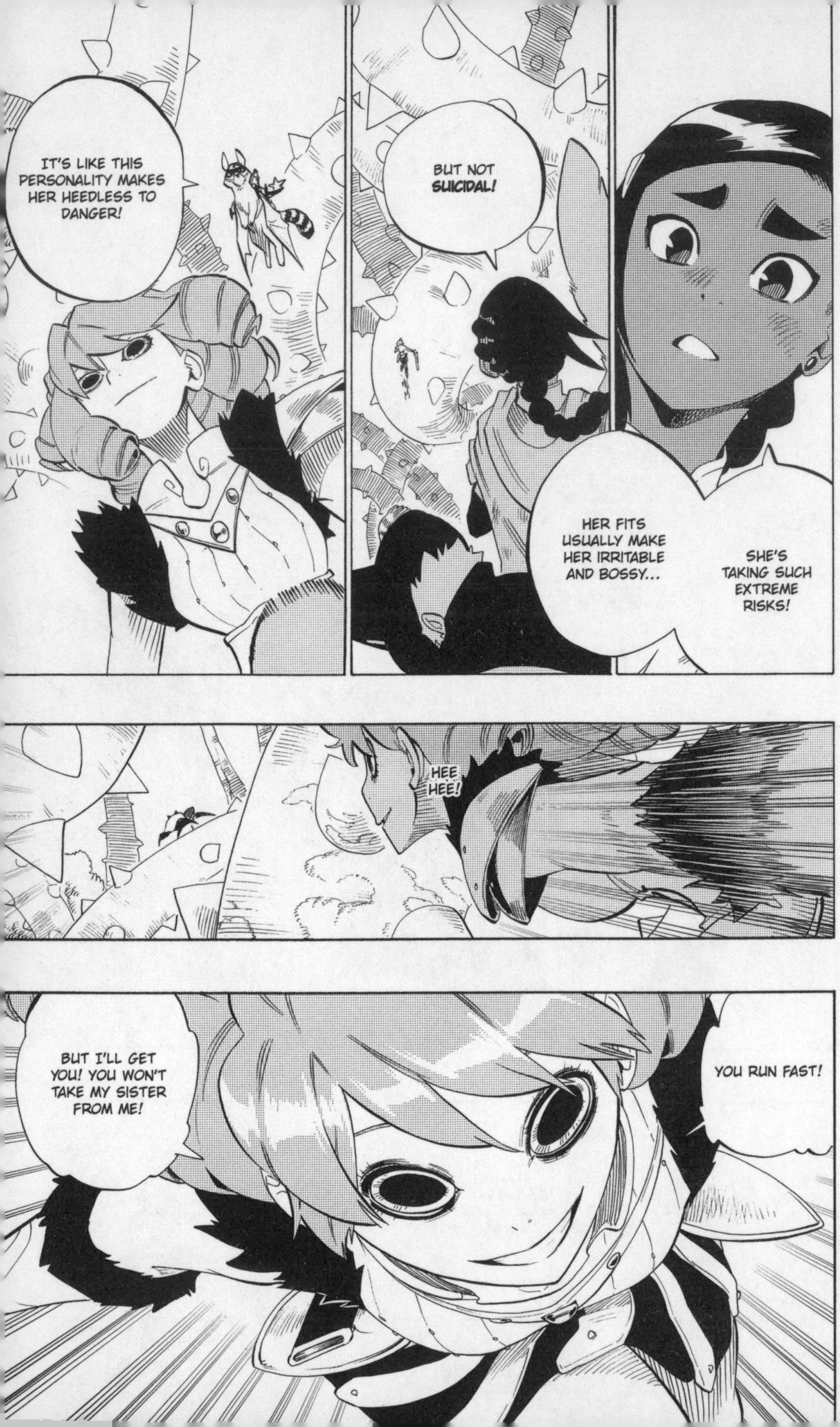
SHE'S TAKING SUCH EXTREME RISKS!
HER FITS USUALLY MAKE HER IRRITABLE AND BOSSY...
BUT NOT SUICIDAL!
IT'S LIKE THIS PERSONALITY MAKES HER HEEDLESS TO DANGER!
HEE HEE!
YOU RUN FAST!
BUT I'LL GET YOU! YOU WON'T TAKE MY SISTER FROM ME!

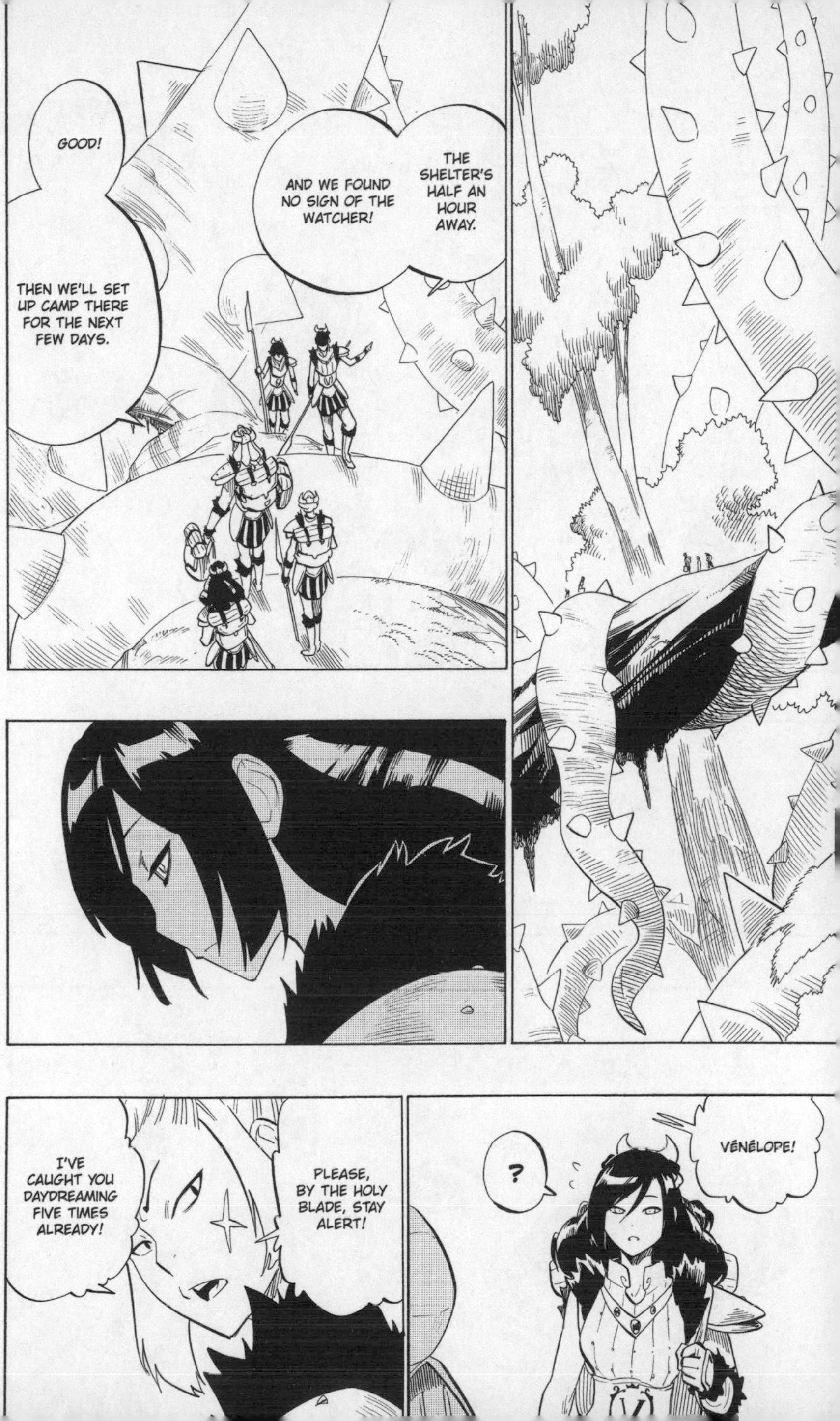
THE SHELTER'S HALF AN HOUR AWAY.
AND WE FOUND NO SIGN OF THE WATCHER!
GOOD!
THEN WE'LL SET UP CAMP THERE FOR THE NEXT FEW DAYS.
VÉNÉLOPE!
?
PLEASE, BY THE HOLY BLADE, STAY ALERT!
I'VE CAUGHT YOU DAYDREAMING FIVE TIMES ALREADY!

YOU INSISTED ON BEING HERE, SO DON'T LET YOUR MIND DRIFT OFF SOMEWHERE ELSE!
I DUNNO ABOUT YOU, BUT THE REST OF US AIM TO COME BACK FROM THIS RITUAL ALIVE AND IN ONE PIECE!
SORRY...
I SAID I'M SORRY!
PFF...
DID YOU FORGET ALL THOSE YEARS OF PREPARATION?
WE CAN'T AFFORD TO HAVE EVEN ONE WEAK LINK IN THE CHAIN! NOT NOW, NOT HERE!
DON'T BECOME LIKE THE ONE BACK IN THE VILLAGE!
HA HA HA!
...

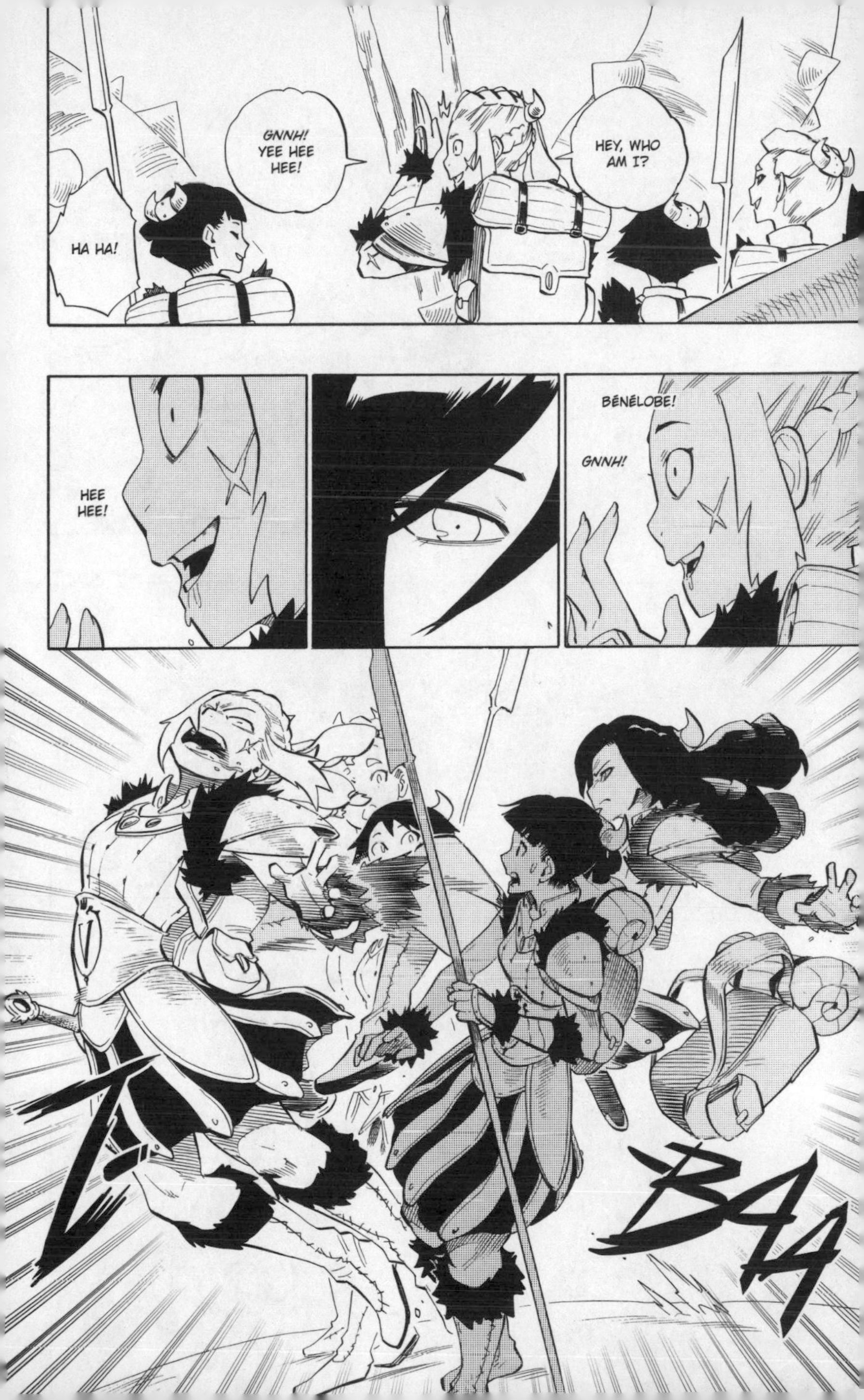
HEY, WHO AM I?
GNNH! YEE HEE HEE!
HA HA!
BÉNÉLOBE!
GNNH!
HEE HEE!

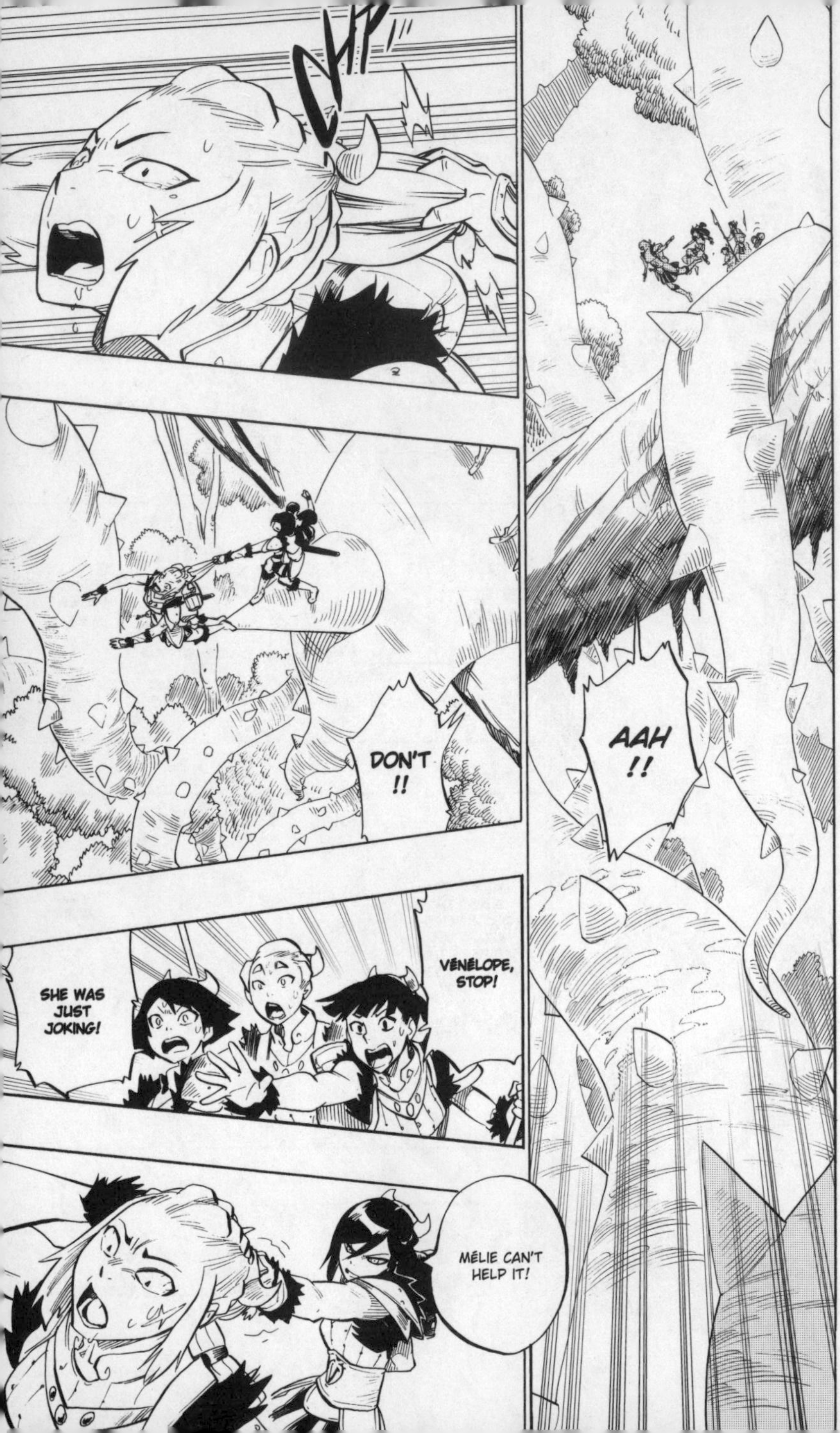
AAH !!
DON'T !!
VÉNÉLOPE, STOP!
SHE WAS JUST JOKING!
MÉLIE CAN'T HELP IT!

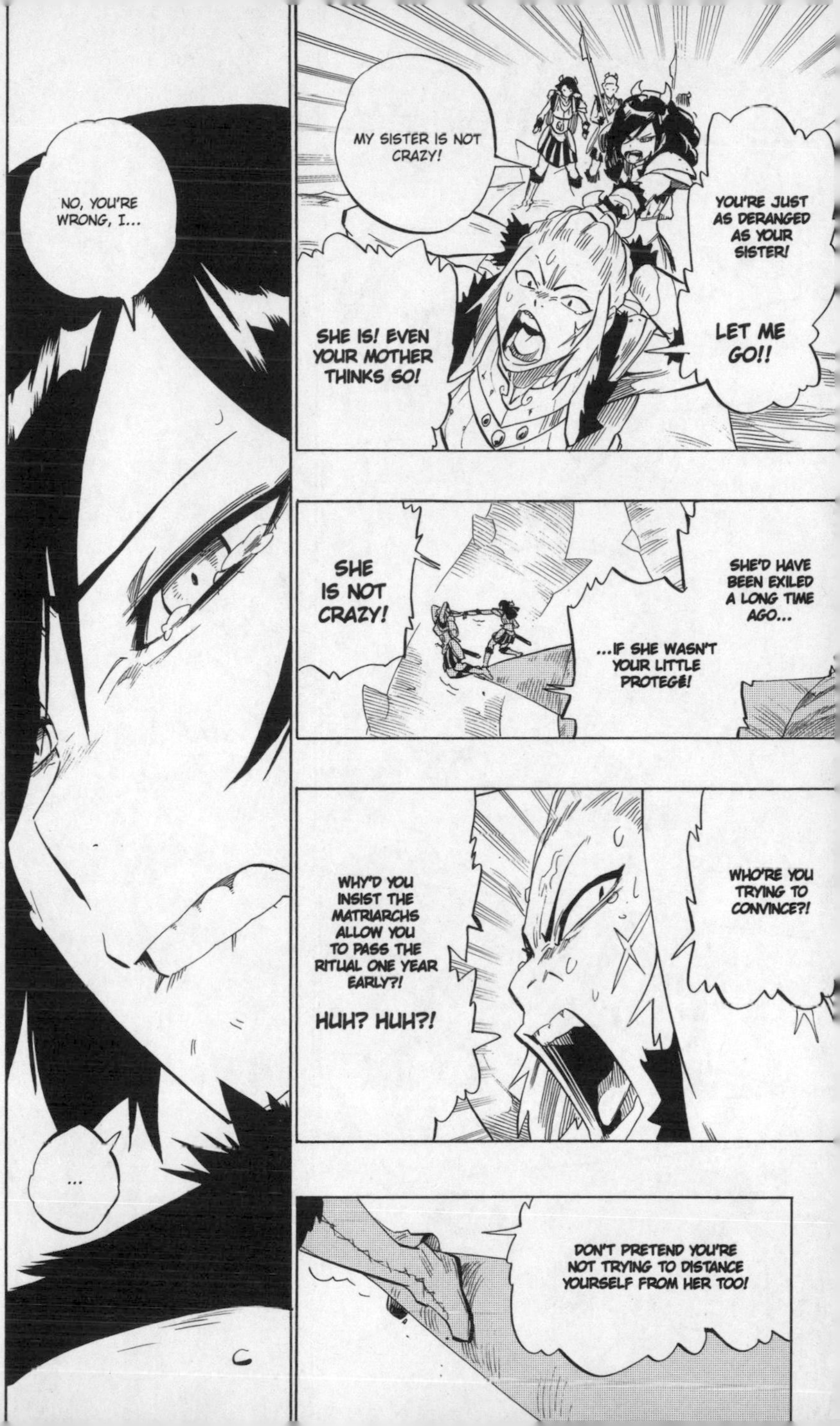
YOU'RE JUST AS DERANGED AS YOUR SISTER!
LET ME GO!!
MY SISTER IS NOT CRAZY!
SHE IS! EVEN YOUR MOTHER THINKS SO!
SHE'D HAVE BEEN EXILED A LONG TIME AGO...
...IF SHE WASN'T YOUR LITTLE PROTEGÉ!
SHE IS NOT CRAZY!
WHO'RE YOU TRYING TO CONVINCE?!
WHY'D YOU INSIST THE MATRIARCHS ALLOW YOU TO PASS THE RITUAL ONE YEAR EARLY?!
HUH? HUH?!
DON'T PRETEND YOU'RE NOT TRYING TO DISTANCE YOURSELF FROM HER TOO!
NO, YOU'RE WRONG, I...
...

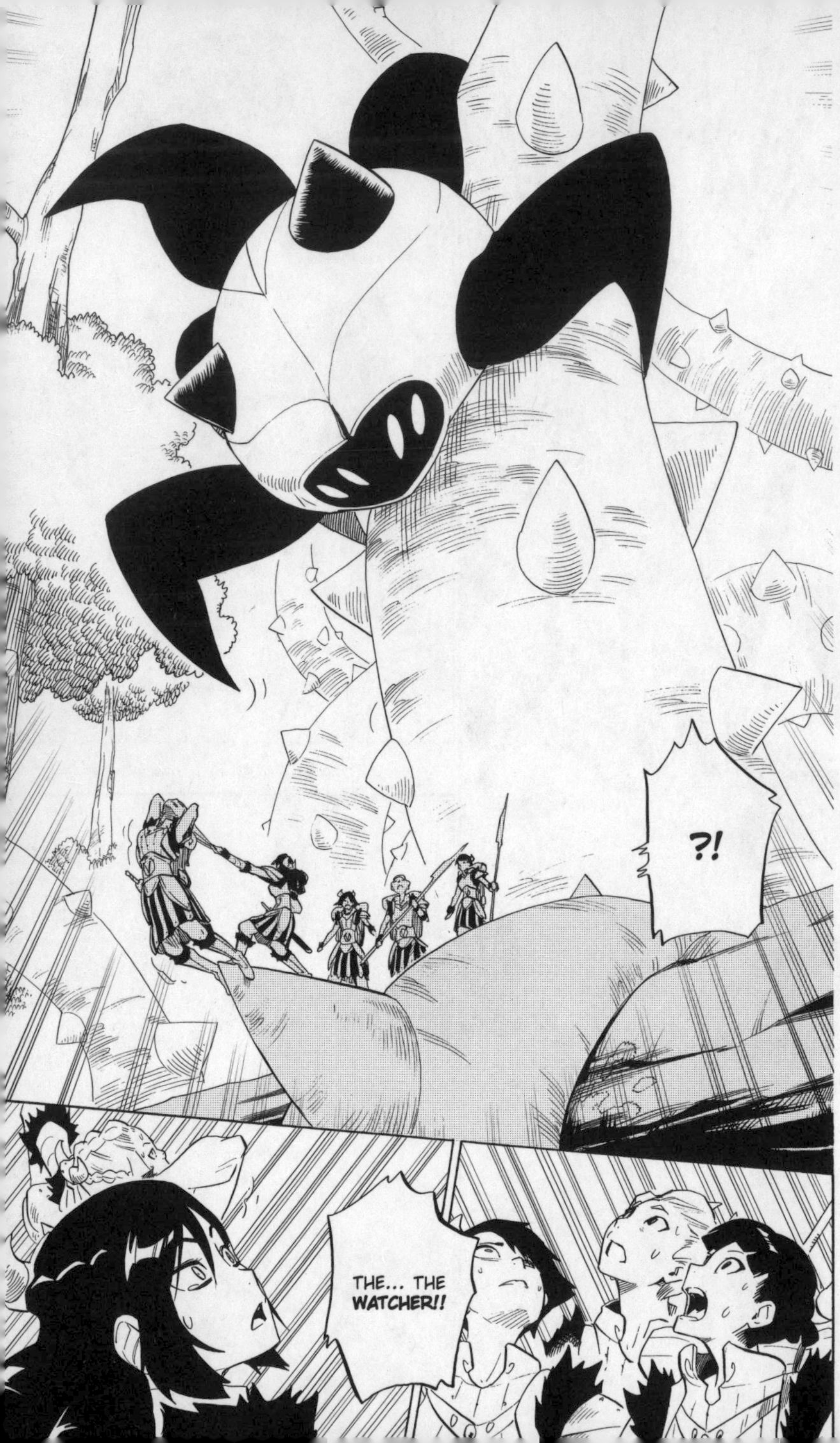
?!
THE... THE WATCHER!!

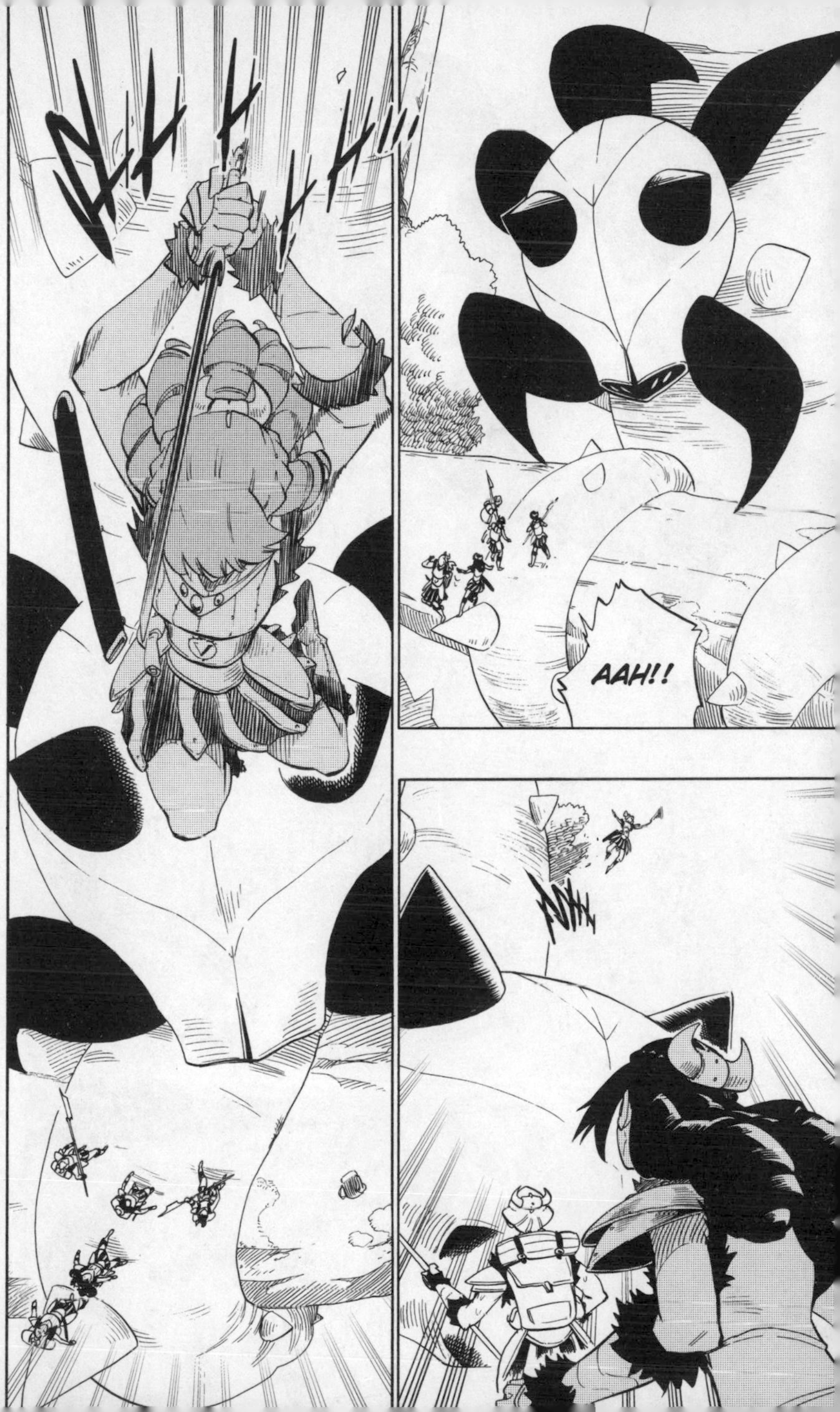
AAH!!

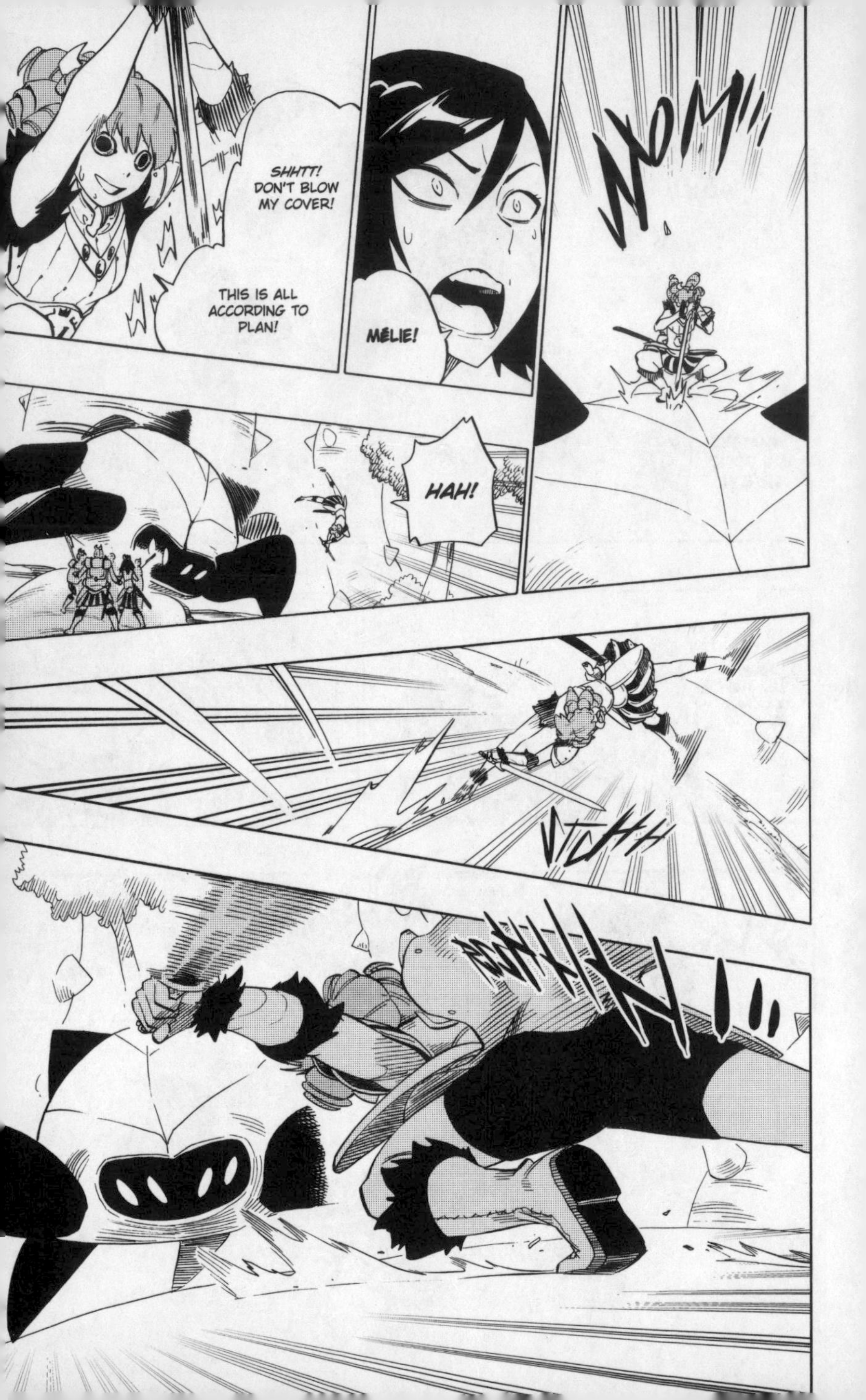
MÉLIE!
SHHTT! DON'T BLOW MY COVER!
THIS IS ALL ACCORDING TO PLAN!
HAH!

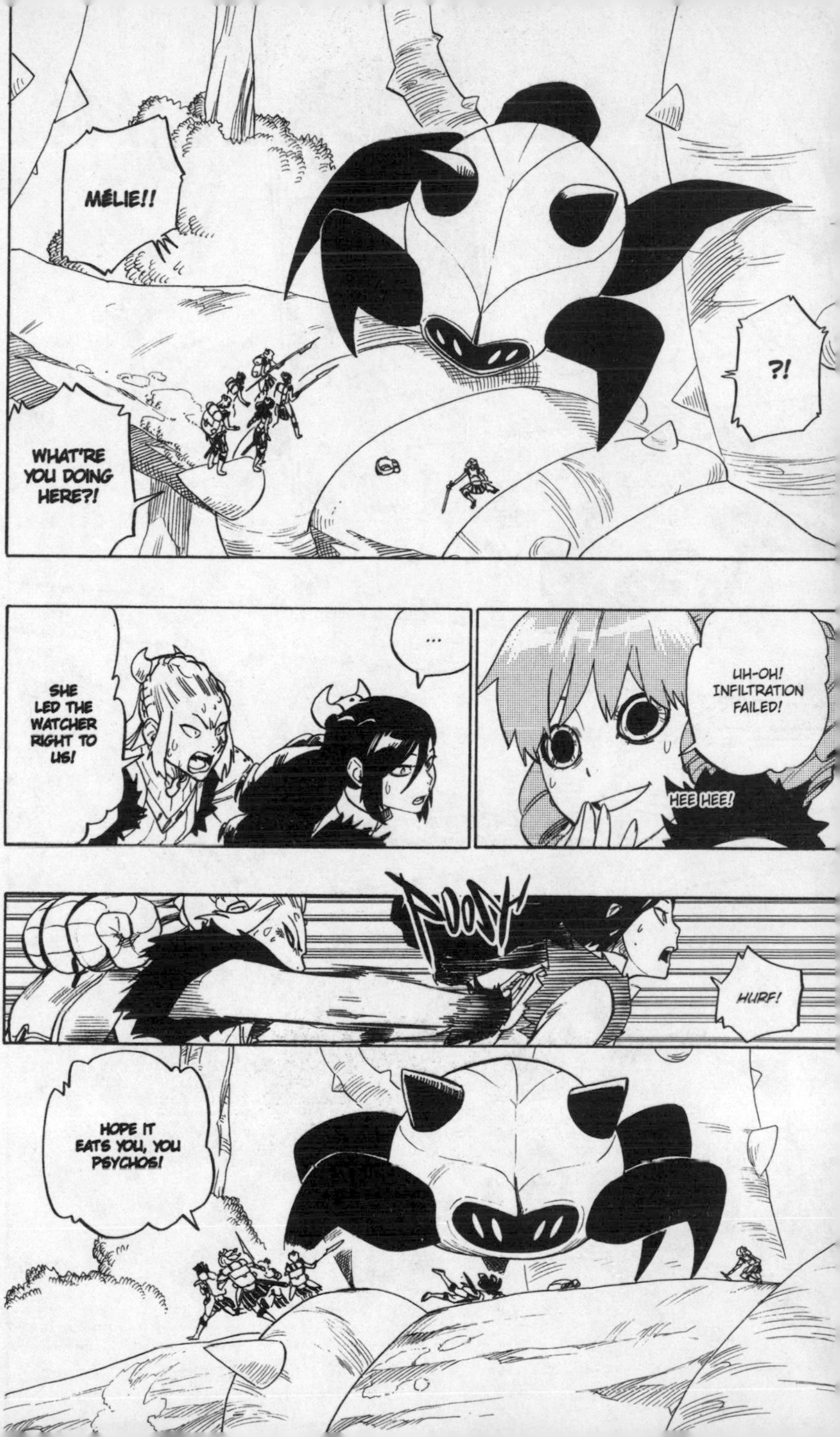
?!
MÉLIE!!
WHAT'RE YOU DOING HERE?!
UH-OH! INFILTRATION FAILED!
HEE HEE!
...
SHE LED THE WATCHER RIGHT TO US!
POOSH
HURF!
HOPE IT EATS YOU, YOU PSYCHOS!

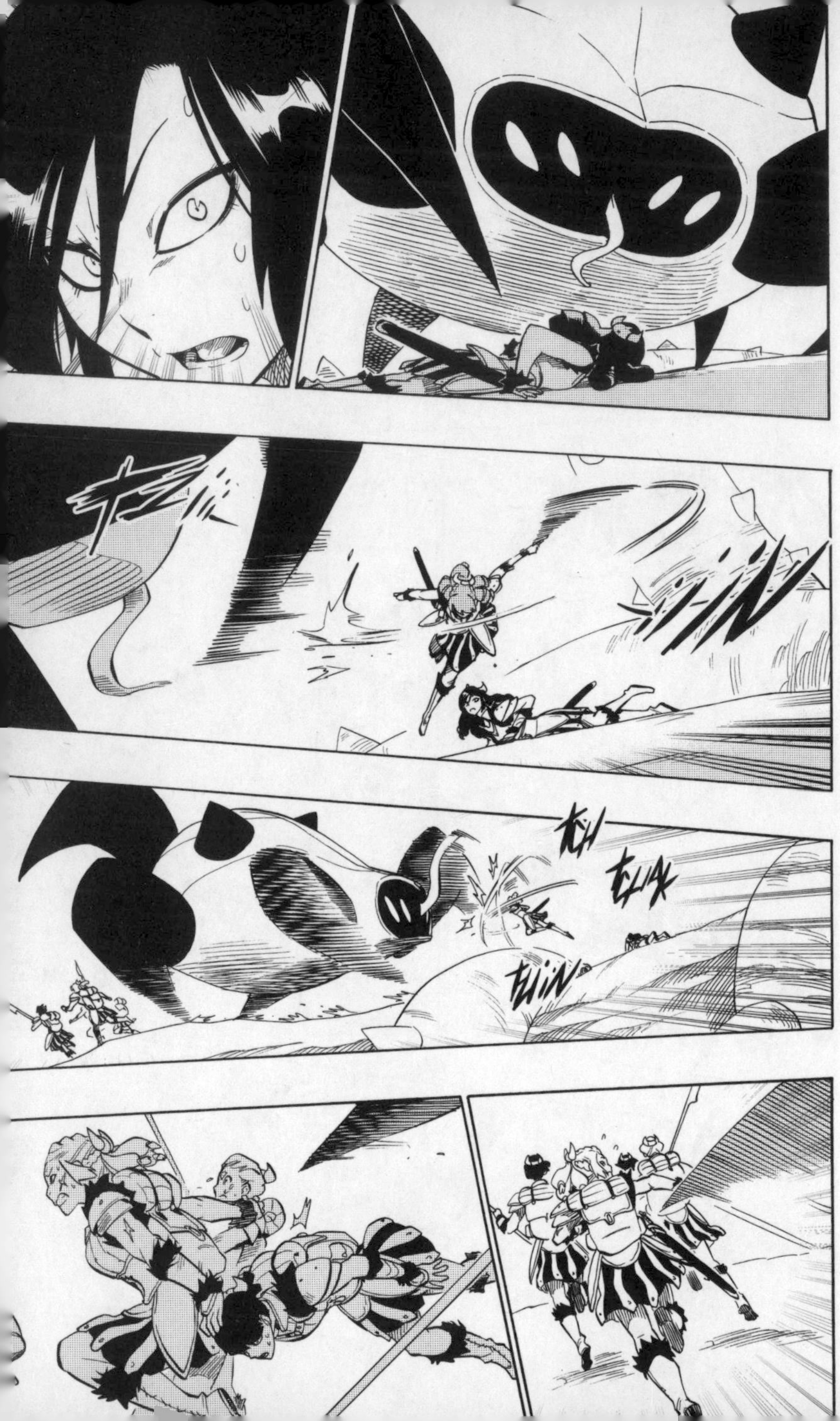
TCH

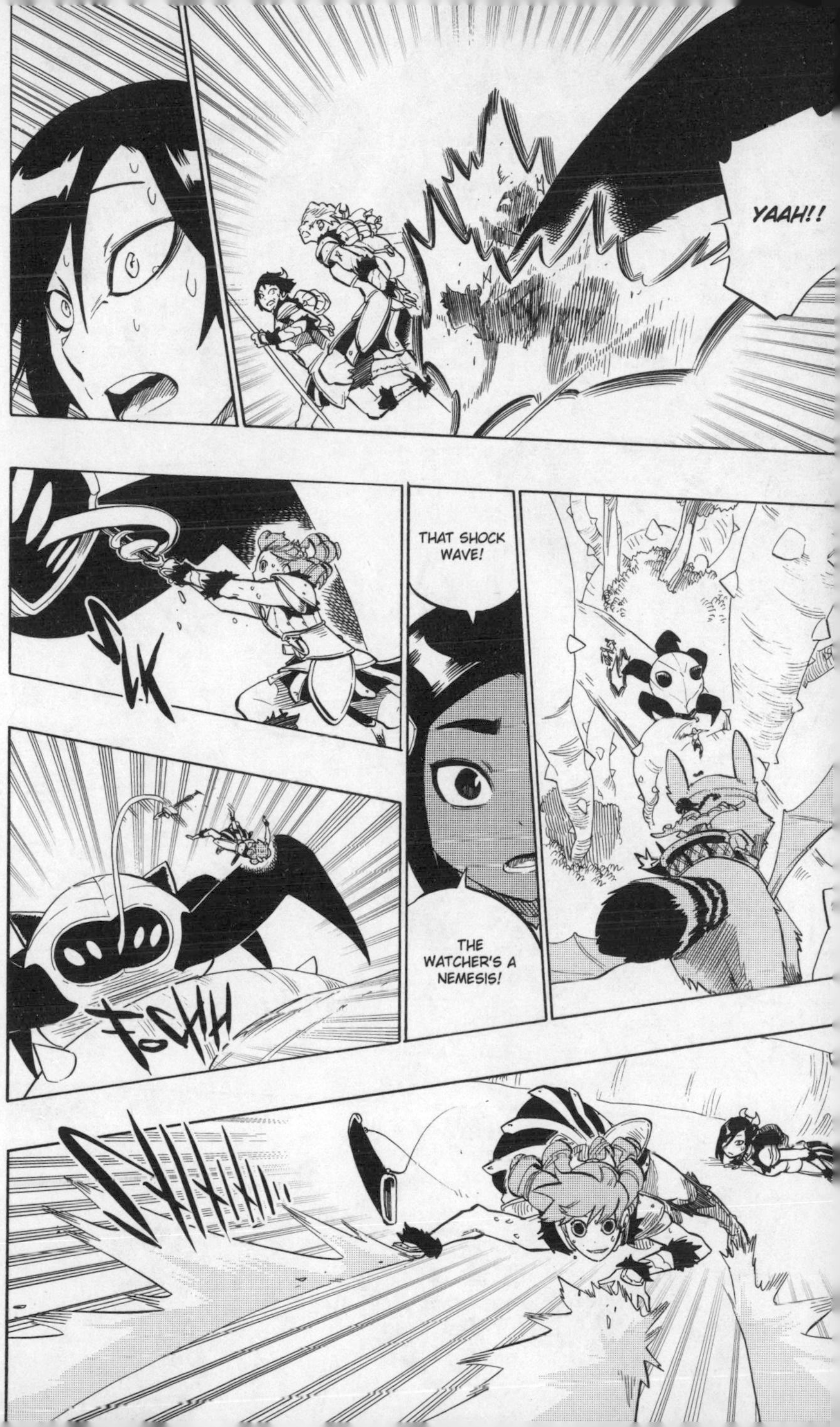
YAAH!!
THAT SHOCK WAVE!
THE WATCHER'S A NEMESIS!

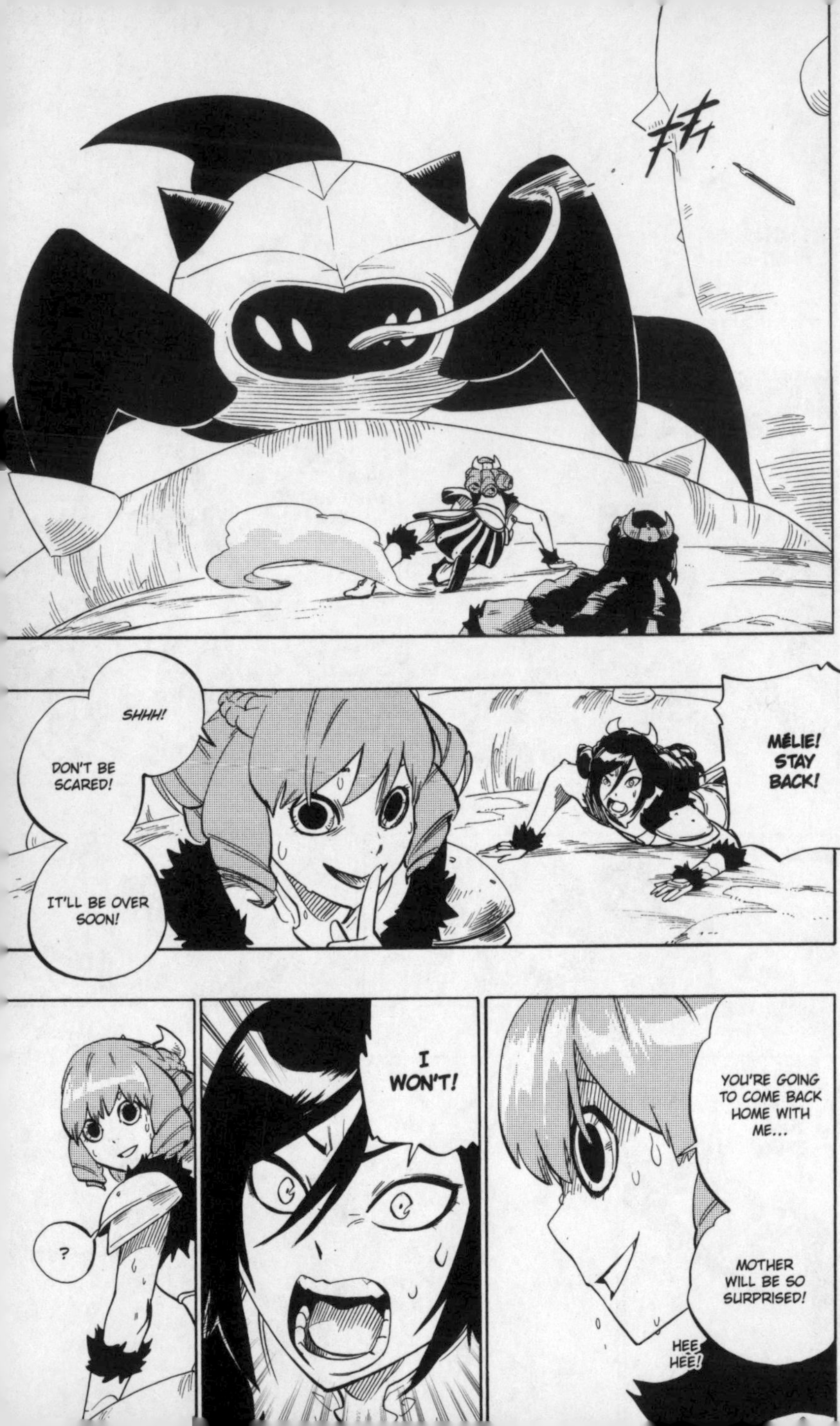
MÉLIE! STAY BACK!
SHHH!
DON'T BE SCARED!
IT'LL BE OVER SOON!
YOU'RE GOING TO COME BACK HOME WITH ME...
MOTHER WILL BE SO SURPRISED!
HEE HEE!
I WON'T!
?

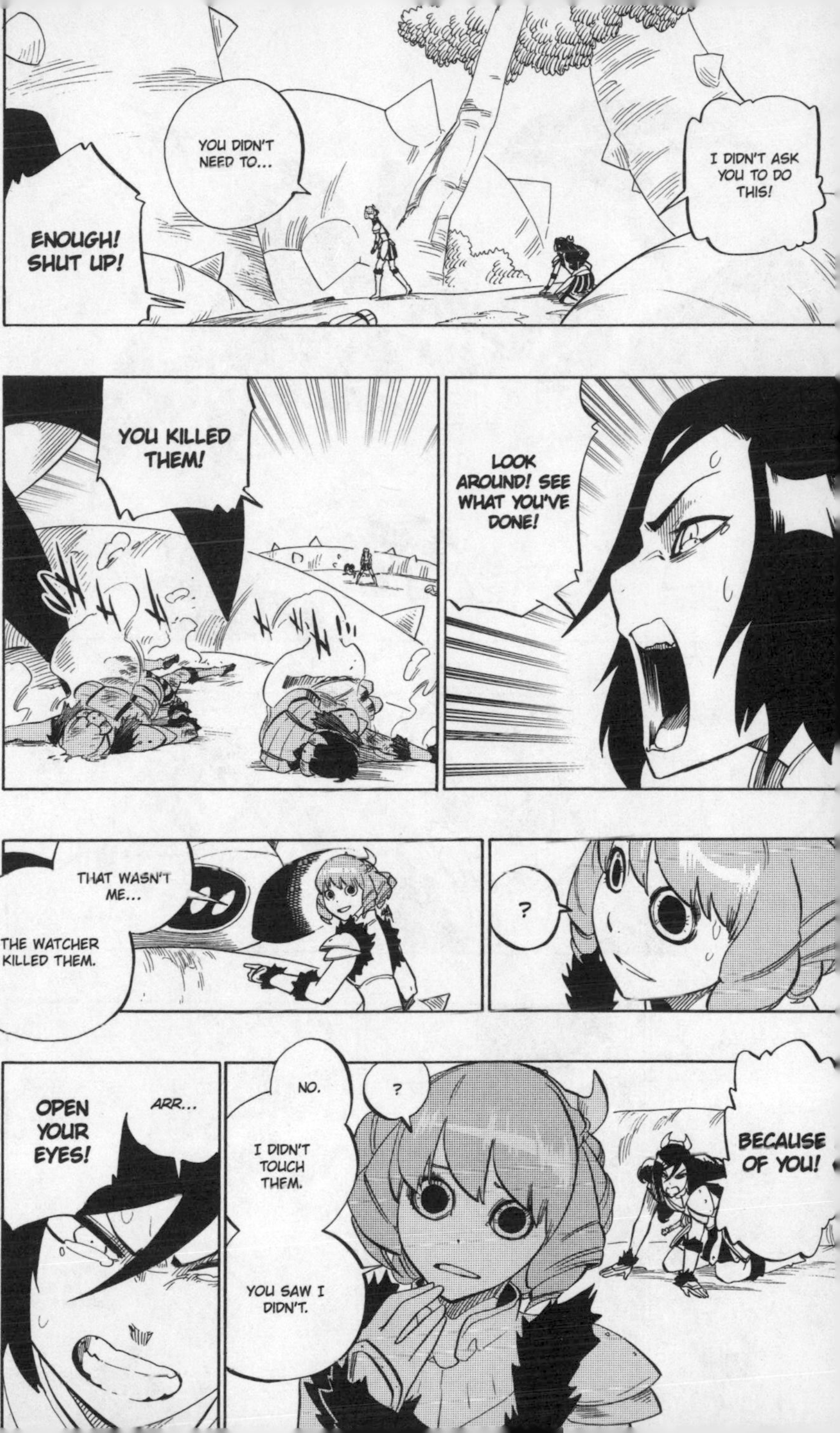
I DIDN'T ASK YOU TO DO THIS!
YOU DIDN'T NEED TO...
ENOUGH! SHUT UP!
LOOK AROUND! SEE WHAT YOU'VE DONE!
YOU KILLED THEM!
?
THAT WASN'T ME...
THE WATCHER KILLED THEM.
BECAUSE OF YOU!
?
NO.
I DIDN'T TOUCH THEM.
YOU SAW I DIDN'T.
OPEN YOUR EYES!
ARR...

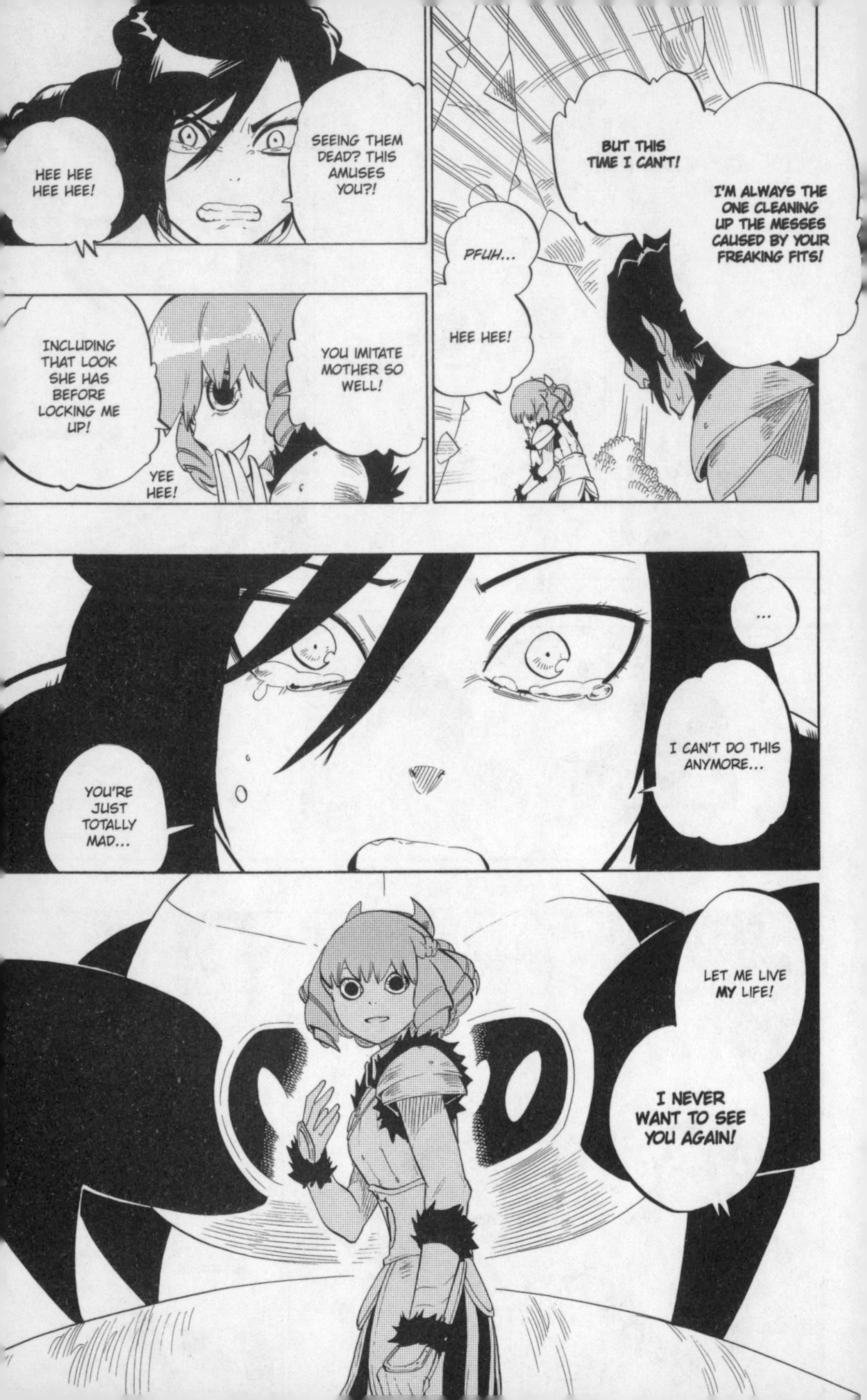
BUT THIS TIME I CAN'T!
I'M ALWAYS THE ONE CLEANING UP THE MESSES CAUSED BY YOUR FREAKING FITS!
PFUH...
HEE HEE!
SEEING THEM DEAD? THIS AMUSES YOU?!
HEE HEE HEE HEE!
YOU IMITATE MOTHER SO WELL!
INCLUDING THAT LOOK SHE HAS BEFORE LOCKING ME UP!
YEE HEE!
...
I CAN'T DO THIS ANYMORE...
YOU'RE JUST TOTALLY MAD...
LET ME LIVE MY LIFE!
I NEVER WANT TO SEE YOU AGAIN!

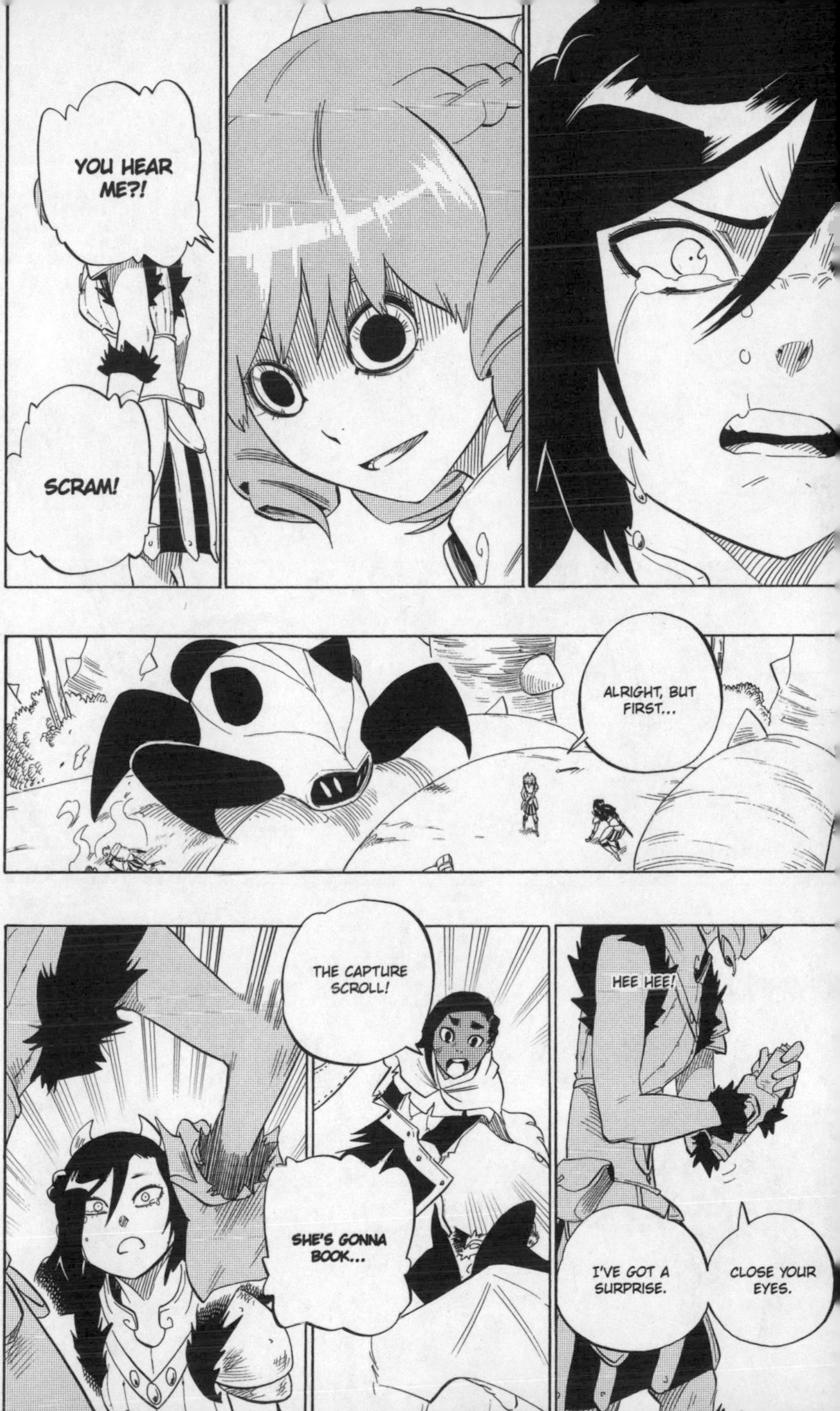
YOU HEAR ME?!
SCRAM!
ALRIGHT, BUT FIRST...
HEE HEE!
CLOSE YOUR EYES.
I'VE GOT A SURPRISE.
THE CAPTURE SCROLL!
SHE'S GONNA BOOK...

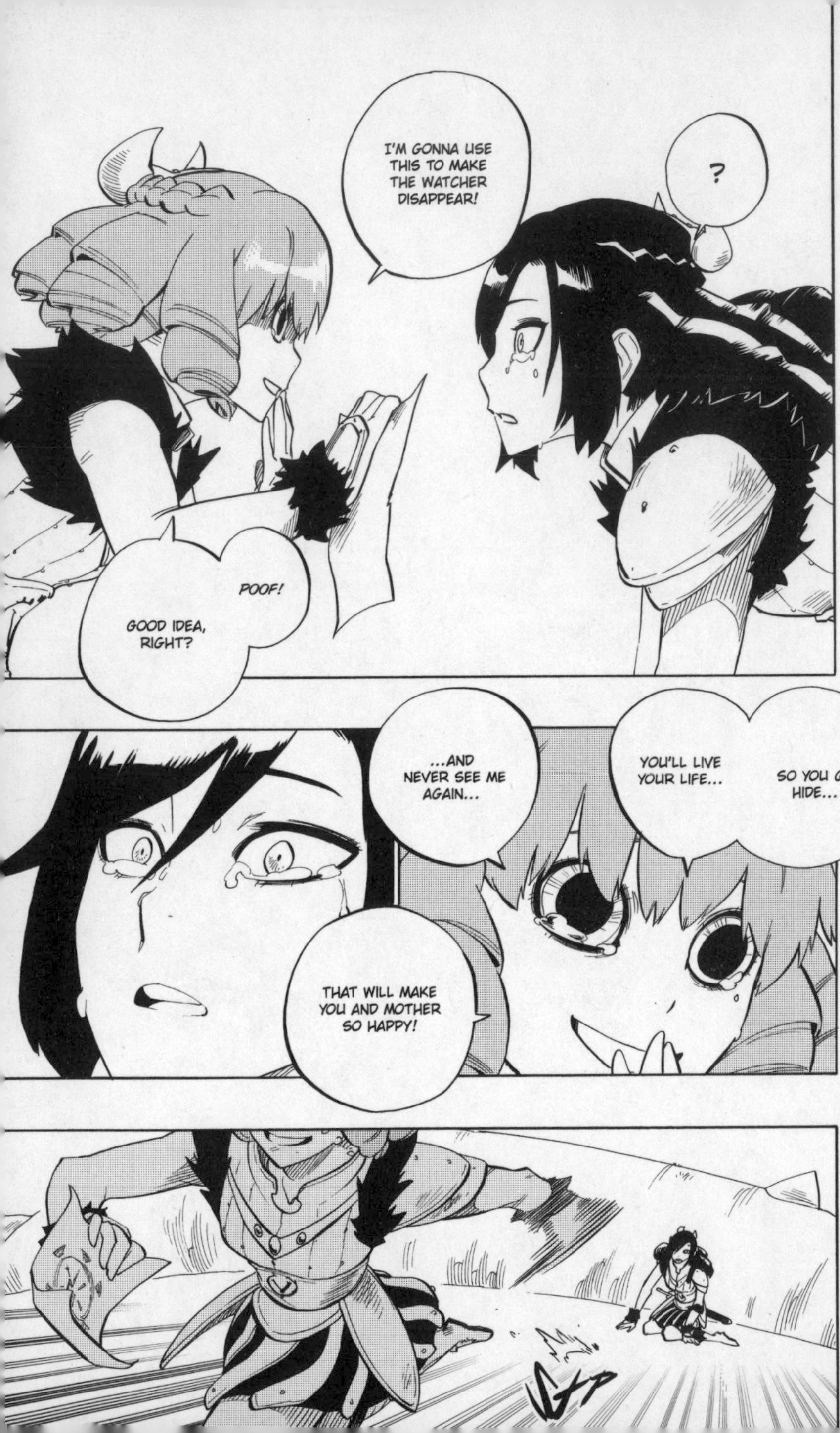
I'M GONNA USE THIS TO MAKE THE WATCHER DISAPPEAR!
?
POOF!
GOOD IDEA, RIGHT?
SO YOU GO HIDE...
YOU'LL LIVE YOUR LIFE...
...AND NEVER SEE ME AGAIN...
THAT WILL MAKE YOU AND MOTHER SO HAPPY!

Chapter 99 Vénélope's Eyes

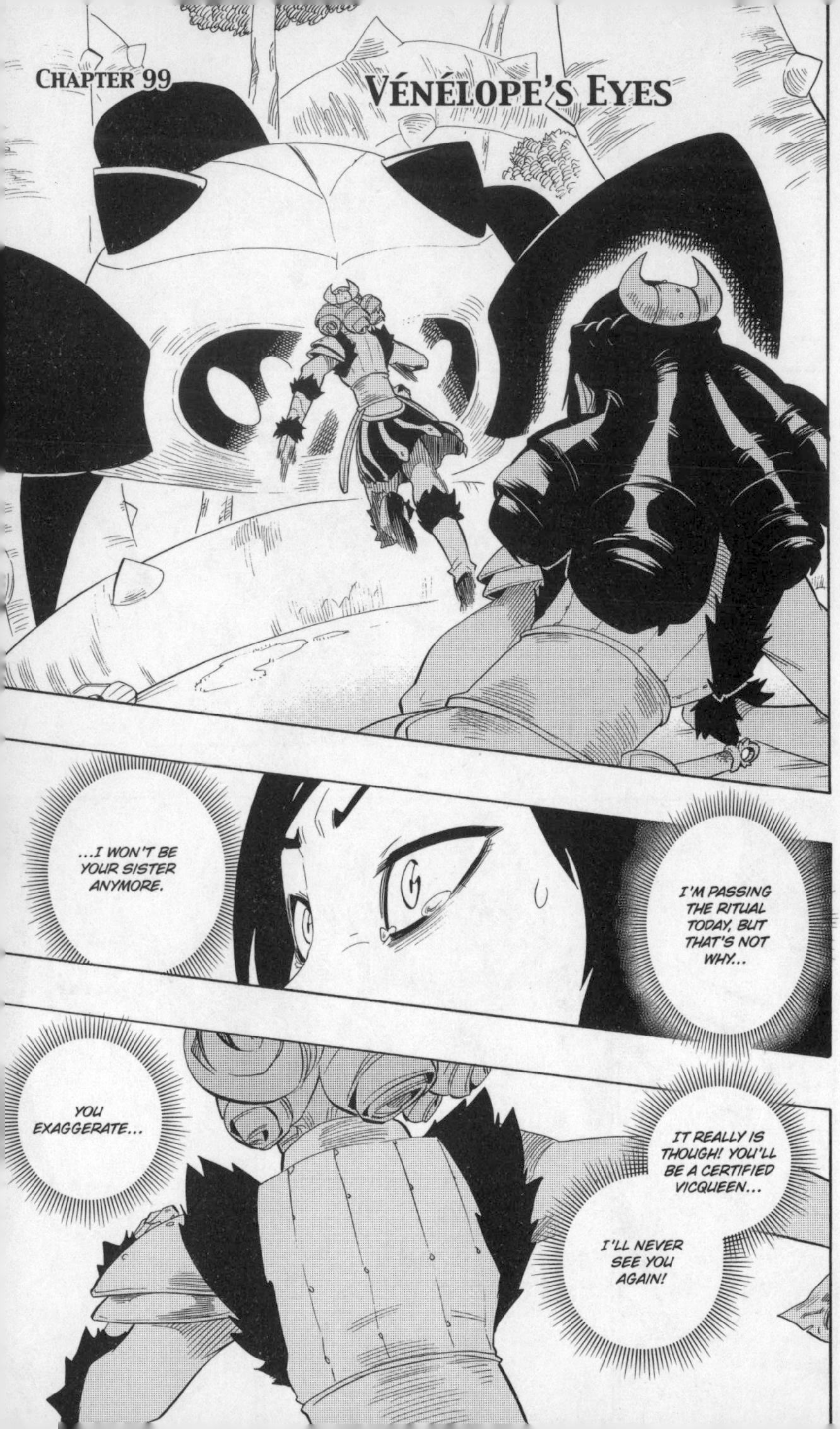
I'M PASSING THE RITUAL TODAY, BUT THAT'S NOT WHY...
...I WON'T BE YOUR SISTER ANYMORE.
YOU EXAGGERATE...
IT REALLY IS THOUGH! YOU'LL BE A CERTIFIED VICQUEEN...
I'LL NEVER SEE YOU AGAIN!

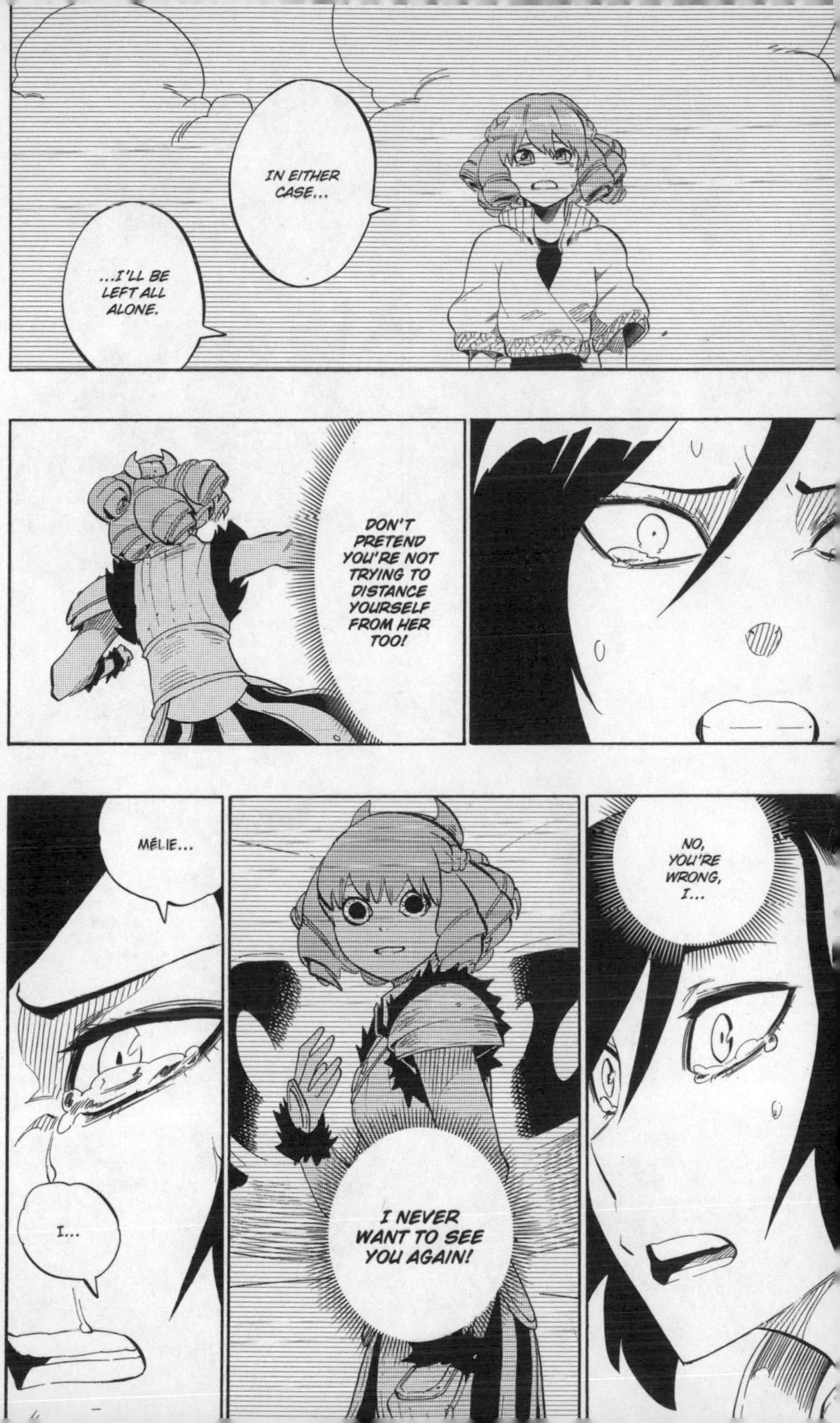
IN EITHER CASE...
...I'LL BE LEFT ALL ALONE.
DON'T PRETEND YOU'RE NOT TRYING TO DISTANCE YOURSELF FROM HER TOO!
NO, YOU'RE WRONG, I...
I NEVER WANT TO SEE YOU AGAIN!
MÉLIE...
I...

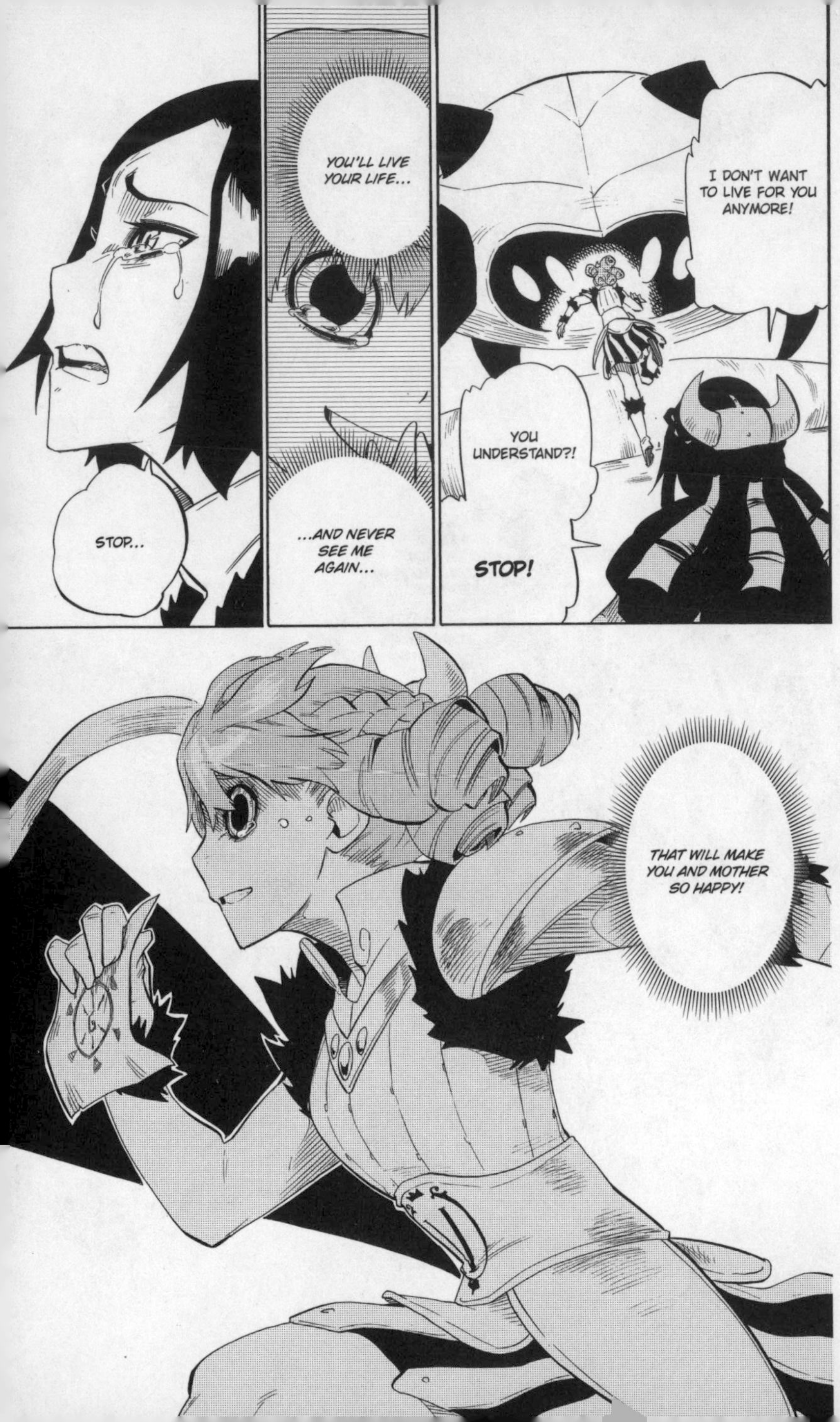
I DON'T WANT TO LIVE FOR YOU ANYMORE!
YOU UNDERSTAND?!
STOP!
YOU'LL LIVE YOUR LIFE...
...AND NEVER SEE ME AGAIN...
STOP...
THAT WILL MAKE YOU AND MOTHER SO HAPPY!

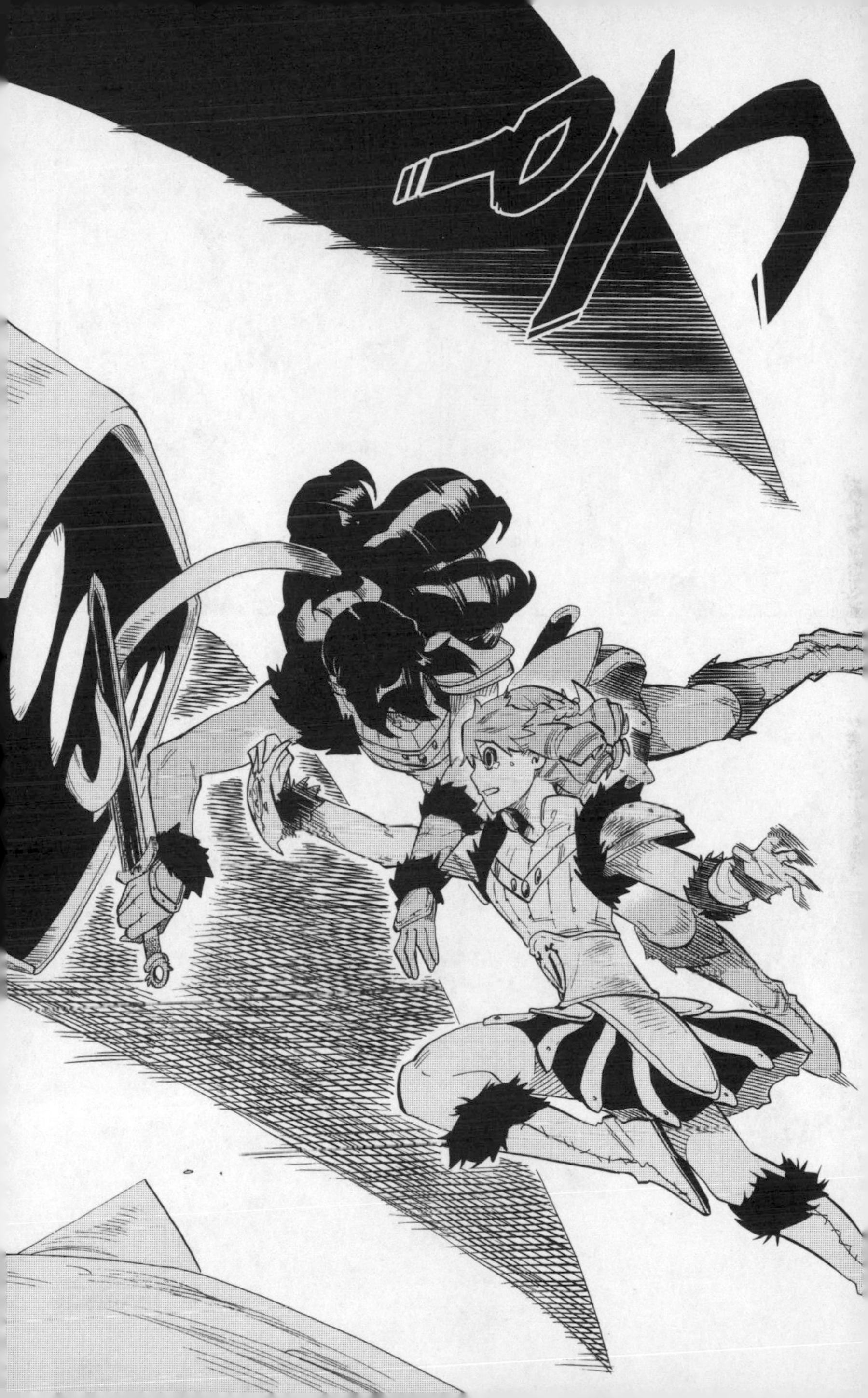

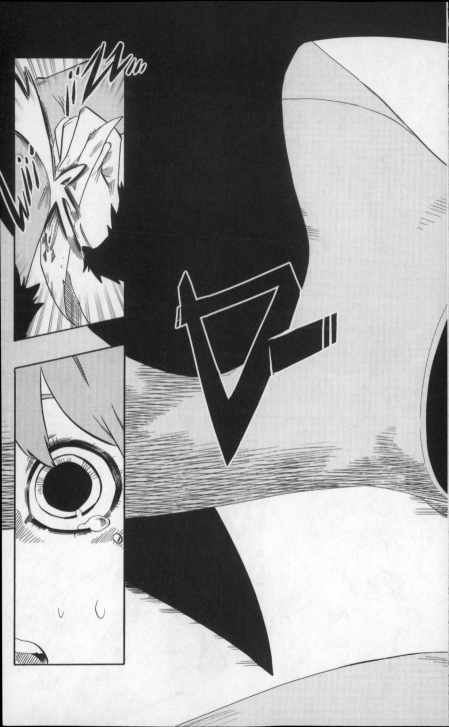

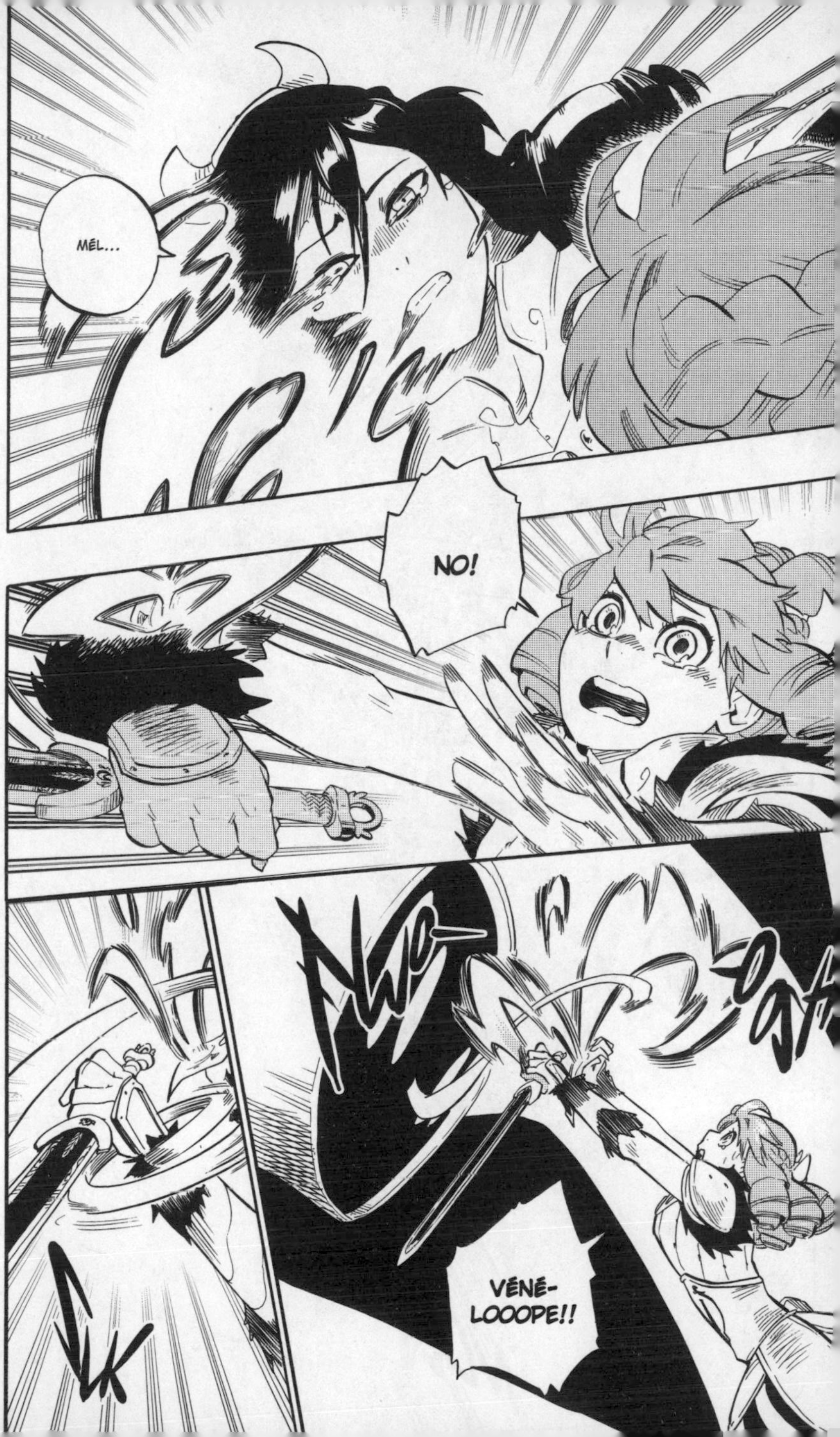
MÉL...
NO!
VÉNÉ-
LOOOPE!!

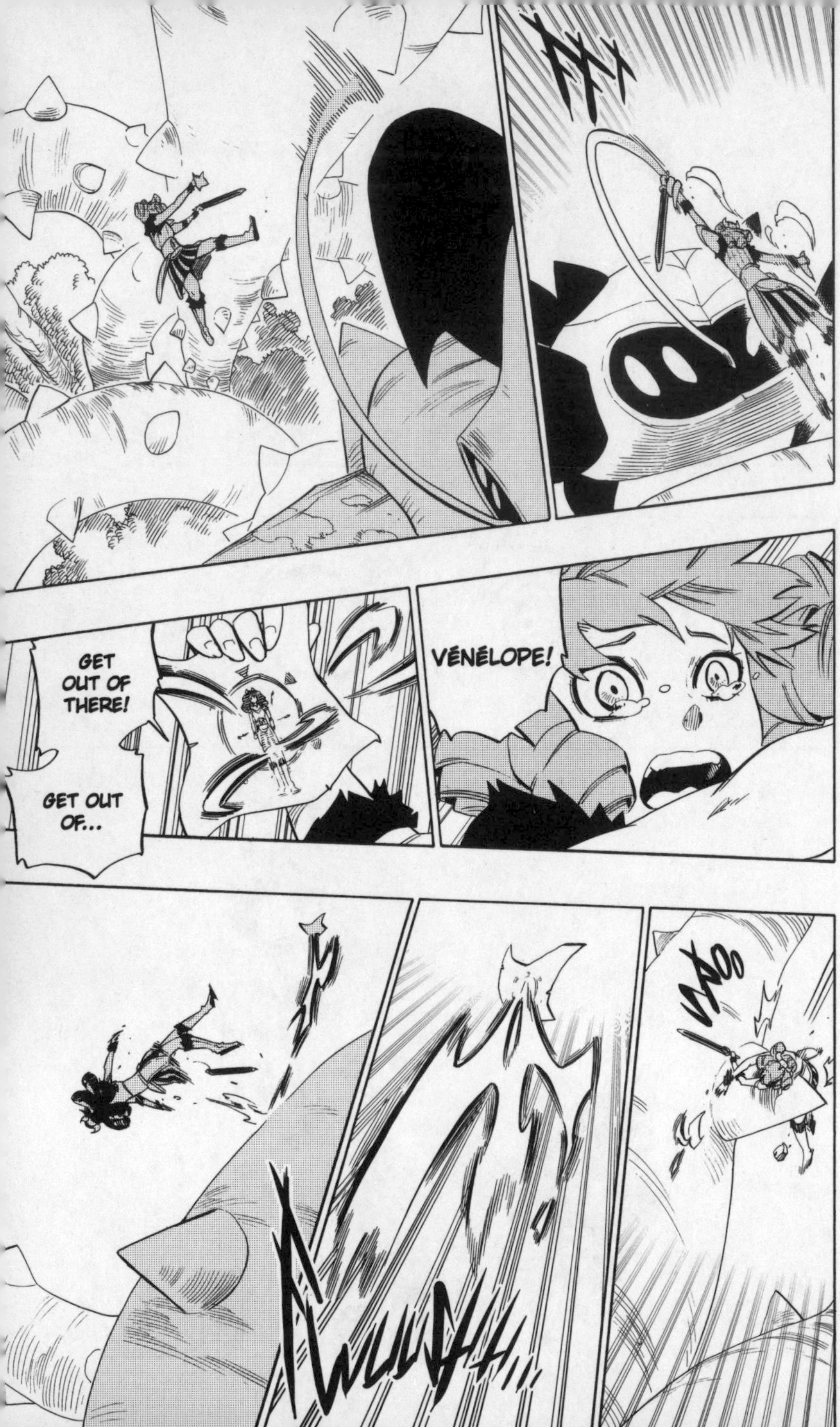
VÉNÉLOPE!
GET OUT OF THERE!
GET OUT OF...

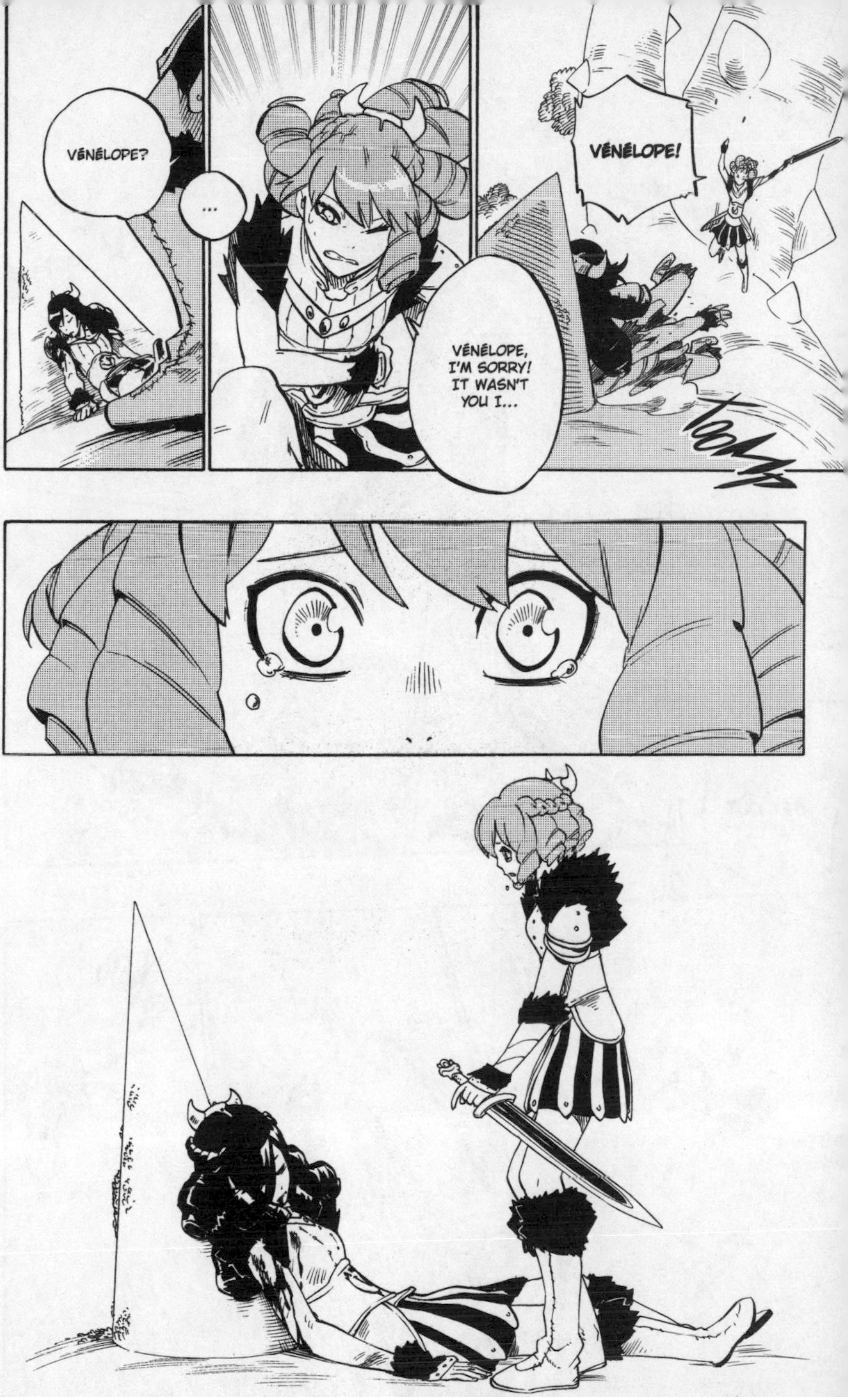
VÉNÉLOPE!
VÉNÉLOPE, I'M SORRY! IT WASN'T YOU I...
VÉNÉLOPE?
...

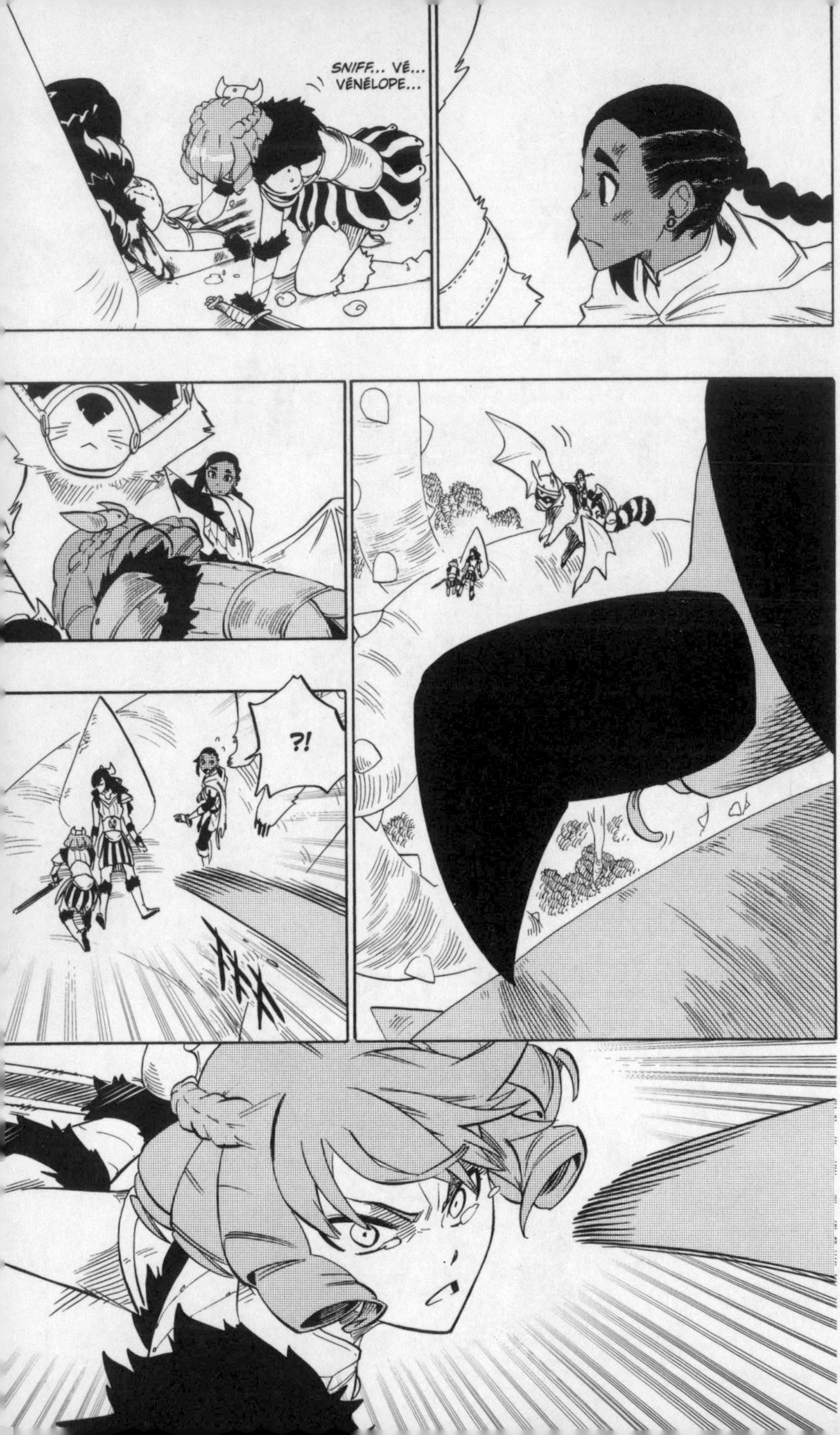
SNIFF... VÉ...
VÉNÉLOPE...
?!

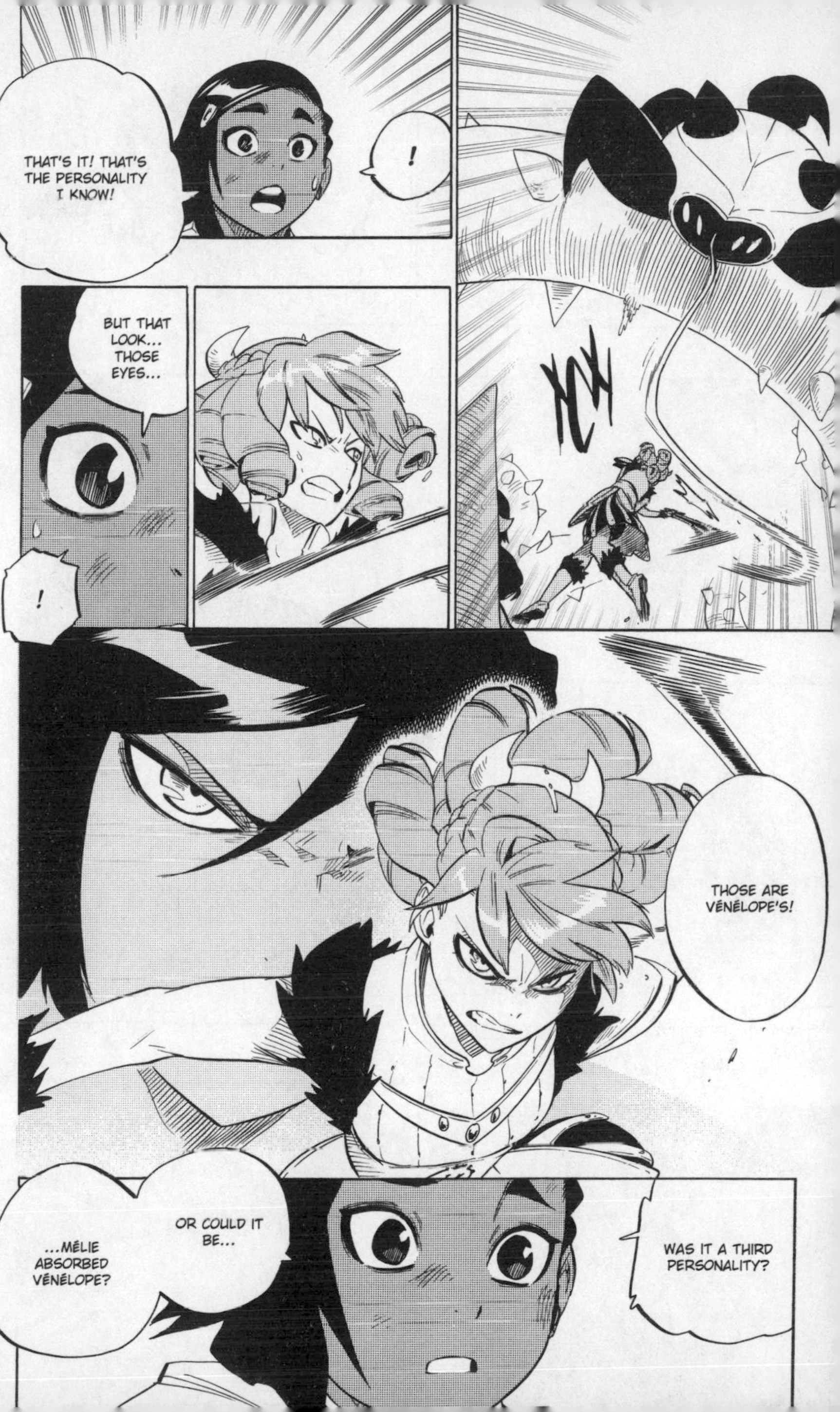
!
THAT'S IT! THAT'S THE PERSONALITY I KNOW!
BUT THAT LOOK... THOSE EYES...
!
THOSE ARE VÉNÉLOPE'S!
WAS IT A THIRD PERSONALITY?
OR COULD IT BE...
...MÉLIE ABSORBED VÉNÉLOPE?

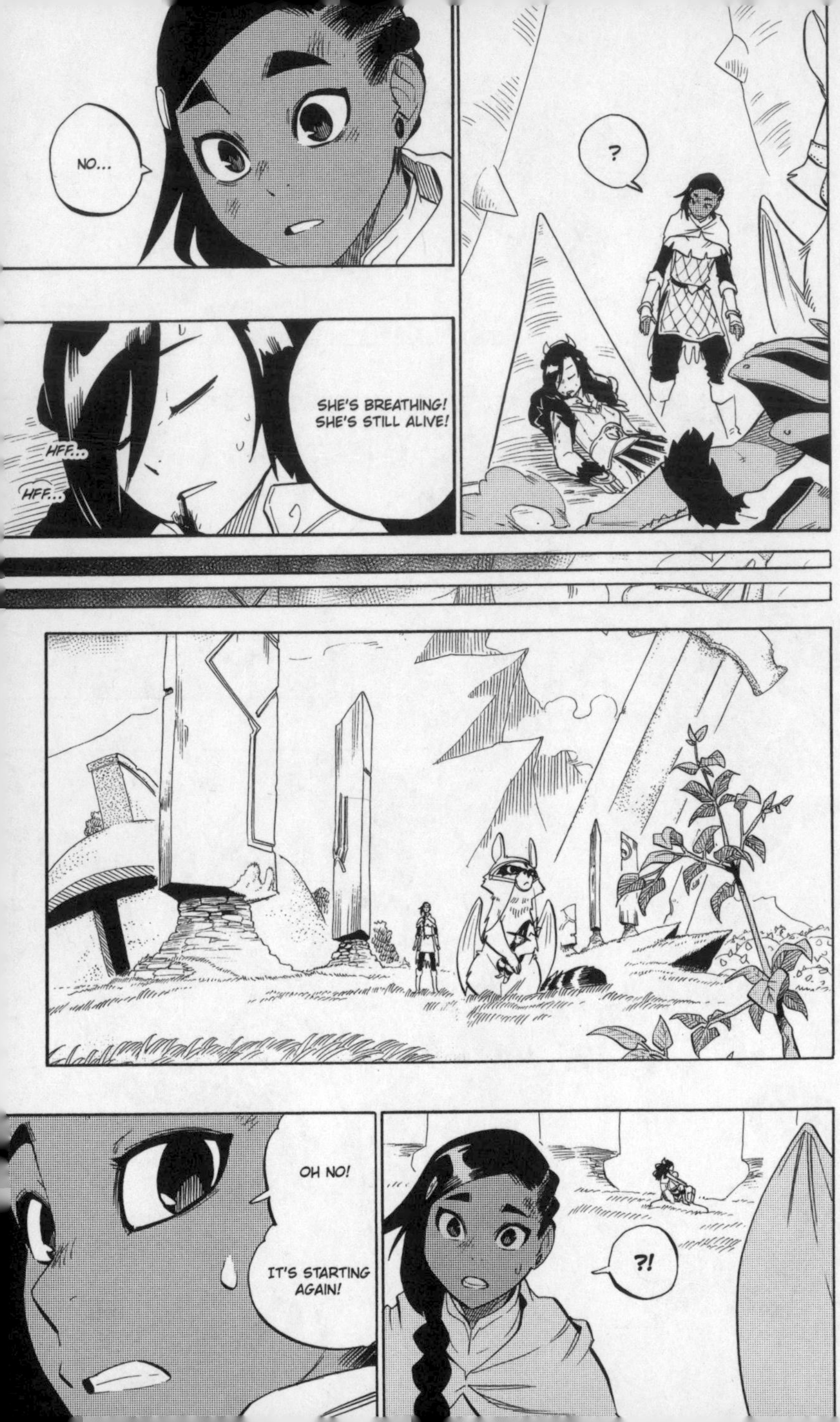
?
NO...
SHE'S BREATHING! SHE'S STILL ALIVE!
HFF...
HFF...
?!
OH NO!
IT'S STARTING AGAIN!

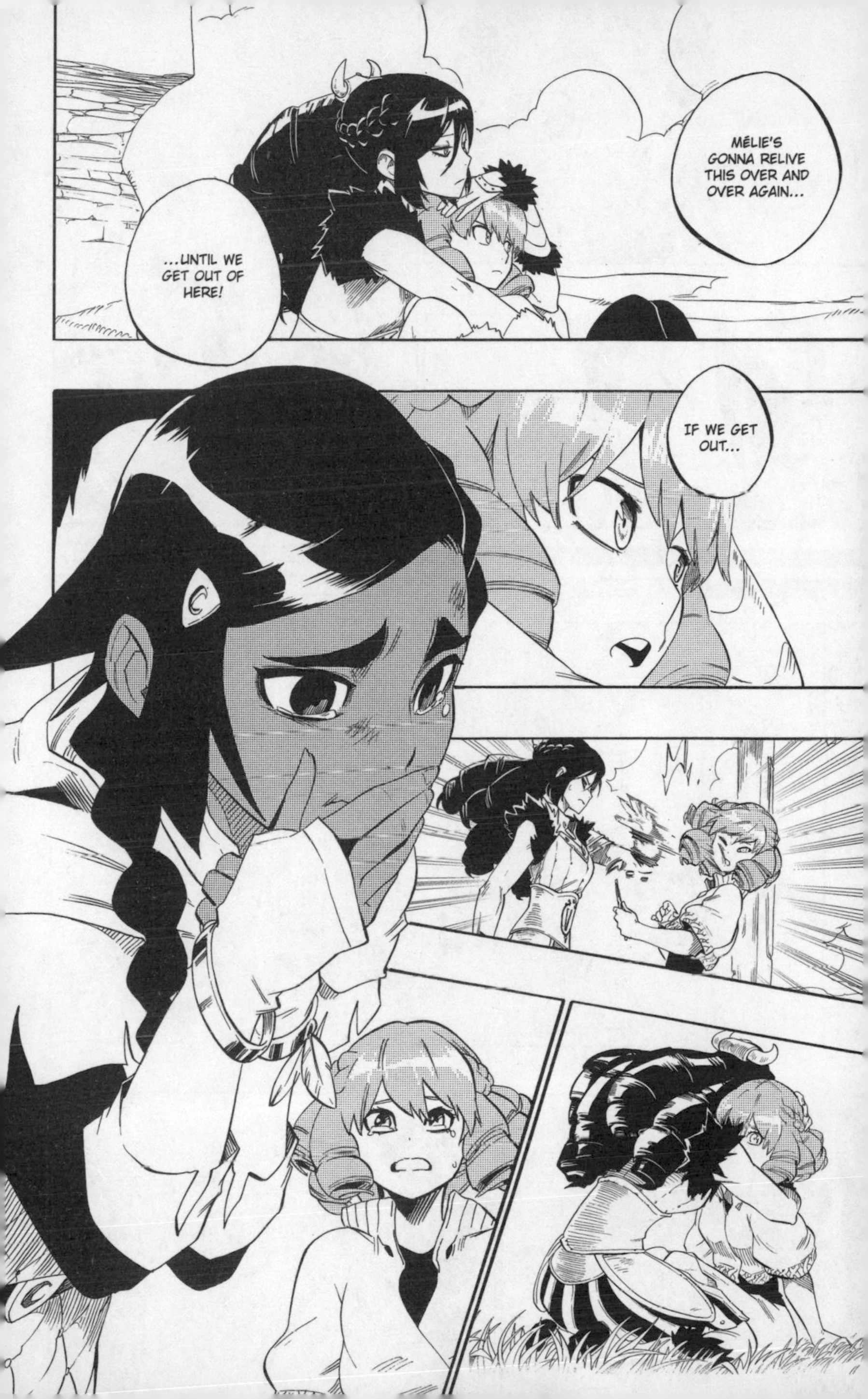
MÉLIE'S GONNA RELIVE THIS OVER AND OVER AGAIN...
...UNTIL WE GET OUT OF HERE!
IF WE GET OUT...

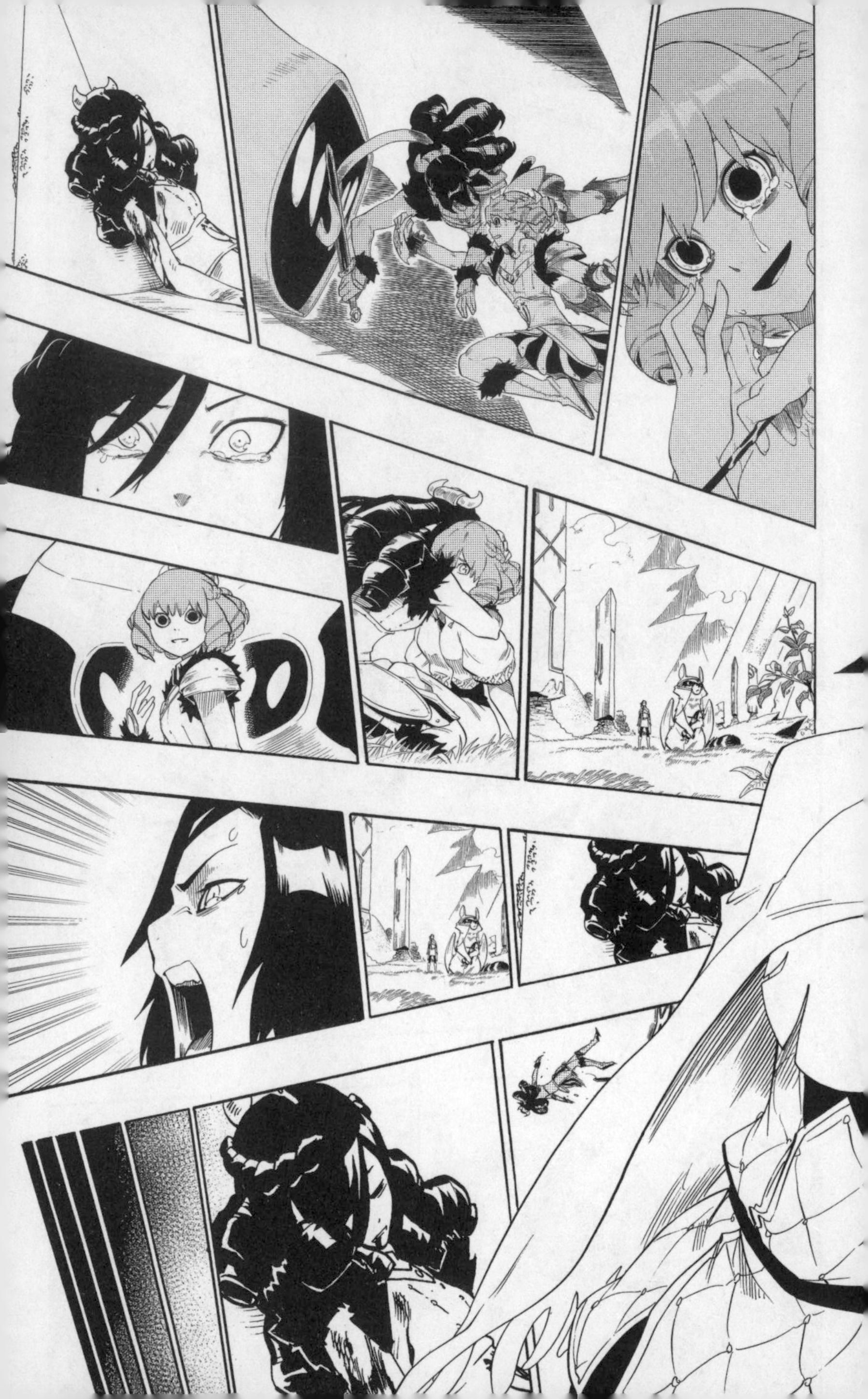

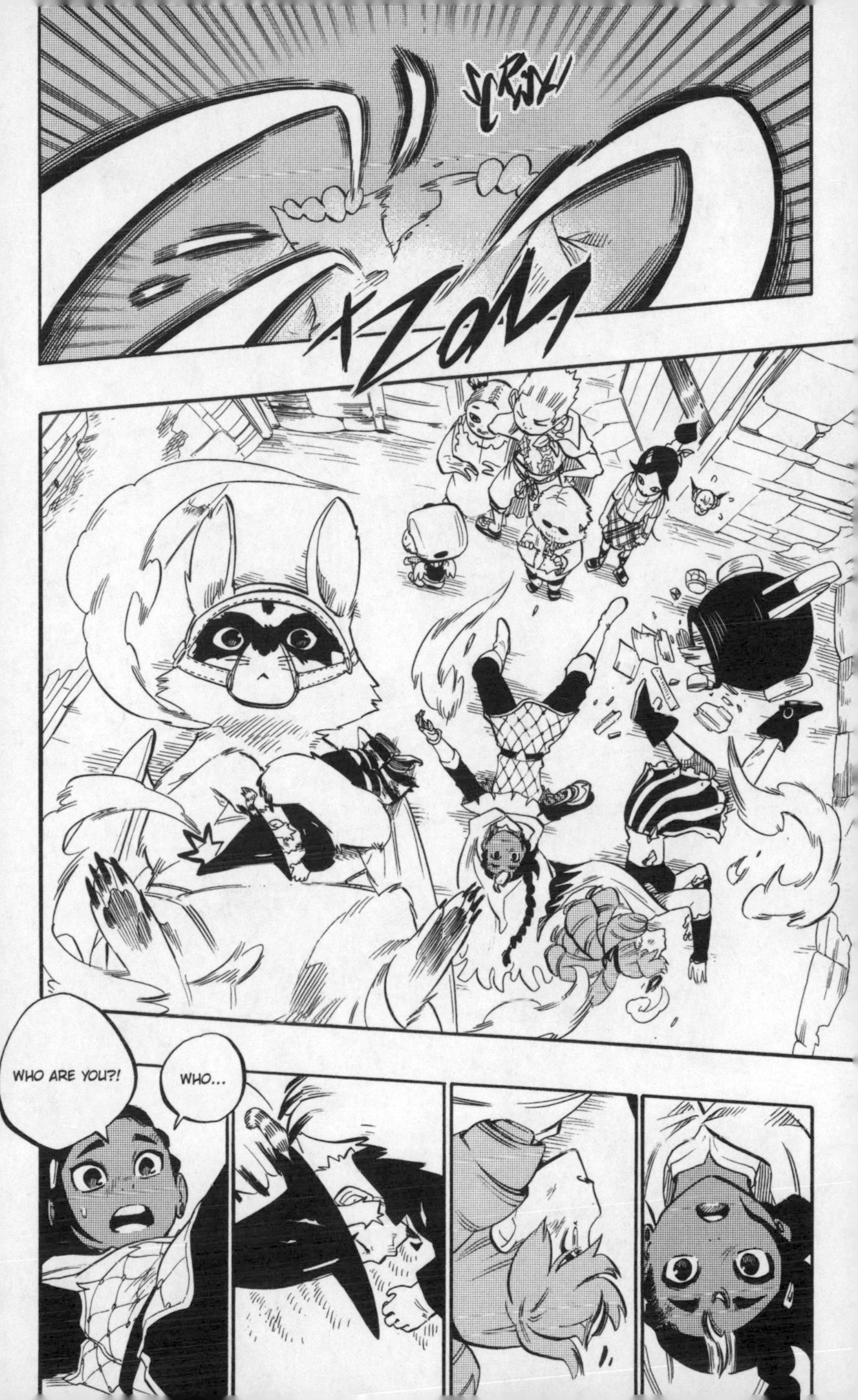
WHO...
WHO ARE YOU?!

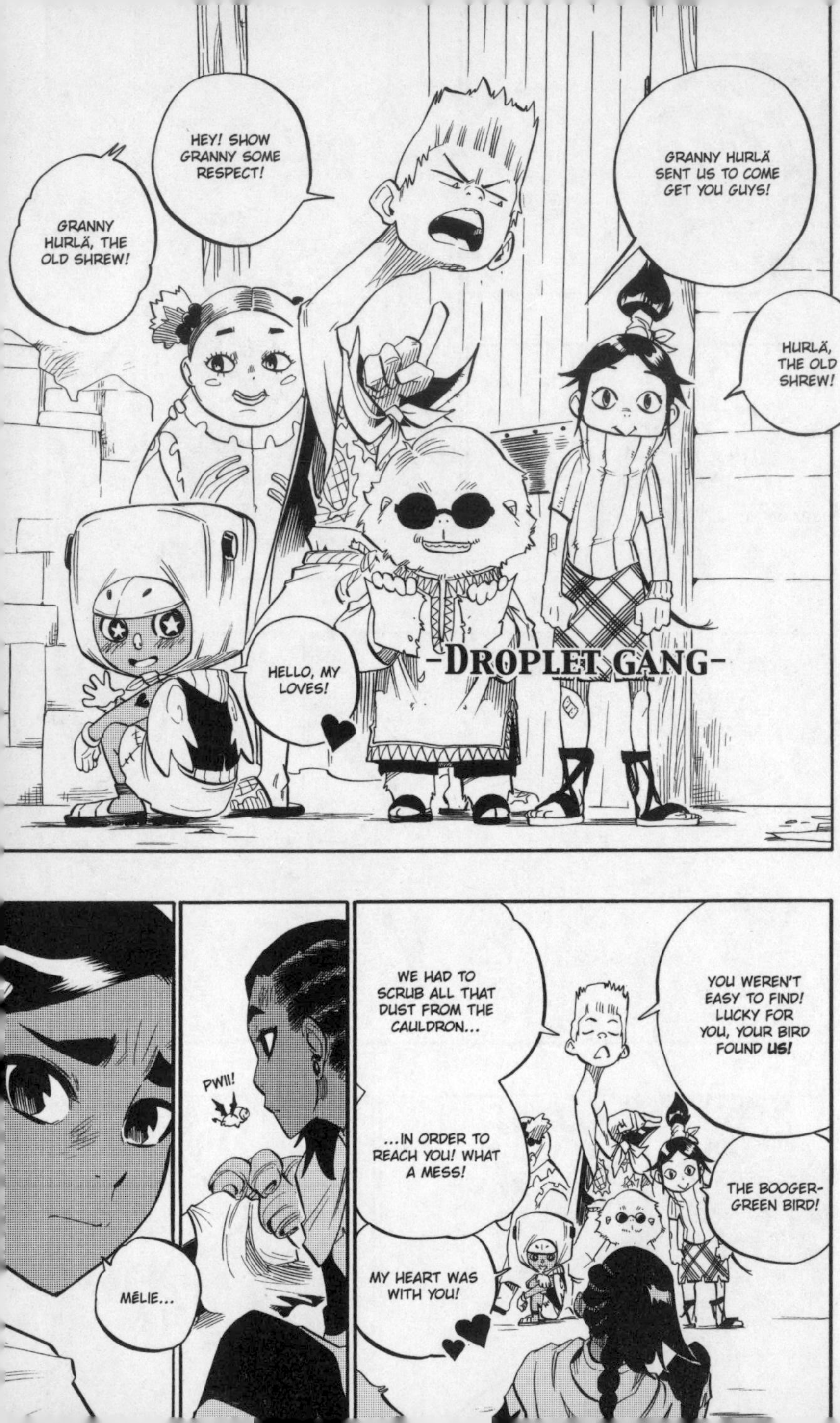
GRANNY HURLÄ SENT US TO COME GET YOU GUYS!
HURLÄ, THE OLD SHREW!
HEY! SHOW GRANNY SOME RESPECT!
GRANNY HURLÄ, THE OLD SHREW!
-DROPLET GANG-
HELLO, MY LOVES!
YOU WEREN'T EASY TO FIND! LUCKY FOR YOU, YOUR BIRD FOUND **US!**
WE HAD TO SCRUB ALL THAT DUST FROM THE CAULDRON...
...IN ORDER TO REACH YOU! WHAT A MESS!
THE BOOGER-GREEN BIRD!
MY HEART WAS WITH YOU!
PWII!
MÉLIE...

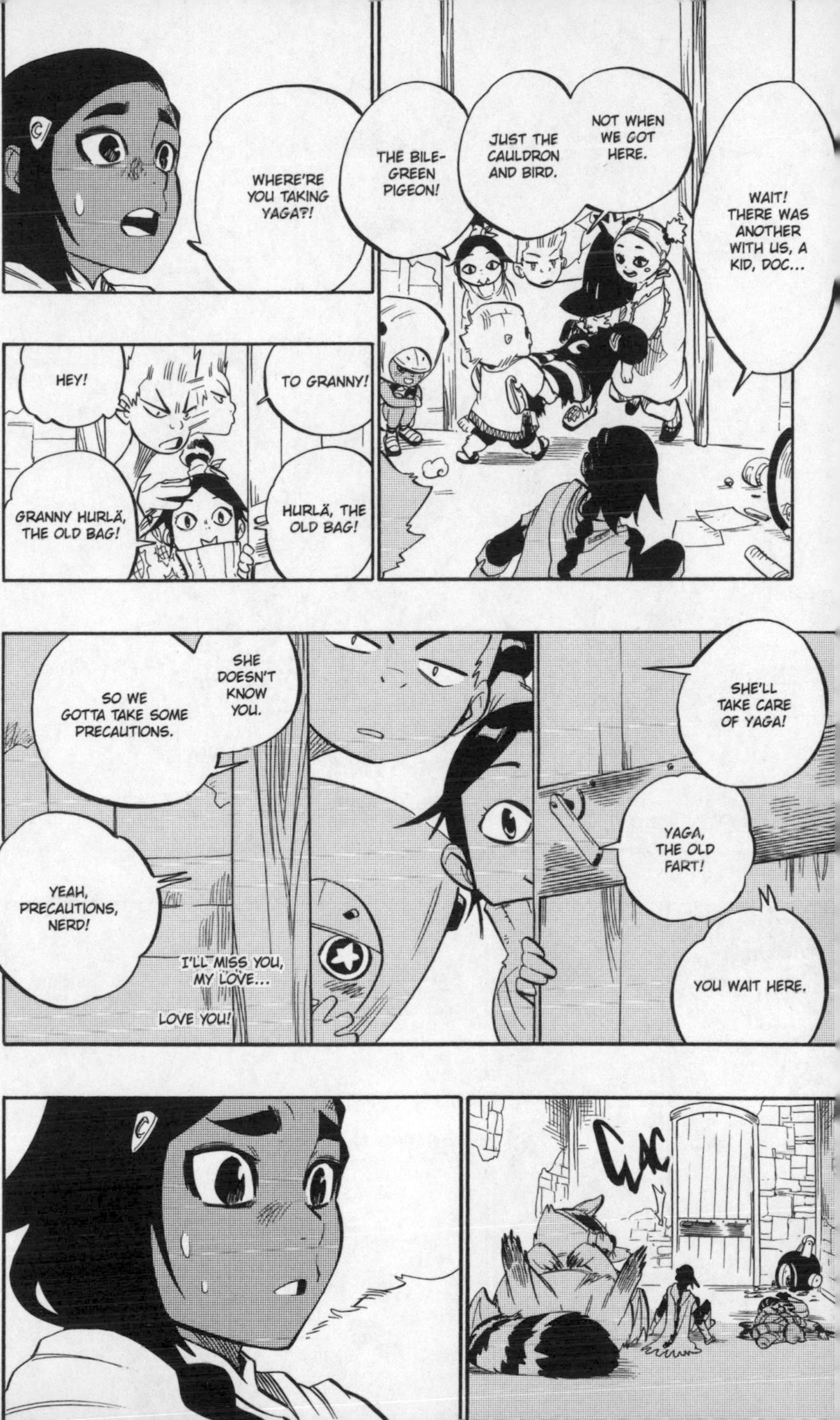
WAIT! THERE WAS ANOTHER WITH US, A KID, DOC...
NOT WHEN WE GOT HERE.
JUST THE CAULDRON AND BIRD.
THE BILE-GREEN PIGEON!
WHERE'RE YOU TAKING YAGA?!
TO GRANNY!
HURLÄ, THE OLD BAG!
HEY!
GRANNY HURLÄ, THE OLD BAG!
SHE'LL TAKE CARE OF YAGA!
YAGA, THE OLD FART!
YOU WAIT HERE.
SHE DOESN'T KNOW YOU.
SO WE GOTTA TAKE SOME PRECAUTIONS.
YEAH, PRECAUTIONS, NERD!
I'LL MISS YOU, MY LOVE...
LOVE YOU!
CLAC

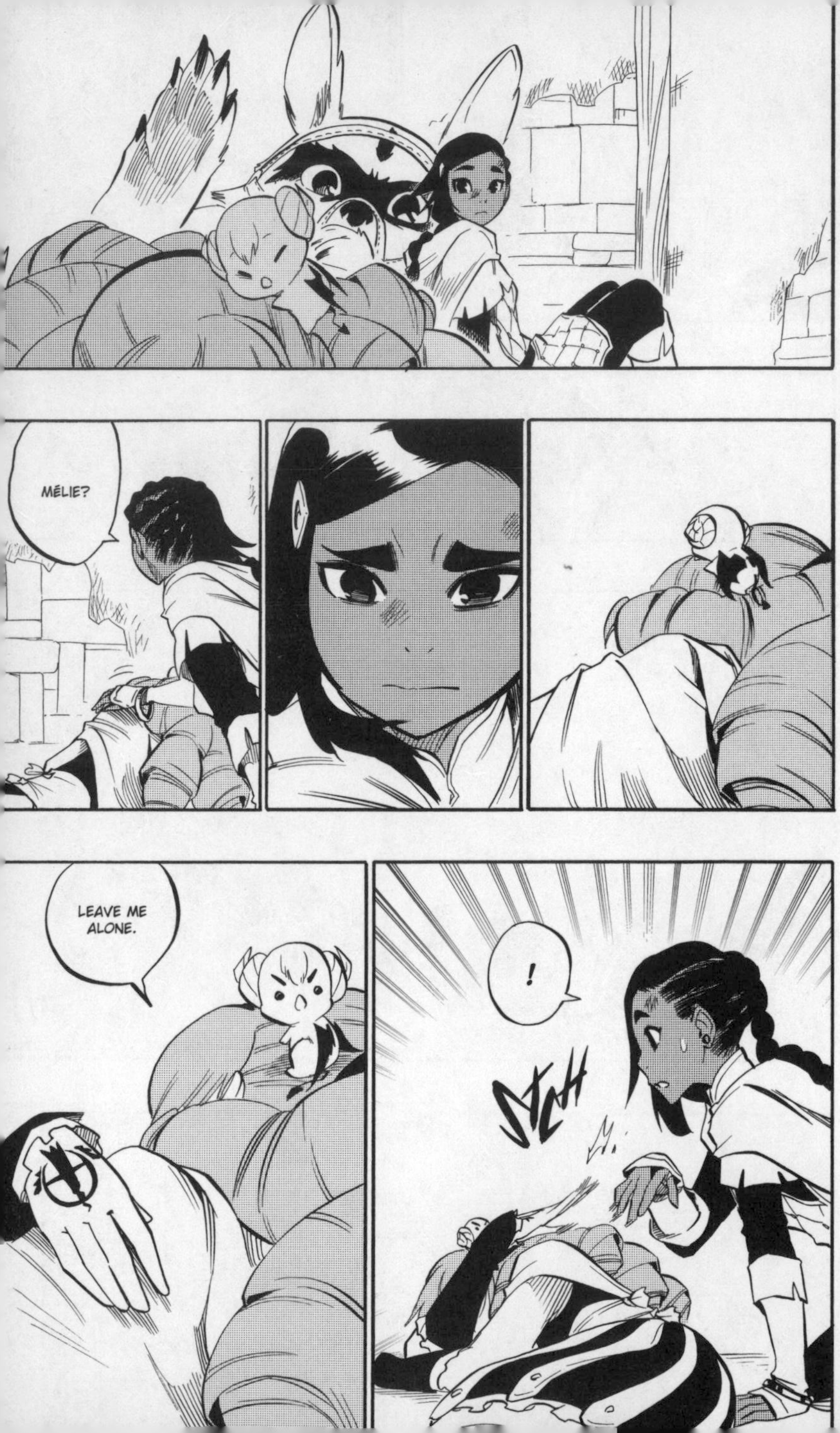
MÉLIE?
!
STCH
LEAVE ME ALONE.

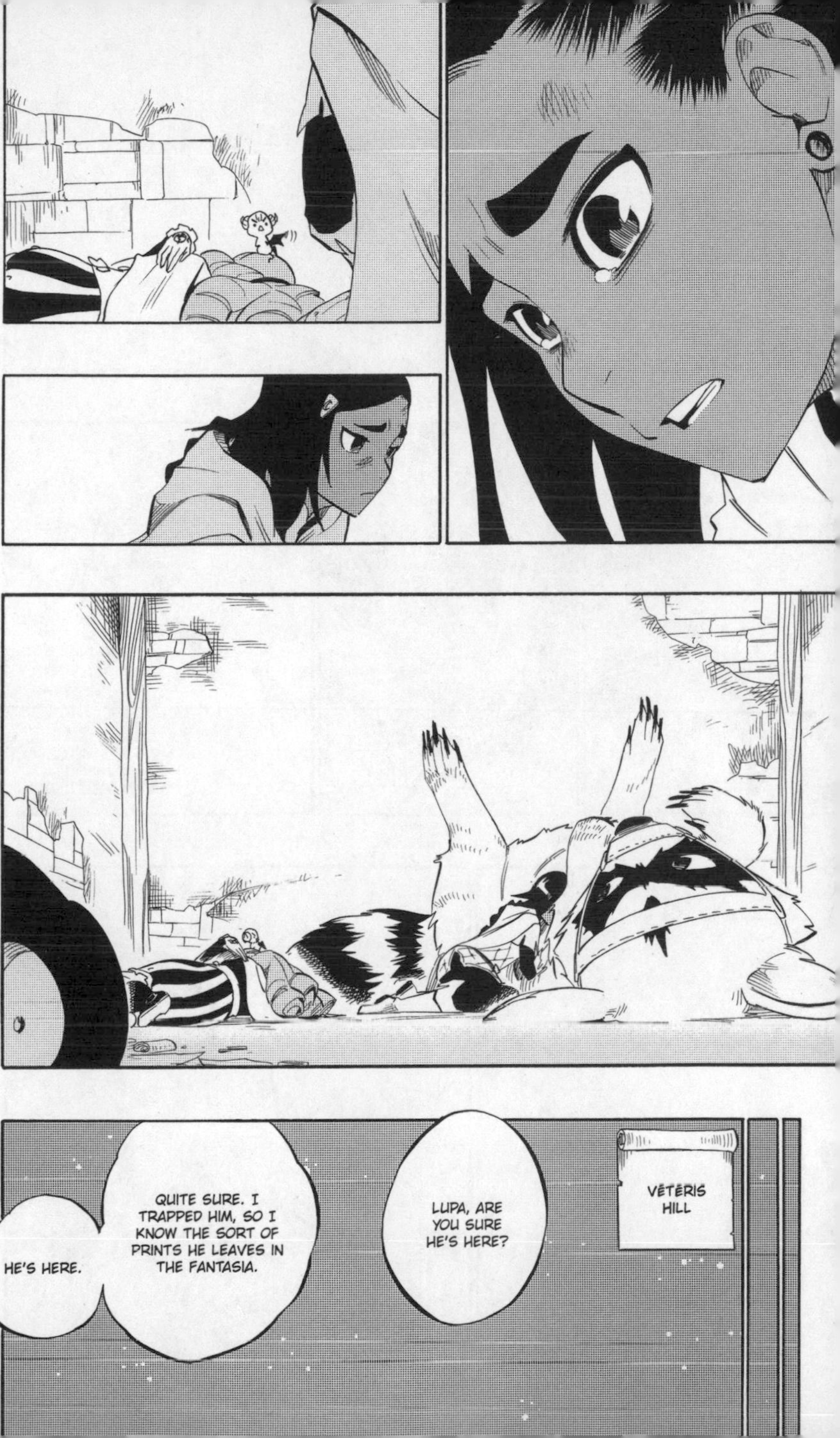
VĒTERIS HILL
LUPA, ARE YOU SURE HE'S HERE?
QUITE SURE. I TRAPPED HIM, SO I KNOW THE SORT OF PRINTS HE LEAVES IN THE FANTASIA.
HE'S HERE.

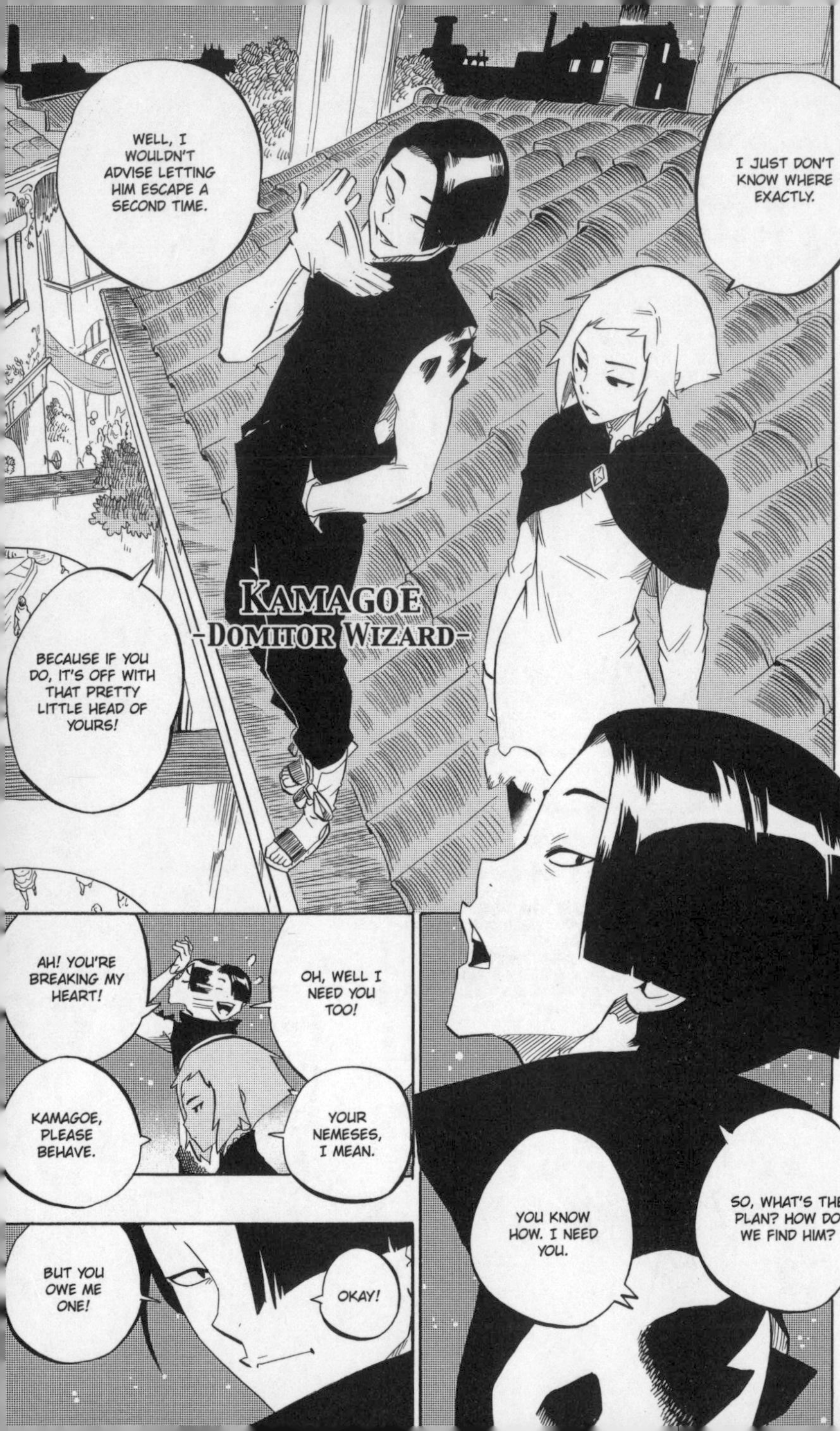
I JUST DON'T KNOW WHERE EXACTLY.
WELL, I WOULDN'T ADVISE LETTING HIM ESCAPE A SECOND TIME.
KAMAGOE
-DOMITOR WIZARD-
BECAUSE IF YOU DO, IT'S OFF WITH THAT PRETTY LITTLE HEAD OF YOURS!
SO, WHAT'S THE PLAN? HOW DO WE FIND HIM?
YOU KNOW HOW. I NEED YOU.
OH, WELL I NEED YOU TOO!
AH! YOU'RE BREAKING MY HEART!
YOUR NEMESES, I MEAN.
KAMAGOE, PLEASE BEHAVE.
OKAY!
BUT YOU OWE ME ONE!

MY DEAREST LOVE,

I CAN'T WAIT TO SEE YOU AGAIN.
THIS WAIT IS KILLING ME...
SOMETIMES, IT FEELS LIKE YOU'RE STILL HERE BY
MY SIDE, BUT THEN I TURN AND... NOTHING. AH,
WHENEVER I THINK BACK TO THE TIME WE MET, MY
HEART LIGHTS UP!
I STILL REMEMBER OUR FIRST CAREFREE MOMENTS
TOGETHER. SO PURE, SO NEW, WHEN OUR LIVES
TOGETHER WERE JUST STARTING.
BE STRONG, FOR THIS LONG-DISTANCE
RELATIONSHIP WILL SURELY SOLIDIFY OUR LOVE.
AS FOR ME, I WOULDN'T CHANGE ANYTHING ABOUT
THESE 12 MINUTES I HAVE SPENT LOVING YOU.

COME BACK TO ME SOON.
YOUR PIPOU

Pipou ♡

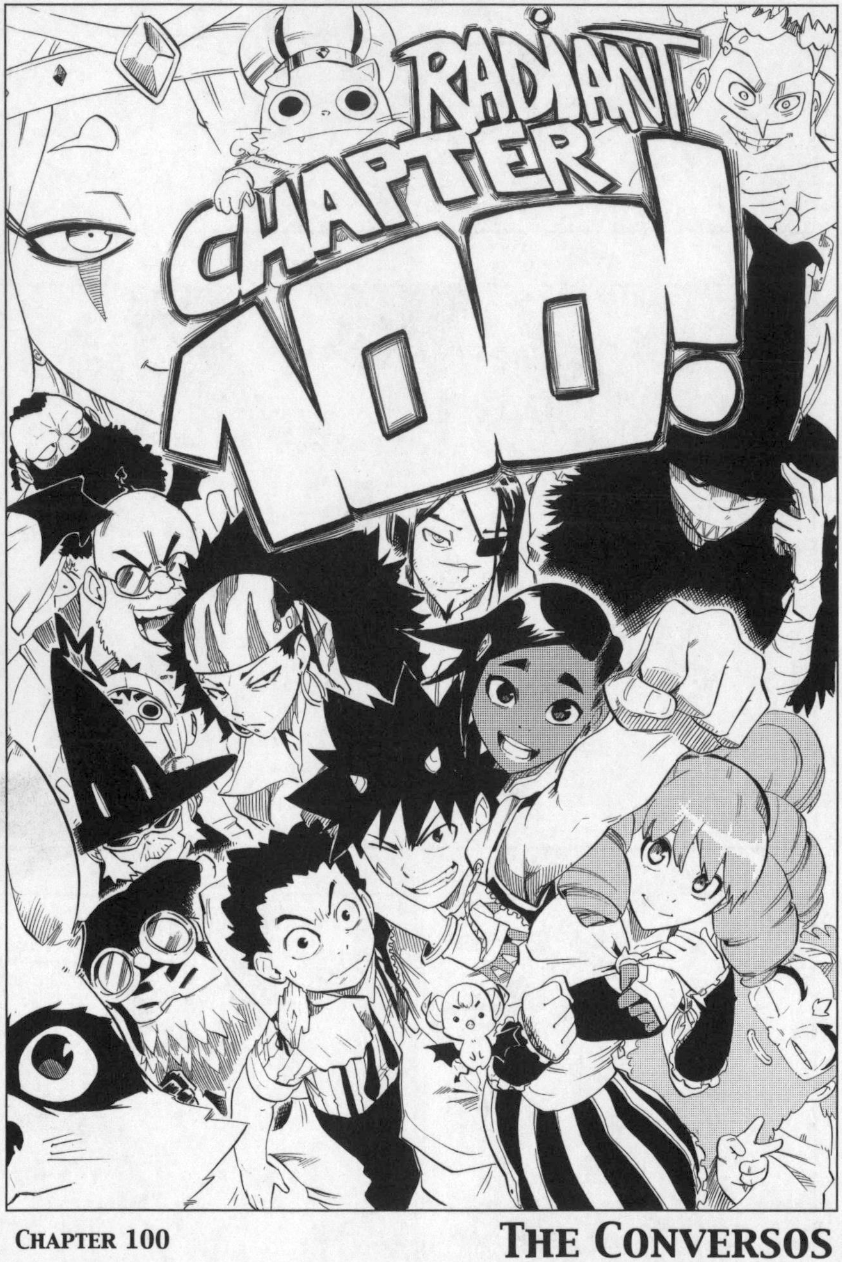
RADIANT
CHAPTER 100!

Chapter 100 **The Conversos**

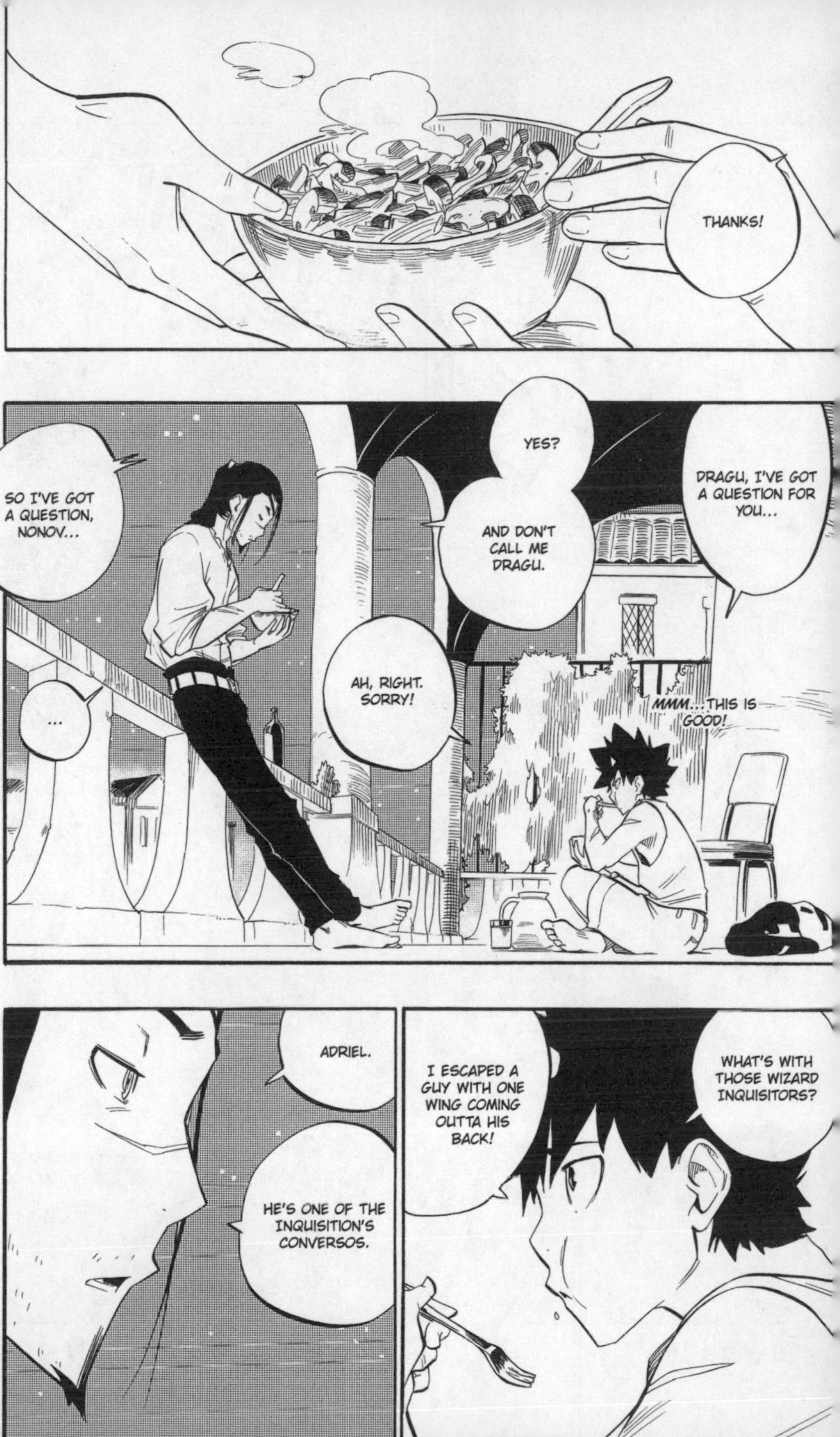
THANKS!
DRAGU, I'VE GOT A QUESTION FOR YOU...
YES?
AND DON'T CALL ME DRAGU.
AH, RIGHT. SORRY!
MMM... THIS IS GOOD!
SO I'VE GOT A QUESTION, NONOV...
...
WHAT'S WITH THOSE WIZARD INQUISITORS?
I ESCAPED A GUY WITH ONE WING COMING OUTTA HIS BACK!
ADRIEL.
HE'S ONE OF THE INQUISITION'S CONVERSOS.

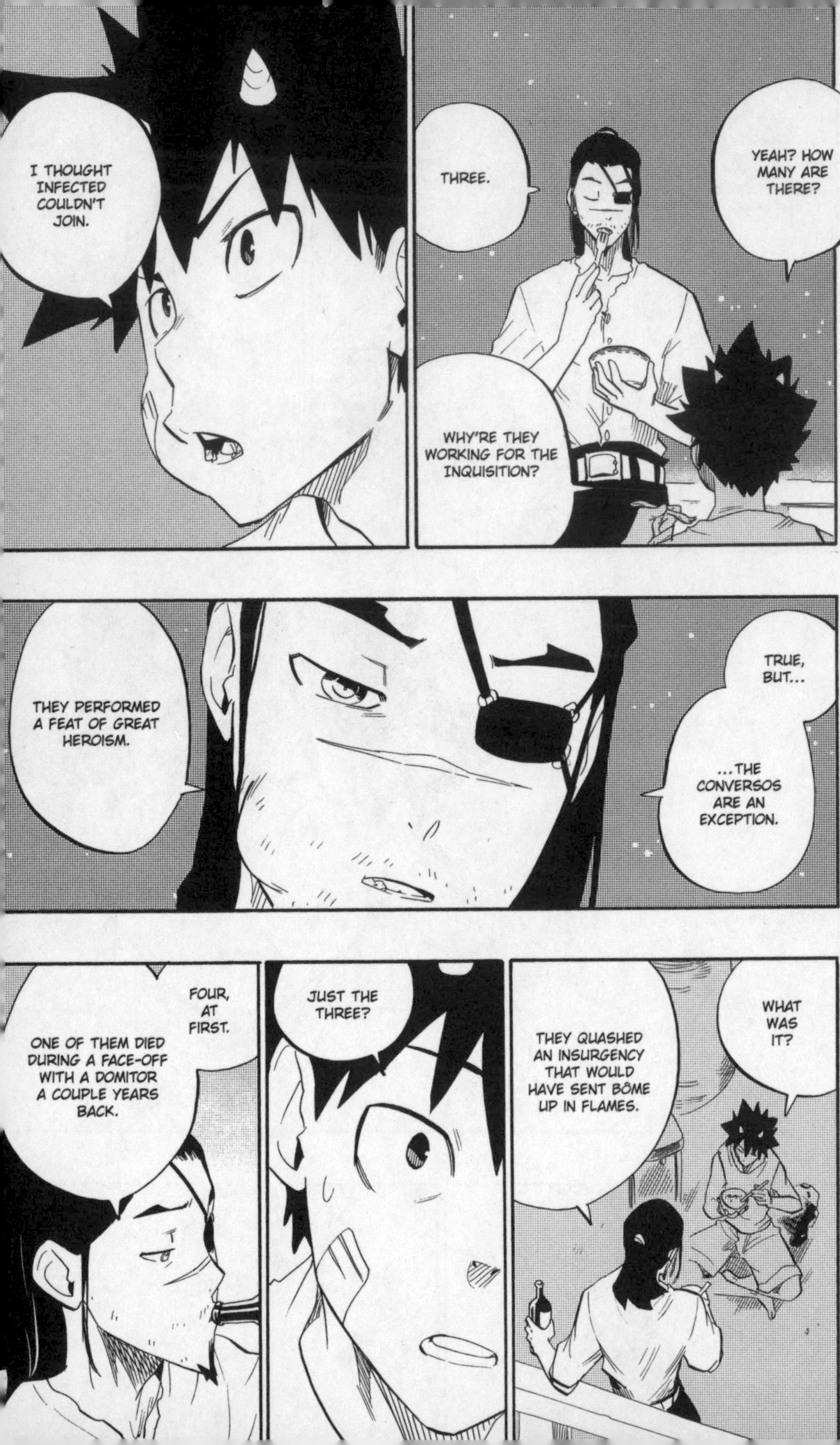
YEAH? HOW MANY ARE THERE?
THREE.
WHY'RE THEY WORKING FOR THE INQUISITION?
I THOUGHT INFECTED COULDN'T JOIN.
TRUE, BUT...
...THE CONVERSOS ARE AN EXCEPTION.
THEY PERFORMED A FEAT OF GREAT HEROISM.
WHAT WAS IT?
THEY QUASHED AN INSURGENCY THAT WOULD HAVE SENT BÔME UP IN FLAMES.
JUST THE THREE?
FOUR, AT FIRST.
ONE OF THEM DIED DURING A FACE-OFF WITH A DOMITOR A COUPLE YEARS BACK.

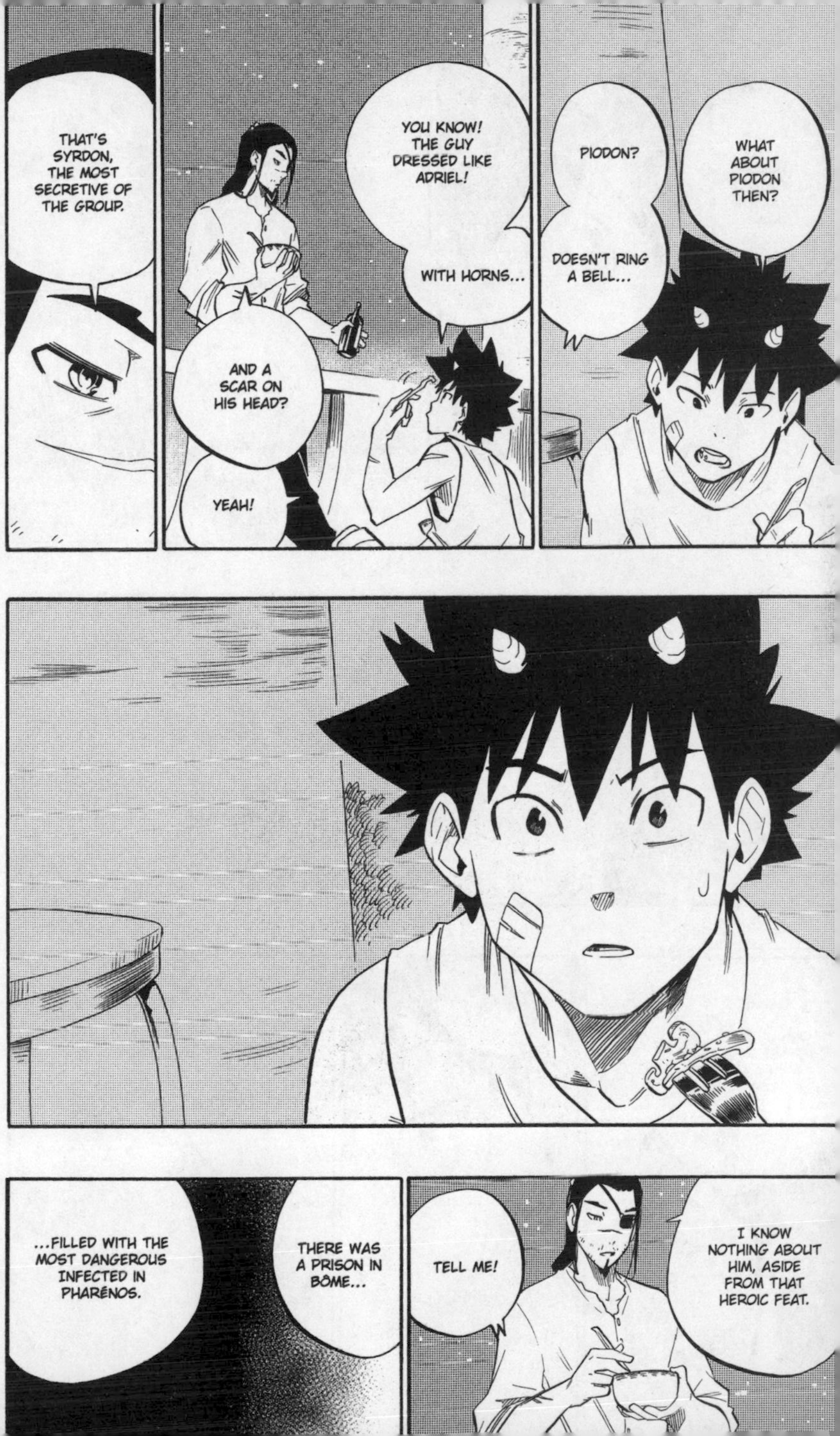
WHAT ABOUT PIODON THEN?
PIODON?
DOESN'T RING A BELL...
YOU KNOW! THE GUY DRESSED LIKE ADRIEL!
WITH HORNS...
AND A SCAR ON HIS HEAD?
YEAH!
THAT'S SYRDON, THE MOST SECRETIVE OF THE GROUP.
I KNOW NOTHING ABOUT HIM, ASIDE FROM THAT HEROIC FEAT.
TELL ME!
THERE WAS A PRISON IN BÔME...
...FILLED WITH THE MOST DANGEROUS INFECTED IN PHARÉNOS.

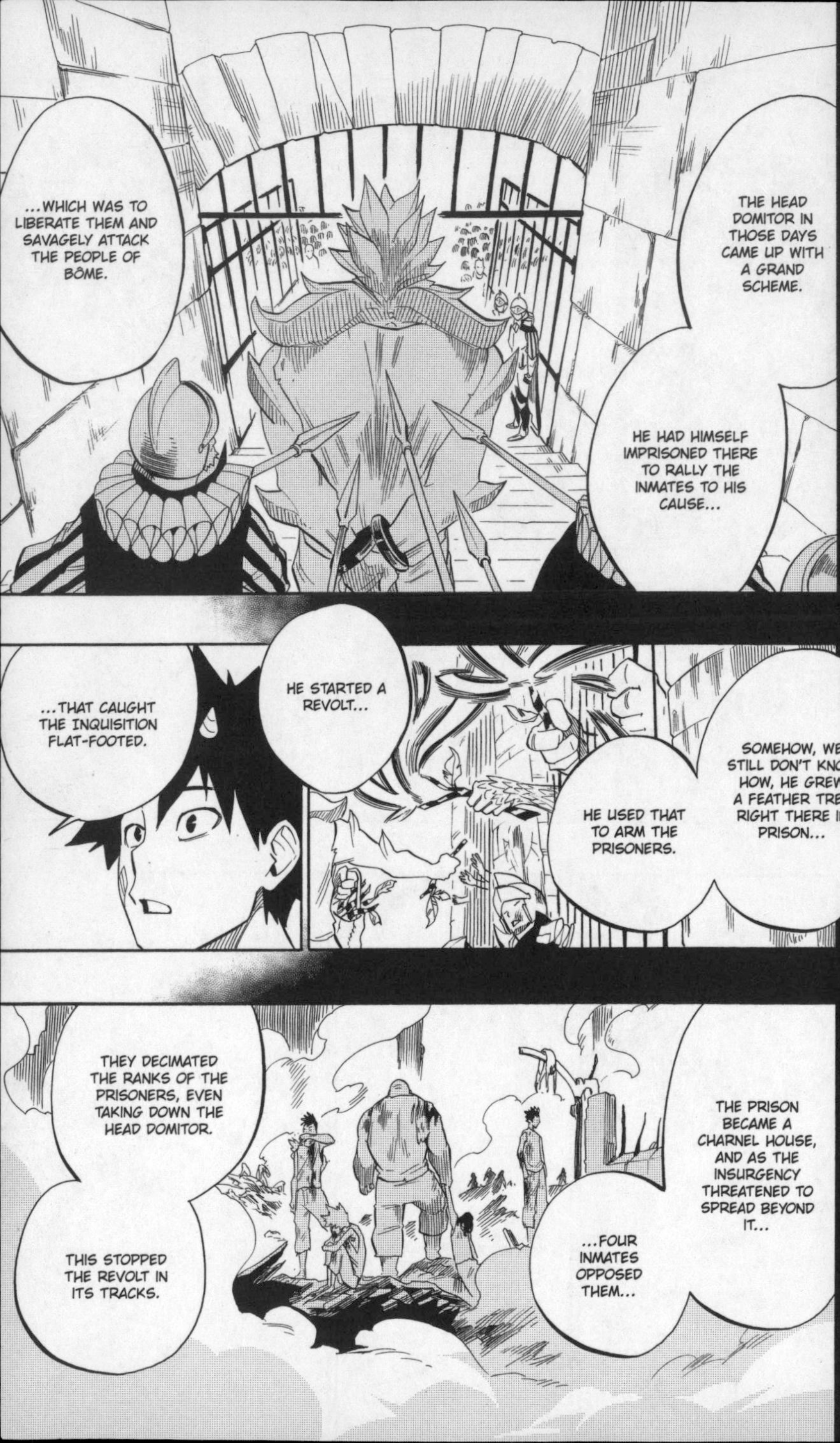
THE HEAD DOMITOR IN THOSE DAYS CAME UP WITH A GRAND SCHEME.
HE HAD HIMSELF IMPRISONED THERE TO RALLY THE INMATES TO HIS CAUSE...
...WHICH WAS TO LIBERATE THEM AND SAVAGELY ATTACK THE PEOPLE OF BÔME.
SOMEHOW, WE STILL DON'T KNOW HOW, HE GREW A FEATHER TREE RIGHT THERE IN PRISON...
HE USED THAT TO ARM THE PRISONERS.
HE STARTED A REVOLT...
...THAT CAUGHT THE INQUISITION FLAT-FOOTED.
THE PRISON BECAME A CHARNEL HOUSE, AND AS THE INSURGENCY THREATENED TO SPREAD BEYOND IT...
...FOUR INMATES OPPOSED THEM...
THEY DECIMATED THE RANKS OF THE PRISONERS, EVEN TAKING DOWN THE HEAD DOMITOR.
THIS STOPPED THE REVOLT IN ITS TRACKS.

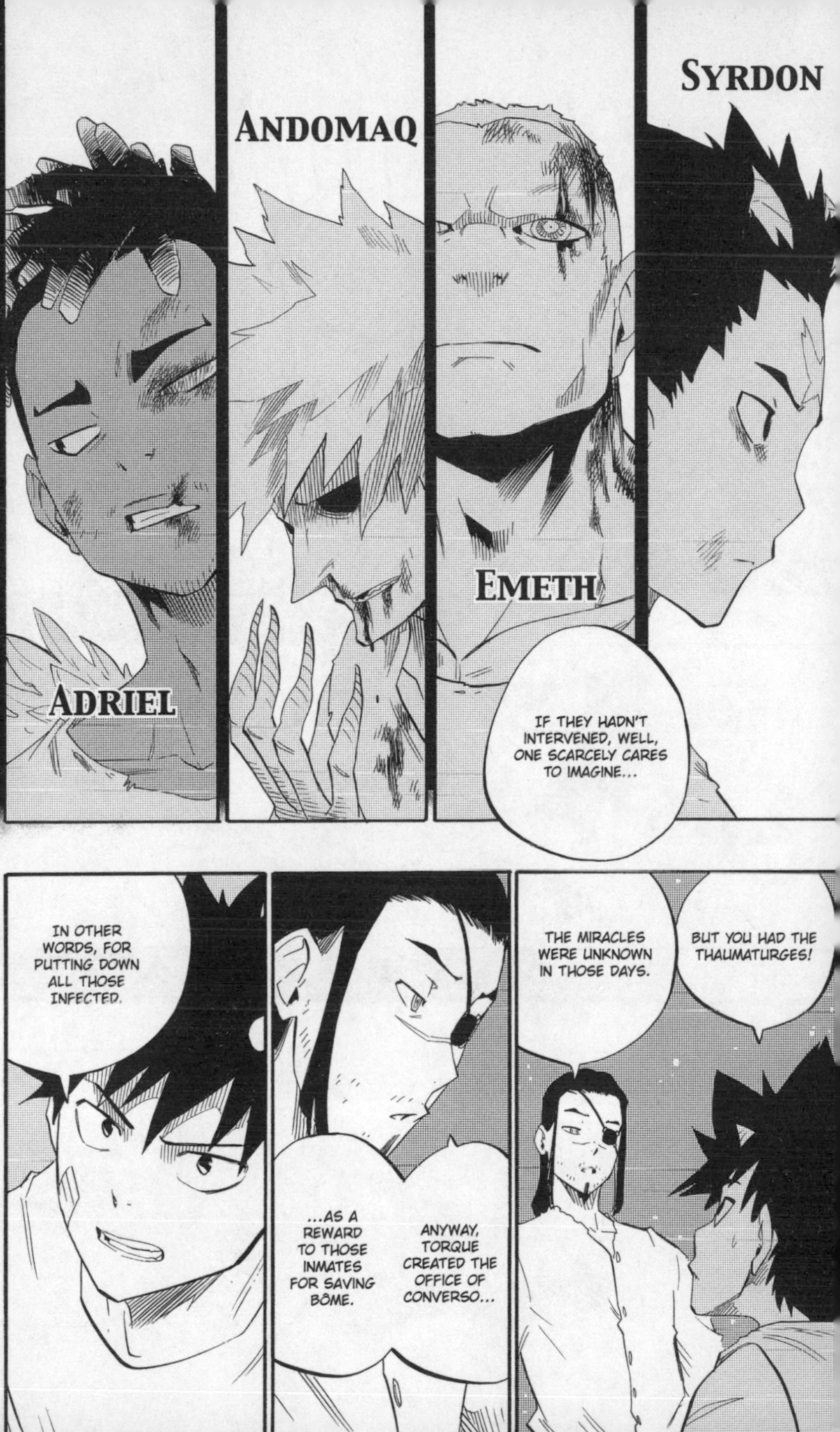

SYRDON
EMETH
IF THEY HADN'T INTERVENED, WELL, ONE SCARCELY CARES TO IMAGINE...
ANDOMAQ
ADRIEL
BUT YOU HAD THE THAUMATURGES!
THE MIRACLES WERE UNKNOWN IN THOSE DAYS.
ANYWAY, TORQUE CREATED THE OFFICE OF CONVERSO...
...AS A REWARD TO THOSE INMATES FOR SAVING BÔME.
IN OTHER WORDS, FOR PUTTING DOWN ALL THOSE INFECTED.

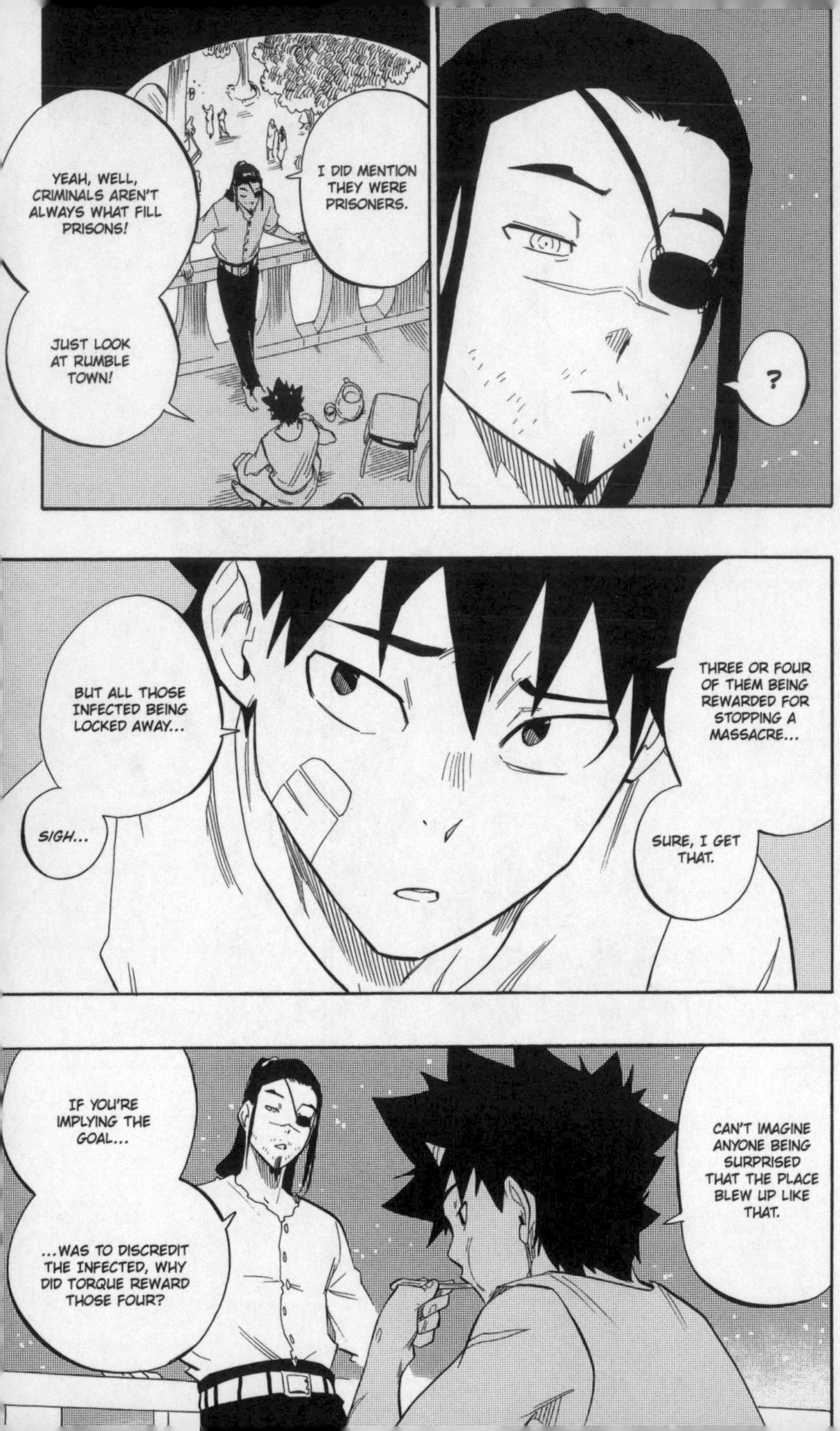
?
I DID MENTION THEY WERE PRISONERS.
YEAH, WELL, CRIMINALS AREN'T ALWAYS WHAT FILL PRISONS!
JUST LOOK AT RUMBLE TOWN!
THREE OR FOUR OF THEM BEING REWARDED FOR STOPPING A MASSACRE...
SURE, I GET THAT.
BUT ALL THOSE INFECTED BEING LOCKED AWAY...
SIGH...
CAN'T IMAGINE ANYONE BEING SURPRISED THAT THE PLACE BLEW UP LIKE THAT.
IF YOU'RE IMPLYING THE GOAL...
...WAS TO DISCREDIT THE INFECTED, WHY DID TORQUE REWARD THOSE FOUR?

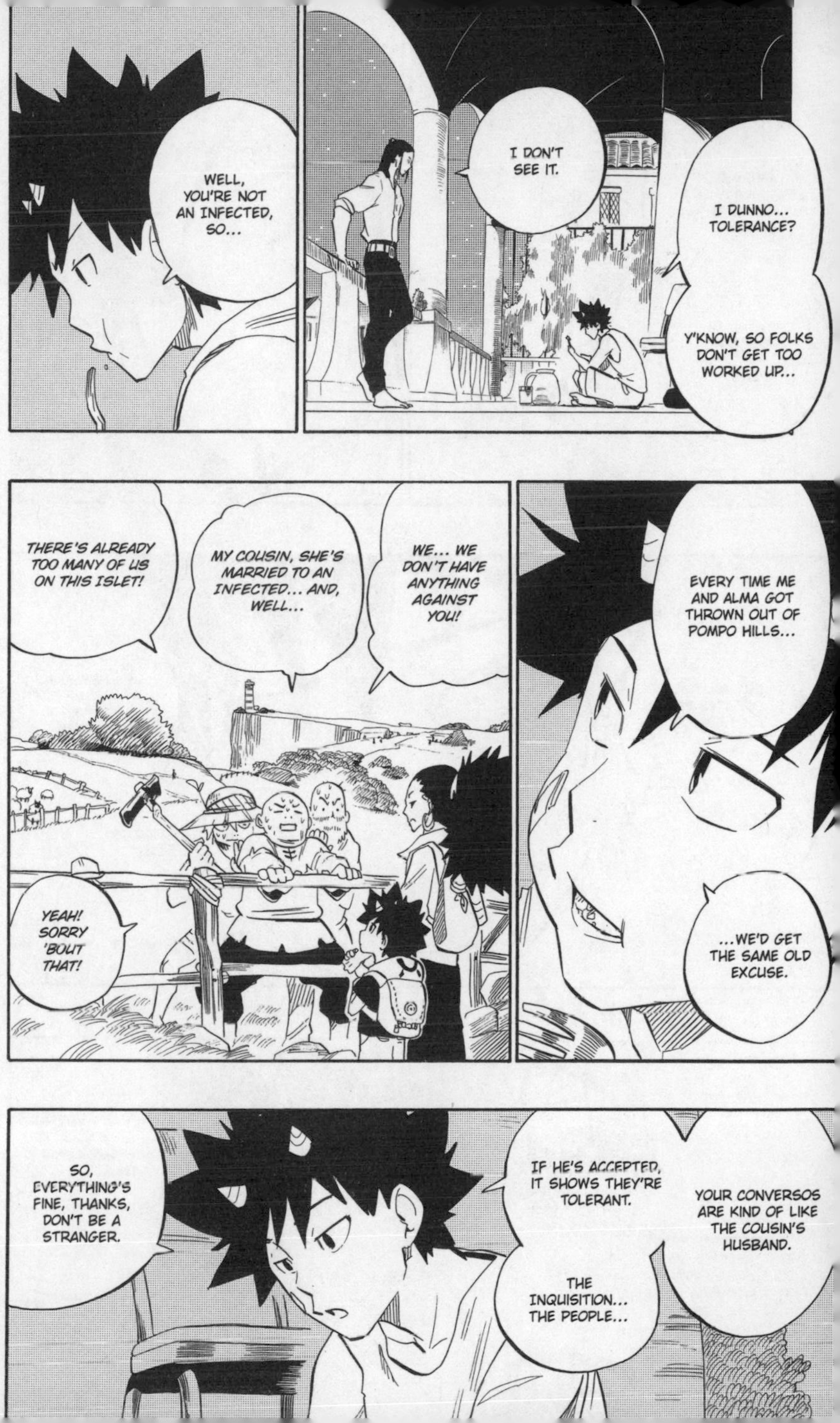
I DUNNO... TOLERANCE?
Y'KNOW, SO FOLKS DON'T GET TOO WORKED UP...
I DON'T SEE IT.
WELL, YOU'RE NOT AN INFECTED, SO...
EVERY TIME ME AND ALMA GOT THROWN OUT OF POMPO HILLS...
...WE'D GET THE SAME OLD EXCUSE.
WE... WE DON'T HAVE ANYTHING AGAINST YOU!
MY COUSIN, SHE'S MARRIED TO AN INFECTED... AND, WELL...
THERE'S ALREADY TOO MANY OF US ON THIS ISLET!
YEAH! SORRY 'BOUT THAT!
YOUR CONVERSOS ARE KIND OF LIKE THE COUSIN'S HUSBAND.
IF HE'S ACCEPTED, IT SHOWS THEY'RE TOLERANT.
THE INQUISITION... THE PEOPLE...
SO, EVERYTHING'S FINE, THANKS, DON'T BE A STRANGER.

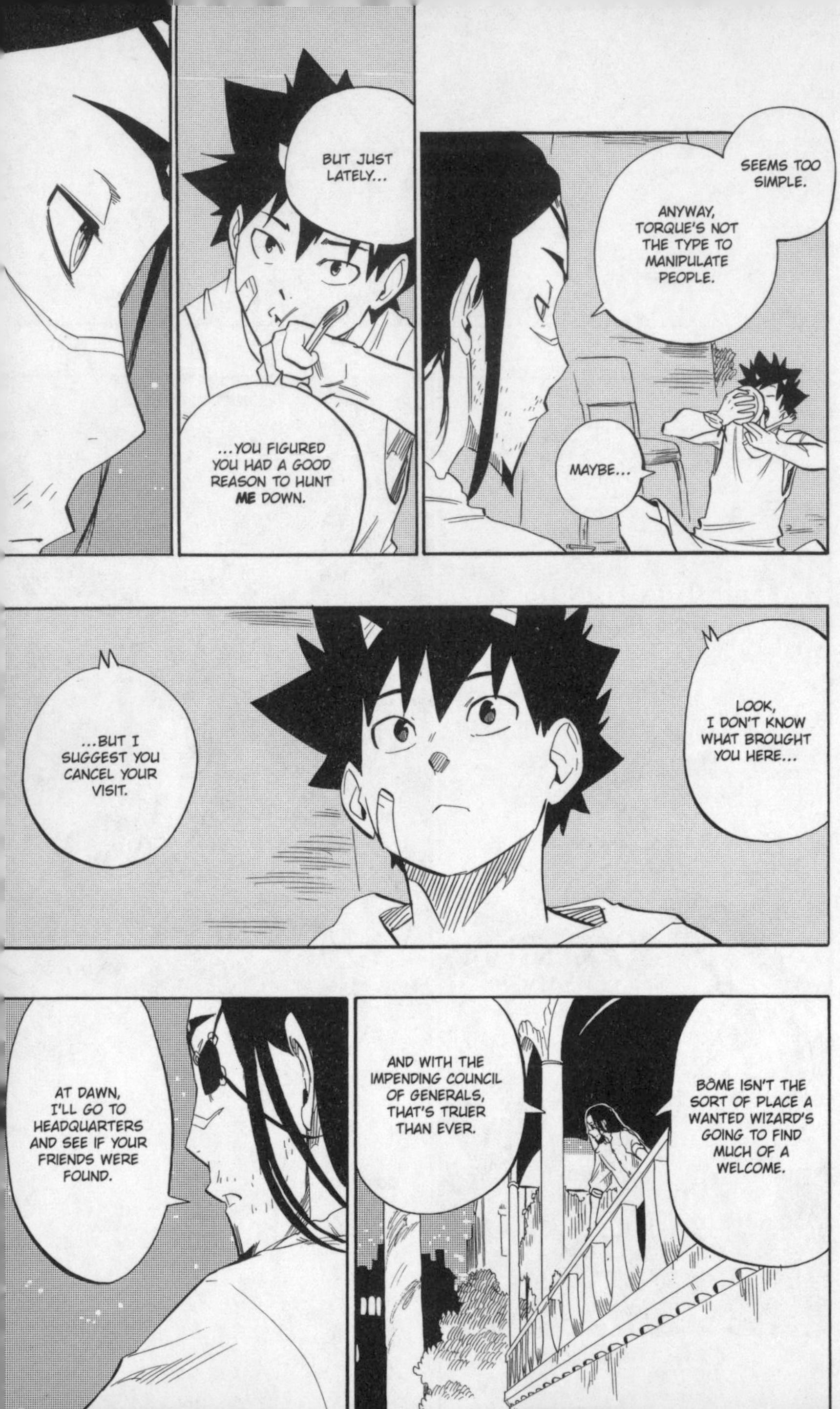
SEEMS TOO SIMPLE.
ANYWAY, TORQUE'S NOT THE TYPE TO MANIPULATE PEOPLE.
MAYBE...
BUT JUST LATELY...
...YOU FIGURED YOU HAD A GOOD REASON TO HUNT **ME** DOWN.
LOOK, I DON'T KNOW WHAT BROUGHT YOU HERE...
...BUT I SUGGEST YOU CANCEL YOUR VISIT.
BÔME ISN'T THE SORT OF PLACE A WANTED WIZARD'S GOING TO FIND MUCH OF A WELCOME.
AND WITH THE IMPENDING COUNCIL OF GENERALS, THAT'S TRUER THAN EVER.
AT DAWN, I'LL GO TO HEADQUARTERS AND SEE IF YOUR FRIENDS WERE FOUND.

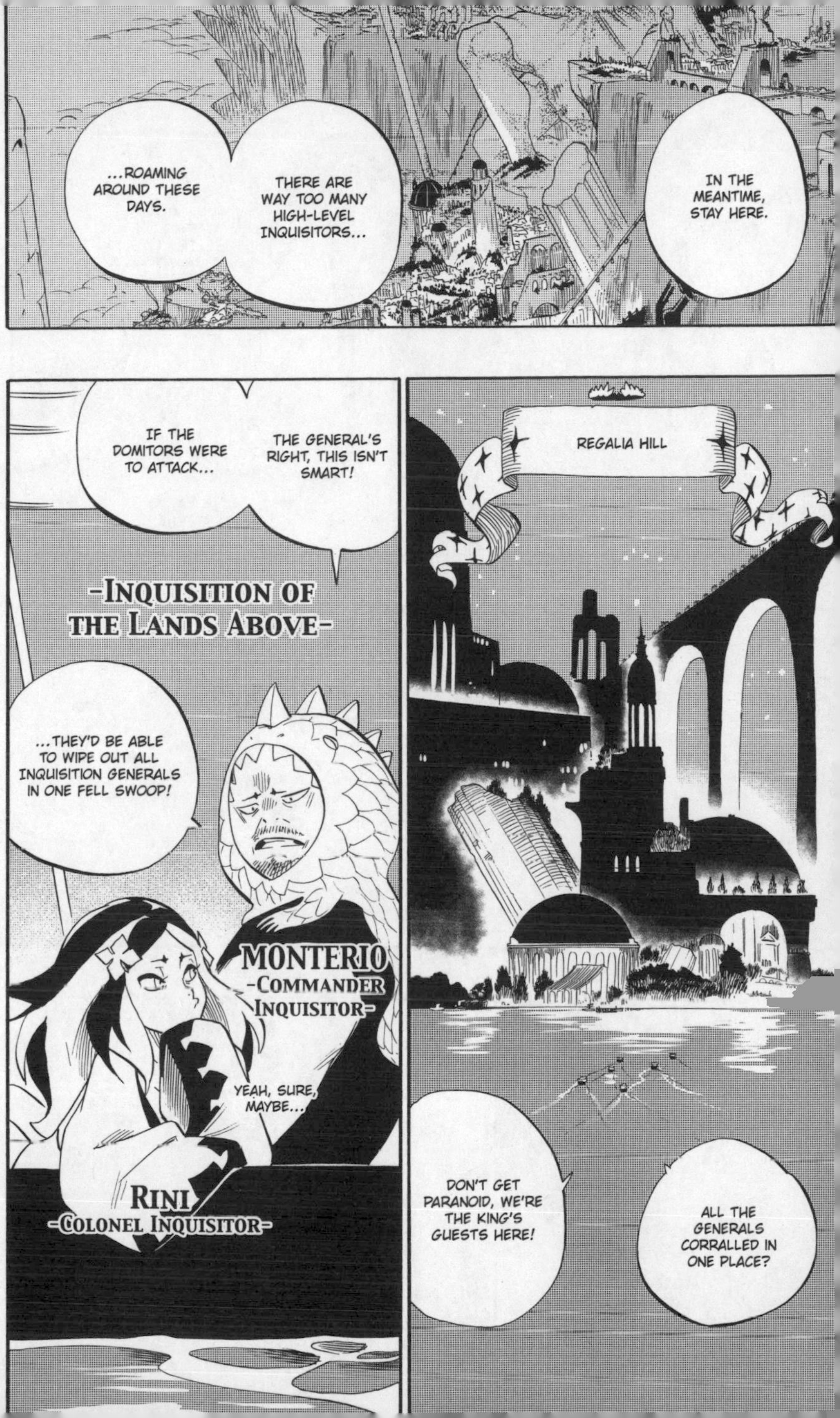
IN THE MEANTIME, STAY HERE.
THERE ARE WAY TOO MANY HIGH-LEVEL INQUISITORS...
...ROAMING AROUND THESE DAYS.
REGALIA HILL
ALL THE GENERALS CORRALLED IN ONE PLACE?
DON'T GET PARANOID, WE'RE THE KING'S GUESTS HERE!
THE GENERAL'S RIGHT, THIS ISN'T SMART!
IF THE DOMITORS WERE TO ATTACK...
-INQUISITION OF THE LANDS ABOVE-
...THEY'D BE ABLE TO WIPE OUT ALL INQUISITION GENERALS IN ONE FELL SWOOP!
MONTERIO -COMMANDER INQUISITOR-
YEAH, SURE, MAYBE...
RINI -COLONEL INQUISITOR-

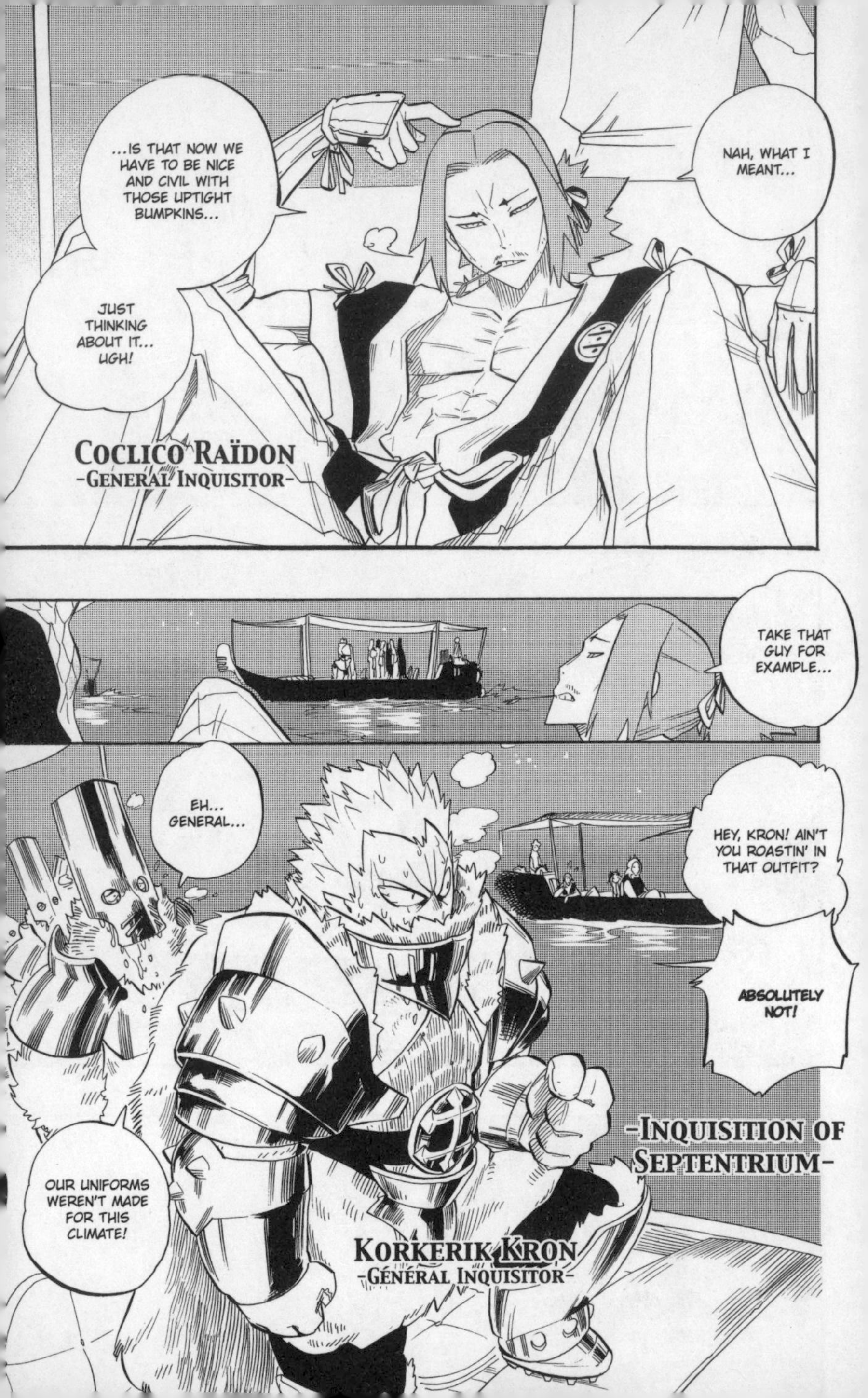
NAH, WHAT I MEANT...
...IS THAT NOW WE HAVE TO BE NICE AND CIVIL WITH THOSE UPTIGHT BUMPKINS...
JUST THINKING ABOUT IT... UGH!
COCLICO RAÏDON
-GENERAL INQUISITOR-
TAKE THAT GUY FOR EXAMPLE...
HEY, KRON! AIN'T YOU ROASTIN' IN THAT OUTFIT?
ABSOLUTELY NOT!
-INQUISITION OF SEPTENTRIUM-
EH... GENERAL...
KORKERIK KRON
-GENERAL INQUISITOR-
OUR UNIFORMS WEREN'T MADE FOR THIS CLIMATE!

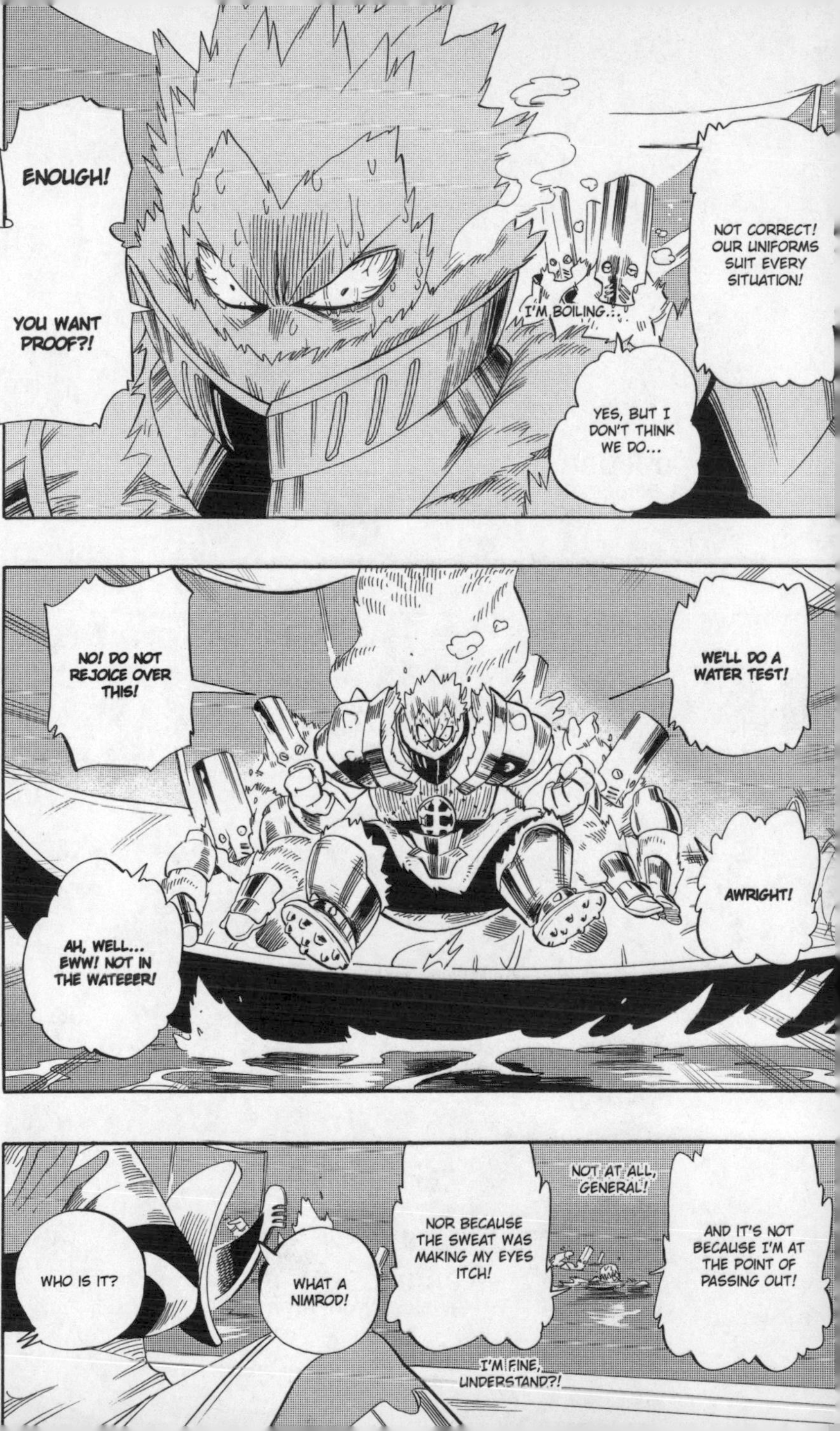
NOT CORRECT! OUR UNIFORMS SUIT EVERY SITUATION!
I'M BOILING...
YES, BUT I DON'T THINK WE DO...
ENOUGH!
YOU WANT PROOF?!
WE'LL DO A WATER TEST!
AWRIGHT!
NO! DO NOT REJOICE OVER THIS!
AH, WELL... EWW! NOT IN THE WATEEER!
AND IT'S NOT BECAUSE I'M AT THE POINT OF PASSING OUT!
NOT AT ALL, GENERAL!
NOR BECAUSE THE SWEAT WAS MAKING MY EYES ITCH!
I'M FINE, UNDERSTAND?!
WHAT A NIMROD!
WHO IS IT?

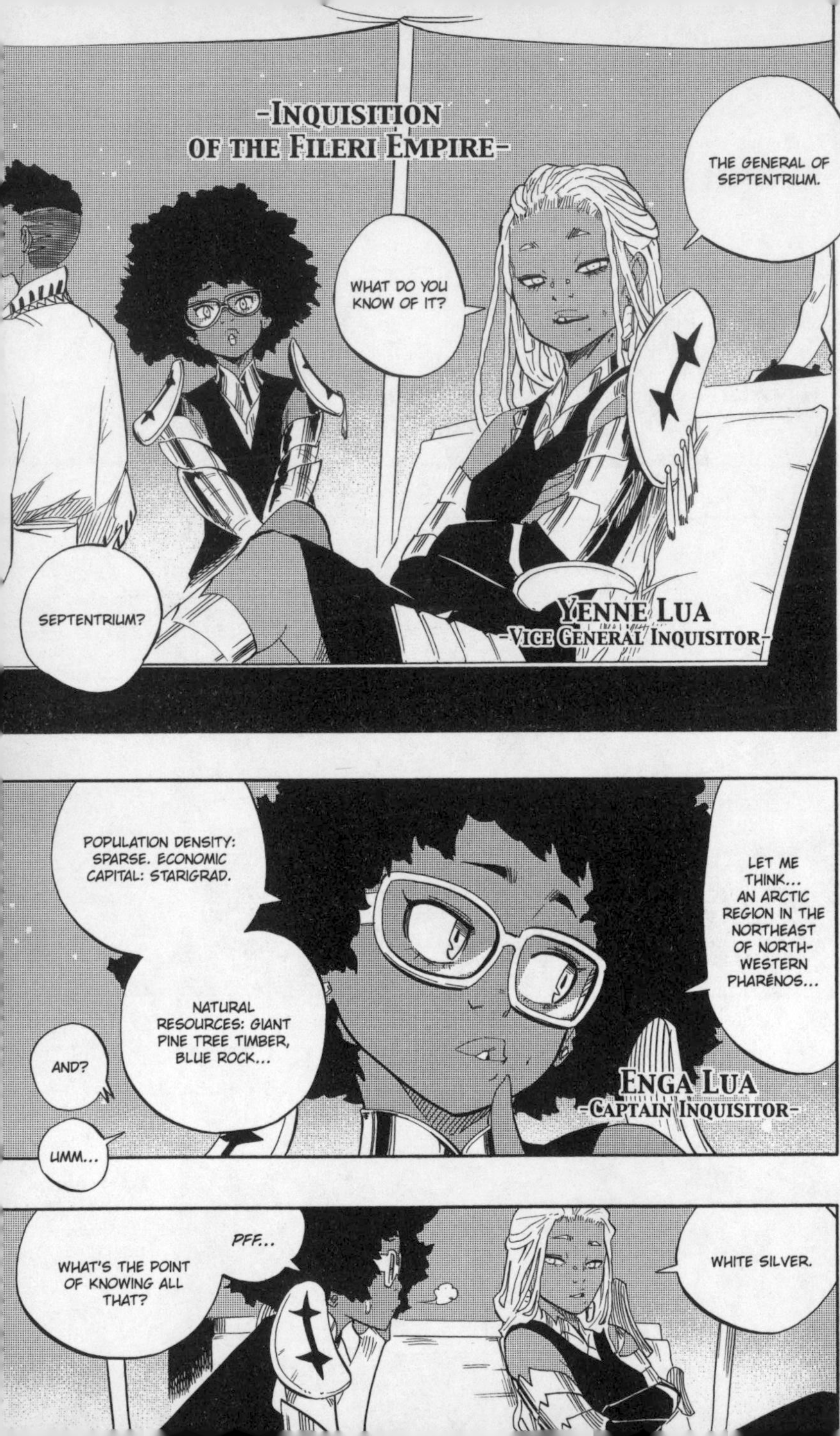
-Inquisition of the Fileri Empire-
THE GENERAL OF SEPTENTRIUM.
WHAT DO YOU KNOW OF IT?
SEPTENTRIUM?
Yenne Lua
-Vice General Inquisitor-
LET ME THINK... AN ARCTIC REGION IN THE NORTHEAST OF NORTH-WESTERN PHARÉNOS...
POPULATION DENSITY: SPARSE. ECONOMIC CAPITAL: STARIGRAD.
NATURAL RESOURCES: GIANT PINE TREE TIMBER, BLUE ROCK...
AND?
Enga Lua
-Captain Inquisitor-
UMM...
WHITE SILVER.
PFF...
WHAT'S THE POINT OF KNOWING ALL THAT?

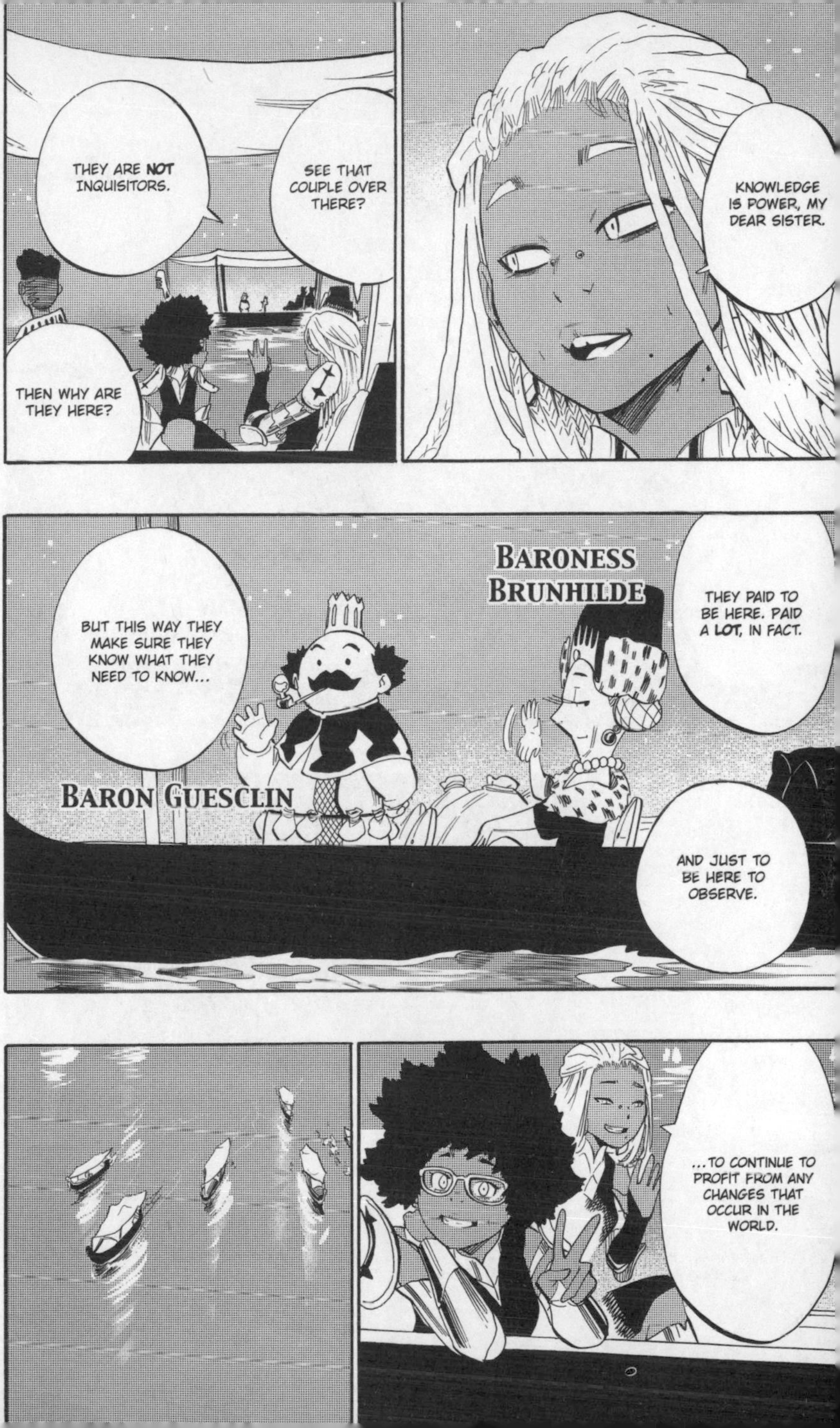
KNOWLEDGE IS POWER, MY DEAR SISTER.
SEE THAT COUPLE OVER THERE?
THEY ARE **NOT** INQUISITORS.
THEN WHY ARE THEY HERE?
THEY PAID TO BE HERE. PAID A **LOT**, IN FACT.
BARONESS BRUNHILDE
BUT THIS WAY THEY MAKE SURE THEY KNOW WHAT THEY NEED TO KNOW...
AND JUST TO BE HERE TO OBSERVE.
BARON GUESCLIN
...TO CONTINUE TO PROFIT FROM ANY CHANGES THAT OCCUR IN THE WORLD.

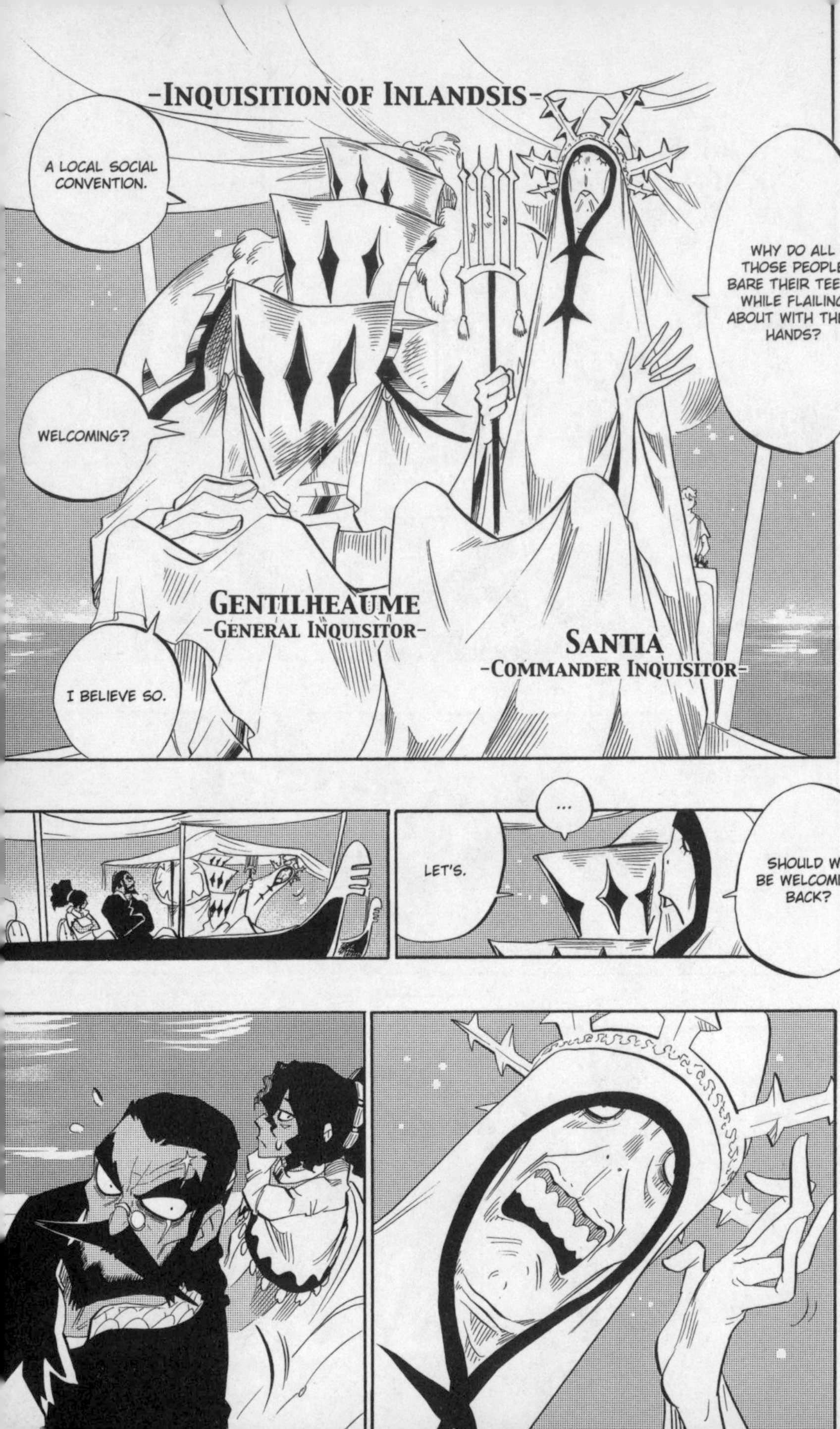
-Inquisition of Inlandsis-
Why do all those people bare their teeth while flailing about with their hands?
A local social convention.
Welcoming?
Gentilheaume
-General Inquisitor-
Santia
-Commander Inquisitor-
I believe so.
Should we be welcoming back?
...
Let's.

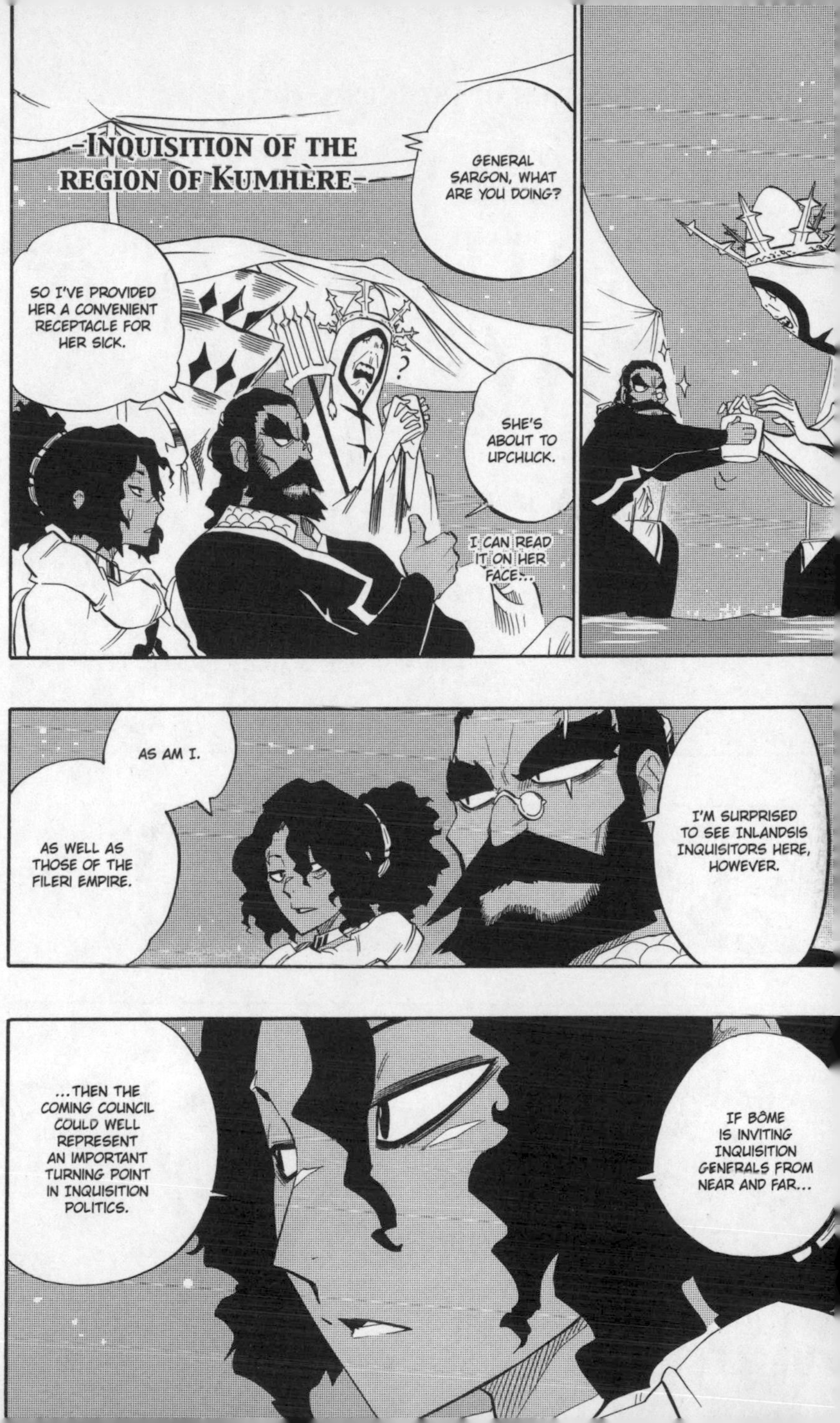
INQUISITION OF THE REGION OF KUMHÈRE
GENERAL SARGON, WHAT ARE YOU DOING?
SHE'S ABOUT TO UPCHUCK.
I CAN READ IT ON HER FACE...
SO I'VE PROVIDED HER A CONVENIENT RECEPTACLE FOR HER SICK.
I'M SURPRISED TO SEE INLANDSIS INQUISITORS HERE, HOWEVER.
AS AM I.
AS WELL AS THOSE OF THE FILERI EMPIRE.
IF BÔME IS INVITING INQUISITION GENERALS FROM NEAR AND FAR...
...THEN THE COMING COUNCIL COULD WELL REPRESENT AN IMPORTANT TURNING POINT IN INQUISITION POLITICS.

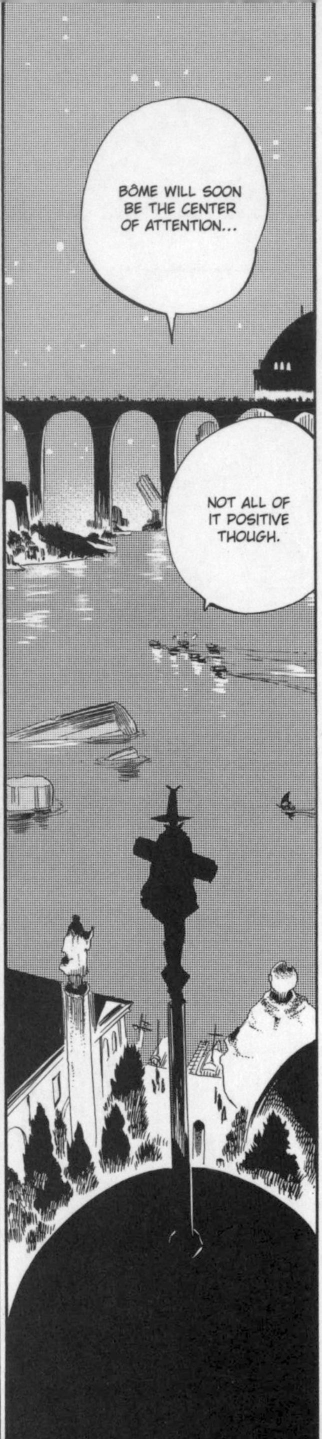
BÔME WILL SOON BE THE CENTER OF ATTENTION...
NOT ALL OF IT POSITIVE THOUGH.
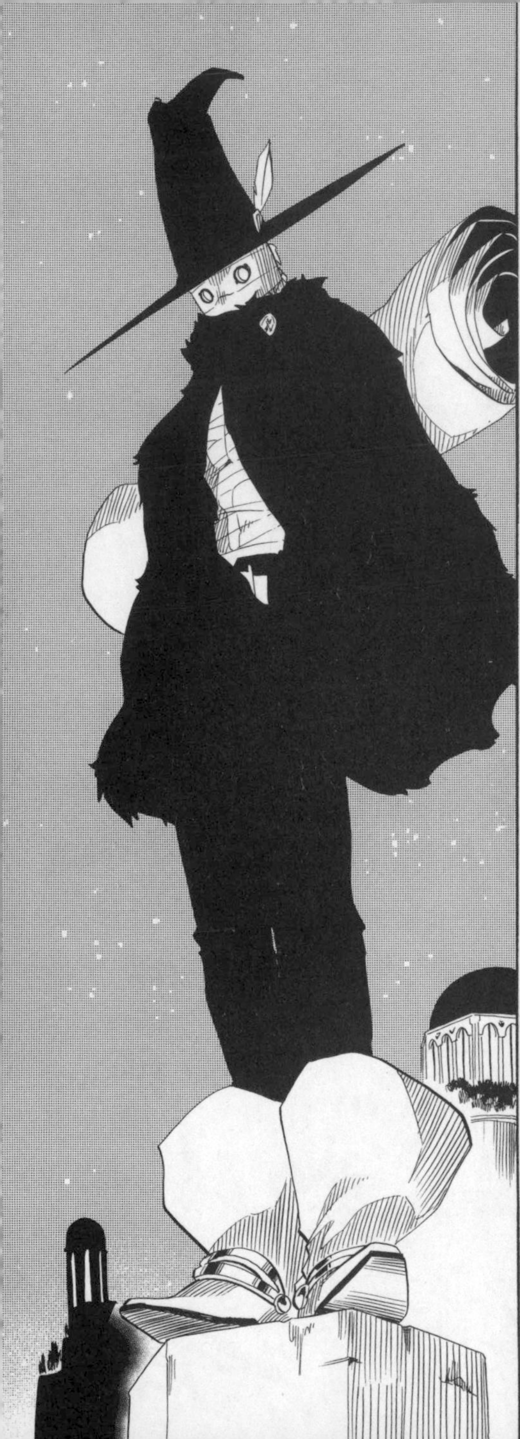

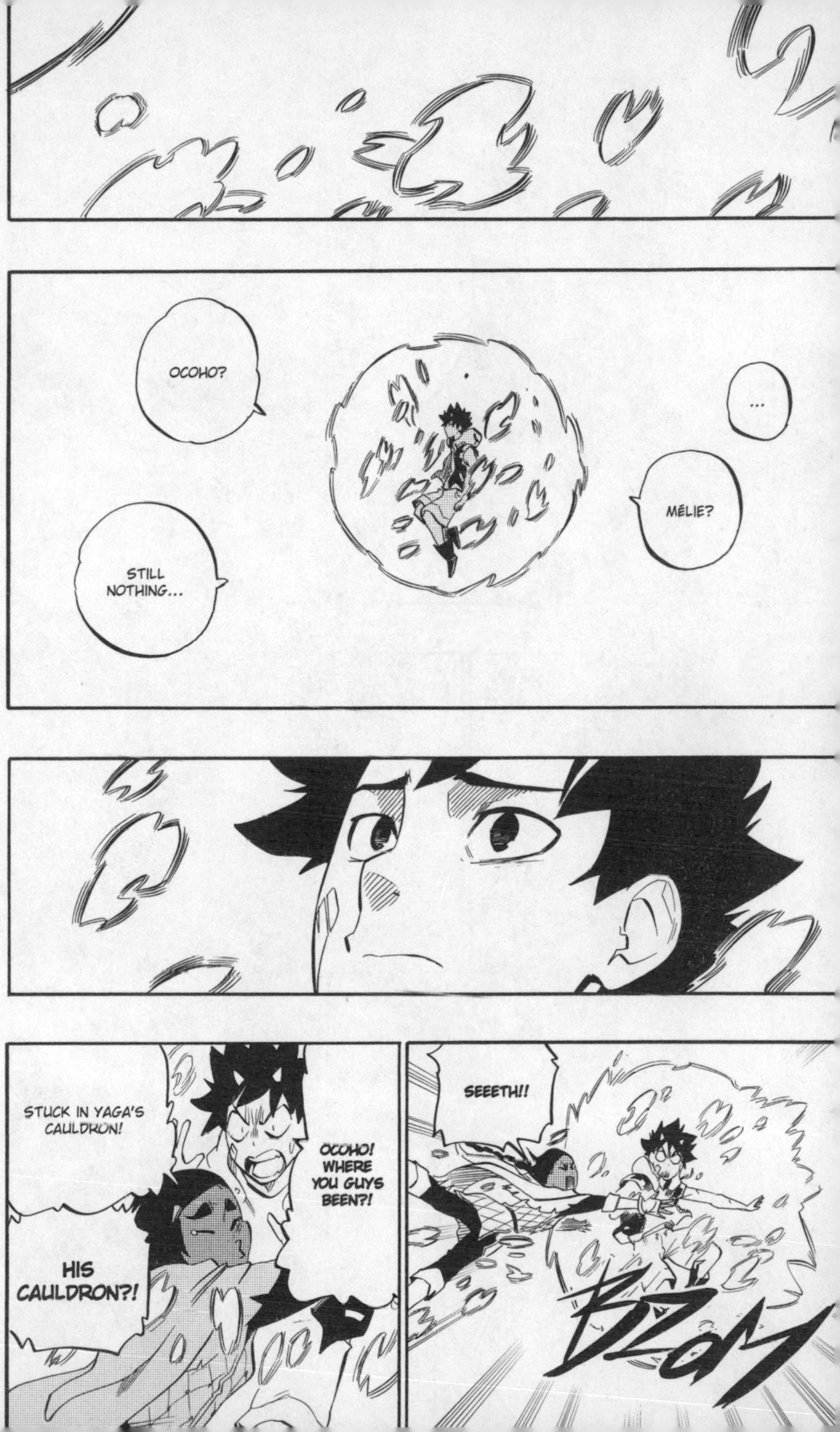
...
MÉLIE?
OCOHO?
STILL NOTHING...
SEEETH!!
BZOM
OCOHO! WHERE YOU GUYS BEEN?!
STUCK IN YAGA'S CAULDRON!
HIS CAULDRON?!

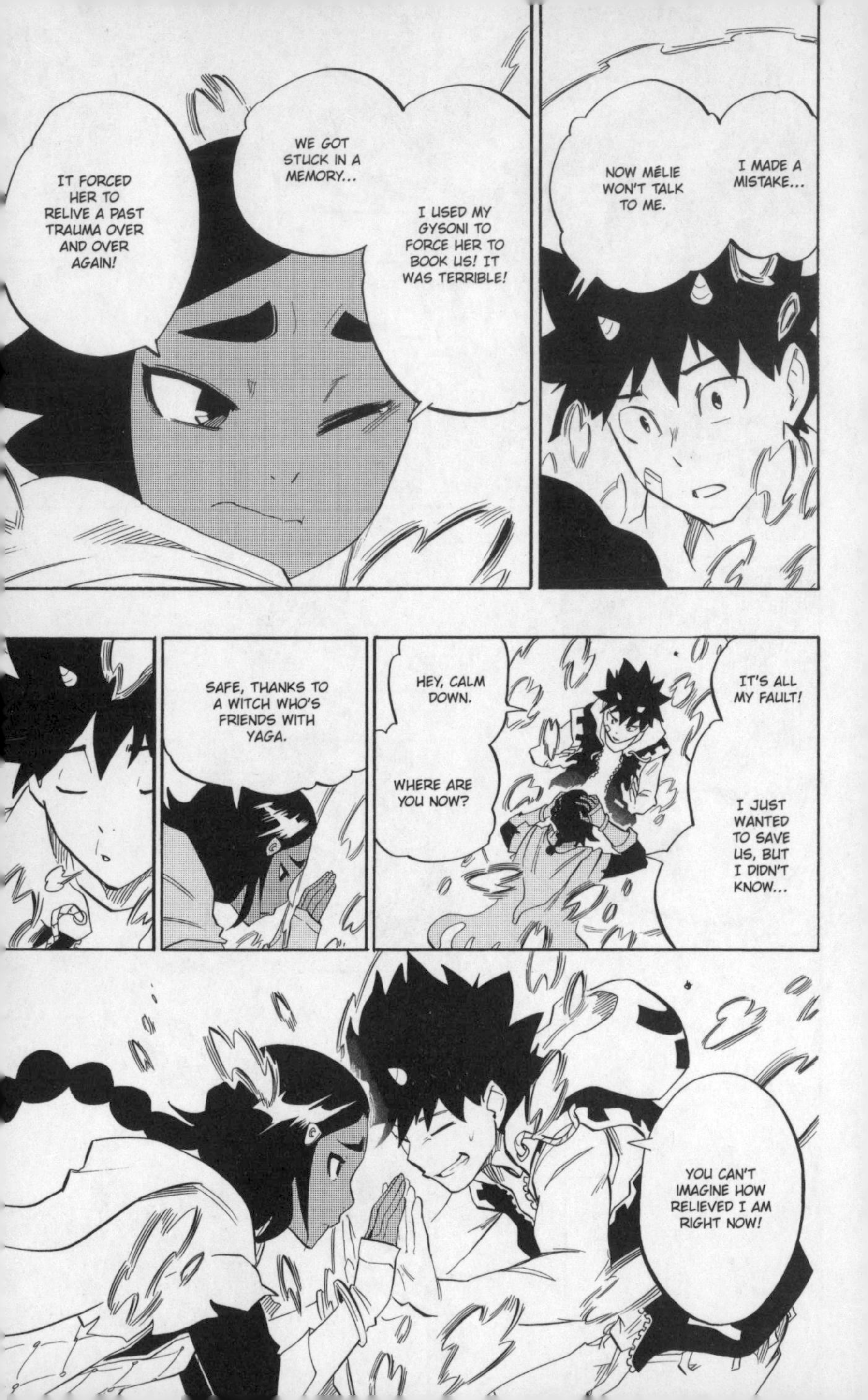
I MADE A MISTAKE...
NOW MÉLIE WON'T TALK TO ME.
WE GOT STUCK IN A MEMORY...
I USED MY GYSONI TO FORCE HER TO BOOK US! IT WAS TERRIBLE!
IT FORCED HER TO RELIVE A PAST TRAUMA OVER AND OVER AGAIN!
IT'S ALL MY FAULT!
I JUST WANTED TO SAVE US, BUT I DIDN'T KNOW...
HEY, CALM DOWN.
WHERE ARE YOU NOW?
SAFE, THANKS TO A WITCH WHO'S FRIENDS WITH YAGA.
YOU CAN'T IMAGINE HOW RELIEVED I AM RIGHT NOW!

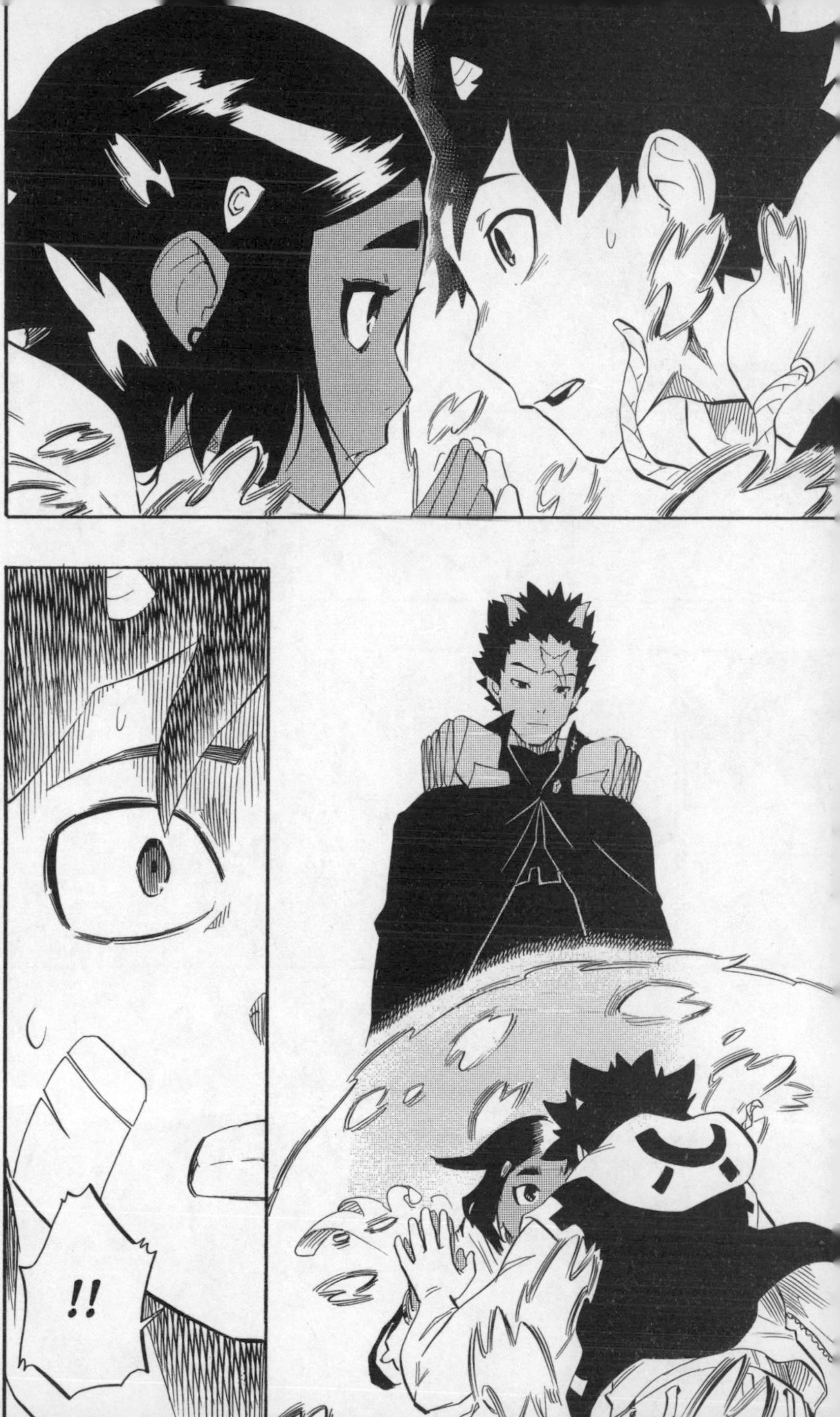
!!

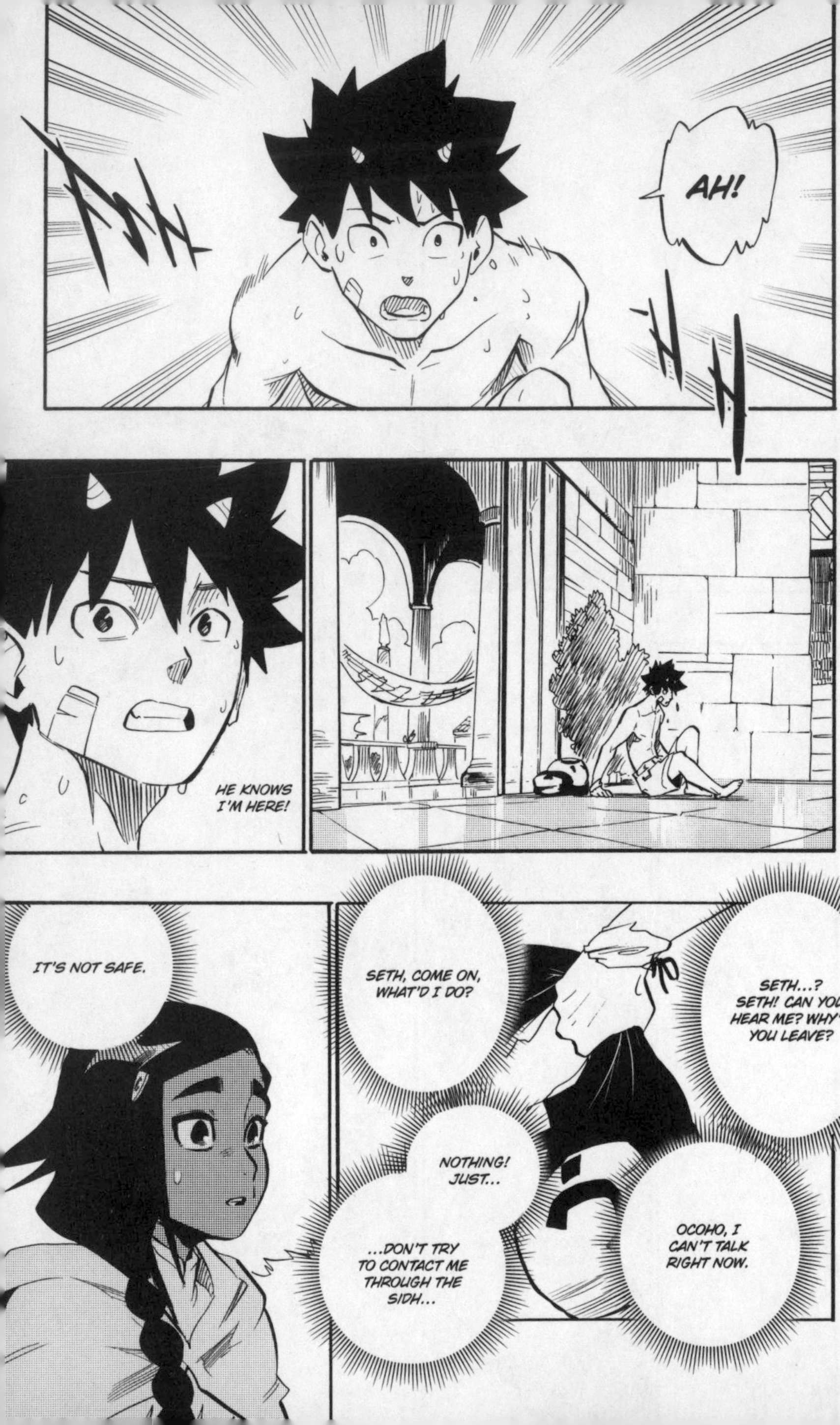
AH!
HE KNOWS I'M HERE!
SETH...? SETH! CAN YOU HEAR ME? WHY'D YOU LEAVE?
OCOHO, I CAN'T TALK RIGHT NOW.
SETH, COME ON, WHAT'D I DO?
NOTHING! JUST...
...DON'T TRY TO CONTACT ME THROUGH THE SIDH...
IT'S NOT SAFE.

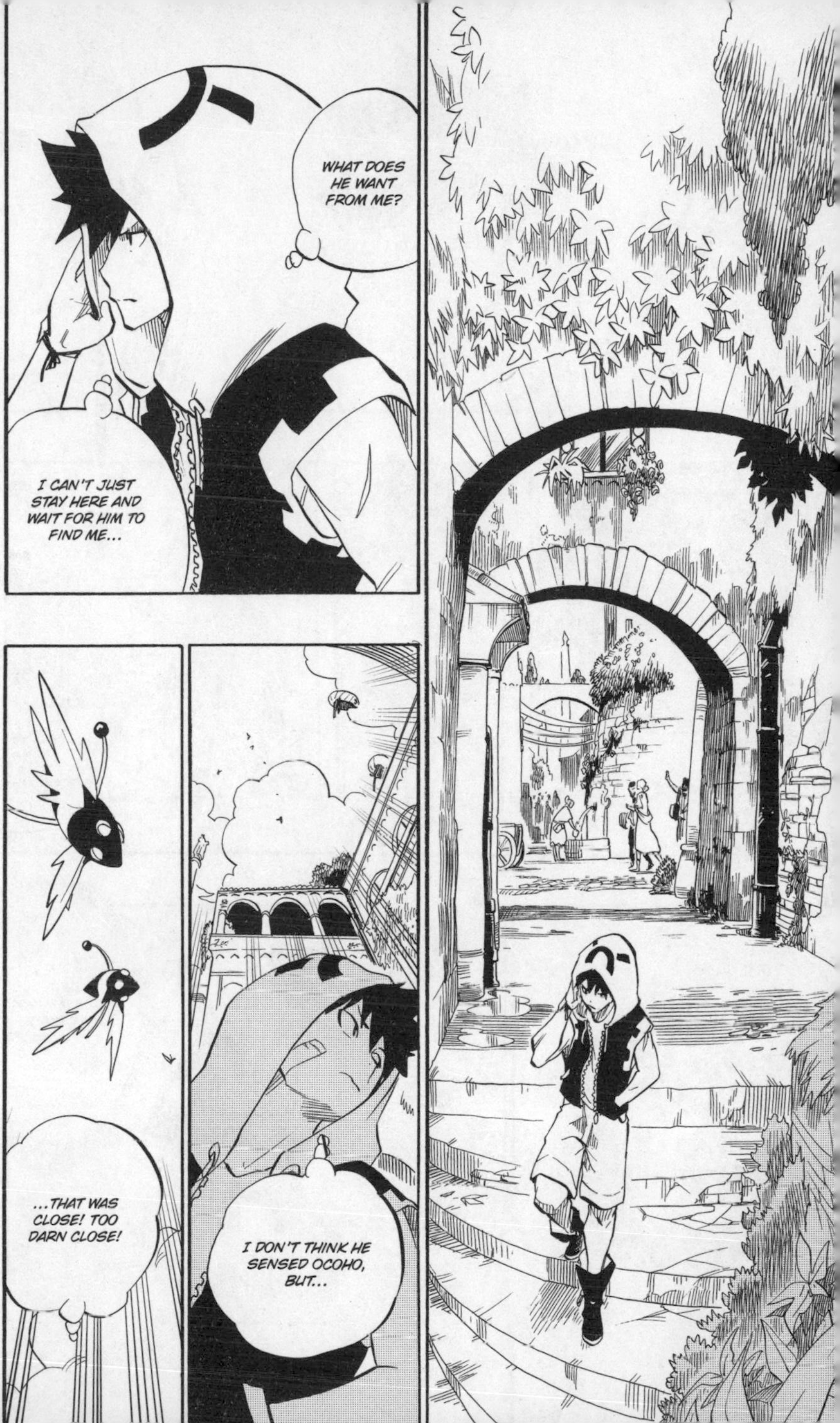
WHAT DOES HE WANT FROM ME?
I CAN'T JUST STAY HERE AND WAIT FOR HIM TO FIND ME...
I DON'T THINK HE SENSED OCOHO, BUT...
...THAT WAS CLOSE! TOO DARN CLOSE!

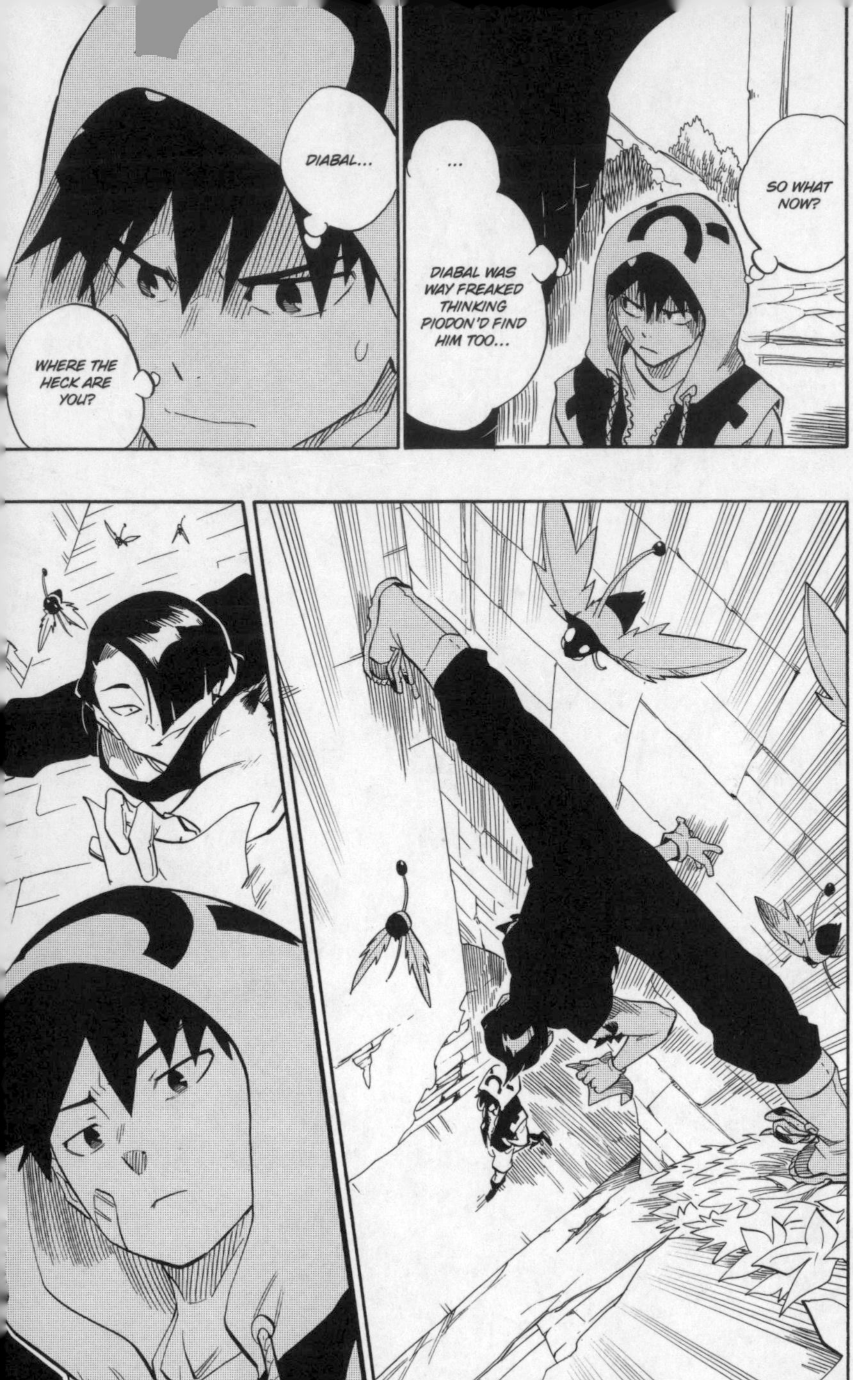
SO WHAT NOW?
...
DIABAL WAS WAY FREAKED THINKING PIODON'D FIND HIM TOO...
DIABAL...
WHERE THE HECK ARE YOU?

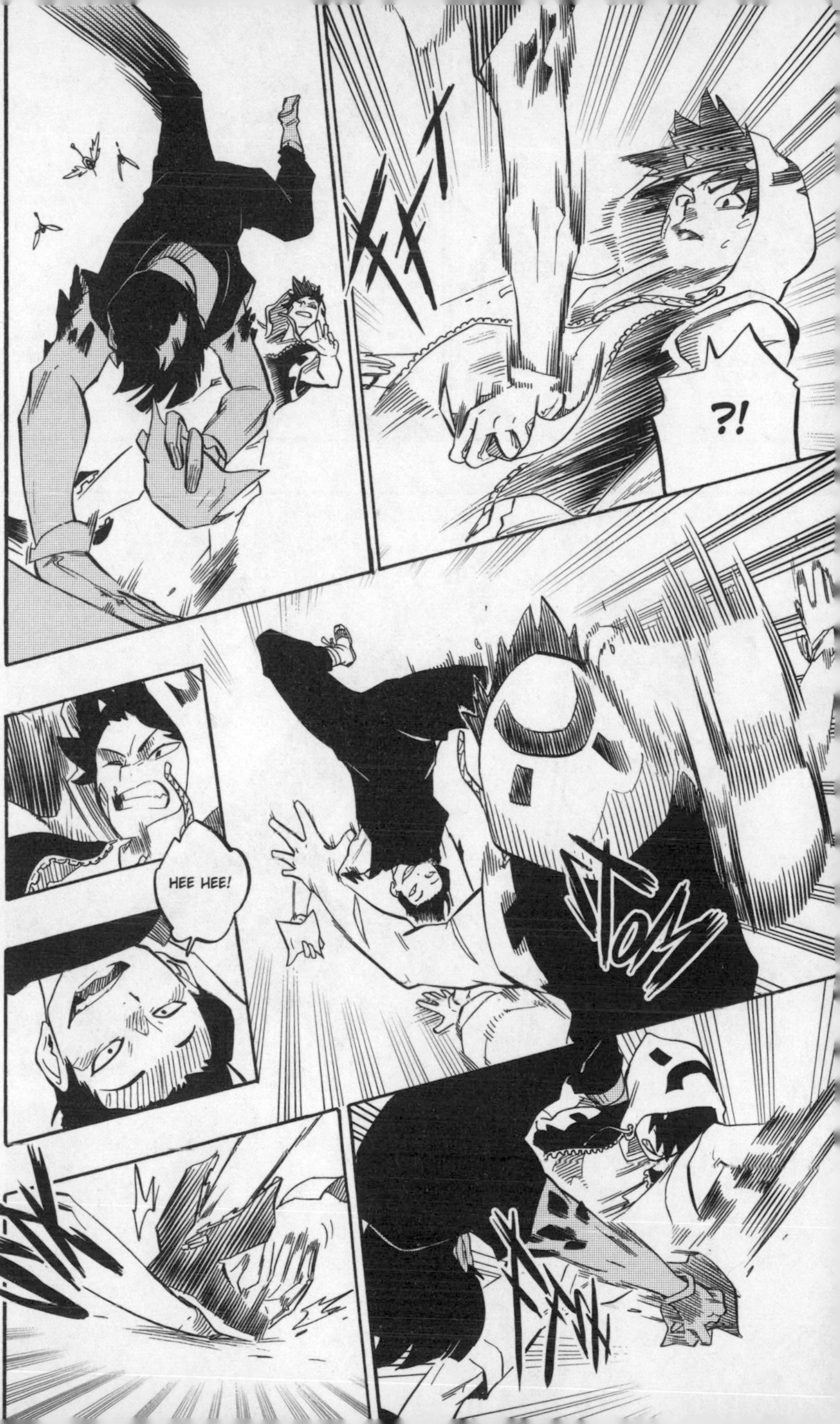

?!
HEE HEE!

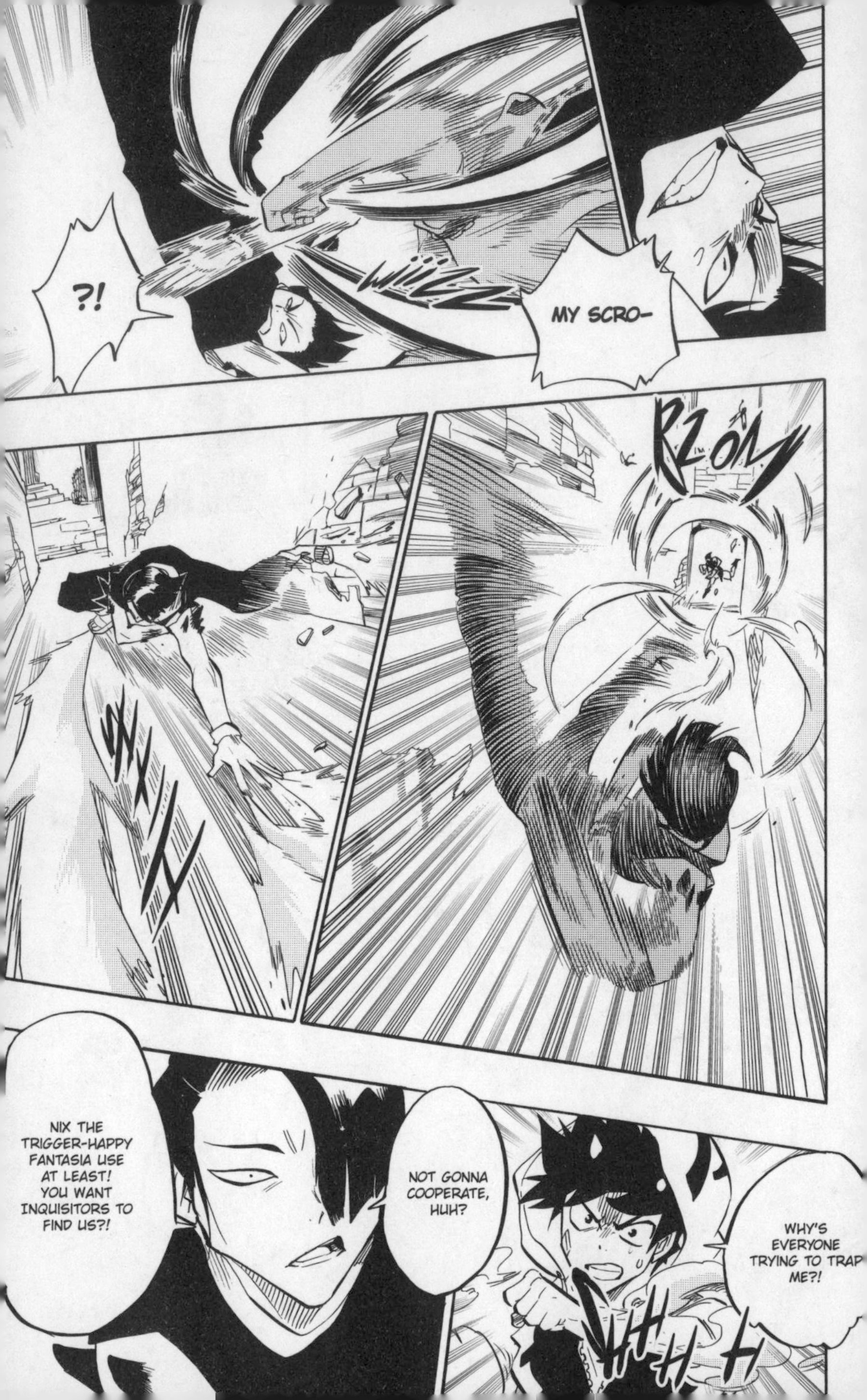
MY SCRO-
?!
RZOM
WHY'S EVERYONE TRYING TO TRAP ME?!
NOT GONNA COOPERATE, HUH?
NIX THE TRIGGER-HAPPY FANTASIA USE AT LEAST! YOU WANT INQUISITORS TO FIND US?!

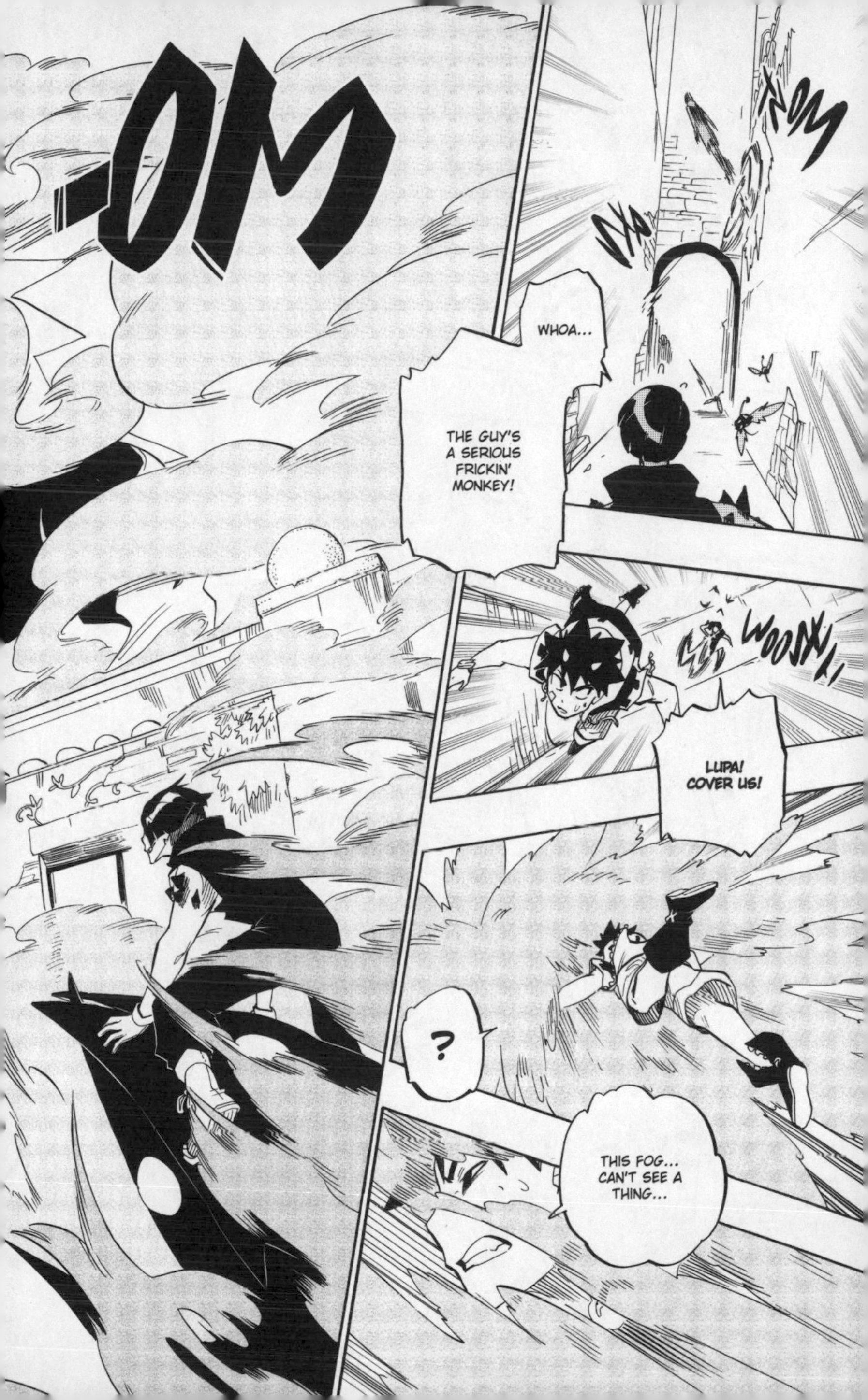
WHOA...
THE GUY'S A SERIOUS FRICKIN' MONKEY!
LUPA! COVER US!
?
THIS FOG... CAN'T SEE A THING...

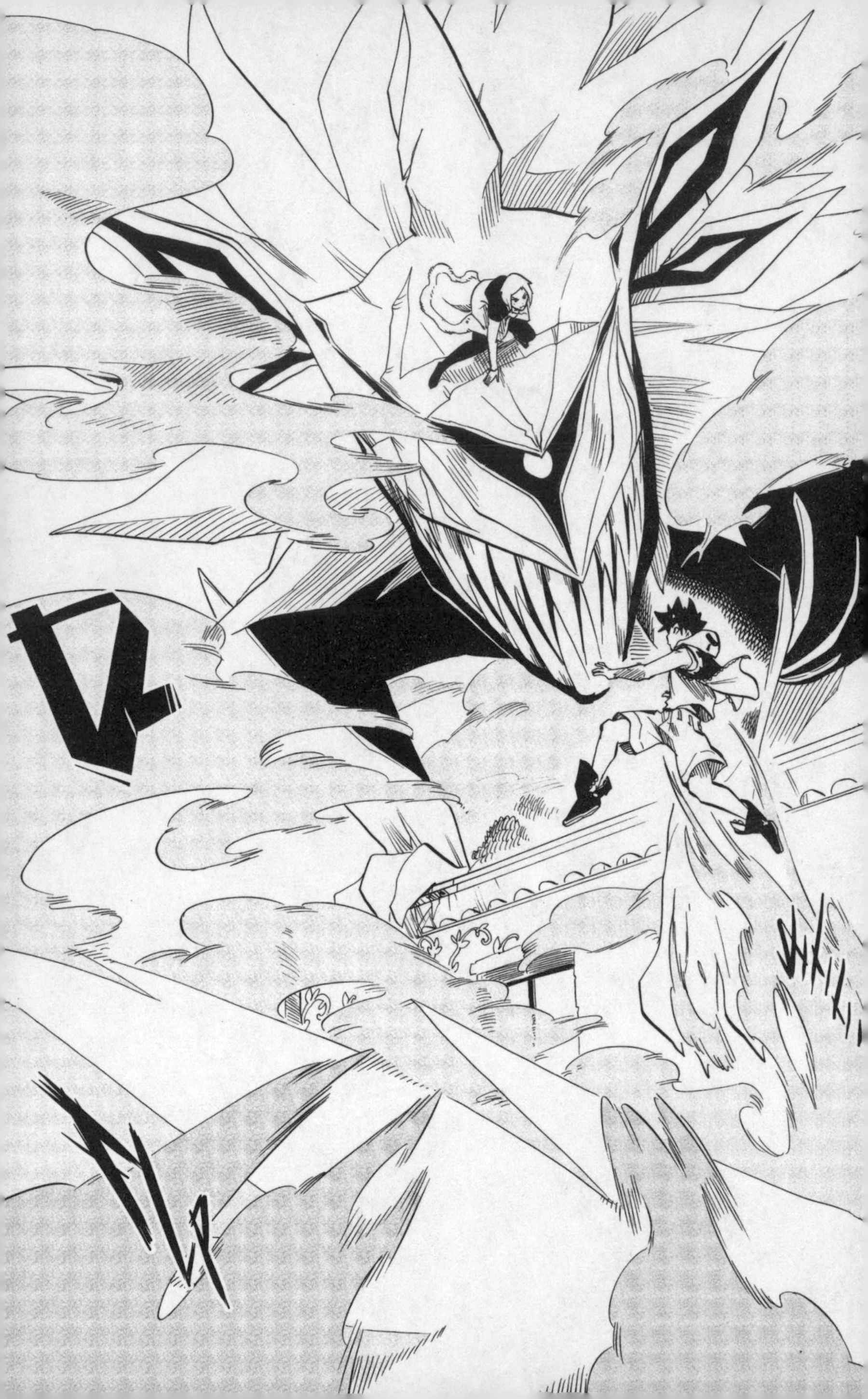
FLP

TO BE CONTINUED...

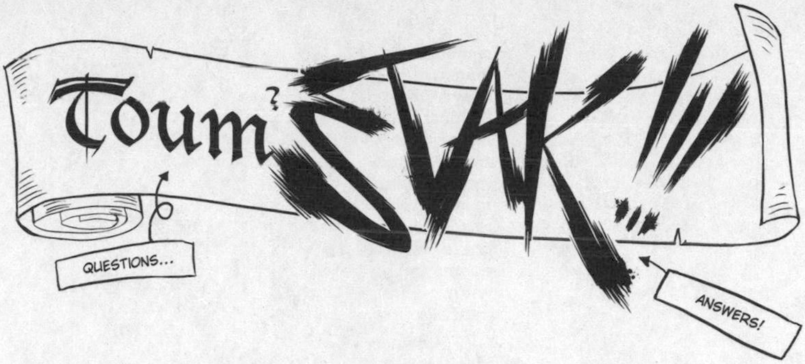
Toum? STAK!!!
QUESTIONS...
ANSWERS!

Gulfur Wulfrod, great barbarian of the Badlands: Ahoy, Tony! I love your manga and the entire world in it (especially Ocoho, who more than earned that title of hers). There is, however, one small thing that's been bothering me: We don't hear a lot about the 9,999 people for every person who becomes a wizard (Source: Jiji, volume 1, page 47, second panel: "There's about 0.01 percent who *do* survive.")

Tony Valente: If you read the Caislean Merlin Arc thoroughly, you'll know that these numbers are being questioned by Mordred and Sagramor. There's a real big gap between what the Inquisitors say and the actual percentage of Infected.

-Just out of curiosity, can a thaumaturge become a wizard? Could he then mix wizardry with miracles?

Technically, the two are not incompatible!

Thanks Tony, and good luck on the rest of *Radiant!*

Lucas M.: Hi, my name is Lucas, I've been reading your manga since the beginning (it's absolutely amazing, definitely in my top 10) and was wondering: if we were to rank wizards by power, would Grimm be ranked high, or is he only a character of medium strength?

Tony Valente: Hmm... Good question. If we were to make a ranking of wizards we've seen until now, then Grimm would be of a burning red rank, with a bonus dragon... Knowing Seth is ranked 178th, parallel roundoff. You know, just so you get the idea of the order.

Zendar Z.: Hello, Mr. Valente! I think your manga is really wonderful, your art fantastic and the plot gripping! Volume 10 especially got me all over! *Schaalk!* Like that! And then I started wondering a couple of things...

-Why are Seth's "memories" in the Sidh in a bubble shape, while Mélie's are just floating around her? Meanwhile, Myr and Jill have none, are they sick? Or maybe Seth's the one who's sick...

Tony Valente: Seth has a protective bubble around him, which presumably is linked to Alma (they mention it in Volume 5). But he still has his memories floating inside, as they are with Mélie, Doc and Ocoho. As for Myr and Jill, they're very used to the Sidh and are able to change even their outer appearance (like they did the first time they find Seth). They can act on a lot of things in there and even avoid leaving unwanted memories lying around all over the place.

-And, more importantly, are we going to see Myr again? Or is he going to stay with the Queen all the time to take care of his kids? Because I'd love to see him again. At least a thousand times...

Aah, well, I love Myr too! And yes, I'm not planning on leaving him behind. We'll definitely see him again!

Jordi D.: Hello mister Valente, I discovered your manga *Radiant* by chance and I've been fascinated ever since by this world you created. You definitely deserve your current success. I was lucky enough to become a father recently, and I was thinking I'd make this the first manga I'd introduce to my little girl when she'll be old enough to understand it.

Unfortunately, this bundle of joy was accompanied by a health issue; a rare abnormality of the spinal cord (diastematomyelia) will handicap my baby girl for the rest of her life. To each their own "Infection" I guess you could say. Nevertheless, I want to give her the best childhood possible. So an idea came to mind. I don't know if you'll even read this message, but if you do, I would be so happy if you could draw a character with a handicap, a girl called Taïna (like my little girl). I wouldn't want to disturb your story, but maybe you could have her show up in the background of one of your amazing double page spreads? It'd be such an amazing pleasure to be able to someday show my little Taïna the character that was inspired by her. I know my request is quite presumptuous, or even out of place, so if this isn't doable, I'll still be happy to continue reading your radiant stories. I wish you all the best for the rest and thank you for bringing us along on Seth's adventures.

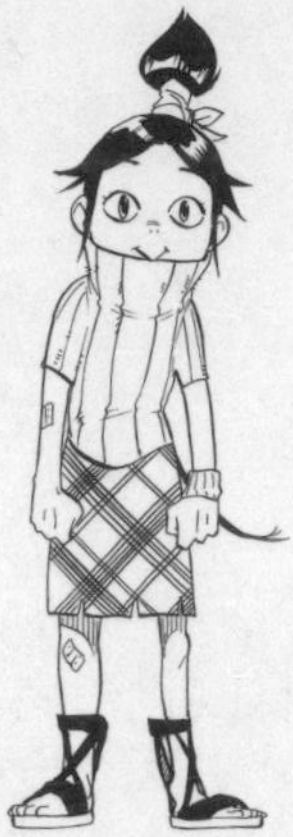

Tony Valente: And there, done, I gave her an official spot amongst the "droplet gang" who help out Urlä! She helps them, teases everyone, all with joy and good humor!
All my love to little Taïna and good luck!! <3

Gabrielle: Hi Tony! How's it going? You must get a lot of messages, so I have no idea if mine will get to you, but might as well try!
Tony Valente: I read all the messages! But unfortunately I can't respond to all of them…

-I wanted to know if it's possible that Mr. Boobrie is a baby dragon. Because he's got the same wings as the Wizard-Knights' dragons.
There're a lot of you asking the same question lately… And *fwoop,* a new question dodging technique.

-Also, I also wanted to be sure, but in volume 1, the Nemesis isn't attacking. Actually, it looks like it's just defending itself, while in the anime it's attacking that kid. Doesn't that change quite a lot? Or not?
Symbolically, yes, it changes things. But behaviorally speaking, if we see a Nemesis as a wild animal, then it can display the behavior shown in the anime, but still stay faithful to the Nemesis in the manga. It all depends on your point of view, really.

-And what about this: "Is perception the basis of knowledge?" Since I've gotta write a paper about that in my philosophy class, I thought, might as well ask some questions for it =DDD. As I said, might as well try!
Answer: "Sometimes yes, other times as well." With that you'll get even better than a good grade! Definitely.

Grégoire H.: So, so, so… First of all: CONGRATULATIONS! When I heard *Radiant* was going to be turned into an anime, I almost fainted… But when I discovered the opening! Man, the chills that gave me, seriously (=^-ω-^=). And while on the subject of the opening, is it you who chose "04 Limited Sazabys" for the song? Did they come to you with a couple of options or what?
Tony Valente: I did not choose it. To be honest, I know nothing of Japanese music, so I wouldn't have been of much help I'm afraid… But I reaaaaaaaly loved it. Same for the season 2 opening, aaaah, love it!

-Anyway, it's nice to see a French anime finally getting made…
It's nice, it's fun, and it's a lot of work too.

-And a last little question: will all the volumes that've been published until now be adapated into an anime? I read an article saying only the first four volumes would get put in the anime. Anyway, I wish you the best of luck for the future, as well for you as for us!
Season 2 will cover volumes 5 to 10, so it goes beyond the info you heard of. As for the continuation, there's no way to tell, since I'm in the middle of a new arc here, and it's far from being over…

Please send your questions to: radiant@ankama.com

I've got this unsettling feeling linked to a frequently recurring memory...

This happened when I was a kid. I was making myself a slice of bread with honey on it, minding my own business. So I'm putting the jar of honey back in the cupboard, on a shelf too high for me, really reaching as far as I can with my arms... and I suddenly feel this warm thing sliding through my sleeve. I panic and stand still. Is it a snake? A rat? An otter? A gouviard? (Don't look it up, I made that one up) The thing is getting bigger, pulling on the hairs of my forearm... It goes all the way to my elbow... And then, on my hand I see it, oh no... The jar of honey was open. I have honey in my sleeve all the way to my elbow. I stand still for a little while longer.

I'm going to be late for school.

—Tony Valente

Tony Valente began working as a comic artist with the series *The Four Princes of Ganahan*, written by Raphael Drommelschlager. He then launched a new three-volume project, *Hana Attori*, after which he produced *S.P.E.E.D. Angels*, a series written by Didier Tarquin and colored by Pop.

In preparation for *Radiant*, he relocated to Canada. Through confronting caribou and grizzlies, he gained the wherewithal to train in obscure manga techniques. Since then, his eating habits have changed, his lifestyle became completely different and even his singing voice has changed a bit!

RADIANT VOL. 13
VIZ MEDIA Manga Edition

STORY AND ART BY **TONY VALENTE**
ASSISTANT ARTIST **SALOMON**

Translation/(´･∀･｀)ﾅｧ?
Touch-Up Art & Lettering/**Erika Terriquez**
Design/**Julian [JR] Robinson**
Editor/**Gary Leach**

Published by arrangement with MEDIATOON LICENSING/Ankama.
RADIANT T13
© ANKAMA EDITIONS 2020, by Tony Valente
All rights reserved

Printed in the U.S.A.

Published by VIZ Media, LLC
P.O. Box 77010
San Francisco, CA 94107

10 9 8 7 6 5 4 3 2 1
First printing, October 2020

VIZ MEDIA
viz.com

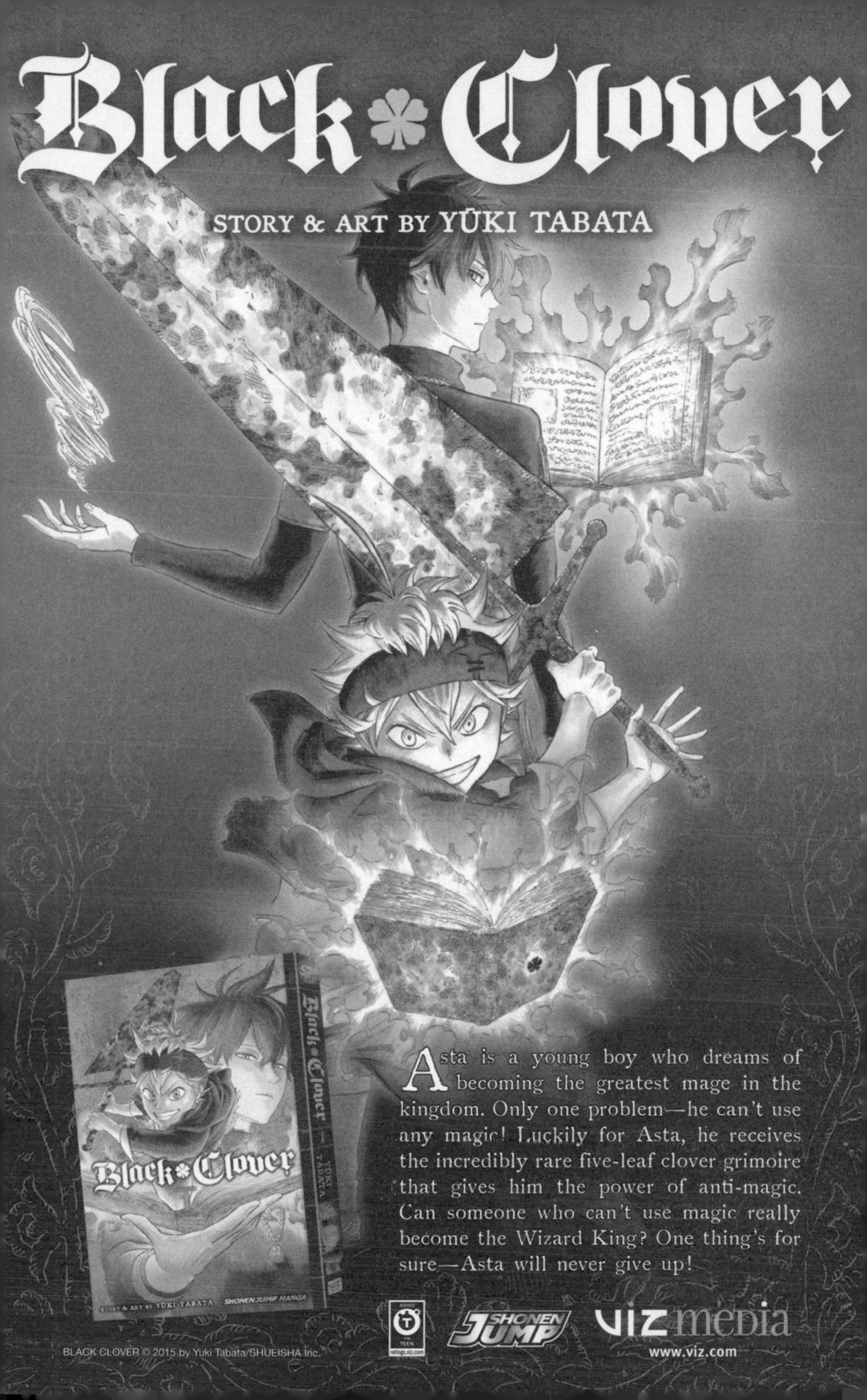
Black Clover
STORY & ART BY YŪKI TABATA
Asta is a young boy who dreams of becoming the greatest mage in the kingdom. Only one problem—he can't use any magic! Luckily for Asta, he receives the incredibly rare five-leaf clover grimoire that gives him the power of anti-magic. Can someone who can't use magic really become the Wizard King? One thing's for sure—Asta will never give up!
Black Clover
STORY & ART BY YUKI TABATA
SHONENJUMP MANGA
RATED T FOR TEEN
ratings.viz.com
SHONEN JUMP
VIZ media
www.viz.com
BLACK CLOVER © 2015 by Yuki Tabata/SHUEISHA Inc.

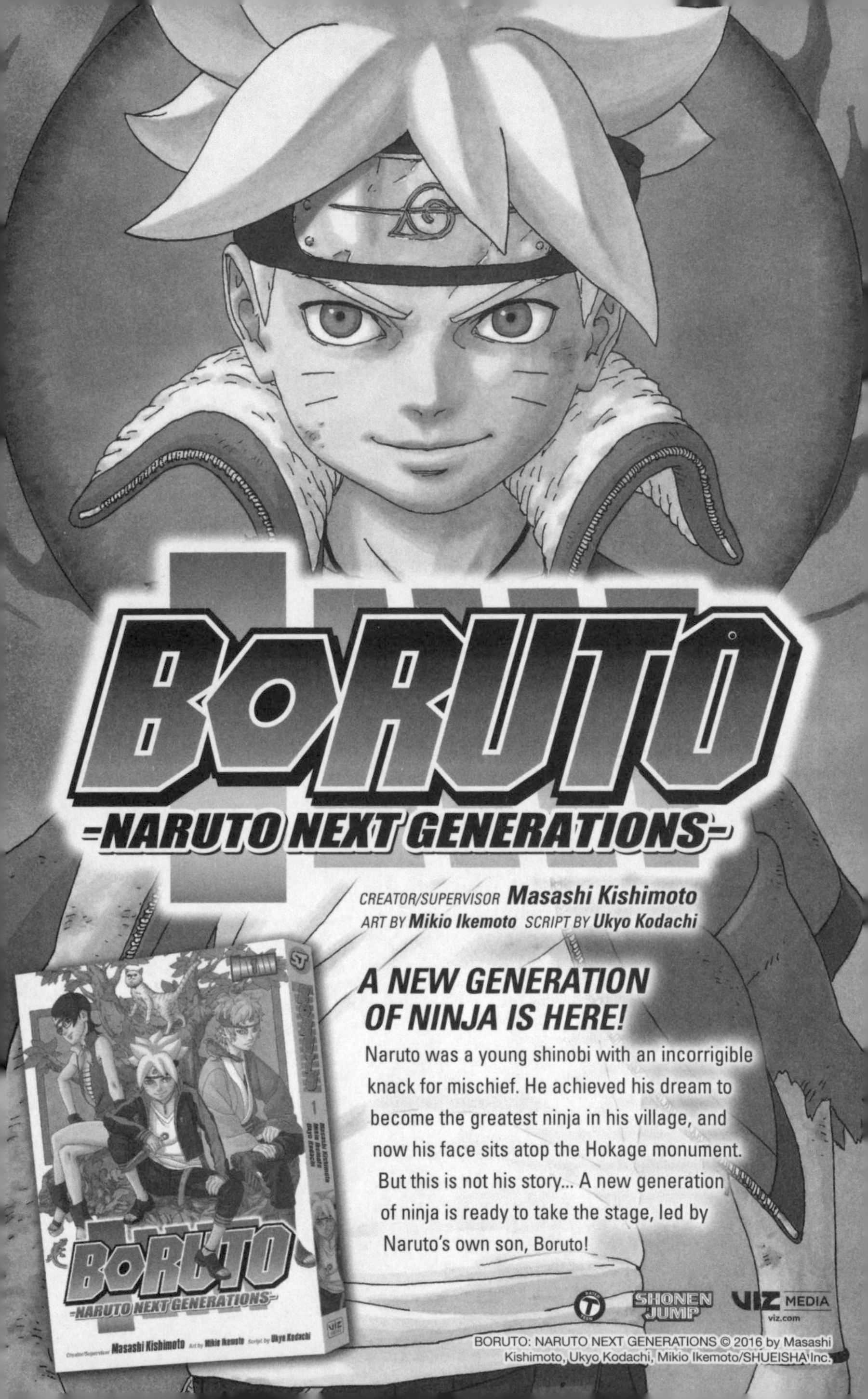
BORUTO
-NARUTO NEXT GENERATIONS-
CREATOR/SUPERVISOR Masashi Kishimoto
ART BY Mikio Ikemoto SCRIPT BY Ukyo Kodachi
A NEW GENERATION OF NINJA IS HERE!
Naruto was a young shinobi with an incorrigible knack for mischief. He achieved his dream to become the greatest ninja in his village, and now his face sits atop the Hokage monument. But this is not his story... A new generation of ninja is ready to take the stage, led by Naruto's own son, Boruto!
BORUTO
-NARUTO NEXT GENERATIONS-
Creator/Supervisor Masashi Kishimoto Art by Mikio Ikemoto Script by Ukyo Kodachi
SHONEN JUMP
VIZ MEDIA
viz.com
BORUTO: NARUTO NEXT GENERATIONS © 2016 by Masashi Kishimoto, Ukyo Kodachi, Mikio Ikemoto/SHUEISHA Inc.

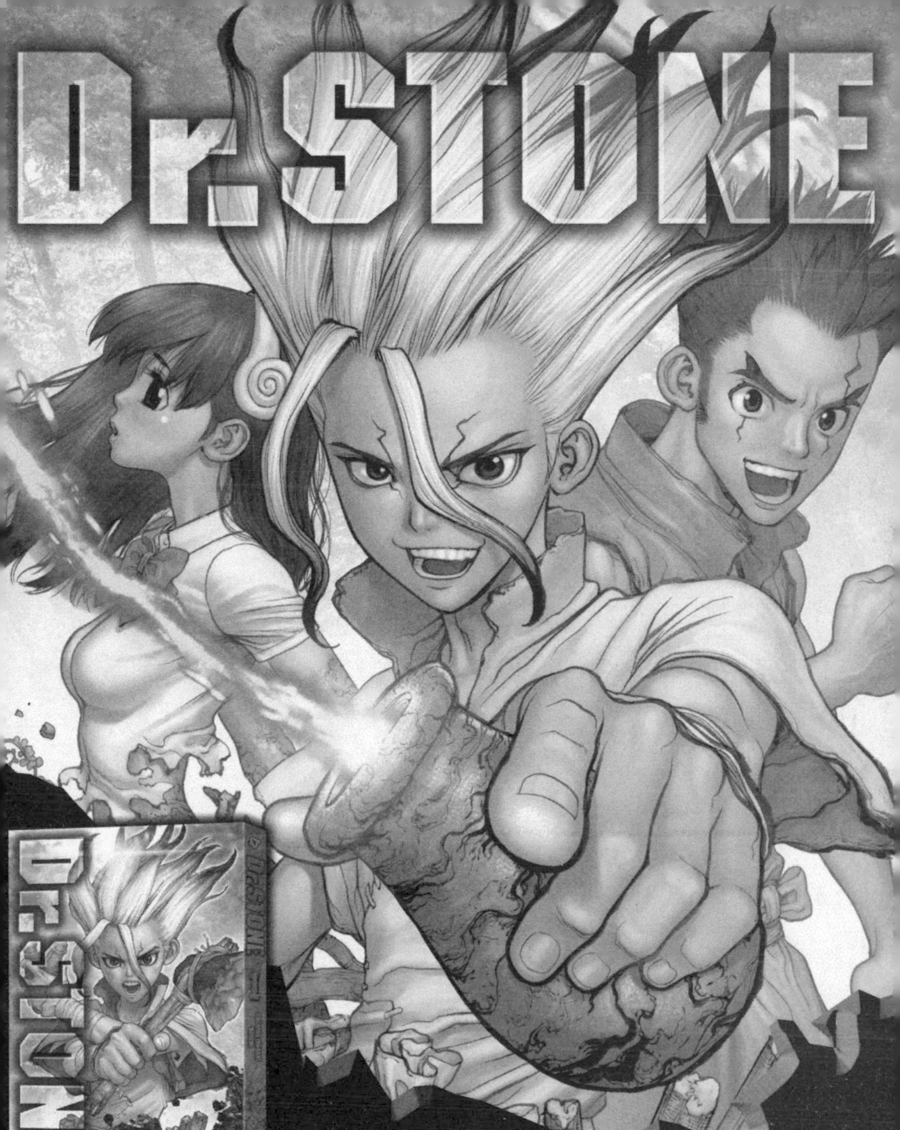
Dr.STONE
Dr.STONE 1
STORY BY
RIICHIRO INAGAKI
ART BY
BOICHI

One fateful day, all of humanity turned to stone. Many millennia later, Taiju frees himself from petrification and finds himself surrounded by statues. The situation looks grim—until he runs into his science-loving friend Senku! Together they plan to restart civilization with the power of science!

VIZ RATED T TEEN

Ruby, Weiss, Blake and Yang are students at Beacon Academy, learning to protect the world of Remnant from the fearsome Grimm!

RWBY

MANGA BY **Shirow Miwa**

BASED ON THE ROOSTER TEETH SERIES
CREATED BY **Monty Oum**

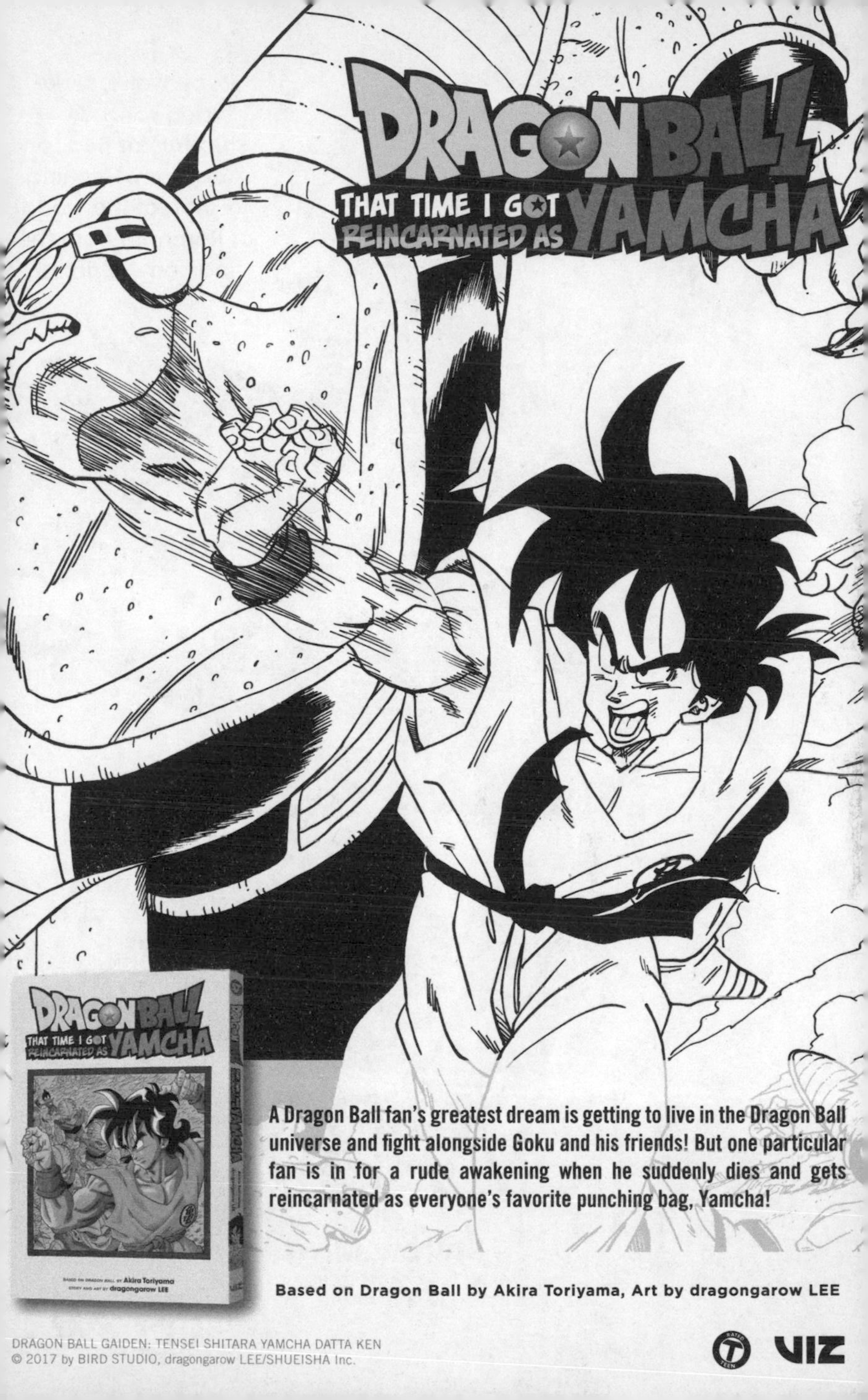
DRAGON BALL
THAT TIME I GOT REINCARNATED AS YAMCHA
A Dragon Ball fan's greatest dream is getting to live in the Dragon Ball universe and fight alongside Goku and his friends! But one particular fan is in for a rude awakening when he suddenly dies and gets reincarnated as everyone's favorite punching bag, Yamcha!
Based on Dragon Ball by Akira Toriyama, Art by dragongarow LEE
DRAGON BALL GAIDEN: TENSEI SHITARA YAMCHA DATTA KEN
© 2017 by BIRD STUDIO, dragongarow LEE/SHUEISHA Inc.
VIZ

YOU'RE READING THE WRONG WAY!

RADIANT reads from right to left, starting in the upper-right corner, meaning that action, sound effects, and word-balloon order are completely reversed from English order.

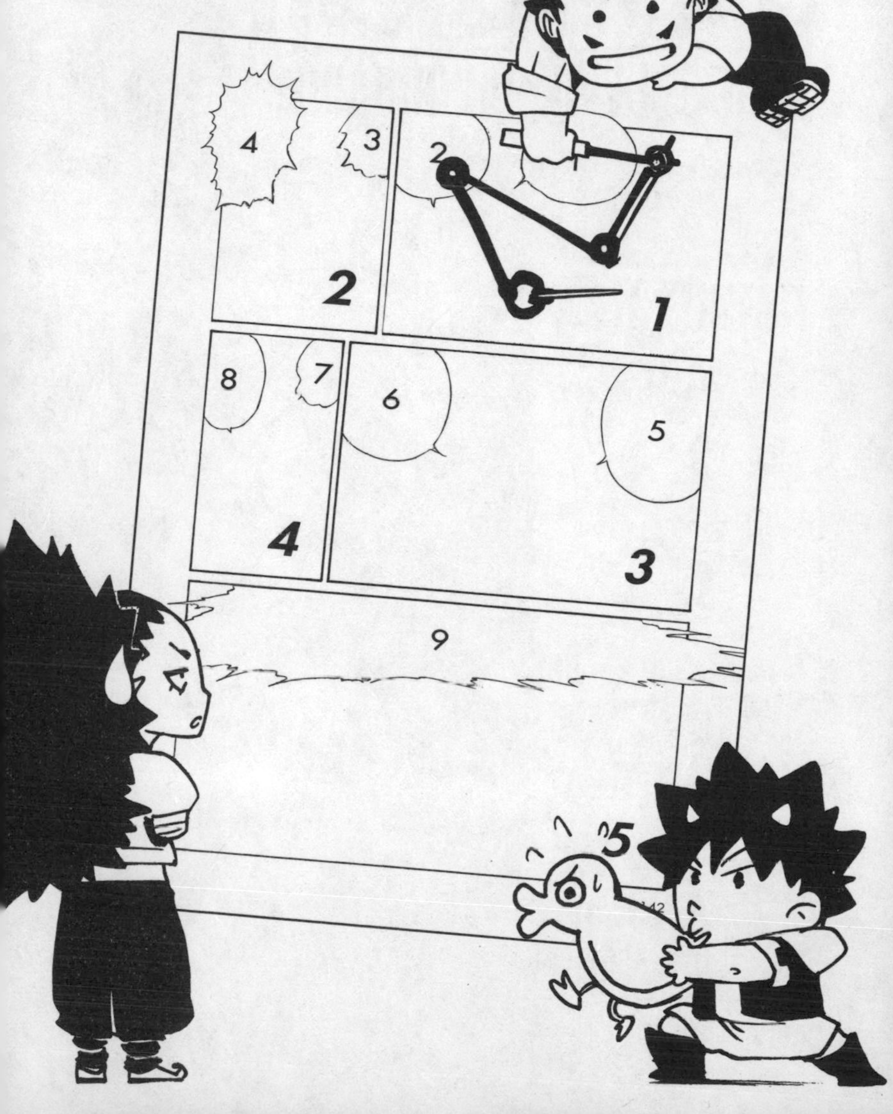

1
2
1
3
4
2
5
6
3
7
8
4
9
5